Thinking and Reasoning

Thinking and Reasoning

■ An introduction to the psychology of reason, judgment and decision making

Ken Manktelow

Ψ Psychology Press
Taylor & Francis Group

LONDON AND NEW YORK

First published 2012
by Psychology Press
27 Church Road, Hove, East Sussex BN3 2FA

Simultaneously published in the USA and
Canada
by Psychology Press
711 Third Avenue, New York, NY 10017

[www.psypress.com]

*Psychology Press is an imprint of the Taylor &
Francis Group, an informa business*

© 2012 Psychology Press

Typeset in Century Old Style and Futura by
RefineCatch Ltd, Bungay, Suffolk

Cover design by Andrew Ward

*British Library Cataloguing in Publication
Data*
A catalogue record for this book is available
from the British Library

*Library of Congress Cataloging in Publication
Data*
Manktelow, K. I., 1952–
    Thinking and reasoning : an introduction
to the psychology of reason,
judgment and decision making / Ken
Manktelow.
        p. cm.
    Includes bibliographical references and
index.

1. Reasoning (Psychology)
2. Thought and thinking.
3. Cognition.   4. Decision making.
I. Title.
BF442.M354 2012
153.4'2–dc23

                            2011031284

ISBN: 978-1-84169-740-6 (hbk)
ISBN: 978-1-84169-741-3 (pbk)
ISBN: 978-0-203-11546-6 (ebk)

Printed and bound in Great Britain by
TJ International Ltd, Padstow, Cornwall

Contents

CONTENTS

Preface

Psychology is the most important subject anyone can study. What could possibly justify such an outrageous and self-serving claim? Well, all the trouble in the world stems from human thought and behaviour; the most important task facing humanity is to try to sort out the world's troubles; and psychology is the study of human thought and behaviour. If you accept these premises, then that opening statement seems to go through. The argument is a kind of *syllogism*, and such arguments have been discussed over four millennia. They are dealt with in various chapters here, and we shall look at a huge array of types and foibles of human thought along with them. Some of what we discuss does indeed address profoundly important matters to do with human life.

This book developed out of an earlier one called *Reasoning and Thinking*, which appeared in 1999. Few of the words in the earlier edition have made it into this one. This is because in the decade or so in between, psychological research on thinking has boomed. There have been two explosions in particular – in theoretical depth and in conceptual breadth – by which I mean that the nature of explanation in this area is now at a greater stage of maturity than it was even a decade ago, with a variety of schools of thought contending, leading to ever more subtle and inventive investigations. Indeed, some of the work you will read about here is staggering in its ingenuity. Not only that, but there are increasingly rich connections between other areas, and not just of psychology: ideas from biology, philosophy, linguistics, economics, computer science and others have influenced the ways in which research on thinking is done, and there are live feedback loops between all these enterprises when it comes to explaining human reason.

The study of our reason has, to some degree, always been at the centre of inquiry about what it means to be human. A great early psychologist, Hermann

Ebbinghaus, once remarked that the subject has a long past but a short history. The study of thought and reason is long in both, as you will see: ideas from more than 2000 years ago are still being discussed alongside those that are hot off the presses. You will find connections not only to other areas of human science, but connections to your own life experience too: that has been another hallmark of the recent study of reason, and you will find this reflected in the book's organisation. Not so long ago, you would have had to work hard to make these connections; now they are clear and striking.

How the book is organised

The book is sequenced so that each section leads on to the next, and so that, as you go through it, you can make these connections, and others as well. Some will be flagged up, but some I hope you will discover for yourself. By the time you get to the end, you should have a thorough grasp of what the interesting issues are, why they are interesting, and where you can go for more detailed information.

One conceptual development that is worth focussing on right at the start is a shift in the way that human reason is thought about. Part of the long history of the study of thought lies in logic, which was first systematised in ancient Greece around two and a half thousand years ago. Until quite recently, theories of reasoning all looked to logic for their normative standards. Around the turn of this century, though, a new paradigm has risen to prominence. Instead of logic, probability is its foundation stone. Why is this important? Logic largely deals in binary, true/false statements. Think about the one that opened this preface: does my conclusion about the importance of psychology follow or not? You might feel that you could come down on one side or the other, yes or no. Or perhaps you feel that 'maybe' or 'it depends' might be wiser. If so, you are using probability. We do not live in a yes/ no world; psychological theory reflects that more and more.

The place of probability in current explanations of reasoning follows the precedent set by its place in the study of judgment and decision making, which has been established for much longer, as you will see. The study of judgment directly concerns how we think about probability, and the study of decision making is probabilistic through and through. In view of its importance, we therefore get straight into probability in Chapter 1. Here we shall consider probability judgment. Once we have done that, you will have a set of tools to think with when probabilistic explanations come into view in later chapters.

In Chapter 2, we shall go back to that ancient history and review how the logical paradigm developed, through the study of syllogisms. These arguments are still being studied, and continue to deliver findings that influence theory in the present day. But they have been rivalled in the modern era by the study of arguments based on *If*, or conditionals to give them their technical name. We look at the classic work on conditional reasoning in Chapter 3, along with research on reasoning using a related connective term, *Or*. Then we shall go further into the study of reasoning as it occurs in more everyday areas, and using more realistic methods, in Chapter 4. These methods have led to huge advances in our understanding. After that, there are two chapters on how reasoning has been explained.

Chapter 5 reviews logic-based explanations, which include the theory of mental models. This has been the most influential of all reasoning theories, and has generated an ocean of research. Chapter 5 will help you navigate it. Chapter 6 is where we review the 'new paradigm' approaches, based on probability, and including the dual process theory, one of the most active of current research areas. In Chapter 7, we bring many of the themes from the first half of the book together and focus on an aspect of thinking that defines us as humans: hypothetical thinking, the kind of thought we use when we formulate new explanations of the world, and test them.

From there, we pass to the area of thinking in which we apply our reason to make choices: the study of decision making. In Chapter 8, we again look back to the founding ideas in this area, and then come up to date with modern explanations. As mentioned above, probability takes centre stage in this. In Chapter 9, we extend our survey into areas of life where puzzling complications and intriguing new findings about our decision-making tendencies emerge, and encounter ideas that pose fundamental challenges to the standard explanations of our decision making. Finally, in Chapter 10, we turn around and look at the person in all of this. What does it mean to describe yourself, or someone else, as rational or irrational? What is extreme irrationality like? What do your personality and culture imply for these labels? As with many of the other areas reviewed in this book, there has been an upsurge in work on all of these questions in the last few years.

I had better say something about the word 'normative', which appeared above. It is an important word that is used a lot by researchers in this field, and you may not be familiar with it. A normative theory is one that states what judgment, decision or conclusion you should, objectively, arrive at. This can be contrasted with a descriptive theory, one whose focus is on what people actually do. A great deal of research effort has gone into exploring and explaining the gaps that appear between the ideal and the actual in human thinking. Normative–descriptive is one of many dualities that you can look out for in the following pages. There is one in the book's title: thinking and reasoning. This alludes to the distinction, now receding because of the new paradigm, between reasoning, the part of human thought that involves explicit inference, and the rest, a category that mainly includes judgment and decision making – another duality. Within reasoning itself, we shall talk about inductive and deductive reasoning, and about indicative and deontic reasoning. There are dual process theories of thinking, dual rationality theories, individualist and collectivist thinking cultures. Perhaps the mind loves contrasts.

The credits

Finally, a brief vote of thanks to a few, only a few, of the many people who have helped get me to the position of being able to write these words, and have generally added to the rewards of being involved in psychological research. Firstly to my academic mentors, David Over and Jonathan Evans. You won't have to look far to find their influence. Kathryn Russel, Tara Stebnicky, and especially, Sharla Plant and Michael Fenton at Psychology Press have helped the text over the finish line. Parts have been read by Anke Büttner, Niall Galbraith, Erica Lucas and Ed

Sutherland. The whole manuscript was reviewed by Linden Ball, Jonathan Evans, Mike Oaksford and David Shanks, to whom I owe the advice to open with the chapter on probability. All the improvements in the text are down to these people. Nicky Hart, head of the department I work in, has helped me more than anyone else through my working day there. And Linda Miller has made all the difference.

Ken Manktelow
Wolverhampton
January 2012

Judging and thinking about probability

If you have read the Preface, you will have been cued into the importance of probability in how we now understand and explain thinking and reasoning. We therefore open with this central topic: it forms the basis of explanation across the spectrum of thought. In this chapter, we shall look at research that assesses how people judge probability directly. You may have come across the word in statistics classes, and already be stifling a yawn. If so, wake up: probability is far from being just a dry technical matter best left in the classroom. Everyone judges probability, and does so countless times every day. You might have wondered today whether it is going to rain, how likely you are to fall victim to the latest flu outbreak, whether your friend will be in her usual place at lunchtime, and so on.

How do we make these judgments? We can make a comparison between *normative* systems, which tell us what we ought to think, and *descriptive* data on how people actually do think. To get you going in doing this, here are some questions devised by my statistical alter ego, Dr Horatio Scale. Answering them will raise the probability that you will appreciate the material in the rest of this chapter. We shall look at the answers in the next section.

1 a What is the probability of drawing the ace of spades from a fair deck of cards?
   b What is the probability of drawing an ace of any suit?
   c What is the probability of drawing an ace or a king?
   d What is the probability of drawing an ace and then a king?

2 You are about to roll two dice. What is the chance that you will get 'snake eyes' (double 1)?

3 a What is the chance that you will win the jackpot in the National Lottery this week?
   b What is the chance that you will win any prize at all this week?

(The British lottery lets you choose six numbers from 1 to 49. You win the jackpot if all your six numbers are drawn; you win lesser prizes if three, four or five of your numbers are drawn.)

4 Yesterday, the weather forecaster said that there was a 30% chance of rain today, and today it rained. Was she right or wrong?

5 What is the chance that a live specimen of the Loch Ness Monster will be found?

6 Who is more likely to be the victim of a street robbery, a young man or an old lady?

7 Think about the area where you live. Are there more dogs or cats in the neighbourhood?

Defining probability

The phrase 'normative systems', plural, was used above because even at the formal level, probability means different things to different people. It is one of the puzzles of history that formal theories of probability were only developed comparatively

recently, since the mid-17th century. Their original motivations were quite practical, due to the need to have accurate ways of calculating the odds in gambling,
investment and insurance. This early history is recounted by Gigerenzer, Swijtink,
Porter, Daston, Beatty and Krüger (1989) and by Gillies (2000). Gillies solves the
historical puzzle by pointing to the use of primitive technology by the ancient
Greeks when gambling, such as bones instead of accurately machined dice, and to
their lack of efficient mathematical symbol systems for making the necessary
calculations – think of trying to work out odds using Roman numerals. All four of
the formal definitions of probability that are still referred to have been developed
since the early 20th century. Here they are.

Logical possibility

Probability as logical possibility really only applies to objectively unbiased situations such as true games of chance, where there is a set of equally probable alternatives. We have to assume that this is the case when working out the odds, but it
is hard to maintain this stipulation in real life. This is behind Gillies' explanation of
why the ancient Greeks and Romans could not develop a theory of probability from
their own games of 'dice' made from animal bones: these have uneven sides that
are consequently not equally likely to turn up.

To see how we can work out odds using logical possibility, let us take
Dr Scale's first question, and assume that we are dealing with a properly shuffled,
fair deck of cards, so that when we draw one from it, its chances are the same as
any other's. There are 52 cards in the deck, only one of which is the ace of spades,
so its odds are 1:52. Odds are often expressed in percentages: in this case, it is
about 1.92%. Probability in mathematics and statistics is usually given as a decimal
number in the range between 0 and 1: in this case, it is .0192. An ace of any suit?
There are four of them, so we can work out 4:52 (i.e. 1:13) in the same way, or
multiply .0192 by four to obtain the answer: .077.

The odds of an ace *or* a king are the odds of each added together: there is one
of each in each suit of 13 cards, so the joint odds are 2:13, or .154. Question 1d is a
bit more complicated. It introduces us to the idea of *conditional probability*, because
we need to calculate the probability of a king *given* that you have drawn an ace.
Each has the probability .077, and you obtain the conditional probability by multiplying them together, which gives the result of just under .006, i.e. 6:1000 – a very
slim chance.

Now you can address Dr Scale's third question, the lottery odds. With 49
numbers to choose from, the odds of the first are clearly 1:49. This number is no
longer available when you come to choose the second number, so its odds are 1:48,
and so on. Sticking with just these two for a moment, the odds of your first one and
then your second one coming up can be worked out just as with the ace and king:
$1:49 \times 1:48$, or $.0204 \times .0208 = $ just over .0004. But with the lottery, the order in
which the numbers are drawn does not matter, so we have to multiply that number
by the number of orders in which these two numbers could be drawn. That is given
by the factorial of the number of cases, in this case $2 \times 1 = 2$. This number replaces
the 1 in the odds ratio, which now becomes $2:49 \times 48$. You simply expand this

procedure to work out the chances of 6 numbers out of 49 being drawn in any order. If you want to do this yourself, it is probably easiest to use the numbers in the following form and then use cancelling, otherwise the long strings of zeroes that will result if you use the decimal notation will boggle your calculator:

$$\frac{6 \times 5 \times 4 \times 3 \times 2 \times 1}{49 \times 48 \times 47 \times 46 \times 45 \times 44}$$

The top line is factorial 6, for the number of orders in which six numbers could appear. The resulting odds are approximately 1:13.98 million. So if you play once a week, you can expect to win the jackpot about once every quarter of a million years.

Question 3b asked about the odds of winning any prize at all. You can work out the odds of three, four or five of your numbers coming up in exactly the same way as just described. You don't just add all these results together, however, because there are numerous ways in which, say, three numbers from the six you have chosen can come up. So you have to multiply each odds result by this number, and then add them all up. In case you don't feel up to it, I can tell you that the odds of winning any prize in any one week are around 1:57. So a regular player should get a prize about once a year, although this will almost certainly be the lowest prize (the odds of three of your numbers coming up are about 1:54). I shall deal with whether, in the face of these odds, playing the lottery is a good decision in Chapter 8.

Frequency

Frequency theory has roots that go back to the 19th century, but it was developed in most detail in the mid-20th, and has been highly influential ever since. In psychology, this influence has been even more recent, as we shall see later in this chapter. People who adopt frequency theory are called *frequentists*, and they regard probability as the proportion of times an event occurs out of all the occasions it could have occurred, known as the *collective*. There are two kinds of collectives, referred to by an early frequentist, von Mises (1950), as *mass phenomena* or *repetitive events*.

Dr Scale's sixth question can be taken as a frequency question about a mass phenomenon: you could count up the number of street robberies and look at the proportions where the victims were old ladies and young men, and see which was the greater. Games of chance, such as coin flips, dice and lotteries, can also be analysed in terms of frequencies: these are repetitive events. Instead of working out the odds mathematically, you could count up the number of jackpot winners as the proportion of players, for instance. Over time, the results of the two probabilities, frequency and odds, should converge; if they don't, you have detected a bias. Gamblers can be exquisitely sensitive to these biases: Gillies (2000) tells us about a 17th century nobleman whose was able, through his extensive experience with dice games, to detect the difference between odds of .5000 and .4914, a difference of 1.7%. Question 7 (cats and dogs) is also a frequency question, again about a mass phenomenon. Beware: this question has a catch, which we shall return to later in the chapter.

Propensity

For a true frequentist, it makes no sense to ask for the probability of a single event such as how likely you are to win a game of chance, because the only objective probabilities are frequencies – things that have actually happened – and frequencies cannot be derived from one-off observations or events that have not yet occurred. Nor can frequencies have any 'power' to influence a single observation: suppose there are twice as many dogs as cats in your area, does that fact determine in any way the species of the next pet you see? How could it? But everyone has a strong feeling that we can give such odds: we do feel that the next animal is more likely to be a dog than a cat. This clash of intuitions was addressed by the celebrated philosopher of science, Karl Popper (1959a), who introduced the *propensity theory*. He needed to do so because of single events in physics, such as those predicted by quantum mechanics. The probabilities of such events must, he thought, be objective, but they could not be based on frequencies.

Dr Scale's second question is about propensity: note that it asks you specifically about a single event, the next throw, whereas Question 1 was more general. Popper used a dice game example when he tried to solve the intuitive riddle just described (i.e. an example involving logical possibility). Consider two dice, one fair and one weighted so that it is biased in favour of showing a 6 when tossed: it tends to show a 6 on one-third of the throws (i.e. twice as often as it would if unbiased). Suppose we have a long sequence of dice throws, most involving the biased die with occasional throws of the fair one. Take one of these fair tosses. What is the probability that it will show a 6? Popper argued that a frequentist would have to say 1:3, because the 'collective' set of throws has produced this frequency. However, you and I know that it must be 1:6, because we are talking about the fair die, and fair dice will tend to show each of their six sides with the same frequency.

Popper's solution was to appeal to the difference in causal mechanisms embodied in the two dice to resolve this paradox: the collective really consists of two sub-collectives that have been produced by two different generating conditions. The biased die has the *propensity* to show a 6 more often than a fair die does because of its different causal properties. (We shall look in detail at causal thinking in Chapter 4.)

There are problems with propensity theories (others have come after Popper), one of which is that invoking causal conditions just replaces one set of problems with another. In the real world, it can be very difficult to produce the same generating conditions on different occasions, as all psychology students know from the discussion of confounding variables in their methodology courses. If it is not realistically possible to repeat these conditions, then is an objective single-event probability therefore also not possible? And if so, what is the alternative?

Degree of belief

We have strong intuitions about the probability of single events, so the alternative to objective probabilities must be subjective probabilities, or *degrees of belief*.

Look at Dr Scale's fifth question. If you have heard of the Loch Ness Monster, you will have some view as to how likely it is that it really exists. However, this cannot be based on a logical possibility, nor can it be based on a frequency: there is not a 'mass' of equivalent Scottish lochs, some with monsters and some without. Perhaps you can even assign a number to your belief, and perhaps you use objective facts in doing so, to do with the known biology and ecology of the species that you presume the beast to be. But your degree of belief can only be subjective.

Now look at Dr Scale's fourth question, about the weather forecast. Weather presenters often use numbers in this way, but what do they mean? Once again, it is hard to see how this can be a logical possibility: weather is not a series of random, equivalent events, even in Britain. Could it then be a frequency? If so, what of? This particular date in history, or days when there has been a weather pattern like this? Baron (2008) uses weather forecasts as an example by which we can assess how well someone's probabilistic beliefs are *calibrated*. That is, if someone says that there is a 30% chance of rain, and it rains on 30% of days when she says this, then her judgment is well calibrated (this is another kind of frequency). This may be useful information about the climate, but it is not a useful attitude to weather fore-casting: we want to know whether to cancel *today's* picnic, a single event. And if the forecaster said 30%, and it rained today, isn't she more wrong than right? She implied that there was a 70% chance that it would not rain. Thus you can be well calibrated in frequency terms but hopeless at predicting single events.

Confusion over the use of percentages like this was addressed by Gigerenzer, Hertwig, van den Broek, Fasolo and Katsikopoulos (2005), following up an earlier study by Murphy, Lichtenstein, Fischhoff and Winkler (1980). First of all, they set the normative meaning of this figure: that there will be rain on 30% of days where this forecast figure is given. So they are adopting the frequentist approach. They tested people's understanding of the figure in five different countries, varying according to how long percentage forecasts had been broadcast. The range was from almost 40 years (New York, USA: they were introduced there in 1965) to never (Athens, Greece). The prediction was that the degree of 'normative' under-standing would be correlated with length of usage of percentage forecasts. It was. Alternative interpretations produced by participants were that the 30% figure meant that it would rain for 30% of the time, or across 30% of the region. Note, by the way, that even among the New Yorkers about one-third did not give the 'days' interpretation. And keep in mind that people listen to weather forecasts to find out about particular days, not climatic patterns. Gigerenzer et al. urge that forecasters be clear about the *reference class* when giving numerical probabilities. This is an important issue that we shall return to in a short while.

By the way, my degree of belief in the Loch Ness Monster is close to zero. If, as most of its publicity says, it is a plesiosaur (a large aquatic reptile of a kind that existed at the end of the Cretaceous period, 65 million years ago), we would have to have a breeding population. They were air breathers – heads would be bobbing up all over the place. They would not be hard to spot.

Of course, our beliefs in rain or monsters can be changed if we encounter some new evidence. You go to bed with a subjective degree of belief in rain tomorrow at .3, and wake up to black skies and the rumble of thunder: that will cause you to revise it.

Belief revision: Bayes' rule

The subjective view of probability opens up a range of theoretical possibilities, which all come under the heading of the *Bayesian* approach to cognition. It is hard to overestimate the influence of this perspective at the present time (see Chater & Oaksford, 2008, for a recent survey), and we shall see it applied to theories of reasoning in later chapters. Most of the rest of this one will be concerned with Bayesian matters in some form or other. The word 'Bayesian' comes from Thomas Bayes, an 18th century English clergyman who laid the foundations for this area in a paper published after his death (Bayes & Price, 1763/1970). It is one of the most influential papers in all of science.

To illustrate Bayesian belief revision, Dr Scale has another question for you:

8   Inspector Diesel and his sidekick, Sergeant Roscoe, are on the trail of noto-
     rious Dick Nastardley, who is on the run. They know that he is often to be
     found in his local pub, the Ham & Pickle, on Friday nights – about 80% of the
     time, they understand.
         It is Friday, and Diesel and Roscoe are outside the Ham trying to see
     whether Dick is inside. They can only see half the bar, and he is not in that
     half. So, what is Diesel's estimate of the probability that if he and Roscoe raid
     the pub, they will find their man and nab Dick?

Bayes' rule produces a precise numerical estimate of this kind of probability. It enables us to compute the probability of a hypothesis when given some evidence: a conditional probability. In doing so, we start off with some *prior knowledge* that the hypothesis is true, before the evidence comes in. This can be combined with the *likelihood* of the evidence, given this hypothesis and any alternative hypotheses. These numbers can be combined to derive an estimate of the *posterior probability* that the hypothesis is true, given the evidence.

Question 8 provides you with all the information you need to compute Diesel's degree of belief that Dick is in the bar. The prior probability is his existing belief (based on a frequency) that he is in the bar – 80%, or .8. The alternative hypothesis – there is only one in this case – is that he is not there: Diesel holds this at .2. Now comes the evidence, or data: Dick is not in the visible half of the bar. If he were in the Ham & Pickle, the probability that he would not be visible is obviously .5, because he could be in the half that is visible or the half that is out of sight; if he were not there, this probability must be 1: he could not be in either half.

In Table 1.1, you can see a formula for Bayes' rule (there are different versions, but I shall just use this one) and how these numbers are plugged into it. The result is a posterior probability of .67. That is, Diesel's degree of belief is now lower than it was before they looked in through the windows, when it was at .8. That makes sense: Dick was *not* in the half they could see, which must reduce Diesel's confidence. However, there is still a greater than .5 probability that Dick is in there. The two sleuths now have a decision to make. We shall review the kinds of thinking that they might use to make it in Chapters 8 and 9.

In the rest of this chapter, we shall look at the research evidence on what people do when they think about probability, and at how this performance has been

Table 1.1 Inspector Diesel's belief revision, using Bayes' rule

The Bayesian formula:

$$\text{prob }(H|D) = \frac{\text{prob}(D|H) \times \text{prob}(H)}{[\text{prob}(D|H) \times \text{prob}(H)] + [\text{prob}(D|\neg H) \times \text{prob}(\neg H)]}$$

prob(H): Diesel's prior belief that Dick is in the Ham & Pickle 80% of the time, i.e. .8
prob(¬H): the prior probability of his alternative hypothesis that Dick is not
  there, i.e. .2
D: Dick is not in the visible half of the bar
prob(D|H): the likelihood that he is not visible, given Diesel's hypothesis, i.e. .5
prob(D|¬H): the likelihood that he is not visible, given the alternative hypothesis, i.e. 1

$$\text{prob }(H|D) = \frac{.5 \times .8}{[.5 \times .8] + [1 \times .2]} = \frac{.4}{.4 + .2} = .67$$

explained. We shall look firstly at 'plain' probability judgments, where people are asked to estimate likelihoods or frequencies, and then go on to belief revision, where we address the question of the degree to which people like you, me and Inspector Diesel are good Bayesians when we update our beliefs. So we shall be comparing normative (Bayesian) theory and descriptive accounts of human performance.

Judging plain probabilities

Dr Scale's first seven questions are about these, and you will be able to recall having thought about, or being asked about, similar probabilities many times. What are your chances of dying in an air crash compared to a car crash, or being struck by lightning? These questions are not always as easy to answer as they first appear, and explaining how we answer them is not always easy either.

Logical possibilities

People usually have a secure grasp of simple problems such as the ace of spades one above: in the classroom, I have not come across any people who have been truly baffled by questions like this. However, there is a sting in the tail even with these, and it is to do with people's understanding of randomness and what it implies for expected frequencies. People seem to assume that an equal chance means that there will be an even distribution, and are more surprised than they should be when the resulting pattern actually looks quite lumpy.

Here are two examples, one involving mass phenomena and one involving repetitive events. The first is quoted by Blastland and Dilnot (2007), in their splendid popular statistics book: cancer clusters. It is quite common to read in the press that there is anxiety about a higher than average incidence of cancer in some locality, sometimes following a change in the environment, such as the siting of a phone mast. With something as serious as cancer, people naturally want to know what might have caused it. When there is no known cause, they will advance hypothetical causal models, such as possible carcinogenic properties of the radiation emitted by phone masts. (The World Health Organization, in 2009, advised that there is no convincing evidence that these induce or promote cancer, or any other illness.) They may even take action, such as sabotage, as Blastland and Dilnot report. But suppose cancer were distributed in the population at random, with respect to phone masts (we know quite a bit about actual causal mechanisms for some cancers, of course): what would the patterns of this distribution look like? They would not be even: that really would tell you that something fishy was going on. They would be lumpy: some areas would report a much higher incidence than average, some lower – they might even be right next door to each other. With real games of chance, such as coin tossing, people are uncomfortable with clusters of more than three, whereas 'lumps' of five or six heads or tails are quite common. Blastland and Dilnot report three sets of 30 coin tosses: there were three runs of five or six heads or tails in these sets.

The second example comes from the psychological literature, and was reported in a famous paper by Gilovich, Vallone and Tversky (1985), concerning people's beliefs about the 'hot hand' in US basketball players. This is a version of the general notion of 'form' in sports performers: that during a period of good form, a player is more likely to hit following a hit compared to following a miss than would be expected by chance. People strongly believe in form, and will swear that this elusive property is causing a higher than normal probability of hits. However, Gilovich and colleagues found no evidence for this effect in several studies of players' actual performance when they looked at the conditional probabilities of hits following hits and misses. What is happening, they say, is that people are oblivious of the statistical effect of *regression to the mean*. Each player will, over the long term, produce a personal average hit rate. In the short term, there will be deviations from this mean that are essentially random, and these deviations will sometimes occur in lumps. Just as with the cancer clusters, people then produce a causal hypothesis, form, to 'explain' the effect.

The *gambler's fallacy* is the most extreme version of this error. Think again about coin tosses, and suppose that there has been a run of five heads. It is quite common for people to believe that there is therefore a high probability of tails on the next throw, but, as the saying goes, the coin has no memory. The *logical possibility* of tails is still .5; this gives an *expected frequency* of 50/50, which is what it will approach in the long run. People who fall for the gambler's fallacy or the hot hand hypothesis are confusing the one for the other.

Alter and Oppenheimer (2006) review numerous studies of the hot hand fallacy and show how it and the gambler's fallacy can be seen as two sides of the same coin (forgive me). The hot hand idea incorporates the notion of skill as a causal mechanism, so that when there is a long streak of one particular outcome, such as hits, people expect the streak to continue. However, when the streak comes from a random, skill-free process such as coin tossing, people expect the streak to end, so that the general sequence balances out. An exception occurs with gamblers playing roulette or dice games in casinos: these are random processes and yet people do often believe in hot hands when gambling. This shows that gamblers have mythical beliefs about the processes that generate outcomes at the tables – a very dangerous state of affairs for the gambler, but a very happy one for the house.

Frequencies

We are now going to see how people approach Dr Scale's Questions 4, 6 and 7 and similar ones. One thing we can ask is how well calibrated people's estimates are compared to the statistical facts. We have already seen that there is a complication, which Question 4, about the weather forecast, brought out, and which applies when we try to use frequency expressions to convey single-event probabilities: you can be well calibrated in frequency terms but useless as a forecaster. Question 6, about robberies, is different. Now you are being asked a frequency question: how often do two things happen?

Evidence that people deviate from statistical norms comes from a classic piece of research by Lichtenstein, Slovic, Fischhoff, Layman and Combs (1978; see also Lichtenstein, Fischhoff & Phillips, 1982). They asked Americans in the 1970s to estimate how many deaths in the USA were due to various causes, such as different forms of disease, accidents, natural events (such as floods) and crime. People tended to overestimate the likelihoods of very uncommon events, such as deaths from botulism (a kind of food poisoning caused by infected meat), but underestimate the likelihoods of deaths from common causes, such as heart disease. As Baron (2008) points out, you would expect this kind of pattern anyway, given that people make mistakes: if something never actually happens, but some people think it does, its prevalence will come out as overestimated. The same will occur at the top end: anyone who mistakenly thinks that something does not happen, when it happens a lot, will pull down its average estimate.

There is a particular and very important difficulty with estimating frequencies: the *reference class* to which the event in question is being compared; this was mentioned earlier when discussing numerical weather forecasts. Remember that probability as frequency is reckoned by the number of times the event happens compared to the number of times it could have happened. This estimate clearly depends crucially on the latter number, so what should that number be?

Consider someone's chances of being struck by lightning. According to the BBC's weather website (accessed in October 2009), a Briton has a 1 in 3 million chance of being struck by lightning, and they make the point that this is a much higher chance than of winning the lottery jackpot (see above). However, it is hard to make sense of this claim without knowing what the 3 million refers to. This is the reference class problem. Probing further on the web, I found that about 50 people are struck by lightning in Britain every year (about 5 are killed). With a population of around 60 million, this is a strike frequency of about 1 in 1.2 million. But that is just in 1 year. In the USA, the 1-year risk is said to be 1 in 700,000, with a lifetime risk of 1 in 5000. However, even when we are clearer about such figures, we still do not have a clear reference class. These are the figures for national populations, and nations are made up of different kinds of people. Compare the chances of farm workers and miners: the former are obviously much more likely to get struck (one British agricultural worker has been struck seven times in 35 years). And if you live in Uganda, take especial care with your life insurance: Uganda has the most lightning storms of any country. So to judge your own chances of being struck, you need to know which class you belong to: there is a lot of difference between British miners and Ugandan farmers in this respect. We shall come back to the reference class problem when we deal with belief updating.

Taking samples: where our information comes from

Think about Dr Scale's Questions 6 and 7 again, about street robberies and dogs and cats. People readily give responses to this kind of question, but what are they basing these responses on? There are two possibilities: prior knowledge and current information. We shall concentrate on the former, since that is where most of the research has been done. I doubt whether, when thinking about street robberies, you retrieved official government statistics, or, when thinking about dogs and cats, you had actually gone round your neighbourhood with a clipboard counting them up. So what did you use as the basis of your estimates?

The most influential answer to this question was proposed by Daniel Kahneman and Amos Tversky in an extensive research programme that has been compiled into two large volumes (Gilovich, Griffin & Kahneman, 2002; Kahneman, Slovic & Tversky, 1982). You use some kind of *heuristic*. A heuristic is a rough rule of thumb, as opposed to an algorithm, which is a set of exactly specified steps. If you are cooking, and faithfully following a recipe, you are using an algorithm; if you are vaguely tossing handfuls of this and that into the mixing bowl, you are using heuristics. The heuristic that applies to Dr Scale's two questions is *availability*, introduced by Tversky and Kahneman (1973). This is their own definition: 'A person is said to employ the availability heuristic whenever he estimates frequency or probability by the ease with which instances or associations could be brought to mind' (p. 208). They add that you do not actually have to bring examples to mind, just estimate how easy it would be to do so. Thus one estimate, ease of thinking, is used to stand for another, probability.

Tversky and Kahneman argue that such a heuristic is ecologically valid (i.e. is true or useful in the real world), because if something is common it should be easy to recall instances of it. However, in some circumstances, its use can lead to biased estimates. This will happen if something other than frequency has led to availability. This is why Kahneman and Tversky's research has come to be known as the *Heuristics and Biases* programme. It is as if the mind commits a logical fallacy (we shall deal with these in Chapter 3): given that *If something happens often then examples will be easy to recall*, and *I can easily recall an example*, you infer *therefore it is happening often*. This would only be valid if nothing else led to ease of recall. The observation of such biases would be crucial evidence that people use heuristics when judging probability.

This prediction was confirmed in a series of experiments, the hallmark of which is their ingenuity and simplicity (see Part IV of the Kahneman et al., 1982 volume and Part One of the Gilovich et al., 2002 volume for collections of these studies). Here is an example from Tversky and Kahneman's original 1973 paper. They chose the letters, K, L, N, R and V, and asked 152 people to judge whether each was more likely to appear as the first letter or as the third letter in a sample of English text. More than two-thirds (105) thought that the first position was more likely for a majority of the letters. In fact, all the letters are more common in the third position. The availability heuristic would predict this since we are far more used to thinking about initial letters, such as in alphabetical name lists, than third letters. In the same paper, they gave people two lists of names. In one there were 19 women and 20 men, and in the other, 19 men and 20 women. In both cases, the 19 names were famous and the 20 were not. When asked to estimate which were more frequent in the lists, men or women, the participants reported that there were more women in the first list and more men in the second – the opposite of the truth. They were biased by the greater ease of recalling the famous names, as was confirmed in a memory test when they recalled 50% more of these than the unfamiliar names.

Evidence that availability can affect more real-life judgments comes from a study by Ross and Sicoly (1979). It concerned people's perceptions of their share of the credit when they have joint responsibility for some event or activity: students will think about this when doing group projects, for instance, and sports team members will ponder who contributed most to their team's performance. Ross and Sicoly studied married couples, thinking about 20 household events (19 for those without children): who did each partner think did the most of each? He and she both thought they made a greater contribution to most of the events, including negative ones such as starting arguments. They cannot both be right. Ross and Sicoly ruled out a motivational bias, because the effect occurred with both good and bad events. The availability explanation is that your own contributions are simply easier to remember: you are always there when you do something, but not when your partner does, and you may also attach greater significance to your own deeds.

Anything that makes an event easy to bring to mind should increase our judgment of its probability whether or not it has anything to do with frequency, according to availability. An example is *vividness*: how much impact does the information make on you? Nisbett and Ross (1980) devote a whole chapter of their classic book to this factor. The street robbery question above was designed to illustrate it. If you thought that old ladies are more often victims than young men are, you may well have thought so because you could easily call to mind vivid instances: you may have seen news stories with graphic pictures, and these are not easy to forget. The memorability of such stories may in turn be due to a factor that Nisbett and Ross identify as contributing to vividness: emotional impact. Proximity in time or space is another: for instance, if the houses on either side of yours have noisy dogs in them.

They also point out that vivid information is usually more information, for instance in the reporting of an elderly crime victim, where a lot about the person and the circumstances of the crime will be given. Celebrity illness is another instance of this: it was observed by Nisbett and Ross over 30 years ago, and can be observed today, that a famous person reported as suffering from a particular disease leads to a flood of people seeking tests for that disease. Politicians and commentators know all about vividness: you will often hear them invoking single striking cases to attack an opposing view, when the statistics actually back up that view. Nisbett and Ross sum up the vividness factor with a chilling quote attributed to the Soviet dictator Josef Stalin: that a single death is a tragedy, while a million deaths is a statistic.

There is another way in which factors such as vividness could affect probability judgment without the availability heuristic: they could bias the sample on which you base your judgment. Think of the news reports of elderly crime victims:

how often do such stories appear, compared to stories about young male victims? It is possible that, when making the kinds of judgments that Question 6 called for, you are responding accurately to the sample that the media present you with. News stories are often about unusual occurrences – that is what makes them news – and so the unusual will come to be represented more often in current experience and memory than it should be, statistically speaking. This would explain the apparent bias in people's assessments of likelihood of death from various causes: they will overestimate rare causes because they are talked about more than common causes, and underestimate common causes for the same reason. Similarly, consider Ross and Sicoly's married couples. Perhaps each thinks they do more than the other simply because they observe more of their own contributions than their partners'.

Klaus Fiedler (2000), in an extensive survey, makes the point that our judgments are always based on samples, and that if the sample that is presented to us is biased, as with sexy stories in the media, then so will our judgments be, especially if our judgment processes themselves tend to be accurate. The bias is in the sample, not in the mind. What we need in order to evade bias is a skill that seems very hard to acquire: that of critically assessing the nature of sampling. The letter task (K, L, N etc.) used by Tversky and Kahneman (1973) in their initial proposal of availability (see above) was criticised on sampling grounds by Sedlmeier, Hertwig and Gigerenzer (1998). They point out that the set of letters used in this study was a biased sample of letters of the alphabet: all five are more common in the third position in English words, whereas 60% of all consonants are in fact more common in the first position. Sedlmeier et al. proposed that people would be sensitive to the relative frequencies within the whole class of consonants, while tending to underestimate the most common letters and overestimate the rare ones, as in the death estimates in the Lichtenstein et al. (1978) study reviewed earlier. A model based on this hypothesis predicted people's judged ordering of frequencies of 13 letters in German words better than did two versions of the availability heuristic. We shall come back to the question of sampling later in the chapter.

The notion of availability was elaborated in later work by Tversky and his colleagues, in the form of *support theory*. Tversky and Koehler (1994; see also Rottenstreich & Tversky, 1997) distinguished between the event itself and mental representations (or descriptions, of events) which they called *hypotheses*. When you judge a hypothesis, you consider the weight of evidence for it: its support. Hypotheses can be explicit or implicit. For instance, suppose you were asked to judge how many people die each year of natural versus unnatural causes. You are given heart disease, cancer and other natural causes to assess; or accident, homicide and other unnatural causes. In each case, the named causes are explicit hypotheses and 'other' is an implicit hypothesis. Explicit mention of factors such as accident or homicide provides cues to search for support that are absent from the implicit hypothesis: it is hard to search for 'other'.

Both earlier research and experiments run by Tversky and Koehler (1994) showed that when implicit hypotheses are unpacked into explicit components and their probabilities judged, the sum of judgments of the explicit hypotheses is greater than the judgment of the implicit hypothesis. This is called *subadditivity*: the implicit support comes to less than the quanta of explicit support when you add them up. It follows from this that the degree of subadditivity should be greater when there are more unpacked explicit components. Objectively, of course, there should be no difference: 'natural causes' should just be the sum of all the causes that come into this category. Both tendencies, subadditivity and its increase, were confirmed by Tversky and Koehler (1994). In one experiment, they asked US students to estimate the probability of death from various causes, either by thinking about the probability of an individual dying from them, or by assessing the frequency of each from the 2 million annual deaths in the USA. These students assessed the probability of 'natural causes' as .58, but their estimates of 'heart disease + cancer + other natural causes' came to .73, a subadditivity factor of 1.26 (i.e. .73/.58). When seven rather than three components were used, subadditivity was increased, as support theory predicted: the factor was now 2.19. The same tendencies were found for unnatural causes.

Interestingly, and consistent again with the findings of Lichtenstein and colleagues (1978) mentioned earlier, the unnatural causes were greatly overestimated relative to the actual frequencies of recorded causes of death. For instance, estimates of frequency of deaths due to accidents were around 30%, but the true figure was 4.4%. Support theory is not about people's accuracy relative to the facts, but about the way they judge their *representations* of events, their hypotheses. These hypotheses can only be formed about what is available, hence unpacking and subadditivity can be affected by the sorts of factors, such as vividness, that influence availability.

Belief updating

In many everyday cases of probability judgment, we do not judge probabilities by themselves, but judge them in response to some information. That is, we start out with some estimate of belief and then have to revise it. Medicine is an obvious case: you have some symptom that leads you to suspect that you may have a certain disease, you get yourself tested, and the test result comes back. Dr Scale has one last problem for you to illustrate this, adapted from an example in Eddy (1982):

9   A friend of yours went on holiday to the Costa del Sol last year and, in between bouts of inadvisable partying, fried in the sun on the beach for two weeks. Recently, he noticed a large new mole on his arm. He went to the doctor, who decided to test him for skin cancer. She told him that (a) in people who have cancer, the test shows positive in 90% of cases, while (b) the false positive rate, where people without cancer test positive, is 20%. People with new moles like your friend's actually turn out to have cancer 1% of the time (c). Your friend is shaken: his test has come out positive. He wants you to tell him what the probability is that he has cancer. What is your answer?

Give a quick estimate before going on: that is what your friend did. And then work it out. As with the Diesel and Roscoe problem (Question 8) earlier, you have all the information in front of you to work out a precise numerical answer, using Bayes' rule, which was given in Table 1.1. To help you along, the prior probability that he has cancer, prob(H), is .01 (c above). The probability that he will test positive if he

Table 1.2 Bayesian answer to the skin cancer problem

The test shows positive in 90% of cases in patients who have cancer: prob(D|H) = .9
The test shows positive in 20% of cases in patients who do not have cancer:
 prob(D|¬H) = .2
1% of people like this patient actually have cancer: prob(H) = .01

Using Bayes' rule from Table 1.1:

$$\text{prob}(H|D) = \frac{.9 \times .01}{[.9 \times .01] + [.2 \times .99]} = \frac{.009}{.009 + .198} = \frac{.009}{.207} = .043$$

has cancer, prob(D|H), is .9 (a), while the probability that he will test positive even though he is clear, prob(D|¬H), is .2 (b). You can now put these numbers into the Bayesian formula in Table 1.1 and work out the posterior probability, prob(H|D), that he has cancer given a positive test result. It will do you good if you do, but Table 1.2 shows the workings if you want to check or avoid it.

The answer is that prob(H|D) = .043, or just over 4%. Or to put it another way, the probability that he does not have cancer is .957: he almost certainly does not have it, even though he tested positive. The test therefore is useless.

You probably find that result surprising, and your friend may take some convincing of it too. This intuition is a clue as to why there has been a huge volume of research into belief updating. If your initial estimate was around .9, which is the result many people give, you have committed the *inverse fallacy* (Koehler, 1996): you have given prob(D|H) instead of prob(H|D). There are two reasons why the latter figure is so low: the false positive rate of 20% is high, and the prior probability of .01 is low. The latter is known as a *base rate*: the amount of the disease that there is in this population to begin with. It looks as if people tend to neglect base rates with problems like this. Base rate neglect is the most researched aspect of belief updating, so we shall begin our detailed examination of this kind of judgment with it. If you found the Bayesian descriptions above rather hard going, rest easy: later on you will see a method that makes deriving the answer to problems like this much clearer – not just for people like you and me, but for experts such as doctors too. The method in question is at the very heart of debates about just how people revise their beliefs, and what determines their accuracy when they do so.

Base rates: neglect or respect?

The medical problem just given shows that it is possible to induce people to neglect base rates when updating belief in the light of evidence. Eddy (1982) actually tested doctors with this kind of medical problem. You might imagine they would be less prone to base rate neglect than non-medics in this context. They were not. This rather alarming state of affairs shows how potentially important base rate neglect is.

As with so much research in this area, the modern study of base rate neglect was kick-started by Kahneman and Tversky in the 1970s. Neither they nor Eddy invented the diagnosis problem (credit for that goes back to Meehl & Rosen, 1955), but characteristically they did introduce some striking new experiments and, equally importantly, a provocative theory to account for their findings. Both their methods and their theory have generated hundreds of research papers and volumes of debate, culminating in two major reviews in the journal *Behavioral and Brain Sciences*, by Koehler (1996) and Barbey and Sloman (2007); each paper is followed by dozens of commentaries from other experts.

Kahneman and Tversky (1973) introduced one kind of problem that has formed part of the bedrock of research into base rate neglect: the personality problem. It comes in two guises. In the first, participants were told about a room full of 100 people, some of whom are engineers and some lawyers. They were given a personality description of an individual said to have been picked at random from the hundred, and asked to judge whether it is more likely that he is an engineer or a lawyer; the description was designed to resemble the stereotype of engineers, say. One group of participants was told that there were 70 lawyers and 30 engineers in the room, while another group had the figures reversed, so that there were 30 lawyers and 70 engineers. These were the base rates, and they should have influenced judgments: the random person is more likely to be an engineer than a lawyer in the second group than the first. But they made no difference: each group's judgment of how likely the random man was to be an engineer was the same.

In the second version, 69 students were asked to estimate the percentage of students across the country studying nine academic subjects. This provided the base rates, as they were understood by these participants. A second group drawn from the same student population was given a personality description of 'Tom W.', portraying him as something of a nerd, and asked how similar he was to the typical student in each of the nine fields. Finally, a third group was told about Tom and asked to predict which field of study he was likely to be involved in. Their predictions correlated almost perfectly with the second group's similarity judgments, and were negatively related to the first group's base rate judgments. For instance, 95% of the prediction group judged that Tom was more likely to be studying geeky computer science than Bohemian humanities and education, but the base rate of the latter was three times that of the former.

Faced with these results (and others), Kahneman and Tversky proposed that the people were using a non-statistical heuristic to arrive at their judgments: *representativeness*. This word is related to ideas such as similarity and resemblance. In an earlier paper, they defined representativeness in this way:

> A person who follows this heuristic evaluates the probability of an uncertain event, or a sample, by the degree to which it is: (i) similar in essential properties to its parent population; and (ii) reflects the salient features of the process by which it is generated.
>
> (Kahneman & Tversky, 1972, p. 431).

The personality tasks are to do with (i): people are noting the similarity between the individuals described and the typical features of a stereotyped engineer or computing student. These are the parent populations, as far as the participants are concerned.

The second kind of representativeness was explored using perhaps the best known base rate task of all, the taxicab problem. Here it is:

A taxi is involved in a hit-and-run accident at night. In the city, there are two taxi firms, the Green Cab Company and the Blue Cab Company. Of the taxis in the city 85% are Green and the rest are Blue.

A witness identifies the offending cab as Blue. In tests under similar conditions to those on the night of the accident, this witness correctly identified each of the two colours 80% of the time, and was wrong 20% of the time.

What is the probability that the taxi involved in the accident was in fact Blue?

We pause here for you to work out the Bayesian answer. If you need some help, look at Table 1.3, where, as with the Diesel and Roscoe and diagnosis problems, the numbers just given are put into the Bayesian formula.

We are trying to work out the probability that the taxi was Blue given that the witness said it was Blue: prob(H|D). For that, we need the prior probability, prob(II), that the cab was Blue. From the problem description we can infer this to be .15, the figure for 'the rest' once the 85% Green taxis are taken into account. Now we need the data, D. This is the witness's testimony, and he or she was 80% accurate. So we compare the times when the witness says Blue and it really is Blue to the times when he or she says Blue and it is actually Green, taking into account the proportions of Blue and Green cabs.

In Table 1.3 you can see these various bits of information put into the Bayesian formula. The result is that the posterior probability that the cab was in fact Blue is .41 which means that, on these figures, the cab was actually more likely to be Green (.59)!

Tversky and Kahneman (1982a) report data from experiments in which people were given the taxicab problem. They report that, like the personality problems, judgments were largely unaffected by base rate: most were around .8, which is the figure for the witness's accuracy, and is prob(D|H). This is a case of what

Table 1.3 Bayesian answer to the taxicab problem

What is the probability that a taxi involved in an accident was Blue, given that a witness identified it as Blue: prob(H|D)?

The city's cabs are 85% Green and 15% Blue: prob(H) = .15, prob(¬H) = .85
The witness is accurate 80% of the time and mistaken 20% of the time
prob((D|H), that the witness says Blue when the cab is Blue, is therefore .8
prob(D|¬H), that the witness says Blue when the cab is Green, is .2

Using Bayes' rule:

$$prob(H|D) = \frac{.8 \times .15}{[.8 \times .15] + [.2 \times .85]} = \frac{.12}{.12 + .17} = \frac{.12}{.29} = .41$$

Kahneman and Frederick (2002) call *attribute substitution*, as is the use of the availability heuristic: we answer a question to which the answer is inaccessible by addressing another one, whose answer is more accessible. In the availability problems we think about recallability: in the cab problem we think about the witness's reliability.

Base rate neglect is in fact only one facet of the inverse fallacy. With base rate neglect, people are underweighting prob(H), but, as Villejoubert and Mandel (2002) point out, the inverse fallacy also involves neglect of prob(D|¬H) – the false positive rate in the diagnosis problem, or the witness's mistaking Green cabs for Blue in the taxicab problem. In an experiment, they showed that judgments varied according to the degree of difference between prob(H|D) and prob(D|H) with base rates held constant, thus confirming that the inverse fallacy and base rate neglect can be teased apart. We shall return to other aspects of the inverse fallacy shortly, when we consider a radical alternative proposal to Kahneman and Tversky's heuristics in explaining belief revision. We shall turn from medicine to the law when we do so.

Belief revision by natural frequencies

Are you still worried about those doctors that Eddy (1982) tested, who were just as bad at judging the probability that a patient has a disease, given a positive test result, as you were? Relief is at hand. Eddy gave his medical participants Bayesian problems described in the way they have been here: in words. Think about the relation between these word problems and probability judgments in real life. Two differences jump out straight away: the words themselves – is this the way real people talk about probability?; and the data the problems present – in real life, we don't often encounter summary statistics, but build up our representation of the statistical world bit by bit. This is called *natural sampling*. Might doctors do this? Christensen-Szalanski and Beach (1982) found evidence that they do: doctors who learned the relation between the base rates of disease and the outcomes of tests through their clinical experience did not neglect base rates when making diagnostic judgments.

Natural sampling is at the core of a gigantic research programme into probability judgment, decision making and rationality conducted since the 1980s by Gerd Gigerenzer and his colleagues. As this list of areas implies, we shall look at this research not only in this chapter but in later chapters too, especially Chapters 9 and 10. For the moment, let us consider the Gigerenzer approach to probability judgment and belief revision.

Gigerenzer is a frequentist, and frequentists accept only repeated observations as the basis for probability judgments; they do not accept that there is any coherent way to judge the probability of unique events. In his landmark paper with Ulrich Hoffrage, Gigerenzer gives an evolutionary justification for this position:

> Evolutionary theory asserts that the design of the mind and its environment evolve in tandem. Assume. . . that humans have evolved cognitive algorithms that can perform statistical inferences. . . For what information format were these algorithms designed? We assume that as humans evolved, the 'natural'

format was *frequencies* as actually experienced in a series of events, rather than probabilities or percentages.

(Gigerenzer & Hoffrage, 1995, p. 686)

The point at the end is that probabilities (from 0 to 1) and percentages are recent cultural developments, whereas natural frequencies could, they propose, have been used by any person at any time in history. It is important to be clear about natural frequencies. It is not that any frequency format will make Bayesian belief revision easier, but that *natural* frequencies will. For instance, relative frequencies will not have the effect, because these are 'normalised' numbers, not instances actually encountered. Percentages, such as those you have just seen in the diagnosis and taxicab problems, are a form of relative frequency: 85 out of every 100 cabs are Green, and so on. This is not the same as saying that 100 cabs have been observed, of which 85 were Green. The dice-playing nobleman we heard about at the beginning of this chapter was using natural frequencies.

Now let us re-word the diagnosis problem set out above in terms of natural frequencies. Take 1000 patients who see their doctor about a new mole on their skin. Of these people, 10 (the 1% given in the original problem) actually have skin cancer. The test will give a positive result for nine of these (90% of them). There will be 990 people who do not have cancer, and the test will show positive in 198 cases (the 20% false positive rate). So what is the likelihood of cancer when given a positive test? There are 207 people with positive test results (9 + 198), of whom 9 have cancer; 9 out of 207 = .043.

That wasn't so hard, was it? If you look back at Table 1.2 you will see these figures, in decimal form, emerging from the Bayesian formula. It is not the figures that are different, but their representation. Gigerenzer and Hoffrage make this representation even clearer by using a tree diagram, and in Figure 1.1 the diagnosis and the taxicab problems are represented in this way. As you can see, and as they emphasise, the computations needed to derive the Bayesian answer with the natural frequency format are very much easier than they are with Bayes' rule itself. In fact, they reduce to

$$\text{prob}(H|D) = \frac{a}{a+b}$$

where a is the frequency of prob(D|H) observations – people with positive test results who actually have cancer, cabs identified as Blue which really are Blue – and b is the frequency of prob(D|¬H) observations – positives without cancer, wrongly identified cabs. Notice what is missing here: prob(H), the base rate. If you represent these problems in natural frequency terms, *you don't need a separate expression for the base rate*; since natural frequencies are derived from the base rate, they contain base rate information within themselves (see Kleiter, 1994, for earlier steps in this argument).

In an experiment, Gigerenzer and Hoffrage (1995) confirmed that presenting problems like this (they used 15 problems, including the cab problem and various medical ones) in a frequency format that promoted representation of just the a and

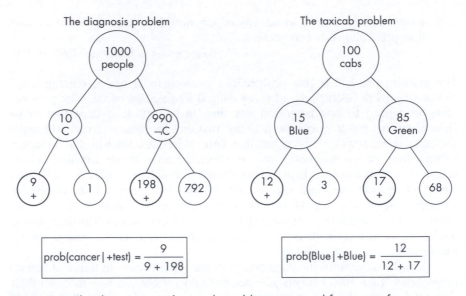

$$\text{prob(cancer | +test)} = \frac{9}{9 + 198}$$

$$\text{prob(Blue | +Blue)} = \frac{12}{12 + 17}$$

Figure 1.1 The diagnosis and taxicab problem in natural frequency form

Note: In the diagnosis problem + means prositive test, C means has cancer and ¬C means does not have cancer; in the taxicab problem, + means witness says Blue

Source: Adapted from Gigerenzer and Hoffrage (1995)

b components resulted in significantly more Bayesian answers than did the standard probability format: 50% versus 16%.

Bear in mind that the question their participants were asked was not the likelihood that a single person had a disease or that a single accident involved a Blue taxi: that would be asking for a single-event probability. In order to ask this, you really do need the base rate, because base rates depend on reference classes (see above): a base rate frequency is the proportion of times an event occurs out of the times it could have occurred. The latter part depends on the reference class. The trouble with this is that there are infinitely many possible reference classes for any single base rate. Consider the diagnosis problem. What is the right reference class for your friend with the mole? Men, young men, young men who have recently been sunburned, young sunburned men with a particular skin type? It is impossible to say. Ultimately, your friend is his own reference class. In natural frequency experiments, people are asked how many ___ out of ___ have the disease, were Blue, and so on. The blanks are filled in with absolute frequencies (i.e. simple counts of actual occurrences), which do not depend on reference classes.

Gigerenzer is not the only researcher to address belief revision in this way. Two leading evolutionary psychologists, Leda Cosmides and John Tooby (1996), also conducted a series of experiments on frequency formats. They used variations on the diagnosis problem. In their basic reformulation of the problem, they found that 56% of people produced the Bayesian solution with a frequency format, a figure comparable to Gigerenzer and Hoffrage's result. However, they included redundant percentages in their experiment (e.g. including the phrase 'a "false posi-tive" rate of 5%' alongside the frequency of 50 out of 1000 people testing positive without the disease) and discovered that performance rose to 72% when this infor-mation was removed. Using further manipulations, such as presenting the problem information pictorially as well as in figures, they raised the rate of Bayesian responding as high as 92%. We shall return to this particular factor below.

Not surprisingly, results like these, along with the theory that predicted them, have generated a large research literature. It is the latter, the theory, that explains this boom. Frequency formats had appeared in research papers before, sometimes to explain the problems to readers (Hammerton, 1973; Pollard & Evans, 1983), sometimes as part of the experimental materials (Fiedler, 1988; Tversky & Kahneman, 1983), but Gigerenzer's approach offered a rationale for their success – a rationale that has not gone unchallenged, as we shall see.

Gigerenzer and his colleagues have devoted enormous energy to their research programme, and I shall give some more examples of this work here. It has been collected into a series of books, for specialist and non-specialist audi-ences. For specialist references, go to Gigerenzer and Todd (1999a) and Gigerenzer and Selten (2001); for more 'popular' treatments, try Gigerenzer (2002, 2007).

This work has obvious potential applications, because people need to make probability judgments in order to make informed decisions. We shall look closely at decision making in later chapters, and will return to Gigerenzer's approach to it when we do so, but for now let us look at two areas in which the natural frequency approach has been applied in the real world: health and the law. In both cases, it is no exaggeration to say that probability judgment can be a matter of life and death.

In his popular book, Gigerenzer (2002) recounts a personal experience. He needed to take an HIV test as a condition of obtaining a work permit for the USA. HIV, the virus that leads to AIDS, is rather like lightning: your chances of being struck by it depend on who you are and what you do. So the first thing to work out is your reference class. Gigerenzer's was low-risk German males, to whom the following data applied at the time:

Base rate: .01%
Test sensitivity: 99.9% (i.e. chance of testing positive if you have HIV)
False positive rate: .01% (i.e. chance of testing positive even though you do
        not have HIV)

Now suppose such a person tests positive: what is the chance that he has HIV? You could construct a tree diagram like the one in Figure 1.1, but you hardly need to in this case. You can use natural frequencies in your head. Start by thinking of 10,000 low-risk German men. How many have HIV? In frequency terms, .01% is 1 in 10,000, so the answer is 1. He will be detected with almost total accuracy (99.9%, or .999). Now think about the remaining 9999 men. The risk of testing positive is also 1: 10,000, so we can be almost certain that there will be one misfortunate man among them. How many positive test results do we have then? Two, of which one is true. On these (real) figures, his chances of actually having HIV, given a positive test result, would be 1:2. He should take another test.

The really important figure in making these judgments is the false positive rate. These can only be derived from observed frequencies because they are by nature unpredictable. We then need to know how to use them in our calculations. As just mentioned, these judgments can have the most profound consequences for people: there is a big difference between thinking there is just a 50/50 chance of having HIV and thinking it is almost certain that you have it. You might not get your work permit; you might, if you are sure you have HIV after testing positive, wind up a victim of suicide, assault or even murder (such incidents are related in Gigerenzer, 2002).

One thing you can be sure of when taking an HIV test is that you will want some good advice. Gigerenzer, Hoffrage and Ebert (1998) conducted a field study of AIDS counsellors in Germany: Ebert had himself tested and counselled at 20 health centres, presenting himself as a low-risk client. You would hope, indeed expect, that counsellors would know how to interpret test results. The ones in this study did not. Ebert asked the counsellors about a number of aspects of the test, such as its sensitivity and false positive rate, and, most importantly, what the result would mean for the likelihood that he actually had HIV, if it came out positive. Five of the counsellors said that the test was 100% sensitive, while thirteen were accurate on this point; only three were clear about false positives from the beginning; while three-quarters told Ebert that he was certain or almost certain to have HIV if he tested positive (against the true figure of 50%). Needless to say, Gigerenzer et al. recommend that counsellors be retrained to interpret, and talk to their clients about, natural frequencies.

Now for the law. In 1999, Sally Clark, an English lawyer, was convicted of the murder of two of her sons. Each had been found dead in their cots when only a few weeks old. Part of the case against her was the testimony of an eminent paediatrician, who told the court that the probability of two children in the same middle-class family dying of sudden infant death syndrome, or SIDS (a residual category, not a diagnosis, arrived at after all other possible causes such as injury and disease have been eliminated), was 1:73 million. Clark served over 3 years in prison before her conviction was quashed on a second appeal in 2003. At that appeal, two sorts of statistical error were pointed out. Firstly, the 73 million: this was arrived at by multiplying the single probability of one SIDS death, about 1:8500, by itself, just as we did with the calculation of 'snake eyes' at the start of this chapter. This is a factual mistake: SIDS deaths are not random events. There are factors within families that make some more prone to suffer this tragedy than others, so if there has been one SIDS death the probability of another is much higher than the random probability. Secondly, the jury might well have committed the *prosecutor's fallacy*: using the paediatrician's figure as the probability that Clark was innocent (see Nobles & Schiff, 2005, for a brief account of this case).

The prosecutor's fallacy is a version of the inverse fallacy: mistaking prob(D|H) for prob(H|D). Even if the figure given was correct, it is the expression of the probability that two children will die in this way (D) given that the alternative in this case – murder – has been eliminated (i.e. that the defendant is innocent (H)). It is *not* the probability that the defendant is innocent given these deaths. Jurors should have compared any such estimate with the prior probability of the alternative hypothesis: that two babies were murdered by their mother. This is likely to be even lower. Here is a parallel, again reaching back to the start of this chapter. You have won the lottery, the odds against this happening being 1:13.98 million. Someone accuses you of cheating. The odds just quoted are the odds that you will win (D) given that you don't cheat (H); they are not the odds that you didn't cheat given that you won. We need to know the prior probability that you cheated, and this is vanishingly remote, because of the design of the lottery machine. Jurors could no doubt see this quite readily, and yet they have fallen prey to the inverse fallacy in cases like Clark's (other women have had similar convictions overturned since her case) – Sally Clark died of alcoholic poisoning 4 years after her release from prison.

The inverse fallacy bedevils the use in criminal trials of the most important aid to crime investigation to have emerged in a century: DNA profiling. TV dramas present this as a failsafe index of a suspect's culpability, but there is no such thing as an infallible test. Even if there is a tiny chance of error, as in the case of the HIV statistics above, this must be taken into account. And these chances must be presented to juries in a way that their minds can handle, otherwise miscarriages of justice will happen.

Suppose that a sample of DNA is taken from a crime scene, it matches the suspect's DNA profile, and the probability that a person selected at random would also match the sample (the random match probability) is 1:1 million. Does that mean that the odds against the suspect's innocence are a million to one? No. Once again, 1:1 million is prob(D|H), the probability that the sample would be found if the suspect were innocent, not prob(H|D), the probability that he is innocent given that this sample has been found. We need to know some other things in order to compute prob(H|D): we need the false positive rate, or prob(D|¬H), and the prior probability that the suspect could have been the perpetrator in the first place, prob(H). A cast-iron alibi, for instance, drastically reduces this figure. And we need to know about the prior probability of the alternative hypothesis, that someone else did it.

Lindsey, Hertwig and Gigerenzer (2003) report a study in which over 100 advanced law students and academics were presented with trial statistics, based on real cases, in frequency and probability formats. The two versions are given in Table 1.4. The first two questions concern the interpretation of the statistical information. Question 1 requires thinking about false positives, and with the probability version performance was appalling: hardly any of the students or academics found the correct answer, which is .09 (there are 110 men with a reported match, of whom 10 actually have a matched profile; 10/110 = .09). These figures rose to 40% (students) and over 70% (academics) with the frequency presentation. The picture was almost identical with Question 2: while again the academics were better than the students, the difference between the probability and frequency conditions for both groups was massive (the probability is .0091, or 1 in 110). And the verdicts (Question 3)? Fifty per cent more law students and academics returned a guilty verdict in the probability condition. Their level of reasonable doubt was higher in the frequency condition. Now, imagine you are the suspect in the previous paragraph, who happens to have a DNA profile that matches the one found at the scene; there is no other evidence against you; you are, in fact, innocent. You live in or near London, where there are about 10 million people. This means that there will be

Table 1.4 Probability and frequency versions of the DNA problem in Lindsey et al. (2003)

Probability version

The expert witness testifies that there are about 10 million men who could have been the perpetrator. The probability of a randomly selected man having a DNA profile that is identical with the trace recovered from the crime scene is approximately 0.0001%. If a man has this DNA profile, it is practically certain that a DNA analysis shows a match. If a man does not have this DNA profile, current DNA technology leads to a reported match with a probability of only 0.001%.

A match between the DNA of the defendant and the traces on the victim has been reported.

Question 1. What is the probability that the reported match is a true match, that is, that the person actually has this DNA profile?
Question 2. What is the probability that the person is the source of the trace?
Question 3. Please render your verdict for this case: guilty or not guilty?

Frequency version

The expert witness testifies that there are about 10 million men who could have been the perpetrator. Approximately 10 of these men have a DNA profile that is identical with the trace recovered from the crime scene. If a man has this DNA profile, it is practically certain that a DNA analysis shows a match. Among the men who do not have this DNA profile, current DNA technology leads to a reported match in only 100 cases out of 10 million.

A match between the DNA of the defendant and the traces on the victim has been reported.

Question 1. How many of the men with a reported match actually do have a true match, that is, that the person actually has this DNA profile? [sic]
Question 2. How many men with a reported match are actually the source of the trace?
Question 3. Please render your verdict for this case: guilty or not guilty?

---

10 people from this region who match: you and nine others. The odds on your innocence are 9:1, not 1:1 million. If you ever find yourself in the dock, you had better hope your lawyer knows how to talk to juries about probability.

People tend to find that the re-presentation of probability problems in natural frequency formats makes them strikingly clearer, so you may be wondering whether there have been any moves to incorporate this way of dealing with probability into the education system. As Bond (2009) reports, there have: Gigerenzer himself has been involved in educational programmes with doctors and judges, and primary school children in Germany have been given classes where they manipulate frequency information. However, we should remember one of the messages of the previous few pages: consider alternative hypotheses. Sure, natural frequencies can lead to clearer probability judgments, but how? Is it possible that they have their effect through a different mechanism from the one favoured by Gigerenzer's school?

Probability from the inside and the outside

Not all psychologists in this area have accepted the frequency research and theory – particularly the theory, with its argument for an evolutionary adaptation for understanding frequencies but not single-event probabilities. The natural frequency theory would be in trouble if it could be shown either that this format did not facilitate probability judgment or that some probability formats did. Evans, Handley, Perham, Over and Thompson (2000) claimed to have found little difference between hard and easy frequency formats and a probability format. However, their 'hard' frequency format presented normalised frequencies (such as the 85 in every 100 referred to above), which Gigerenzer and Hoffrage have always maintained would not facilitate because they obliterate base rate information. The low level of performance with the 'easy' problem, at 35%, is not easy to explain. Evans et al. used tasks based closely on those used by Cosmides and Tooby (1996), which, as we saw earlier, sometimes produced different levels of performance from those observed by Gigerenzer and Hoffrage. Sloman and Over (2003) also report not obtaining such high levels of performance as Gigerenzer and Hoffrage and Cosmides and Tooby did. This may be the most important point from these various studies: natural frequency formats do not always bring forth accuracy from a majority of the people presented with them, which is a problem for a theory that says they should.

Girotto and Gonzalez (2001) tested natural frequency presentations against a novel probability format: chances. It is novel for psychological research, but, as Girotto and Gonzalez remark, this format is often used in real life, and it was used in considering Dr Scale's card-playing questions earlier: saying that there are 4 chances in 52 of finding an ace is expressing probability in this way. They found that it promoted accurate judgments as well as natural frequencies did. Hoffrage, Gigerenzer, Krauss and Martignon (2002) counter that the chances format merely mimics natural frequencies, something that Girotto and Gonzalez do not accept, using playing cards as an example: such problems are easy, but they are not easy because you have sampled sets of cards, but because you know about their logical proportions in advance.

What all these authors focus on, both the Gigerenzer school and its critics, is an idea originally put forward, yet again, by Kahneman and Tversky: that probability problems asking for judgments of single events – this patient, this taxi – encourage a focus on the properties of the individual case in question, an 'inside' view, while frequency problems encourage a focus on the class of which the individual case is a member, an 'outside' view (Kahneman & Tversky, 1982b). We shall see how this applies to base rate problems, with which we have been mainly concerned up to now, and then look at some others that have figured prominently in the literature: the planning fallacy, overconfidence, and the conjunction fallacy.

As far as base rate problems are concerned, both Evans et al. and Girotto and Gonzalez strongly emphasise what has come to be known as *nested-sets theory*. This has also been advocated in the recent review by Barbey and Sloman (2007). Gigerenzer and his colleagues (see Gigerenzer & Hoffrage, 2007; Hoffrage et al.,

2002) argue vehemently that this has always been an inherent aspect of the natural frequency theory in any case. It can be stated very easily. Refer back to the little equation above, which expresses what you need to compute from the information provided in Gigerenzer and Hoffrage's tree diagrams (see Figure 1.1): prob(H|D) = $a/a+b$. What Gigerenzer's critics argue is that anything that helps you to see that a is part of $a+b$ should help you to the Bayesian solution, and that natural frequencies just happen to do this, whereas Gigerenzer argues that natural sampling is the only reliable way to this insight. The diagrams used by Cosmides and Tooby (see above) may have helped in this, and in producing such high levels of performance.

Sloman and Over (2003; see also Sloman, Over & Slovak, 2003) also report that diagrams aid Bayesian reasoning, but only when attached to tasks presented in single-probability format: they did not boost the already good performance brought about by frequency presentation, unlike in Cosmides and Tooby's research. Importantly, they also used purely verbal means to clarify the nested-sets relation, for example:

> The probability that an average American has disease X is 1/1000. A test has been developed to detect if that person has disease X. If the test is given and the person has the disease, the test comes out positive. But the test can come out positive even if the person is completely healthy. Specifically, the chance is 50/1000 that someone who is perfectly healthy would test positive for the disease.

> Consider an average American: what is the probability that if this person is tested and found to have a positive result, the person would actually have the disease?

The answer is 1/51, or 1.8%, or .018. Forty per cent of participants produced an answer at or near this value, a figure close to that commonly observed with frequency formats. Notice that the information is given in the form of normalised relative frequencies, and the question asks for a single-probability judgment, all aspects that, according to the Gigerenzer school, should fog your mind. Results such as this do not mean that the natural frequency findings should be rejected, of course. But it does seem safe to conclude that natural frequency formats have their effects primarily by making set relations transparent, and that they are perhaps the most effective presentational tool for doing this.

The outside view, then, is to think about the two sets, a and $a+b$. The inside view is to focus on the characteristics of the single case, the patient, accident, crime or suspect in question. When you take the inside view, you lose sight of the essential information about sets or classes and the relation between them. Here are some other aspects of thinking where this inside/outside conflict seems to be operating, beginning with one with which you are sure to be familiar through personal experience.

The planning fallacy

Think about a project that you are about to engage in, such as writing a piece of coursework, fixing a car or redecorating a room. How likely do you think it is that you will complete the task on time? Now think about similar projects that you completed recently. Did you bring them in on time? Research and common experience show us that our predictions tend not to be matched by reality: we are much less likely to meet deadlines than we think we will be before we start a project. We are also likely to underestimate the costs, problems and effort involved. This is the planning fallacy.

Once again, the early running in identifying and researching this problem was made by Kahneman and Tversky (1979a; reprinted 1982c); they even seem to have coined the term 'planning fallacy'. Its essence, as Buehler, Griffin and Ross (2002) explain, is the clash between an overly optimistic prediction about the project in hand and a more realistic history of past performance. Kahneman and Tversky refer to these as the *singular* and *distributional* aspects of planning. These correspond to the inside and outside views. Thus when estimating completion time for a project, we tend to focus on the ways in which this project is unique and forget about the ways in which it is similar to things we have done before.

Of course, there is more to it than just this, because our planning predictions tend to be inaccurate in one direction: overoptimistic. Buehler et al. identify two possible reasons for this. Firstly, planning is by nature about the future, and this orientation may prevent you looking back into the past. Secondly, when you plan a project you plan for its successful completion, not its failure; you will therefore think more about those factors that are likely to promote its success and ignore those that might undermine it – even if you have plenty of experience of them. Buehler, Griffin and Ross (1994) collected verbal reports from students estimating when they would complete an assignment (only 30% met their predicted time). Three-quarters of their collected thoughts concerning these projects were about the future; only 7% referred to their own past experience, another 1% to others' and only 3% referred to possible snags.

Reports of the adverse impact of the planning fallacy are legion, and it can be very costly, indeed lethal. Buehler et al. (2002) quote the case of the Sydney Opera House as 'the champion of all planning disasters' (p. 250): in 1957, it was estimated that it would be completed in 1963 at a cost of $7 million; it opened 10 years late at a cost of $102 million. On an individual level, every year we hear of tourists who think they can get to the top of a mountain and back by tea-time, in their t-shirts and shorts, and are proved wrong in the most drastic way possible: they wind up dead.

How then can we escape the fallacy? Buehler and colleagues put forward three possibilities. The first is to think about sets, that is, to take the outside view; Kahneman and Tversky (1979a) also recommended this remedy. However, this seems hard to do, for a variety of reasons. For instance, Griffin and Buehler (1999) had people make planning predictions about either a single project or a set of ten projects. They contend that the frequentist school of Gigerenzer and his associates would predict that the latter should have reduced the planning fallacy. But it did not: the fallacy was committed to the same extent in both conditions. According to Buehler et al. (2002), this failure was because people were unable to detach themselves from the inside view even when thinking about frequencies. The richness of real-world problems masks their statistical aspects. Taking the outside view is difficult because you have to see the current project as a sample from a population, which, as we saw above, is a sophisticated skill not available to untutored people;

and you have to construct a reference class of similar cases in the past. Sometimes, as Kahneman and Tversky remark, the case at hand is all you have, as in the planning of an opera house.

Secondly, you could think about alternatives to success: how might the project come unstuck? Although this kind of alternative scenario planning is popular in business circles, Buehler and colleagues found, as with the previous remedy, that it failed to overrule the planning fallacy. Even when instructed to generate pessimistic possibilities that were highly plausible, people neglected them in favour of optimistic scenarios. They did, thankfully, find more encouraging support for their third option, which they called the *recall-relevance* manipulation. That is, people were encouraged to focus on their past planning history and think about what it might imply for their prospects of current success. This significantly reduced the gap between prediction and reality.

Finally, it is worth recording aspects of the planning fallacy that Buehler and colleagues point to as a positive advantage for researchers interested in human judgment. It is a clear and simple test-bed for this work because it does not require any reference to logical or mathematical norms, since 'accuracy and bias can be measured by the calendar and the clock' (Buehler et al., 2002, p. 270); it has obvious real-world implications; and it concerns a central psychological question, about how we use memory to guide our thoughts and actions.

Overconfidence

This is another kind of optimistic bias, and has been subject to a lot of attention from researchers: indeed, Griffin and Brenner (2004) call it 'the poster child of judgmental biases' (p. 180). It is related to the calibration of probability judgments, which was discussed earlier. The overconfidence effect is commonly observed with general knowledge questions, such as:

1   Absinthe is: (a) a precious stone; (b) an alcoholic drink.
2   Which city is further north, Paris or New York?
3   Which city has the higher population: (a) Bonn; (b) Heidelberg?
4   What is the capital of New Zealand: (a) Auckland; (b) Wellington?

You can try this for yourself: take each question and, when you have an answer, rate how confident you are that the answer is correct, on a scale of 50–100%. The scale starts at 50% because it is possible to get half these questions right if you know nothing at all about them, just by guessing; 100% means you are certain that you are right.

As long ago as 1980, it was possible to sum up an already large literature on studies of the relation between people's reported confidence and their actual performance. Lichtenstein et al. (1982), in their review of calibration studies, reported that on questions where people said they were 100% confident, they tended to be only about 80% accurate; with 90% confidence, they were 75% accurate, and so on. Their confidence exceeded their performance, just as it does with the planning fallacy.

It did not take long to discover that there is more to this bias than this, and in fact 'overconfidence' may be a misleading term for the overall effect. One early complication was the *hard–easy effect*. Lichtenstein and Fischhoff (1977) gave people three kinds of tests designed to differ in their difficulty: there was an easy test (people got 85% of these questions right), a difficult test (61%) and a test with impossible questions (51% – close to the guessing rate of 50%). There was maximum overconfidence with the impossible test: no matter what the participants thought was their probability of correctness, its actual average rate was always around 50%. The usual overconfidence effect was found with the difficult test: a declining slope from 100% confidence (around 75% accurate) down to 60% (around 55% accurate). However, with the easy set, there was evidence of *underconfidence* at the lower levels: when people were only 50% confident, they were around 60% accurate. They were overconfident when they expressed a high degree of confidence.

Evidence that overconfidence is influenced by more than difficulty was provided by Griffin and Tversky (1992). They distinguished between the *strength* of evidence and its *weight*. In the general knowledge case, strength is your impression about what you know about, say, geography questions such as 2–4 above. Weight is how well that evidence predicts performance. To give another example, you get a very strong tip from someone about the stock market or a horse race, but they know very little about these things (we all know people like that): their advice is strong, but it carries little weight.

Griffin and Tversky gave US students pairs of American states and asked them to choose which one scored more on various attributes: the states' populations, their voting rates in presidential elections and their high-school graduation rates. They predicted that people would be quite accurate and highly confident with the population questions and quite inaccurate and less confident with the voting questions – they were. Most interestingly, they used the graduation question to separate strength and weight: people are likely to have a strong impression that one state is more 'educated' than another, perhaps through availability of well-known universities, but such factors have little predictive validity with respect to school attainment. So there should be low accuracy and high confidence on these questions (i.e. a high degree of overconfidence), which is exactly what Griffin and Tversky found.

The inside–outside dynamic also turns out to be relevant. Several researchers, most notably Gigerenzer and his colleagues, have pointed to the difference in categories between the assessment that you give of your confidence in an answer and the data on your accuracy. The first is a single-case judgment, while the second is a frequency. What would happen if the confidence judgment were also asked for in frequency terms? Gigerenzer, Hoffrage and Kleinbölting (1991) addressed this question. Instead of asking people to rate their confidence in single questions, they asked them to assess how many of the whole set of test questions they thought they had got right. If people were truly overconfident, this should make no difference. However, Gigerenzer et al. found that the overconfidence effect disappeared with this frequency task. In fact, it went into reverse: in one experiment, there was a 14% overconfidence effect when it was tested for in the normal way, with single questions; but with the frequency question, there was a difference between confidence ratings and accuracy of more than –2%, indicating a slight degree of underconfidence.

Gigerenzer has a particular explanation for this effect, among others, which we shall return to in Chapter 9 since it relates to decision making as well as judgment. For now, we can note that we have again what appears to be an inside–outside difference to do with the reference classes that the two types of task, single-question and whole-test rating, invite you to invoke. In the case of the single question, you might ask yourself what you know about questions like that particular one: geography, say, or weird drinks. With the whole test question, you ask yourself about how well you tend to do on general knowledge quizzes. As with the planning fallacy, we tend to be better calibrated when it comes to our past histories than we are when we need to apply them to the case in hand.

The conjunction fallacy

This is also a very well researched aspect of thought, and one that brings the inside–outside distinction into sharp focus. It involves possibly the most famous fictional character in cognitive psychology. She is called Linda, and this is the Linda problem:

> Linda is 31 years old, single, outspoken and very bright. She majored in philosophy. As a student, she was deeply concerned with issues of discrimination and social justice, and also participated in anti-war demonstrations.
>
> Which descriptions are most likely to be true of Linda? Rank them in order of probability.
>
> a   Linda is a primary school teacher.
> b   Linda works in a bookshop and takes yoga classes.
> c   Linda is active in the feminist movement.
> d   Linda is a psychiatric social worker.
> e   Linda is a member of the League of Women Voters.
> f   Linda is a bank clerk.
> g   Linda sells insurance.
> h   Linda is a bank clerk and is active in the feminist movement.

As always with these problems, it will do you good to have a go at it before reading on.

The original version of the problem was reported by Tversky and Kahneman (1982b, 1983); I have altered the wording slightly. Linda appeared alongside another problem involving Bill, but he lacked Linda's charisma and has been largely forgotten. Now look at your rankings, and especially at the numbers you wrote against sentences c, f and h. These are the important ones; the others are merely fillers.

If you are like most people given this task, you ranked c above h and h above f. If you did the second of these, as 89% of participants did in an experiment reported by Tversky and Kahneman (1983), you have made a logical error. Why? Because it is impossible for a conjunction, $x + y$, to be more probable than one of its components. You cannot be more likely to be a female student than just a student, or a feminist bank clerk than just a bank clerk. Note that people tend not to judge that Linda is more likely to be a feminist bank clerk than just a feminist; they rank *c* above *h*. This gives a clue as to what is going on here. Tversky and Kahneman interpreted their findings in terms of the representativeness heuristic, which was discussed earlier: one of the aspects of this heuristic was that people judge an item, such as sentence *f*, as likely to the extent that it is similar in essential properties to its parent population. Linda sounds a bit of a radical, doesn't she? The parent population then is something like 'radical women'. So people think that it is more likely that she is a radical bank clerk than just a bank clerk: sentence *f* might imply that she is *not* a feminist (Politzer & Noveck, 1991).

Thinking about Linda in this way is taking the inside view and focussing on her individual attributes. What happens when people are asked to take the outside view, and focus instead on the relation between classes? This was in fact done in the Tversky and Kahneman (1983) paper, and a replication, using a slightly different method, was reported by Fiedler (1988). Fiedler used a ranking task, as in the example above, whereas Tversky and Kahneman had people give probability ratings to each item. Hertwig and Gigerenzer (1999) brought the natural frequency theory to bear on the problem. In essence, what all these studies did was to ask participants to think about 100 people just like Linda, and then assess statements *f* and *h*. In all cases, the conjunction fallacy was committed far less often, sometimes disappearing altogether.

Sloman and Over (2003) present evidence that, once again, it is not frequency presentation itself that brings about this insight, but its ability to make set relations transparent: in this case, people need to see that $x + y$ is a subset of x. They found that this facilitation could be suppressed if the set relation was obscured by having the critical statements (*f* and *h* above) separated by seven filler items rather than just one. This happened with both rating and ranking tasks, and they also found, as previous researchers had, that the ranking task produced much higher rates of the fallacy; this point is discussed in detail by Hertwig and Chase (1998), as well as by Hertwig and Gigerenzer and Sloman and Over. A highly detailed review of the conjunction fallacy, covering more theoretical interpretations of it than I have space to include here, is given by Fisk (2004).

We have seen in this chapter how crucial probability judgment is in real-life thinking, and as stated at the outset it is also crucial in explaining human reasoning: it is central to the 'new paradigm' view of reasoning that has recently emerged from the schools of Oaksford and Chater and Evans and Over (Over, 2009). It is also at the core of two other forms of thinking that we shall deal with: inductive thinking and decision making. So let us first delve into the history of the study of reasoning, and from there proceed to the new paradigm. Then we shall head off into these other areas.

Summary

1   Probability is at the heart of the explanation of many areas of thinking and reasoning. It is a research topic in itself, and has always been a cornerstone

of theories of decision making, but has recently come to the fore in the psychology of reasoning as well.

2 Probability can be formally defined in four ways: as logical possibility, frequency, propensity or subjective degree of belief.

3 People's judgments of probability may systematically depart from mathematical norms: they have an insecure understanding of randomness, and tend to overweight low probabilities, among other biases.

4 Sampling is a major problem in naïve probability judgment: people are unaware of sampling biases and how they can bias judgment.

5 The most influential school of thought in the psychology of probability judgment is the *Heuristics and Biases* research programme of Kahneman and Tversky. They explain sampling biases through the availability heuristic.

6 Belief updating is the revision of beliefs in response to evidence. Its normative theory is derived from Bayes' rule, which weights prior belief by the conditional probability of the evidence, given that belief and its alternatives, to derive a posterior probability.

7 Kahneman and Tversky explain deviations in human performance in belief updating through heuristics such as representativeness.

8 Biases such as base rate neglect have been explained by Gigerenzer using the construct of natural sampling, that gives rise to representations of frequencies that obviate the need to consider base rates. This approach has been successfully applied to improve judgment in medical and legal contexts.

9 Recent research implies that the natural sampling effect may come about through its making set relations transparent. It facilitates an 'outside' view of probabilities (the set of cases) while bias often results from taking an 'inside' view (of the case at hand).

The study of reasoning: classic research

In this chapter, we reach back to the very beginnings of inquiry into human reason, a process that spans over 2000 years. Some of these ancient notions are still traceable in modern work. We begin with syllogistic reasoning. This was for centuries the central concern of people interested in how we think. While it may no longer be number 1, it is still an active area, with a continuous stream of ideas and results appearing. In the next chapter, we proceed to an area that can claim to have shoved syllogisms off their perch: conditional reasoning. We also look at thinking with disjunctive – *Or* – sentences. You will see that similar issues arise with all these apparently distinct aspects of thought.

The classical syllogism: reasoning with quantities

Syllogisms were developed by Aristotle, who lived in the fourth century BC; they form the basis of his logic, and dominated logical analysis for hundreds of years. They are sometimes known as Aristotelian syllogisms for this reason, and you will also find them referred to as categorical or quantified syllogisms. The latter term tells you something about their properties: they contain *quantifier* expressions: *All, No, Some, Some . . . not*. These are given code letters A, E, I and O, respectively, from the Latin terms **a**ffi**r**mo and **ne**go: A and I are affirming, E and O are negating. *All* and *No* are known as universal statements, while *Some* and *Some . . . not* are particular.

By convention, a syllogistic argument contains two premises, from which you can draw a conclusion. Here is an example, using just A sentences:

Premises:	All *a* are *b*
	All *b* are *c*
Conclusion:	All *a* are *c*

The essential syllogistic inference is thus about the relation between the 'end terms' *a* and *c*; the 'middle term' *b* drops out. Note that some authors use different sets of letters for the terms: X, Y and Z or the traditional S, M and P are the most common. We shall stay at the front of the alphabet.

Restricting syllogistic arguments in this way to just four expressions and two premises might seem guaranteed to detach them from real life. After all, we use lots of different quantifiers, such as lots, many, most, few and so on, and don't stop dead when an argument stretches beyond two premises. To see how researchers have recently tried to 'expand the universe' of syllogisms, look at: Stenning (2002), who considers 'u-conclusions' such as Some not-*a* are not-*c*; Copeland (2006), who deals with arguments containing more than two premises; and Roberts (2005), the person responsible for the 'universe' phrase, who uses premises with additional negatives in them, such as All *a* are not *b*.

Even with the standard restrictions in place, things get complicated very quickly. Firstly, there is the matter of which expressions go into the premises. With four expressions and two premises, there are 16 possible combinations. This is known as the *mood* of the premises; the example above is a syllogism in AA mood.

Then there is the ordering of the *a*, *b* and *c* terms. In the example, the orders are *a-b* and *b-c*, but obviously there are two other possible orders: *b-a* and *c-b*. These orders of terms in the two premises are known as the *figure* (i.e. 'structure') of the syllogism, and are numbered like this:

a-b	b-a	a-b	b-a
b-c	c-b	c-b	b-c
1	2	3	4

Our basic example is therefore an AA1 syllogism: it has two A premises in figure 1. Once again, bear in mind that different authors use different numberings. The system here is the one introduced by Johnson-Laird (1983) and adopted quite widely by present-day researchers. He also favours defining mood in the way I have done here; logicians and some psychologists take into account the form of the conclusion as well when doing so.

We now have arguments with 16 moods in four possible figures. That gives 64 possible argument forms. To that we have to add the mood of the conclusion. These can clearly also be one of the four A, E, I and O sentences, and the terms in the conclusion can be in two orders: *a-c* and *c-a*. That takes the number of possible syllogisms, even with these tight constraints, to 512. Which leads us to the essential question about them.

Validity

When you are constructing or assessing a reasoned argument, your own or somebody else's, there is one thing you want to know above all: is it right? Or, in the context of syllogisms, does the conclusion follow? These are not always the same thing, as we shall see in Chapter 4. For now, let us concentrate on whether the conclusion follows, that is, whether the argument is valid. A valid argument is one where the conclusion *necessarily* follows from the premises; that is, where there is no possibility of reaching a false conclusion when the premises are true (logical arguments require you to assume the truth of the premises).

How many of these sound arguments are there among the 512? You get added complexities when you ask this question: it does not have a straightforward answer. This is because you have to make some assumptions to arrive at a total. One that is usually made by psychologists is that the premises are not 'empty': there is at least one *a*, *b* and *c* being referred to. This is called the existential presupposition. Another, more psychologically controversial, is that weak conclusions are acceptable. Weak conclusions betray the logical heritage of this area of research: they are statements that are entailed by, but less informative than, stronger ones. This happens because, in logic, a statement is true if it is not false; there is nothing in between (which is why philosophers call this the law of excluded middle). Consider the A statement: All *a* are *b*. This is only false if no *a* are *b* or some *a* are not *b*, so Some *a* are *b* is logically acceptable; or, to put it another way, if all *a* are *b*, it must be true that some are. Thus, Some *a* are *c* would be a logically valid conclusion for our AA example. Johnson-Laird and Byrne (1991) allow the existential presupposition but disallow the weak conclusions, and arrive at a psychological rather than logical total of just 27 valid syllogisms.

Reasoning with syllogisms

Theorists down the ages, beginning with Aristotle himself, have thought of a range of devices by which we can derive the valid syllogisms and reject the invalid ones. The early examples are reviewed by Adams (1984), and there are also wide-ranging accounts in Politzer (2004) and Stenning (2002, Ch. 4); Stenning tells us of one such device invented by Lewis Carroll. They can be used as methods of proof, as well as explanatory tools. Some of these devices are graphical, as we shall see. They are necessary because of the central empirical fact about syllogisms: they differ hugely in their difficulty. Some valid conclusions are very much harder to arrive at than others, while some invalid conclusions are readily mistaken as valid. Accounting for these patterns of performance is what psychology is concerned with.

Here is an example of the range of difficulty. You are already familiar with the basic example of the AA1 syllogism, and will probably feel that this is an easy one; I hope so, because that is why it was chosen as an introductory example. You can see without much effort that the conclusion follows validly from the premises. Turning the letters into words to make sensible sentences should make it even clearer:

> All archbishops are believers
> All believers are Christians
> _____
> All archbishops are Christians

Remember, you have to assume the truth of these premises – both of them, especially the second, are factually questionable – and then validity is determined purely by the *form* of the argument. Logic was originally devised by Aristotle to provide an objective way of deciding on the soundness or otherwise of rhetorical arguments in ancient Athens.

Now here is another syllogism (this time in EA1 form, if you want to check the notation):

> No atheists are believers
> All believers are Christians
> _____
> ?

If you are having trouble with this one, you are in good company: Ford (1994) tells us that none of her participants got it right, and Johnson-Laird (2006) reports 'only a handful' (p. 145) doing so. I bet that you came up with one of these two answers: that nothing follows (i.e. there is no valid conclusion), or that no atheists are Christians. Neither conclusion follows. In fact, there is a valid conclusion: that some Christians are not atheists. The key to understanding why this follows is to recall your scepticism about the second premise. This makes it hard to assume its truth, which you have to do in order to reason logically. You also need to bear in mind that 'some' means 'at least one and possibly all'. Another source of difficulty is that the valid conclusion does not quite fit your world knowledge while there is an invalid one that does; more about this later.

Now, here is how a graphical device can be used to solve syllogisms. There are many of these; Guy Politzer, the most historically minded of current reasoning researchers, traces them back to the 17th century (see Politzer, 2004). We shall use Euler's system, which he used in the 18th century to illustrate logic to 'une princesse d'Allemagne' (Euler, 1761, quoted in Politzer, 2004), although the actual invention of this device can be credited to Leibniz a century earlier. But we know them as Euler's diagrams, and they are still in wide use by theorists, as well as tutors, today.

Euler's system involves representing the terms in a syllogism by circles, which in turn represent the 'fields' of items the terms refer to – think of them as like the fences that enclose farm animals. The Euler diagrams for all four of the standard quantifiers are shown in Figure 2.1. You can see that for all except E (No

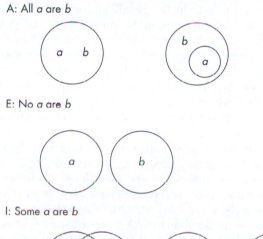

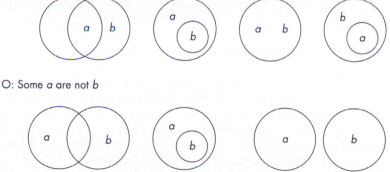

Figure 2.1 Euler circle representations for the four syllogistic premise statements

a are *b*), each statement is compatible with more than one diagram. Taking the A (All) statement first: the left-hand diagram shows the set of *a* items as equivalent to the set of *b*s, but there is another possible arrangement where the *a* set is entirely enclosed in the set of *b*s. That is the case when there are *b*s that are not *a*s, as with believers and archbishops. The I (Some) statement is even more complex. The left-most diagram shows the sets intersecting; that is the diagram for the situation when some (but not all) *a*s are *b*s and some *b*s are *a*s: some archbishops are bachelors, for instance. The next one along shows that the *b*s are enclosed by *a*, which represents the case where some *a*s are *b*s (and some are not) while all *b*s are *a*s. For instance, some animals are bears. The two on the right are the same as the A diagrams, and reflect the logical fact that 'some' is consistent with 'at least one and possibly all'.

Finally, the O (Some ... not) statement. The left-most diagram looks like the intersecting relation shown against the I statement, but note that *a* is in a different place, to refer to those *a*s that are outside the *b* circle, as Euler himself specified (Politzer, 2004). The one on the right reflects again the 'possibly all' connotation.

Solving syllogisms with Euler circles requires you to combine all the possible diagrams in every possible way consistent with the premises, then to read off the relation between *a* and *c* from the resulting composite. This can actually be done in a number of different ways, as Stenning (2002) and Politzer (2004) describe. Figure 2.2 shows how to do it using the original AA1 example. There are only two possible outcomes: where *a* and *c* are equivalent, and where *a* is enclosed by *c* (or *a* is a subset of *c*, if you prefer). Either way, it is true that all *a* are *c*, and there is no other possibility, so this conclusion is valid. In the case of the second example above, the EA1 argument, there are three possible outcome diagrams; in each case, some (and possibly all) *c* are not *a*, and so this is the valid conclusion.

It is worth pausing to note two things about what we have seen by using Euler circles. Firstly, Roberts and colleagues (Roberts, Newstead & Griggs, 2001; Roberts & Sykes, 2005) demonstrate that when you draw Euler diagrams that show only the relation between *a* and *c*, only seven combinations of such outcomes cover all 64 premise pairs. Secondly, since more outcome diagrams are involved with the EA argument, it should be harder than the AA argument: that is a testable psychological prediction. So let us look in more detail at the psychological evidence.

Patterns in human performance

Psychologists have been giving people syllogisms to solve for decades, so we can make a few empirical generalisations. The task of theory is obviously to account for the observed patterns in the data. What exactly those patterns are is not as easy a question to answer as you might think, because there is more than one way of presenting syllogisms to people, and more than one way they might solve them. For instance, some researchers, such as Rips (1994), present people with a complete argument and ask them to judge whether the conclusion follows from the premises; some present a list of possible conclusions from which the participant

The possible representations of the first premise are:

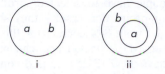

The possible representations of the second premise are:

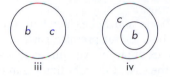

which produce the following possible combinations:

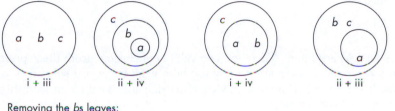

Removing the *bs* leaves:

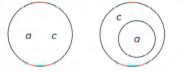

which both support the conclusion that All *a* are *c*.

Figure 2.2 Combining the premises and drawing a conclusion with the AA syllogism using Euler circles

has to select the right one (e.g. Dickstein, 1978); and some present just the two premises and ask their participants to derive their own conclusion. The latter is used by Johnson-Laird and his colleagues (e.g. Bucciarelli & Johnson-Laird, 1999; Johnson-Laird, 2006; Johnson-Laird & Byrne, 1991). In addition, few researchers have presented the complete set of 64 possible premise pairs.

To help you through this maze, I shall refer mainly to papers that have summarised the research data. The most recent such summaries are given by Roberts and Sykes (2005) and by Oaksford and Chater (2007; see also Chater & Oaksford, 1999). Both sets of authors refer to the data sets from the research of Dickstein (1978), Johnson-Laird and Steedman (1978) and Johnson-Laird and Bara (1984); Roberts and Sykes also include data from Roberts et al. (2001). These studies are ones where all 64 possible premise pairs were presented.

As mentioned above, Roberts and Sykes (2005) classify the 64 possible premise pairs in terms of their *outcome categories* – the states of affairs compatible with the inferred relation between *a* and *c*; they use Euler circles to represent these. They consider experiments in which people have to select or produce conclusions separately. Looking at the conclusion-production results, they show that performance on the valid conclusions ranges from 88% correct for the AA syllogisms that have an A conclusion (they also regard the weaker I conclusion as correct) down to 24% for those arguments that have an O (Some . . . not) conclusion. The invalid syllogisms were correctly regarded as having no valid conclusion 29–40% of the time, which means that people were more likely to generate a conclusion they mistakenly thought was valid on these ones.

Classifying performance in this way, Roberts and Sykes point to several general response tendencies. Firstly, there is a bias for AA premise pairs to lead people to produce A conclusions. In our first example above, this conclusion happens to be valid. However, that is not always the case. Consider this argument:

All *b* are *a*

All *b* are *c*

This is an AA4 argument. There are two valid I conclusions from these premises: Some *a* are *c* and Some *c* are *a* (they are both valid because I sentences can be reversed; see below). However, only 8% of participants went along with this; 68% produced an A conclusion.

Secondly, despite this setback, arguments with valid I conclusions were easier overall to get right, with 85% correct. This is psychologically interesting because these arguments are consistent with four of the five possible conclusion representations. They are thus logically more complex than are the arguments that lead to O (Some . . . not) conclusions: these are compatible with only three outcome categories. However – thirdly – these latter arguments are much more difficult: they led to only 20–24% correct conclusions. The second example above, concerning atheists and Christians, is one of them. Most people judge that no valid conclusion follows.

Other general response tendencies have been identified by other authors, and Politzer (2004) shows that some were discovered over a century ago, in what appears to have been the first empirical test of syllogistic reasoning, by G. Störring. One is the figural effect. The figure of the syllogism refers to the structural relation of the premises, and was introduced at the start of this chapter. Störring found that the first two figures (see above) gave rise to a response bias: figure 1 tended to lead to conclusions with terms in the order *a-c*, whereas figure 2 led to *c-a* conclusions. The other two figures are symmetrical and so do not fall prey to these effects. These tendencies were rediscovered by Johnson-Laird and Steedman (1978) and Johnson-Laird and Bara (1984). They explained them in terms of the operation of working memory. With figure 1, *b* is 'contiguous' between the two premises – you go straight from thinking about *b* in the first premise to its appearance in the second. With figure 2, you can bring the two mentions of *b* into contiguity by thinking about the second premise first, which leads you to think of *c* as the first term in the conclusion instead of *a*.

Störring's other discoveries have also reappeared in recent times. One is the use of *strategies*. Different people go about reasoning in different ways, using different kinds of representations and processes. Indeed, Stenning (2002) reports a major research programme concerning the teaching of logic and reasoning, in which he remarks that reasoning can be considered as 'the search for systems that make problems tractable' (p. 94); reasoning is thus 'largely a matter of deciding on a representation' (p. 112). Störring observed two strategies in use among his four participants: verbal and visual. Some people drew circles or clusters of individuals and read the conclusions off the resulting patterns; others re-wrote the arguments in sentences. Ford (1994) noted similar individual differences in her work, where she collected not just people's responses, but verbal reports and written notes produced during the process of finding the solutions. There have been findings from other areas of thinking and reasoning research that show that individual differences are an important aspect of human mentality with profound theoretical implications. We shall come back to them later in the book, especially in Chapter 10.

Explaining the patterns of performance

We have seen that syllogistic arguments vary widely in their difficulty (this applies to both valid and invalid arguments) and that these variations are systematic, not random. There have been numerous attempts over many years to account for these patterns, and these have recently been classified by Maxwell Roberts (2005; Roberts et al., 2001; Roberts & Sykes, 2005) into four theory families. First there are the *surface* or *heuristic* theories. These propose that people do not do much actual reasoning on these problems, but rather attend to their surface features, which they use as a rule of thumb to guide them to a likely solution. Second, there are *search* theories, which explain difficulty in terms of the number of steps needed to solve a problem. Thirdly, there are *interpretation* theories, where difficulty arises because of possible errors in interpreting the quantifiers – remember that three of them are compatible with more than one Euler diagram, and you need to have this knowledge and use it to be completely accurate. Search and interpretation explanations are both to do with how people represent the problem when they reason. Lastly, there are *conclusion identification* theories, where people have trouble forming the conclusion even though they may have represented the problem completely accurately. As with real families, members can share features among each other (e.g. surface theories with conclusion identification components).

The earliest theory of syllogistic reasoning performance was put forward by Woodworth and Sells (1935) and refined by Begg and Denny (1969): the *atmosphere* theory. It is a prime example of a surface theory, since it proposes that the mood of the premise pairs creates an 'atmosphere' that suggests what the mood of the conclusion should be. Thus two universal (A or E) premises will promote a universal conclusion, and two affirmative (A or I) premises promote an affirmative conclusion. The presence of at least one particular premise (I or O) suggests a particular conclusion, and at least one negative premise (E or O) suggests a negative conclusion.

Atmosphere works better as a solution heuristic than it does as a theory of performance. If you use atmosphere, you will in fact produce quite a good level of performance, at least as far as the valid arguments are concerned, and if you make an error there is a good chance that it will be along the lines that atmosphere predicts. However, it fails as a theory in two important ways. Firstly, although it provides quite a good description of performance patterns, it does not explain them. *Why* should people behave in this way? Secondly, it does not predict two central aspects of people's performance: the variation in difficulty between problems, and the conditions under which they will say that no valid conclusion follows.

A less superficial surface theory is the *matching* hypothesis, put forward by Wetherick and Gilhooly (1990). They propose that people prefer a conclusion mood that matches the premise moods. So, for instance, with an AA syllogism, people will be guided to an A conclusion. Our original example, the AA1 argument, was like that, as was the later one, in AA4 form. Both produce high rates of A conclusions, but in the second case this is an error. When the premises contain two different quantifiers, Wetherick and Gilhooly propose that people prefer the one that is most conservative, the one that commits you to the least cases. Thus when All and Some premises are paired, people prefer Some in the conclusion, and when No is in the premises, people prefer No in the conclusion.

Interpretation explanations come in two forms, based on conversion and conversation. Conversion was mentioned above, in noting that the I sentence can be validly reversed: if Some *a* are *b*, it must be true that Some *b* are *a* – there is no Euler diagram for I where this is not the case (see Figure 2.1). So Some *a* are *b* can therefore be validly *converted* into Some *b* are *a*. Looking at Figure 2.1 again we can see that this is also true of the E sentence: No *a* are *b* must also imply that No *b* are *a*. However, the other two statements, A and O, cannot be validly converted, because they have possible representations that are inconsistent with their reversed forms. This is an obvious potential source of error, as Chapman and Chapman (1959; see also Revlis, 1975) noted; people could fall into this error because the illicit conversion of A and O simplifies the problems by reducing the range of representations. For instance, if you assume that All *a* are *b* implies that All *b* are *a*, you have removed the right-hand diagram, where the *a* field is enclosed by the *b* field, from your thoughts.

'Conversational' factors might also play a role in syllogistic performance. Politzer (1986) reviews them and their relation to reasoning in detail. Specifically, the term refers to the pragmatic principles of conversation introduced by the linguist Paul Grice (1975). He argued that human communication has to proceed on the shared assumption that the parties involved are cooperating in their effort at understanding: this is the principle of cooperation. From this Grice derived his conversational maxims: *manner* (be clear), *relation* (be relevant), *quality* (be truthful) and *quantity* (be optimally informative, i.e. don't give too much or too little detail). These, especially the latter, may underlie the problems people have with the logical versus the everyday meanings of 'some'. You will recall that, logically, 'some' can mean 'possibly all', because when All *a* are *b* it is true that Some *a* are *b*. But nobody uses 'some' in everyday life when they know that 'all' is true, because of the maxim of quantity. So when you hear 'some', you think it means, or at least implies, some but not all: interpreting 'some mushrooms are edible' as allowing that they all are could cost you your life. Importing this common understanding into syllogistic reasoning could lead to logical error, but with not quite such serious consequences perhaps.

The extent to which Gricean interpretations actually do lead to error in syllogistic performance has been extensively researched by Stephen Newstead (1995). Newstead noted that while numerous researchers had assumed that Gricean interpretations contributed to syllogistic reasoning errors, there was actually very little experimental evidence to back this up. He used a range of tasks to explore their influence: immediate inference, where people were given single premises and had to indicate which other statements followed from them; a task where they had to match single statements with possible Euler representations; syllogistic arguments involving evaluation of presented conclusions; and arguments requiring participants to produce their own conclusions. The first two tasks provide measures of people's tendency to make Gricean premise interpretations. These can then be linked to their syllogistic responses. Newstead found very little evidence that Gricean interpretations contribute to syllogistic performance, especially when conclusion production was required. He attributes this to the depth of processing demanded by the reasoning tasks, which overrides the surface linguistic features.

Lately, Newstead has continued to explore interpretational factors, considering conversion and Gricean interpretation together: see Roberts et al. (2001). Using two existing data sets (Johnson-Laird's and Dickstein's; see above) and new results of their own, they found once again that Gricean interpretations by themselves seem to play little part in syllogistic reasoning. However, there was better evidence for the involvement of reversible interpretations (e.g. taking All *a* are *b* to imply that All *b* are *a*), sometimes in combination with Gricean interpretations. Thus misinterpretation of the premises (compared to their logical meanings) does influence performance, but this is not a simple matter and seems to be subject to wide individual differences.

Ideas from surface and interpretation theories such as these have not been thrown away, but absorbed into larger-scale theories that do include independent rationales for their motivation. Results from these studies can also be used to test these larger-scale theories. We shall now look at three of them, and you should note that they will reappear when we consider other forms of reasoning later in the book, especially Chapters 5 and 6.

Mental logic

We have seen that the study of reasoning began with syllogisms, and that they have a heritage that ranges back over two millennia, to the time of Aristotle, who developed logic to tell sound from unsound arguments. Logic has to come from somewhere – the human mind – so it does not seem much of a stretch to propose that people have some form of logical rule system in their minds that they use more or less accurately when reasoning. That is the basis of the mental logic view.

The most detailed mental logic theory of syllogisms is that of Lance Rips (1994), which he calls the Psycop theory (from the phrase '**psy**chology of **p**roof'). Psycop is based on the philosophical system of *natural deduction*, whose rule system rests on inference rules containing three basic logical operators: conjunction (and), negation (not) and the conditional (if . . . then). All the syllogistic premises can be expressed using these operators; Table 2.1 shows how this is done

Table 2.1 The four syllogistic sentences (first lines) translated into Psycop's inference rules (second lines) and their implicatures (third lines), with their English language forms in brackets

A	All A are B	
	IF A(*x*) THEN B(*x*)	[If *x* is an A then *x* is a B]
	A(*a*) AND B(*a*)	[there are things, *a*, which are A and B]
E	No A are B	
	NOT (A(*x*) AND B(*x*))	[it is not the case that *x* is A and *x* is B]
	A(*a*) AND NOT B(*a*)	[there are things, *a*, which are A and not B]
I	Some A are B	
	A(*b*) AND B(*b*)	[there are things, *b*, which are A and B]
	A(*a*) AND NOT B(*a*)	[there are things, *a*, which are A and not B]
O	Some A are not B	
	A(*b*) AND NOT B(*b*)	[there are things, *b*, which are A and not B]
	A(*a*) AND B(*a*)	[there are things, *a*, which are A and B]

in Psycop. As Psycop is a descriptive, psychological theory – it proposes what goes on in people's minds when they think – Rips includes purely psychological components, such as the Gricean interpretations and the existential presupposition. These give rise to some *implicatures* (also shown in Table 2.1) that should influence reasoning.

In Psycop, reasoning means finding mental proofs using inference rules and suppositions. The number of different steps needed to find a proof, and the nature of the rules involved, should predict the *difficulty* of a deductive problem, while the type of inference rules and their implicatures should predict the *type* of errors people make. The basic idea behind a mental proof is that reasoners address a problem by generating sentences that link the premises to the conclusion; these links are provided by the inference rules. A simple inference rule is that of *modus ponens*:

If *a* then *b*; *a*; therefore *b*.

In Table 2.1 you can see how this can be used as a translation of the A statement. Applying these rules generates suppositions, which themselves can be used along with further rules to prove subgoals: these subgoals are necessary steps along the way to deriving a proof. You may not always succeed in finding a proof – you may lack a necessary inference rule, or be prevented by working memory restrictions from completing all the steps, or it may be that no possible proof exists – but you will always make an attempt at it.

Inference rules can be applied in a forward or backward direction, a notion that is important in accounting for how some deductions can be made. The difference lies in whether you proceed from the premises to the conclusion (forward) or from the conclusion to the premises (backward). To take the example of modus ponens above, consider an argument of the following kind (adapted from Rips, 1994, Ch. 3):

If John is an archbishop then he is a believer	[premise 1]
If John is a believer then he is a Christian	[premise 2]
John is an archbishop	[premise 3]
John is a Christian	[conclusion]

Does this conclusion follow? Applying forward modus ponens, we combine the first premise with the third and derive the assertion 'John is a believer'. This is a subgoal in the proof. Combining this with the second premise, we derive the assertion 'John is a Christian', and hence prove the conclusion (the main goal). Using backward modus ponens, we start with the conclusion. This matches the second part of the second premise, and backward modus ponens states that this goal is satisfied if we can prove the first part of the premise, so this forms the subgoal. To do this, we apply the same backward rule again: now, the first part of premise 2 matches the second part of premise 1; if the first part of premise 1 is true then the subgoal is proved. Premise 3 asserts just this, so the subgoal is proved and hence so is the conclusion.

There are 10 forward rules and 14 backward rules. Also, for syllogisms and other forms of argument using quantifiers, Rips supplements them with three additional forward rules: transitivity, exclusivity and conversion, since syllogistic inference cannot be captured without them. The transitivity rule takes this form (Table 2.1 shows how the symbols in parentheses are used):

If $A(x)$ then $B(x)$
If $B(y)$ then $C(y)$
If $A(z)$ then $C(z)$

and is sufficient to prove the AA1 syllogism we began with. Since this argument requires only one easily available rule, it should be simple. The exclusivity rule looks like this:

If $A(x)$ then $B(x)$
Not $(B(y)$ and $C(y))$
Not $(A(z)$ and $C(z))$

and suffices to prove the argument:

All a are b	All archbishops are believers
No b are c	No believers are cannibals
No a are c	No archbishops are cannibals

Again, since this is a one-rule argument it should be easy, and it is (85% correct in Rips' own data). The conversion rule simply allows us to reverse the item order in an E sentence, recognising that No a are b is equivalent to No b are a:

$$\frac{\text{Not } A(x) \text{ and } B(x)}{\text{Not } B(y) \text{ and } A(y)}$$

This is an immediate inference, in Newstead's (1995) terms.

Not all syllogisms are easy, as we have seen. Consider the AO syllogism:

$$\frac{\begin{array}{l}\text{All churchgoers are believers}\\ \text{Some agnostics are not believers}\end{array}}{\text{Some agnostics are not churchgoers}}$$

According to Rips, this argument requires the application of four inference rules, known as forward and-elimination, backward and-introduction, backward not-introduction and backward if-elimination (for further explanation of these rules, see Rips, 1994, Chs. 6–7). Not surprisingly, it turns out to be hard: in Rips' own data, only 35% of subjects agreed, correctly, that the conclusion followed. Note that Rips uses a conclusion evaluation method: people have to judge the soundness of the complete argument.

Mental models

The study of reasoning began with syllogisms; so did the theory of mental models, in the research reported by Johnson-Laird and Steedman (1978). Since its detailed development in the 1980s and 1990s (see Johnson-Laird, 1983; Johnson-Laird & Byrne, 1991), mental models has become the most influential theory of reasoning, and it will figure many times in this book, especially in Chapter 5.

Mental models theory proposes that there are three stages of thinking that people go through when reasoning; these are shown in Figure 2.3. The first stage is to understand the premises, using your knowledge of language and any relevant general knowledge. This is called the *comprehension* stage. It results in your constructing models of the states of affairs conveyed by the premises; in the case of syllogisms, this is done by representing an arbitrary number of instances of each premise.

The second stage is to combine the premise models to derive a description of the state of affairs they jointly define: the *description* stage. The composite mental model that results must include new information: it must state something that was not already explicit in the premises – a conclusion, in other words. If you cannot find such a model, you respond that no conclusion follows. If you can, then you pass to the third stage: *validation*. This involves searching for any alternative models that are consistent with the premises but in which the putative (i.e. candidate) conclusion is false. If there is one, then the conclusion is false; you should then search for another conclusion and validate it. A valid conclusion is one where there are no alternative models that falsify it: it must therefore be true if the premises are true.

Johnson-Laird and colleagues include an important psychological constraint to explain the difference in difficulty between syllogisms, which is the central

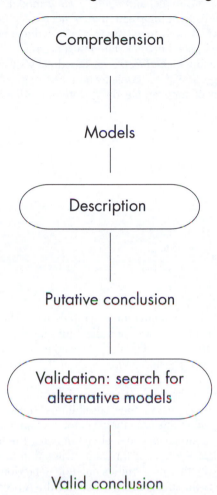

Premises and general knowledge

Figure 2.3 The three stages of reasoning in mental models theory

Source: Johnson-Laird and Byrne (1991), reproduced by permission of Psychology Press

empirical fact about them. This is a principle of *economy*, and it basically means that, because of the restricted capacity of working memory, which has been known about since the earliest days of experimental psychology, reasoners will try to do as little cognitive work as possible. They will thus try to construct a minimum of models, with a minimum of information explicitly represented in each.

These elements of the mental models theory – the stages and the economy principle – lead to clear and testable empirical predictions.

Modelling the premises will depend on the comprehension stage and the economy principle. From these two factors comes a fundamental distinction in the theory, between an *initial* model and a *fully explicit* model. The initial model will contain only so much explicit information as is necessary for the meaning of the premise, but people will be able to extend this knowledge if necessary: they will be aware of what may be implied but not stated by a premise. They keep track of this 'hidden' information using *mental footnotes*. The theory's way of expressing these has changed over the years. In its classic formulation (e.g. Johnson-Laird & Byrne, 1991), the initial model of, for example, the A statement *All archbishops are believers* looks like this:

> [archbishop]   believer
>
> [archbishop]   believer
>
>   . . .

or in abstract terms:

> [*a*]   *b*
>
> [*a*]   *b*
>
>   . . .

You can see that there are two notational symbols here: the square brackets and the three dots. The former is a way of indicating that the *a* items (archbishops) cannot appear in any other possibility; they are said to be exhaustively represented in the initial model. More recent formulations of the theory (see Johnson-Laird, 2006; Johnson-Laird & Byrne, 2002) no longer use the brackets, but simply state that people use a footnote about this. The second symbol, the three dots, is another mental footnote that there are further possibilities; these can be *fleshed out* as required by the task, and in this case they cannot contain *a* items.

We can see how a model can be fleshed out using the fully explicit representation of the A premise. We need a third bit of notation to do this: a symbol for negation, because any further possibilities must be not-*a*. Johnson-Laird uses the ¬ symbol for this. Here is the fully explicit model for the A premise:

> *a*   *b*
>
> *a*   *b*
>
> ¬*a*   *b*
>
> ¬*a*   ¬*b*

This conveys the logical possibilities that while there can only be *a*s that are *b*s, there can be *b*s that are not *a*s, and there may also be things that are not *b* and also not *a*. Table 2.2 gives all the initial and fully explicit models for the four syllogistic statements.

Now we can see how these models can be combined in solving syllogisms, and how the theory predicts patterns of performance. First, the familiar AA

Table 2.2 The initial and fully explicit models of the four syllogistic sentences in Johnson-Laird's theory of mental models

	All a are b		Some a are b		No a are b		Some a are not b	
Initial models	[a]	b	a	b	a		a	
	. . .		. . .			b	a	[b]
					. . .			[b]
							. . .	
Explicit models	[a]	[b]	a	b	[a]	¬b	a	¬b
	[¬a]	[b]	¬a	b	¬a	[b]	a	[b]
	[¬a]	[¬b]	a	¬b	¬a	¬b	¬a	[b]
			¬a	¬b			¬a	¬b

Note: ¬ is the symbol for negation; [ ] denotes exhaustive representation; . . . denotes alternative models with no explicit content

Source: Adapted from Johnson-Laird and Byrne (1991)

syllogism. The initial model for the first premise has just been given; the second premise will look similar:

b   c

b   c

. . .

These can be combined following the constraint that reasoners will not represent explicitly more information than they have to; in this case, they will not represent *b* items twice over, so the combined model will look like this:

a   b   c

a   b   c

. . .

This is the only way in which the information about *a*, *b* and *c* could be combined – there is no need to consider the content of the implicit instances. It is consistent with the conclusion that All *a* are *c*, and, since there is no alternative model that is not consistent with this conclusion, it is valid. This should therefore be an easy syllogism to solve (because it only needs one combined model and does not require consideration of the implicit information) and it is: Johnson-Laird and Byrne (1991) report that 89% of people get it right.

Now let us go back to our EA argument, which we know tends to produce a high rate of errors:

No atheists are believers

All believers are Christians
?

From Table 2.2 you can retrieve the initial models; when combined, Johnson-Laird suggests they will produce the following initial composite:

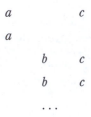

This supports the conclusion 'No *a* are *c*', and is the most common conclusion that people draw. However, the theory says that you will search for alternative models, and the premise models can also be combined in this way:

a   *c*

a

     b   *c*

     b   *c*

    . . .

which is not consistent with the first putative conclusion, because it is possible that there are *c*s which are not *b*s (remember the second Euler diagram for the A statement, where *b* is enclosed in *c*). This opens up the possibility of an *a* that is also a *c*. So you might revise your conclusion to Some *a* are not *c*. That would be consistent with both of the above combined models. But wait: there is a third possible combination as well, where every single *a* is a *c*; that is logically possible, even though it seems, on the basis of our general knowledge, unlikely:

a   *c*

a   *c*

     b   *c*

     b   *c*

    . . .

Is there a conclusion that is consistent with all these three possible composite models? Yes: Some *c* are not *a*. As we saw earlier, very few people arrive at this conclusion, and the model theory attributes the difficulty primarily to the need to consider more than one combined model. These examples illustrate an important general observation made by mental models researchers: that the difficulty of syllogisms varies according to the number of models needed to arrive at a conclusion. The first example was a one-model problem: the premise models can only be combined one way. The second was a three-model problem. One-model problems have consistently been found to be easier to solve than problems that require more than one model. The mental models theory predicts other results as well, since it provides an account of the mental processes people are supposed to be using when they reason; for instance, it can account for the *types* of errors people make, not just their frequency (see Bucciarelli & Johnson-Laird, 1999; Johnson-Laird, 2006; Johnson-Laird & Byrne, 1991, for detailed experimental results). However, the theory has not gone unchallenged, as we shall see in the next section and later in the book.

Probability heuristics

Earlier in this chapter, I mentioned that logical argument, such as the syllogisms we have been dealing with, requires you to assume that the premises are true: that is, they are certain and they permit no exceptions. This is obvious when you consider deductive validity, where the conclusion necessarily follows: no *necessary* conclusion is possible if the premises are less than certain. The trouble with this stipulation is that it is another way in which the study of reasoning can, if we are not careful, detach itself from real life. This is because in real life there are few statements that can be made with certainty.

This insight is the basis of a new approach to the psychology of reasoning that is little short of revolutionary: the probabilistic approach of Oaksford and Chater (2007). It is part of the new paradigm in reasoning research that has been mentioned in the Preface and will be mentioned again at various points in the book. They point out that almost any general factual claim you make about the world is, to use a technical term, *defeasible*: it can be defeated by additional information. That being the case, everyday reasoning cannot be based on logic, which is the calculus of certainty. It must be based on probability, the calculus of uncertainty. Oaksford and Chater invert the relation between psychological research and the everyday world: instead of trying to generalise from the laboratory to the world, they see the task of explanation as one of modelling the relevant aspect of the world, in this case how people make inferences, and using that to explain people's performance when they are tested. This involves using the approach of *rational analysis*, pioneered by John Anderson (1990, 1991).

Reasoning, from the probabilistic perspective, is about gaining information and updating belief (see Harman, 1999, for a similar perspective in philosophy). Gaining information means reducing uncertainty: that is your cognitive goal. A statement is informative the more improbable (i.e. surprising) it is. Thus, finding out that some archbishops are Catholics is unsurprising and hence uninformative, but finding out that some archbishops were cannibals would be very surprising and hence highly informative.

In this example, the probability varies because of the content, but Chater and Oaksford apply this principle to syllogistic reasoning by calculating the informativeness of the four statements A, E, I and O, independent of content. They do this by conducting formal analyses of the probability that each of the four statements is true. They then work through the theoretical consequences of these calculations to predict syllogistic performance, on the assumption that people in experiments are importing their understanding of these probabilities into the laboratory task. The result is the *probability heuristics model* (PHM, from now on), which is set out in great detail by Chater and Oaksford (1999) and slightly more briefly by Oaksford and Chater (2007).

We shall first see how the informativeness of the statements is derived, using Chater and Oaksford's graphical devices; you can go to the original paper for more detail on the mathematics that support the argument. Their first step is to turn the A, E, I and O sentences into probabilistic statements by comparing the *conditional probabilities* associated with them. A conditional probability is the probability that something is a *b* given that it is an *a* (e.g. that you are a believer given that you are an archbishop).

Let us start with the A statement, All *a* are *b*. This must mean that the probability that you are a *b* given that you are an *a*, written prob(b|a), is 1: it is certain that you are a *b* if you are an *a*, if A is true (see Figure 2.1 for graphical confirmation of this). With the E statement, No *a* are *b*, prob(b|a) must be 0. The I statement, Some *a* are *b*, is rather less specific because prob(b|a) now must lie in a range between more than zero and 1 (since 'some' does not rule out 'all'); similarly, with the O statement, Some *a* are not *b*, all that can be ruled out is that all *a* are *b*, so prob (b|a) lies in the range between zero and just less than 1.

These relations are set out graphically in Figure 2.4. This shows the range of prob(b|a), from 0 to 1, and where the statements lie on it. A is represented by a single point on the right and E by a single point on the left because, as we have

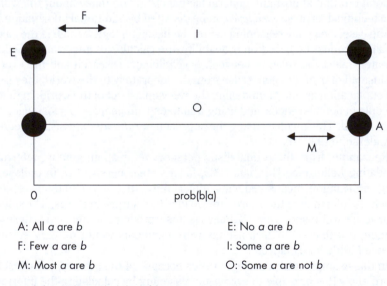

A: All *a* are *b*   E: No *a* are *b*

F: Few *a* are *b*   I: Some *a* are *b*

M: Most *a* are *b*   O: Some *a* are not *b*

prob(b | a): the probability of *b* given *a*

Figure 2.4 Conditional probability ranges of six syllogistic statements

Source: Chater and Oaksford (1999), reproduced by permission of Elsevier

seen, they have exact values, 1 and 0. The range of values that I can take is shown on the top line, which joins a point next to A (where some = all) but leaves a gap before the zero point, since No *a* are *b* is ruled out. Similarly, O joins the zero end, but does not meet the 1 end, because only All *a* are *b* is ruled out.

You will notice something else about Figure 2.4: the two double-headed arrows. These represent the two so-called generalised quantifiers, *Most* and *Few* (M and F), which are beyond the scope of traditional logic because you cannot derive deductively valid conclusions from them and they had never been studied by psychologists before Chater and Oaksford's work. They appear in PHM almost as a free gift, because they can be represented in terms of conditional probability quite naturally. *Most* occupies a narrow range towards, but not quite reaching, the 1 end of the prob(b|a) scale: if Most *a* are *b*, then prob(b|a) is high but less than 1. *Few* occupies a similar narrow range at the zero end: prob(b|a) is low but more than 0. The inclusion of M and F without modification is one of PHM's great strengths.

That is not the end of PHM's generosity. If you look again at Figure 2.4, you can see that other properties fall out of this analysis. For instance, A and O take up the whole range of prob (b|a). This means that if one of these (A or O) is true, the other must be false. The same applies to the E and I pair. We can also derive the 'weak' versions of the various statements. Because A is included in I, then A probabilistically entails (p-entails in the theory's terminology) I; ditto with E and O.

This analysis takes us part of the way towards quantifying informativeness, but we need another component: how do these statements relate to the world? Remember, PHM is based on the principle of rational analysis, and therefore aims to model the part of the world it is concerned with. How probable is it that any of these six statements (A, E, I, O, M, F) will be true? You cannot simply count them up, so Chater and Oaksford give us a formal analysis based on the *rarity assumption*. This assumption comes from the fact that most of the terms in natural language refer only to rare items and properties: the number of archbishops is a tiny proportion of the number of priests or believers, let alone men, humans or living things. From this, we can immediately see that there is a very high probability that any E statement about two random items will be true. Sure enough, no archbishops are birds, books, binoculars . . . to name three things I can see right now. Thus E statements are very unsurprising and hence uninformative. Which means that O statements must be even more uninformative, because O is p-entailed by E.

Chater and Oaksford (1999) provide another graphic device in an appendix to their paper that illustrates how a final order of informativeness of the six statements can be derived, on the basis of conditional probability and rarity. This is shown in Figure 2.5. The frequency of true E statements is shown by the vertical arrow on the left: they are highly likely to be true. The A statements are highly unlikely to be true (not all dogs bark, not all birds fly), and this is represented by the little black square on the right. Transferring the double arrows from Figure 2.4, we can see that there will be more true F statements about the world than M statements: F occupies a larger area than M. Therefore M is more informative than F. The Z region refers to the range of prob (b|a) values that are not specific to any one statement, where I and O overlap. So we can say that the proportion of true I statements will be the sum of F, Z, M and A, while the proportion of true O statements will be the sum of F, Z, M and E. Since

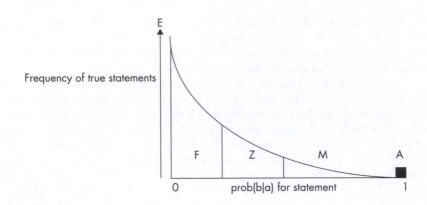

Figure 2.5 Proportions of true statements as a function of conditional probability in PHM

Source: Chater and Oaksford (1999), reproduced by permission of Elsevier

there are vastly more of the latter than the former, O is much less informative – it is only ruled out by A, and so will almost always be true (some dogs don't bark; neither do some archbishops). We thus end up with this order of informativeness:

$$A > M > F > I > E \gg O$$

with the double chevron emphasising how uninformative O statements are.

Now we come to the H part of PHM, the heuristics. A heuristic is a reliable but not totally precise decision rule, a rule of thumb. PHM specifies five of these: three generate conclusions (G) and two test them (T).

- G1: The min-heuristic. An argument is only as strong as its weakest link, so choose the conclusion that takes the form of its least informative premise, the min-premise.
- G2: The p-entailments. The next most preferred conclusion will be one p-entailed by the one predicted by the min-heuristic.
- G3: The attachment-heuristic. This determines whether the conclusion's terms are in the order *a-c* or *c-a*. If the min-premise has *a* as its subject, then choose an *a-c* conclusion; if it has *c* as its subject, choose the *c-a* form. If it does not have *a* or *c* as its subject, use the max-premise as a guide in the same way.
- T1: The max-heuristic. Confidence in the generated conclusion varies according to the informativeness of the max-premise. So you should be most confident if an A conclusion is generated, and least confident in an O conclusion.
- T2: The O-heuristic. Avoid O conclusions because they are so very uninformative.

Here is the example that Chater and Oaksford give to show how they work, using an AI2 syllogism:

All *b* are *a*	the max-premise
Some *c* are *b*	the min-premise
Therefore, Some ...	by the min-heuristic
... *c* are *a*	by the attachment-heuristic

Several testable predictions arise from this analysis but I shall deal only with the main ones here; the min-conclusion should be preferred for all syllogisms; the p-entailments will determine the next most preferred conclusion; the frequency with which a conclusion will be drawn will be determined by the max-heuristic; valid O conclusions will be hard to draw because of the O-heuristic; and conclusion term orders will follow the attachment-heuristic. Chater and Oaksford report analyses of two data sets to test these predictions. The first was a meta-analysis of five studies in which people were given the complete set of syllogisms containing A, E, I and O premises, and the second was data from two new experiments that included the M and F premises – these extend the number of possible premise pairs from 64 to 144. All the predictions mentioned above were confirmed, as were several other subtler tests.

How do these findings compare with tests of other theories, such as mental models? PHM should be able to account for results that favour other theories too. For instance, remember the distinction between single-model and multiple-model problems made by Johnson-Laird: syllogisms that require more than one model should be more difficult than those that require two or three. It so happens that all the valid two- and three-model problems have O conclusions, which PHM says should be difficult on that basis alone; all the one-model problems have A, E or I conclusions. Furthermore, Chater and Oaksford predict and observe differences *within* the classes of two- and three-model problems that mental models theory does not.

Which is not to say game, set and match to PHM. Chater and Oaksford themselves concede that there are times when mental models theory, for instance, wins over PHM. In addition, Roberts and Sykes (2005) also find little evidence for the T2 heuristic – and in fact it does seem like a mere aspect of T1, rather than something distinct. We shall come back to the probabilistic approach of Chater and Oaksford at several points in the book, since, like the other theories we have briefly considered so far, it is concerned with more than just syllogisms.

We have seen in this chapter how an area of logical argument can be subjected to psychological analysis, generating predictions that can be tested in experiments. We have also seen how human performance can be explained theoretically, and how these theories can themselves generate novel predictions and tests. That will be the pattern throughout this book. In the next chapter, we shall begin this further exploration by introducing the most researched area in the whole field of the psychology of reasoning. Before we do that, note that we have not finished with syllogisms quite yet: they will take a prominent position when we consider new paradigm theories of reasoning in Chapter 6.

Summary

1   Research on reasoning began with the quantified syllogism. Syllogistic logic was developed by Aristotle as a means of gauging the soundness of arguments.

2   Classical syllogisms contain four quantifier expressions in two premises, leading to a conclusion that can be valid or invalid. Their structures can be classified according to mood (the form of the premises, along with the conclusion) and figure (the arrangement of the premises).

3   Syllogisms vary widely in the performance they produce, from very easy to very difficult. Explaining this variation is the main task of the psychology of syllogisms.

4   People's performance deviates from logical norms. They can misinterpret premises or be influenced by conversational pragmatics.

5   The main explanation for this deviation is given by three theories: the theory of mental logic, Johnson-Laird's theory of mental models and Chater and Oaksford's probability heuristics model.

Reasoning with propositions

If: conditionals

This little monosyllable has been responsible for more research and theory than any other word in the language. I shall set out the basics of the psychological work on it here, but we shall return to it often in subsequent chapters. *If* is an example of a *connective* term. Connectives do what it says on the label: they connect linguistic propositions. Other connectives are *Or*, which we shall also examine, *Not* and *And*. Because they connect propositions, this form of reasoning is also known as *propositional reasoning*. As with classical syllogisms, propositional reasoning has been studied in a number of ways, and the kinds of tasks used have raised important issues and generated vast amounts of research. First, a bit of technical background.

Knowing p, knowing q: inferences and truth tables

Conditional inferences can be set out in the same way as quantified syllogisms, with two premises and a conclusion, like this:

> If p then q
> $\underline{p}$
> ?

The letters p and q are almost always used when talking about conditionals, so we shall stick with them. They refer to the two parts of the sentence known as the *antecedent* (p) and the *consequent* (q). The first premise in a conditional syllogism is called the *major premise*, and it states the claim being made about p and q using *If*. The second premise is called the *minor premise* (or *categorical premise*), and it states something about one of the components, p or q. That something is either to affirm it, as above, or deny it. So you could call the above argument affirmation of the antecedent, but it is always known by its Latin tag, *modus ponens* ('affirming mood'). It appeared in the description of Rips' Psycop theory of syllogisms in Chapter 2. It is one of the four possible conditional inferences. Here they are, with some realistic content to illustrate them, concerning a person called Alex, whose religious affiliation is in question:

- *Modus ponens (MP)*

  If p then q If Alex is a Christian, then he is a believer
  p Alex is a Christian

  What conclusion are you most likely to draw from these premises? It seems to follow straightforwardly that Alex is a believer. Now for the inference where the antecedent is negated, producing a denial inference.
- *Denial of the antecedent (DA)*

  If p then q If Alex is a Christian, then he is a believer

Not *p*   Alex is not a Christian

You are likely now to conclude that Alex is not a believer. There are two more possible inferences, based on the affirmation and denial of the consequent.

- *Affirmation of the consequent (AC)*

If *p* then *q*   If Alex is a Christian, then he is a believer
q   Alex is a believer

Therefore, Alex is a Christian? This seems reasonable, but you may be having your doubts; we shall address them shortly.

- *Modus tollens (MT; 'denying mood')*

If *p* then *q*   If Alex is a Christian, then he is a believer
Not *q*   Alex is not a believer

Therefore . . . what? This one seems to ask for some quite hard work to see what, if anything, follows, and you might want to pause and reflect on your struggle before we go any further.

These kinds of conditionals are called *indicative* conditionals, as they contain a descriptive, factual claim. Now for the essential logical question about these inferences: their validity. Just as with Aristotelian syllogisms, a valid conclusion is one that necessarily follows from premises that are assumed to be true. Here we run up against the first complication in addressing validity, because logically there are two ways of reading these conditionals. This can be seen clearly if you bear in mind, recalling the section on Rips' Psycop theory in Chapter 2, that *If* sentences can be translated into the syllogistic A premise, in this case, *All Christians are believers*. Referring back to the Euler diagrams in Figure 2.1, you can see that the A premise is consistent with two states of affairs, one where *a* is a subset of *b* and one where the two components are equivalent. An *If* sentence can also be compatible with either of these states of affairs. The subset relation is known as *material implication*, and is the reading that is assumed by logicians to be prime. It is what logicians mean when they refer to the conditional. The equivalence relation is known as material equivalence, or the *biconditional*.

Now let us apply these factors to the arguments above and assess their validity. We first assume that the major premise is an implication conditional. This is consistent with the world we live in as well as with logic, because it is a fact that there are plenty of people who believe in God who are not Christians. So the subset relation applies: every *c* is a *b*, but there are some *b*s that are not *c*s. Taking the MP argument first, is it necessarily the case that a Christian is always a believer, given the truth of the major premise? Yes; all the *c*s are inside the *b* field.

Now let's take the DA argument, where you know Alex is not a Christian. Clearly, you cannot tell whether he is also not a believer, because of the existence of *b*s outside the *c* field (believers who are not Christians). So while it is possible that he is not a believer, it is not necessarily the case: DA is therefore an invalid inference, or *fallacy*.

Next, we take the AC argument, where we know that he is a believer: is he necessarily a Christian? No, for the same reason: there are *b*s outside the *c* field, so again, while the conclusion is possible, it is not necessary, and so AC is also an invalid inference.

Lastly, take the MT argument, where Alex is not a believer. Looking again at the Euler diagram for the subset relation, you can see that anything that is not in the *b* field is not in the *c* field either. Alex therefore cannot be a Christian, given the truth of the two premises in the MT argument: the conclusion is valid.

As far as the biconditional (equivalence) reading is concerned, we can be brief. When *p* and *q* are equivalent, all four inferences are valid. This is because *If p then q* can be validly converted to *If q then p* when the classes are equivalent. Here is an illustration:

Suppose the rule about Alex is that *If he has a Y chromosome (p), then he is male (q)*. As these are equivalent, then we can just as well say that if he is male, then he has a Y chromosome. So what were DA and AC arguments in the first case become MT and MP arguments in the second, and hence are valid.

Truth tables are so called because they set out the conditions under which a sentence can be judged to be logically true or false: its *truth conditions*. Instead of assuming that a conditional is true, we judge its truth or falsity in the light of the affirmation or negation of its components, *p* and *q*. When is the claim about Alex's beliefs true, and when is it false? It seems plain that if he turns out to be both a Christian and a believer, then the claim is true. As for when it would be false, think back to the relation between *If* and the syllogistic A statement, All *c* are *b*: the latter would be false were there a single *c* that was not a *b*. So the claim about Alex is false if he calls himself a Christian but is not a believer.

There are two other possible cases, involving non-Christians and whether or not they believe. Logically, remember, a statement is true as long as is not false. The not-*c*s are the items outside the *c* field in the Euler diagram and so they may be either *b*s or not-*b*s: not-*c*s therefore cannot determine for sure that the *If* statement is true or false. And so finding out that Alex is not a Christian, whether or not he believes, allows the conditional claim to stand as true, because it has not been falsified in these cases. Stating that Alex's being a chiropractor and a believer or a calligrapher and a burglar confirms the claim that *If Alex is a Christian then he is a believer* strikes most people, those untrained in logic, as weird, if not downright wrong. That is a powerful clue that the logical meaning of conditionals departs from their everyday meaning – a fact that has profound psychological implications, as we shall see in later chapters.

We can summarise the relations between the implication conditional and its four factual contingencies in a truth table:

Alex is	*p*	*q*	*If Alex is a Christian then he is a believer* is
a Christian and a believer	true	true	true
a Christian, not a believer	true	false	false

not a Christian, a believer	false	true	true
not a Christian, not a believer	false	false	true

To sum up: *If p then q* is true in all cases except *p and not-q*.

There is also the biconditional interpretation, where *If p then q* can also be read as *If q then p*. This has the following consequences for the truth table:

Alex has/is	p	q	If Alex has a Y chromosome then he is male is
Y, male	true	true	true
Y, not male	true	false	false
not Y, male	false	true	false
not Y, not male	false	false	true

Thus the biconditional is true in the *p, q* and *not-p, not-q* cases, and false in the *p, not-q* and *not-p, q* cases. The last one follows because the sentence is reversible.

Research results

As with research on syllogistic reasoning, psychologists have presented people with arguments and recorded their responses to them, often comparing these responses with what logical norms dictate. One of the problems in reading this literature, particularly where older studies are concerned, is that sometimes responses are reported in the form of error rates (i.e. those that deviate from logic). Classifying behaviour in this way is assuming the answer to the question of what people are doing, which is a serious matter when logical norms themselves are disputed, as we shall see later in this chapter and subsequently. Sometimes, it is debatable whether an error really has been committed. It is much better practice just to record the inferences that people make.

There have been quite a large number of studies that have done this, and they were reviewed by Schroyens, Schaeken and d'Ydewalle (2001). The response patterns on the four conditional inferences were as follows:

	MP	DA	AC	MT
Mean %	96.8	56.0	64.0	74.2

These results come from experiments where over 700 people were given arguments containing abstract materials – those that have been designed to minimise the influence of general knowledge. Such materials may be just letters or numbers, statements about shapes on blackboards, names of imaginary people and places, and so on (reasoning with more realistic materials will be reviewed in detail in the next chapter). There is a wide range of results between studies, which needs to be borne in mind when you read papers in which authors only comment on their own data. Looking at the figures above, we can see straight away that people do not simply respond according to the logic of the implication conditional. If they did, then they would always accept MP and MT, and never accept DA and AC. Nor are they simply adopting the biconditional interpretation, otherwise all four inferences would be accepted. Do the DA and AC figures show that some people – over half – use the biconditional reading while others use implication? If that were the explanation, the MT figure should be much higher, since MT is valid under both readings.

Any theory of conditional reasoning must therefore explain why the fallacies are sometimes made, and why MT is less frequently accepted than MP. We shall see how the three main ones, mental logic, mental models and probabilistic theories, manage in Chapters 5 and 6.

The data from truth-table experiments also need to be accounted for. Results from these started to appear in the 1960s, and the basic data patterns were established by Johnson-Laird and Tagart (1969). They used abstract letter–number rules, such as *If there is a letter A on one side of the card, then there is a number 3 on the other side*, and gave people a set of such cards with different combinations of letters and numbers on them. Their task was to sort these cards into three piles: cards truthfully described by the statement, cards falsely described; and cards to which the statement was irrelevant.

This third category was included following Wason's (1966) argument that false-antecedent items (*not-p, q; not-p, not-q*), such as the non-Christians mentioned above, would be regarded on linguistic grounds as irrelevant to the truth value of a conditional. An *If* sentence, on this argument, was a statement about a presupposition, expressed by *p*, and its consequences, expressed by *q*: when *not-p* was stated, the presupposition was void, so people would see these items as having no bearing on the truth of the sentence. They would, however, see the *p, q* item as verifying the statement and a *p, not-q* item as falsifying. The result would be what Wason called the 'defective' truth table:

p is	q is	If p then q is
true	true	true
true	false	false
false	true	irrelevant
false	false	irrelevant

Johnson-Laird and Tagart found good evidence for this, with 79% of their participants sorting their cards in this way. You might wonder whether they were led to do so by the mere presence of the 'irrelevant' category. There are two reasons to suspect that they were not. Firstly, Johnson-Laird and Tagart also used a rule that is logically equivalent to *If p then q: Not p or q* (they are both false in the case of *p, not-q* and true otherwise). Very few 'irrelevant' judgments were made in this condition. Secondly, Evans (1972) had people construct instances rather than evaluate them: they were given an abstract conditional sentence, about shapes and colours, and had to come up with all the combinations they could think of that would verify or falsify it. The *p, q* instance was most often constructed as verifying and the *p, not-q* instance as falsifying, while the *not-p, q* and *not-p, not-q* items were most often not constructed at all, implying that they were not psychologically relevant. Byrne and Tasso (1999) replicated this finding.

Truth-table tasks have not figured anywhere near as much in conditional reasoning research as have inference tasks. However, both have to take their place alongside a problem that has generated a gigantic pile of research, and to which we now turn.

The Wason selection task

In the same book chapter in which Wason (1966) argued for the defective truth table, he introduced what has often been hailed the most investigated experimental paradigm in the entire field, the selection task. It is hard to overstate the impact that this problem has had: Stenning and van Lambalgen (2008a) call it 'the mother of all reasoning tasks' (p. 44). It has become a widely used instrument for investigating a range of psychological constructs, some of which might not have been discovered without it. At one time, it even formed part of the Human Biology display at the Science Museum in London.

Like the truth-table task, it also first appeared in abstract form. In the first published experimental paper on the task, Wason (1968a) used letters and numbers, and presented people with the following conditional sentence: *If there is a D on one side of any card, then there is a 3 on its other side*. Four cards were placed on a table, and the participants were told that each had a letter on one side and a number on the other. Their task was to decide which of the cards would enable them to determine whether the sentence was true or false; Wason pointed to each one, and the subjects, as they were called then, were asked whether knowing what was on the other side would enable them to make that judgment.

So here is the task:

 Sentence: If there is a D on one side, then there is a 3 on the other side

Cards:

Now, you are a subject. Which of the cards do you need to turn over to determine whether the sentence is true or false? Spend a couple of minutes thinking about your answer before you read any further: it will pay off later.

Here is the solution; you could have used the information in the previous sections on conditional inferences and truth tables to derive it, although chances are you did not. Firstly, you should go looking for instances that could falsify the claim made in the sentence. This is because while no amount of confirming instances can prove a claim true, a single disconfirming instance will prove it false (remember the possible case of a non-believing Christian). We now need to consider which of the cards above could possibly be a falsifying card. The sentence is a conditional in *If p then q* form, and you know from the section on truth tables that such a sentence is false if we find a *p, not-q* case, otherwise it is true. Thinking about the task in this way, the logical status of its contents looks like this:

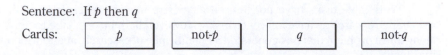

Sentence: If p then q

Cards: | p | not-p | q | not-q |

Which of these cards could be p, *not-q* cards? Clearly, the p card could be: it might have a *not-q* item on the back. A little less clearly, the *not-q* card could be too, because it might have a p item on the back. Neither of the others could have this combination. Thus in this task, you should select the D card and the 7 card, but not the K card or the 3 card.

In Wason's original 1968 experiment, only one of 34 participants did this, and it is highly likely that you did not do so either. Most people pick either the p card alone or the p and q cards together. Reviewing early studies of the selection task, Wason and Johnson-Laird (1972) reported that fewer than 10% of participants made the logically warranted choice of the p, *not-q* cards, and this figure has not deviated since (see Evans, Newstead & Byrne, 1993a; Klauer, Stahl & Erdfelder, 2007). People select the q card when they don't need to, but fail to select the *not-q* card when they should; they rarely select the *not-p* card and usually select the p card. In a detailed meta-analysis of experiments with the basic abstract task, Oaksford and Chater (1994a) report the following percentage frequencies, derived from 34 studies involving 845 participants over a 25-year time span:

Cards:	p	not-p	q	not-q
%	89	16	62	25

Thus we have another data set that any respectable theory of reasoning must be able to handle: the patterns of choices in the selection task. The challenge is all the greater here because of the interest that the selection task sparked among researchers, from its earliest days. This led them to try to get to the bottom of how its 'structural simplicity' led to its 'psychological complexity,' as Wason himself put it (1969a). Why do the great majority of people go wrong on it?

One line of attack to this question is to dissect the problem and try to find out what makes it so difficult, and what can be done to make it easier. Might people have trouble identifying what makes a conditional false? We can dismiss this possibility straight away. The data from truth-table experiments show that people are well able to recognise the p, *not-q* case as falsifying when they see it, as Wason (1968a) confirmed (see also Dominowski, 1995, for more recent evidence). This observation, incidentally, turns out to have serious theoretical implications, as we shall see particularly in Chapter 6 when we go into the dual process theory.

Perhaps, then, people have trouble with the idea of testing claims to destruction. However, Griggs (1995) found that the same selection patterns emerge if you ask participants directly to test whether the sentence is false. That seems to leave a possible difficulty in finding relevant cases on the hidden parts of the cards. There is better evidence for this, because when the task is simplified by leaving out the p and *not-p* cards, where people usually do the right logical thing (they select the former and avoid the latter), people are much more likely to select *not-q* than q cards (Johnson-Laird & Wason, 1970; Wason & Green, 1984).

One way in which the task can be made easier is therefore to give participants less to think about. Griggs (1995) systematically investigated others: task instructions, sentence clarification and decision justification. The first two of these are aimed at reducing ambiguities in the standard task, to do with the kind of search task the participants are presented with and ruling out a possible biconditional interpretation of the sentence, respectively. Decision justification means that people have to explain their card choices, and results using this manipulation have been mixed. Evans (1989) reports abandoning an experiment where participants were asked to give a verbal commentary on their thinking because they seemed quite unable to do so. Asking for retrospective reports, where people say why they chose a card, is fraught with difficulty, as was discovered by Wason (1969b): they are frequently astonished and flustered when they are shown any conflict between what they have chosen and what they should have chosen. In later work, Wason and Evans (1975; Evans & Wason, 1976) showed that people seem to give post hoc rationalisations of their choices, rather than any meaningful account of how they made them – another result that has had profound theoretical implications, and which we shall return to in later chapters.

Griggs (1995) found that when people were given a sentence clarification, were asked to find instances that violated the claim made in the conditional and were asked to justify their choices, up to 81% made the p, *not-q* selection, which is a huge facilitation effect from the usual sub-10% rate.

There are two other ways that have succeeded in elevating selection task performance: the use of negation in the conditional sentence and the use of realistic problem contents. We shall deal with those in the next chapter; some of the most important work on the selection task has involved using these methods. We have not finished with conditionals by a long way: they will also form the focus of Chapters 5 and 6, where we shall look at how well the major theories of reasoning explain people's thinking with them.

Reasoning with Or: disjunctives

Nothing like as much psychological research has been directed at reasoning with this part of language compared to *If*. This is partly because some of the issues that arise are similar, although *Or* does raise some distinct points of its own.

The first similarity to note is that, in parallel with the conditional, there are two possible readings of the disjunctive, termed *inclusive* and *exclusive*. They can be logically related to the implication conditional and the biconditional, respectively. Here is a truth table for inclusive disjunction, with some everyday content for illustration; it is often expressed as '*p or q (or both)*':

Alex has	p	q	Alex has a degree or job experience is
a degree and experience	true	true	true

a degree but no experience	true false true
no degree but experience	false true true
no degree and no experience	false false false

Inclusive *Or* is thus only false in one situation: when neither property is affirmed; otherwise it is true. This is how you can see the logical equivalence between disjunctives and conditionals: *If p then q* has the same truth conditions as *Not p or q*, and both are false in the case of *p* (which is not *not-p*) and *not-q*.

Exclusive disjunction is often expressed as '*p or q (but not both)*' or as '*p or else q*'. The sentence is false when you have both properties, as well as when you have neither, and again you should be able to connect this with *If*, this time the biconditional. Here is a truth table showing its properties:

Alex is	*p*	*q*	*Alex is an atheist or a believer* is
an atheist, a believer	true	true	false
an atheist, not a believer	true	false	true
not an atheist, a believer	false	true	true
an agnostic	false	false	false

Sometimes it is easier to understand these tables if you think not in terms of whether the sentence is true or false, but assume its truth and then judge what is possible or impossible. For instance, if the sentence *Alex is Ed's mother or father* is true, you can see that it is possible that Alex is his mother and that Alex is his father, but it is impossible for Alex to be both and also for Alex to have no children.

Research results

As with the research on conditionals reported in the first half of this chapter, psychologists have looked at both inferences and truth-table judgments involving disjunctives. This work has been going on since the 1970s, and was summarised by Evans et al. (1993a); surprisingly little similar such work has been reported since. Unlike the conditional reasoning results, the patterns in the data with disjunctives are not as clear as one might hope.

Taking the inference results first, just as with *If* sentences, two affirmation inferences and two denial inferences are available, one each for the *p* and *q* parts. Here is an example of an affirmation inference:

p or q	Alex has a degree or experience
p	Alex has a degree

?

Whether you can draw a valid conclusion – one that necessarily follows the premises – depends on whether you are dealing with an inclusive or exclusive reading of the *p or q* sentence. Only with the exclusive does one conclusion – *not-q* – definitely follow; with the inclusive, *q* is also possible. With the affirmation of *q*, the conclusion is about *p*, of course, and the same points apply. Roberge (1976a) found that 92% of people drew the affirmation inference with an exclusive sentence, but Johnson-Laird, Byrne and Schaeken (1992) obtained a rate of only 30%. It is far from clear why there was this difference, but both the materials used and the participant populations differed. With the inclusive sentence, Roberge in two studies found around 36% accepting it (Evans et al., 1993a, Ch. 5); as mentioned, this is an invalid inference here, and so it should not be accepted.

Now here is a denial inference:

p or *q*	Alex has a degree or experience
Not p	Alex has no degree

?

There is a valid conclusion under both readings here: *q*. So people should always accept it. Roberge (1976b, 1978) found that under both readings the denial inference was accepted at rates between 70% and 93%; acceptance was higher with the exclusive reading. Quite why it would ever not be accepted, sometimes by nearly one-third of these participants, is a bit of a mystery. These experiments involved 'arbitrary' materials – sentences and instances somewhat detached from what you come across in real life – and it seems that these sorts of problems are too artificial for many people.

As far as truth-table results are concerned, there is again inconsistency between studies (see Evans et al., 1993a). The *not-p, not-q* instance is always rated as false, which it should be under both inclusive and exclusive readings (see above). However, the *not-p, q* and *p, not-q* instances were only evaluated as true about 80% of the time, and as they are logically true under both readings this figure is actually rather low. The *p, q* instance serves as a kind of litmus test of whether someone is reading the sentence as inclusive or exclusive (Paris, 1973), and you won't be surprised to learn that sometimes there was a clear preference for rating it as true (in line with an inclusive reading), sometimes for rating it as false (in line with the exclusive) and sometimes there was no clear preference at all!

Some psychologists (e.g. Fillenbaum, 1974) have argued that the exclusive reading is the more natural in everyday language and Noveck, Chierchia, Chevaux, Guelminger and Sylvestre (2002) point to a contrast between this everyday usage and results obtained in reasoning experiments. Here, as we have seen, the inclusive reading is sometimes preferred. Noveck et al. argue, backed up with experimental results, that inclusive *Or* is the basic interpretation but that people strengthen it to the exclusive when it would be more informative to do so. Thus they will not endorse a conclusion to an argument that takes the form *q or r* if *q and r* is possible, even though this is logically justified. So in everyday speech *Or* tends to invite the implicature *But not both*: why say *Or* if you could mean *And*? Indeed, sometimes in everyday language you see the form *and/or*, as when a job advert says that you must have a degree and/or experience, indicating that you qualify if you have either or both. This factor is related to the Gricean principle of informativeness, which we met in the context of syllogisms in Chapter 1.

As I mentioned earlier, this kind of research, using inferences or judgments and abstract materials, has rather faded away. Since the pioneering work of the 1970s, research on disjunctives has mainly continued under two flags. The first is their use in testing the mental models theory, which we shall review in detail in Chapter 5. The second is their use in another tricky task devised by Wason: the THOG problem.

Wason's THOG problem

Wason had the Midas touch when it came to inventing tasks that experimenters could use to explore human reasoning. He produced four problems that have each generated hundreds of studies. We have already had our first look at the selection task, and now it is the turn of a second, the THOG problem. We shall go into detail about a third, the 2 4 6 task, in Chapter 7, while the fourth, the verification task (the first one he devised) will be touched on at various points. THOG has recently been reviewed in great detail by Koenig and Griggs (2010).

Wason (1977) claimed to have thought of the THOG problem in 1976, but there is an earlier version in Wason and Johnson-Laird (1972, Ch. 5). The first research paper on it was by Wason and Brooks (1979). Here is their version of the problem. As always with these problems, you will learn much more if you have a go at it yourself before reading on.

In front of you are four designs:

You are to assume that I have written down one of the colours (black or white) and one of the shapes (square or circle). Now read the following rule carefully:

If, and only if, any of the designs includes either the colour I have written down, or the shape I have written down, but not both, then it is called a THOG.

I will tell you that the Black Square is a THOG.

Each of the designs can now be classified into one of the following categories:

a Definitely is a THOG
b Insufficient information to decide
c Definitely is not a THOG

So which, if any, of the other three designs, apart from the black square, is a THOG? When I first encountered this problem, at a conference presentation by Wason himself, I was initially stumped, and then came hesitantly to this conclusion. The white square and the black circle could be THOGs (*b*: insufficient information), while the white circle is definitely not a THOG (*c*). This turns out to be the answer that most people come up with, so you probably did too. It is completely wrong.

The right answer is that the white square and black circle cannot be THOGs, while the white circle definitely is one. The problem depends on the properties of exclusive disjunction (*p or q but not both*) and the biconditional (*If and only if p then q*), which you know about and which determine the right answer. It goes like this. The example the experimenter has written down can have just one colour (black or white) and just one shape (square or circle). You know the black square is a THOG, so the rule for THOGness could be black and circle (i.e. not square), or white (i.e. not black) and square; it cannot be black and square, since that is the *p, q* item, which is prohibited under exclusive disjunction, and it cannot be white and circle, since this would be the *not-p, not-q* item, which is also prohibited (refer back to the truth table above). Now we can classify the three mystery designs. If the THOG rule were black-and-circle, we could rule out the black circle (*p, q*) and the white square (*not-p, not-q*); but the white circle (*not-p, q*) contains just one property, circle, and so gets its THOG status. Similarly, if the THOG rule were white-and-square, we could again rule out the white square (*p, q*) and black circle (*not-p, not-q*) and accept the white circle (*p, not-q*). Either way, the white circle must be a THOG and the other two cannot be.

The common error that I, and perhaps you, fell into was called the *intuitive error* by Wason and Brooks. We responded to the surface features of the problem, in particular the THOG item – black square – that we were given, and neglected the logic. Just as with the selection task, understanding and using the logic do not seem to be the problem; Wason and Brooks found that people were well able to do this when the elements of it were disentangled. Rather, as Newstead, Legrenzi and Girotto (1995) report, much of the difficulty stems from a failure to separate the *hypotheses* arising from the experimenter's statement of the rule from the *data* supplied by the given THOG: black and square.

Newstead et al. call this *confusion theory*. It leads to an obvious move: make this separation easier, and the task should be easier too. Girotto and Legrenzi (1989) did this by using more realistic materials. A character called Charles plays this game with his friends:

> I have brought a deck of cards. It contains only these four shapes [four cards showing shapes such as those above]. I deal one for myself from the deck, and I won't show it to you. Now, I'll deal each of you a card, and I will pay for a dinner for each person who has a card including either the colour of my card or the shape, but not both. [The four cards above are given to Charles' friends Rob, Tim, Paul and John, reading left to right.] Without showing you my card, I can tell you that I owe Rob a dinner. Which card do you think I could have? And do you think I have to pay for a dinner for anyone else? If so, for whom?

The answer to the last question is John, of course, and 89% of participants gave this answer. In a later study, Girotto and Legrenzi (1993) induced 70% of people to give the right answer by giving an actual name, SARS, to a hypothesised design, with THOG defined as having either the colour or the shape of the SARS. However, this result was found to be hard to replicate by Griggs, Platt, Newstead and Jackson (1998), without an additional manipulation introduced by O'Brien, Noveck, Davidson, Fisch, Lea and Freitag (1990): telling people that there actually is one other THOG and challenging them to find it. This of course simplifies the problem – you no longer have to keep in mind the possibility that there might not be another THOG to be found at all. O'Brien et al. also simplified the problem by using a 'blackboard' story, where participants where told that the experimenter had written one colour on the left of a blackboard and one on the other, ditto for the shapes. This made it easier for them to separate the data from the hypotheses, and recalls Stenning's (2002) advice (see Chapter 2) that much of your task as a reasoner concerns finding a representation that works. This principle fits with the findings of Koenig and Griggs (2004), who found that being exposed to one of the easier versions raised performance on the standard abstract task, as long as people were made to generate the hypotheses.

Some final points about the THOG problem. Firstly, it is not as artificial as you might think. As Smyth and Clark (1986) point out, disjunctive concepts can be found in real life. For instance, if you have a half-sister or a half-brother, you have the same father or the same mother as them, but not both: your half-sister is a THOG! Secondly, the powerful intuitive error is a good example of an *illusory inference*, whereby what we think is the whole truth is in fact nothing like the truth. We have to override our initial intuitive responses by more deliberative, analytic thought if we are to solve tricky problems. We shall look in more detail at both aspects of this behaviour – illusory inference and dual thinking processes – in Chapters 5 and 6, and come back to issues raised by problems such as THOG in Chapter 10. In the next chapter, we look at more realistic aspects of the kinds of reasoning that have been outlined so far.

Summary

1   The major focus of research into propositional reasoning has been on how people think about conditional statements, those expressing an *If* relation.

2   *If* statements in reasoning can be used in conditional syllogisms consisting of a major premise (the statement of *If p then q*) and a minor premise (a statement of *p* or *q*, which can be affirmed or denied) leading to a conclusion.

3   Classical logic shows that there are two readings of *If*: implication (where *If p then q* cannot be reversed) and equivalence (where *If p then q* can also be read as implying *If q then p*).

4   Logically, there are four basic inferences, depending on the affirmation or denial of the minor premise, and also four truth conditions.

5   Performance on the four inferences does not fit with the logic of either implication or equivalence: fallacies are often endorsed, and one particular valid inference, *modus tollens*, is often resisted.

6   Similarly, people do not follow logic in evaluating truth conditions: they tend to regard *not-p* cases as irrelevant, not as verifying.

7   One of the most studied research paradigms is the Wason selection task. With the standard abstract task, people tend to select one item that they should not, and neglect one that they should select, against the logical norms of the task.

8   Another logical connective, *Or*, has also been studied in detail, but not to the same extent as *If*. It also has two logical readings, inclusive and exclusive. Human performance when reasoning with *Or* has not produced such clear patterns. A particular paradigm, Wason's THOG problem, has generated findings related to issues that have been addressed by later theories.

Reasoning and meaning

The last two chapters were concerned with the 'basics' of reasoning research in two broad areas, quantified and propositional reasoning. This research was based on a strategy that can strike people as a little peculiar: to strip out meaningful content and use abstract materials (see Evans, 2002, for an extensive discussion of this and related themes). In fact, this strategy has a long and honourable history in psychological science, dating back to Ebbinghaus's pioneering experiments on memory in the 19th century. His famous nonsense syllables were designed so that memories could be studied from their very beginnings: when you remember real words, you already know something about them, and so it is impossible to state when a memory for those words really begins. In the study of reasoning, the argument is similar. If people are given realistic problems to think about, then some of that thinking may reside in the meanings of the materials, and so a pure measure of thinking is impossible.

However, it is still right to be sceptical about this approach. After all, in the real world, we almost always think about things that have meaning to us. What is gained by ditching this meaning? If we want to explain how the mind works, surely we should study mentality in something like its natural context. Of course, any experiment, even when realistic problems are used, is hardly a natural context. That is the central problem in any experimental science: how to trade off the control the laboratory gives us against the rich untidiness of the outside world, so that we end up with results we can interpret and are worth knowing about.

So now we turn our attention to studies using more realistic materials. The main question that thinking and reasoning researchers in all fields have addressed has been the degree to which people's performance keeps to, or deviates from, the standards set by formal systems such as logic. Realistic problem content could have two effects with respect to these standards: to make them easier to attain or harder. There is evidence for both in the literature. When performance gets closer to logical norms, researchers talk about the *facilitation* of reasoning, and when it deviates from them, they talk about *biases*. In this chapter, and in the next two, we shall see under what conditions these effects emerge, and how their study has opened up whole new fields of research.

Facilitation: the study of content effects

We saw in the last chapter how the use of realistic materials can enable the baffling THOG problem to be solvable by the majority of experimental participants. That is actually one of the more recent examples of this kind of research; such work stretches back over a century. Perhaps the best-known early study is that of Wilkins (1928), who investigated what she called 'changed material' in syllogistic reasoning. She used four kinds of content: *abstract* (single letters of the alphabet), *unfamiliar* (rare or made-up words), *thematic* (common words) and *belief bias* – this was her term, and referred to contents where a valid conclusion was in conflict with belief, or where an invalid conclusion was consistent with belief. Participants had to select conclusions from a range of alternatives. There was a higher level of logical performance than one sees these days: over 75% overall. As you might expect, performance was best in the thematic condition. Next best was the belief bias condition, showing that, while there was a benefit from thinking about real-world items, the conflict between logic and belief could lead people astray. Both conditions produced more logical performance than did the abstract and unfamiliar ones.

Thus in this pioneering study we have both aspects of content effects: facilitation (people were more consistent with logic when the content was realistic) and bias (some contents deflected performance from the logical prescription). This last aspect of reasoning will be returned to in more detail in later chapters; belief bias in syllogistic reasoning has been explored extensively and has attained serious theoretical significance along the way. Facilitation, however, has been investigated more through the medium of the Wason selection task.

The selection task is a very different kind of reasoning problem compared to the Aristotelian syllogism, and not just because syllogisms concern quantified statements whereas the selection task usually concerns conditionals. Unlike the syllogism, in the selection task you are not drawing a conclusion, but rather figuring out the conditions under which a claim can be tested. As we saw in the previous chapter, very few people follow the dictates of conditional logic when they have to do this with the abstract task. But what would they do if the task, instead of being about letters and numbers or shapes and colours, were made more realistic?

This question was asked by Wason himself in the early days of research on the problem. Wason and Shapiro (1971) presented the following version to 16 people; you should try it:

> I am making a claim about four journeys that I have made on different days. I have written down on four cards where I went on one side of the card and the means of transport I used to get there on the other side. Here they are:

Monday	Tuesday	Wednesday	Thursday
Manchester	Leeds	Car	Train

> I claim that *Every time I go to Manchester, I travel by car*. Which cards would you need to turn over to decide whether my claim is true or false?

As well as this version, Wason and Shapiro gave another 16 people an abstract letter–number version (see Chapter 3).

Which cards did you pick? You will remember that to establish the truth status of any claim, you need to test it to destruction: try to falsify it. So you need to find the cards that could do so. In this case, I would be wrong if I travelled to Manchester other than by car, so you need to turn over the Manchester card, to see if I did this, and the Train card, in case it says Manchester. Neither of the other cards needs to be checked; it does not matter how I got to Leeds, or where else I might have gone by car. If this was your choice, you are in the same company as 10 of the 16 subjects in Wason and Shapiro's experiment, and it is the answer that fits conditional logic: the claim is equivalent to an *If p then q* sentence, which is falsified by a *p, not-q* instance; and so is the abstract letter–number version, which they also presented, but in this case only two people chose the *p, not-q* item. Wason and Shapiro therefore found a clear facilitation effect.

This finding sparked a series of further investigations, aimed at uncovering the source of this effect. The most spectacular results were reported by Johnson-Laird, Legrenzi and Legrenzi (1972). They gave people a task in which they imagined they were postal workers, sorting the mail. They were given the following kind of rule: *If a letter is sealed, then it has a 50c stamp on it*, and were charged with indicating the letters that needed to be examined 'to find out whether or not they violate the rule' (Johnson-Laird et al., 1972, p. 397). Here are some envelopes; which would you check?

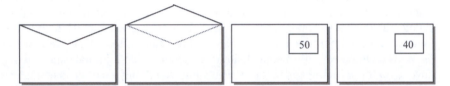

Once again we have an *If p then q* rule and should therefore be looking for the *p, not-q* item. So you need to check the sealed letter, in case it has a lower-valued stamp on it, and the letter with the 40c stamp, in case it is sealed. Twenty-one of 24 participants did this, compared to two in an abstract condition; it remains one of the largest facilitation effects ever obtained.

As to why thematic materials bring about these effects, Johnson-Laird and the Legrenzis were clear: they 'lead the subject to a greater insight into the logical structure of the task' (p. 396). In which case, any task set up like this should have this effect, and several other facilitation results were reported after these two papers. However, not all of them do. In a series of experiments, Manktelow and Evans (1979) completely failed to replicate the facilitation effect. Most of their experiments used materials concerning imaginary meals, with rules such as *If I eat pork then I drink wine*, but they also re-ran the Wason and Shapiro task. In every case, performance with the thematic contents was at the same low level as performance with abstract contents.

Why the discrepancy? Manktelow and Evans, reviewing their results alongside others in the literature at the time, proposed that whenever a facilitation effect had been observed, it was due to the participants *remembering* the correct counter-example, the *p, not-q* case, rather than figuring it out. There had indeed been a two-tier postal rule like the one used by Johnson-Laird et al. in force in Britain, where their experiment was run, at the time. In other words, it is possible that participants were hardly reasoning at all, and so logical insight did not come into it.

This was called the memory-cueing hypothesis by Richard Griggs and his colleagues, who ran a nice series of experiments testing its predictions. An obvious one is that the postal content should not facilitate in a society that had never had a two-tier postal regulation. On the other hand, the effect should emerge if some kind of culturally appropriate content were used. Griggs and Cox (1982) ran the necessary experiments in Florida, USA, where there had never been a two-tier postal regulation. No facilitation was observed with a postal task. They tested their participant population for contents with which they would be familiar, and devised the drinking-age task as a result. Here, you had to imagine you were a police officer, charged with checking whether customers in a bar were breaking this rule: *If a person is drinking beer, then the person is over 19 years of age.* This was the actual legal drinking age. Cards were presented showing a customer's age on one side and what they had been drinking on the other side. The four test cards showed Age 22, Age 16, Beer and Coke. Once again, you should look for possible *p, not-q* items, which here are the beer drinker, who might be under age, and the 16-year-old, who might have been drinking beer. Nearly three-quarters of the participants made this choice.

These results are consistent with the memory-cueing hypothesis, but the hypothesis did not survive for very long. If we pause and look more closely at these experiments, you can begin to see why. Firstly, can it really be true that you have to have actual experience of rules and instances in order to perform well on the selection task? Clearly not: Griggs and Cox's participants were university students, not police officers. In fact, the memory-cueing hypothesis did not explain the results reported by Johnson-Laird et al. (1972) either, for a similar reason. They presented the task to British participants, but used British currency units with some and Italian currency with others. It made no difference. Must those given the Italian version have had experience of posting letters in Italy? It hardly seems likely.

Now look again at the contents of the postal and drinking-age problems, and compare them with the journeys task and the abstract version, and you will see some subtle differences. Firstly, I have used the word 'rule' to describe the target sentence in the first two cases. This was no accident. These are rules in the sense of *regulations* – requirements for certain kinds of behaviour. Secondly, the rules contain or imply the auxiliary verb 'must' in the consequent. We often use this word when we want someone to do something. Thirdly, the participants' task was not to think about how to test whether the rule was true or false, but to search for items (understamped letters or underage drinkers) which broke the rule. These are far from being the same thing. Perhaps, then, what was really happening in the facilitation experiments was not facilitation at all, in the sense of enabling greater logical insight, but rather that a different form of reasoning was being tapped: reasoning about regulations. That was the turn that research took after the early rush of facilitation experiments. It is one of those areas of research that the selection task opened up, as we shall see in the next section.

Deontic reasoning: thinking about rules

The word 'deontic' has philosophical origins, and refers to the study of obligations. Deontic reasoning is therefore the kind of thinking we do when we consider what we should or should not do, or may or may not do. In the previous section, we saw how research on the thematic facilitation effect opened up the possibility that the effect was really to do with people switching from one kind of thinking (true/false judgments) to another (detecting rule violations), in contrast to the possibility that they were just getting better at the first kind.

Pragmatic reasoning schemas

This possibility was directly addressed for the first time in a paper that has become a classic in the field: that of Cheng and Holyoak (1985). Just as Griggs and Cox had done, they gave the postal problem to American participants who had no experience of two-tier stamping. However, they went further, and in one condition introduced a rationale for the rule about higher priced stamps for sealed letters:

> The rationale for this regulation is to increase profit from personal mail, which is nearly always sealed. Sealed letters are defined as personal and must therefore carry more postage than unsealed letters.

What they have done here is make explicit that there was a benefit to the postal service, which lays down the rule, and a cost to the customer, the target of the rule. Cheng and Holyoak compared performance by their US participants on this version with a sample from Hong Kong, where there had been a two-tier postal regulation, as there had been in Britain when Johnson-Laird et al. ran their experiment. With the rationale, the US and Hong Kong groups produced similar, facilitated performance. Without it, the US group's performance was significantly poorer, while the Hong Kong group's stayed high. Thus it seems that it is understanding of regulations – deontic thought – that is crucial, and that this is unlocked either by cultural experience (as in the Hong Kong and British populations) or a clear cost–benefit rationale.

The fame of Cheng and Holyoak's paper is due not just to ingenious experimentation, but to the theory they put forward to account for the facilitating effect of deontic content: the theory of *pragmatic reasoning schemas*. A schema is a package of knowledge about a given domain, containing rules for thought and action. The particular reasoning schema that Cheng and Holyoak focussed on was the permission schema. This, they proposed, contained the following set of four *production rules*:

- P1: If the action is to be taken, then the precondition must be satisfied.
- P2: If the action is not to be taken, then the precondition need not be satisfied.
- P3: If the precondition is satisfied, then the action may be taken.
- P4: If the precondition is not satisfied, then the action must not be taken.

The schema will bring about facilitated performance as follows. Firstly, the content of the problem needs to evoke the schema; it can do this if its target rule matches one of the production rules. You can see that the postal rule maps nicely on to P1. Once that happens, the production rules give you a determinate conclusion – one that must follow – only in the cases of P1 and P4. These rules therefore tell you which cards (letters) to look at: the p card (sealed letter) in case the precondition *q* (the dearer stamp) has not been satisfied, and the *not-q* card (the cheaper stamp) in case the action has been taken without this precondition. You should be able to fit the drinking-age task to this schema as well.

Cheng and Holyoak (1985) tested this theory using a new content, concerning immigration rules at an airport. This is an important move, since it is unlikely that participants would have had experience as immigration officers. They were given this rule:

> If the form says 'ENTERING' on one side, then the other side includes cholera among the list of diseases.

These were in fact the immigration forms; each recorded whether the passenger was entering or in transit on one side, and what inoculations they had had on the other:

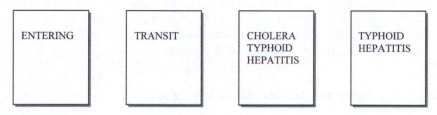

Clearly, this is an *If p then q* rule, and you can see that the forms show, from left to right, the *p*, *not-p*, *q* and *not-q* instances. This task, like the postal task, was presented to both US and Hong Kong participants in two versions, one with a rationale for the rule ('to ensure that entering passengers are protected against the disease'; Cheng & Holyoak, 1985, p. 401) and one without. With the rationale, both groups selected the *p, not-q* combination of cards (representing the possibility of a passenger entering without the required inoculation) at a very high rate of around 90%. Without it, performance dipped to around 60%.

They then went further, using an abstract rule embedded in a violation-checking deontic context:

> Suppose you are an authority checking whether or not people are obeying certain regulations. The regulations all have the form 'If one is to take action A, then one must first satisfy precondition P.' . . . In order to check that a certain regulation is being followed, which of the cards below would you need to turn over?
>
> (Cheng & Holyoak, 1985, p. 403)

The cards showed 'has taken action A', 'has not taken action A', 'has fulfilled precondition P' and 'has not fulfilled precondition P'. This task was compared with a non-deontic abstract task. The result was that 55% of participants chose *p, not-q* (has taken action A, has not fulfilled precondition P) with the deontic task, whereas 30% did so with the non-deontic task, which is a statistically significant difference. Note, however, that this particular experiment has been criticised on methodological grounds, for instance by Jackson and Griggs (1990) and O'Brien (1995; see also

Noveck & O'Brien, 1996). Both sets of authors point to numerous differences between the deontic and non-deontic abstract versions, and find less or no difference in performance when these are addressed. Fiddick (2003) also argues that results with abstract deontic rules favour evolutionary explanations rather than pragmatic reasoning schema theory; see the next section for more on evolutionary theory.

Despite such problems, Cheng and Holyoak (1985) give us good evidence that it was the deontic nature of the task, rather than knowledge about its specific contents, such as the postal service, bars or immigration, that held the key to high levels of performance on these versions. Cheng, Holyoak, Nisbett and Oliver (1986) went on to develop an obligation schema: an obligation rule takes the form *If p happens then q must be done*. Its facilitating effects were confirmed by Politzer and Nguyen-Xuan (1992).

This leaves us with the question of why the deontic content has its effects. Evidently, people have knowledge of rules and how to reason with them, but what does this knowledge consist of and where does it come from? Cheng and Holyoak (1985) proposed that people reason 'using abstract knowledge structures induced from ordinary life experiences' (p. 395). However, this is not the only possibility, and a radical alternative was not long in coming.

Evolutionary approaches to deontic reasoning

Around the time that Cheng and Holyoak's paper appeared, so did a PhD thesis written by Leda Cosmides, who was to become one of the world's leading evolutionary psychologists. The bulk of the work reported in it appeared in a huge paper that had huge effects: it took up an entire issue of the journal *Cognition*, and became one of the most discussed papers in the literature on evolutionary psychology as well as the psychology of reasoning (see Cosmides, 1989; also Cosmides & Tooby, 1992).

Cosmides introduced to reasoning what has come to be known as *social contract theory*. It is based on the biological construct of *reciprocal altruism* or, more usually in the current context, *social exchange*. Reciprocal altruism occurs when I do something for you, and you do something for me. That is, *if* I do something for you, I expect, and you accept, that you will do something for me in return. You will pay me money, or do something else that I value. This dynamic can be expressed in a basic rule of social exchange: that *If you take a benefit, then you pay a cost*. Of course, in the absence of an all-seeing authority to check up on us, we will need something else for efficient social exchange: the ability to detect, and punish, cheaters. This is because there is a powerful incentive to take a benefit without paying any cost – anyone who can get away with that is at a considerable advantage. Thus according to Cosmides we must have what she calls *Darwinian algorithms* in our minds: the benefit–cost rule and a sensitive cheater-detector.

Cosmides argues that we have evolved to understand ourselves in this way; it is a necessary part of what it means to be human. This contrasts with Cheng and Holyoak (1985), who proposed that we learn about rules through our life experiences. The idea that we come pre-wired for this kind of understanding has generated both novel predictions and controversy, as we shall see.

The first thing that Cosmides asked was whether social contract theory could account for existing findings. When she reviewed the literature on the selection task, she found that all the versions that reliably produced facilitation (i.e. a high proportion of *p, not-q* responses), fitted the social contract framework. For instance:

	Benefit	*Cost*
Postal rule	Sealed letter	Dearer stamp
Drinking age	Drink beer	Be over 19
Immigration	Enter the country	Correct inoculations

The original journeys content of Wason and Shapiro (1971) is not on this list because it is not a reliable facilitator (Manktelow & Evans, 1979), but there are several others in the literature that could be, and you can find others all around you. For instance, here is a rule that operates on weekend trains when I travel to London: *If you sit in First Class, you must pay an extra £10.* A cheater is clearly someone who takes the benefit of a First Class seat without paying the surcharge, and the ticket inspectors are adept at detecting them. That's why we have ticket inspectors.

Cosmides went on to test the predictions of social contract theory using her own materials. These were usually quite elaborate stories about imaginary anthropological expeditions reporting observations about the behaviour of aboriginal people encountered on distant islands, stated in the form of *If p then q* conditionals. Here is an example of the kind of sentence used:

If a man eats cassava root, then he has a tattoo on his face.

with four cards representing four men, each showing what they ate on one side and whether they are tattooed on the other:

| Eats cassava root | Eats molo nuts | Has tattoo | Has no tattoo |

Now, this content can be 'spun' so that it becomes either a descriptive, test-the-rule task, where you have to pick the cards that could tell you whether the claim made in the *If* sentence is true, or a social contract task. Cosmides did this by stating in the background story that cassava is a prized aphrodisiac and that only married men have access to it, marriage being signified by a tattoo. So cassava is the benefit for which a man pays the cost of being married (and getting tattooed: a painful business in itself, I'm told). A cheater is someone who gets to eat cassava without getting tattooed or married. The two versions produced the predicted difference: around 75% *p, not-q* selections with the social contract version compared to around 25% with the descriptive version.

Cosmides' next move was highly inventive. She used 'switched' versions of the social contract rules, stating that *If you pay a cost then you take a benefit* (e.g. if a man has a tattoo then he eats cassava). The benefit and cost are the same, cassava and tattoo, but now they make up the q and p parts of the conditional instead of the p and q parts. If people are responding to the social contract structure rather than to conditional logic, they should continue to look for cheaters, who are still unmarried cassava consumers. But this time, they would need to select the *not-p* and q cards to find them, which is the exact opposite of the 'logical' response. Cosmides' participants did just this: around 70% selected this combination, while close to zero did so on the descriptive task. This was the first time that this pattern had been predicted or observed.

A bold new theory and astonishing results: these are catnip to scientists, hence the huge effect of this paper. It stimulated a flood of follow-up studies, which is still going on. One kind of follow-up has involved further testing of the biological aspect of Cosmides' theory by monitoring brain activity. For instance, Canessa, Gorini, Cappa, Piattelli-Palmarini, Danna, Fazio and Perani (2005) recorded this using functional magnetic resonance imaging while people addressed indicative and deontic versions of the selection task. In both cases, there was a high level of activity in the left hemispheric regions usually associated with verbally based thinking, but the deontic problems also caused similar right-hemisphere areas to light up. The authors tell us that these areas are the ones often associated with social cognition. There was the usual superiority of performance with the deontic materials, so having their brains scanned did not affect the participants' thinking.

Psychological follow-ups have tended to take two forms: extensions of the evolutionary theory and critical studies. I shall give you some brief examples of both, which will lead us to the final part of this section, where we look at an alternative to pragmatic and social contract schemas in explaining deontic reasoning.

One response from researchers has been to test for other kinds of evolutionary-based schemas that could not be subsumed under the social contract principle. For instance, Hiraishi and Hasegawa (2001) studied the detection of 'free riders'. A free rider is, of course, someone who takes a benefit without paying a cost: a cheater. However, Hiraishi and Hasegawa proposed that it was possible to be a free rider without reneging on a cost–benefit social exchange. They looked at in-group and out-group differences. There is a tendency within groups to share resources among members (this happens in non-human animals too) so that: *If one receives a resource, one is an in-group member*. It should be possible to detect two kinds of cases where things go wrong: failure to share within the group, and out-group individuals exploiting the in-group's resources. Hiraishi and Hasegawa found evidence for sensitivity to both types of violation, but more so to the second kind.

Several researchers, beginning with Brown and Moore (2000), have used the selection task to study whether people are prone to detect pure altruists – those who give benefits to others without receiving anything in return. Brown and Moore proposed that altruist detection would be useful in solving the problem of what they called subtle cheating, a problem that arises because, owing to the complexity of social interaction, it can be difficult to detect the kind of blatant cheating that Cosmides was talking about. Sure enough, there was evidence for altruist detection. Oda, Hiraishi and Matsumoto-Oda (2006) went on to test whether altruist detection was related to cheater detection or to the Hiraishi and Hasegawa sharing rule. They did this by correlating performance patterns on these various versions, and found that altruist detection was, surprisingly, quite independent of cheater detection, which was, however, associated with the sharing rule. Which implies that we have separate schemas for detecting nice and nasty people!

A different form of evolutionary deontic theory was put forward by Denise Cummins (1996a, 1996b). She also argues that we are evolutionarily prepared for deontic reasoning, but bases her theory not on social exchange but on the construct of dominance hierarchies. All social species, including humans, organise themselves on hierarchical lines, because individuals are both cooperative and competitive. Those at the top, the dominant ones, have access to resources denied to those at the bottom. Thus, she proposes, we have an innate capacity for deontic reasoning based on the need to know what is obliged, permitted and prohibited, given one's rank in whatever hierarchy we are in, as well as how to improve one's ranking. Deontic rules are typically laid down by an authority, which is either a person or a body (such as the law) with influence over us (Cheng & Holyoak, 1985).

Cummins compiles a catalogue of evidence, her own as well as other researchers', in support of her case (although see Chater & Oaksford, 1996, for criticism of it). The most striking piece of her own research involved the youngest set of participants ever known to have been given the selection task: some were only 3 years old. Cummins (1996c) argued that an innate facility should be observable in the very young, who have had a minimal amount of learning time. She gave her tiny participants a simplified version of the selection task involving real objects, not cards. They were a set of toy mice and a toy cat, along with a mouse-house. Some of the mice squeaked when squeezed, others were mute. The children were told that the mice had been given the following rule by Queen Minnie Mouse in view of the threat from the cat:

> It is not safe outside for the squeaky mice, so all squeaky mice must stay in the house. Yes, all squeaky mice have to stay in the house.

Which mice should be tested to see whether they were breaking the rule? The ones outside the house, to see if they were squeakers; the ones inside the house could squeak to their hearts' content and so did not have to be tested. Over two-thirds of the 3-year-olds were correct at this task, as were 85% of the 4-year-olds (see Girotto, Blaye & Farioli, 1989, and Harris & Nuñez, 1996, for related findings; Cummins based her experiment on Girotto et al., who used older children and a less concrete task).

Finally, we have an extension that stems from a criticism. Much of the criticism of social contract theory centres on its extreme domain-specificity. By this, I mean that the theory only applies to a restricted area of knowledge. This is because evolutionary theory leads to the proposal that the mind, like the body, evolved in response to adaptive problems. You will recall Cosmides' observation that consistent facilitating contents could all, at the point at which her work began (in 1983, according to Cosmides & Tooby, 1992), be seen as variations on the social contract theme. This threw down an immediate challenge to other researchers to identify other contents that would also do the job. In fact, as Cheng and Holyoak (1989) pointed out, the Griggs and Cox drinking-age task does not quite fit the social contract framework in any case, since the 'cost' here is being over 19. Your age is not something that can be traded with another person, it is a condition. Social contract theorists have acknowledged this point and now talk of meeting a requirement as part of the contract, with paying a cost as a subset of that (Fiddick, Cosmides & Tooby, 2000).

Manktelow and Over (1990; see also Cheng & Holyoak, 1989) devised a content that certainly did not contain a social contract. They asked people to imagine that they were monitoring the behaviour of nurses in a hospital. The nurses were given the following rule:

If you clear up spilt blood, then you must wear rubber gloves.

and cards showing the records for four nurses, with whether or not they cleared up blood on one side and whether or not they wore gloves on the other side. Who might be breaking this rule? This would be someone who clears up blood (p) without wearing gloves ($not\text{-}q$). Nearly three-quarters of people selected these cards. It is hard to see clearing up blood as a benefit for which you have to pay someone the cost of wearing rubber gloves. Rather, this rule, technically known as a prudential obligation, is concerned with taking precautions in the face of a hazard.

Such results lead to two possible responses. One, taken by social contract theorists, is to propose another schema for a different domain: hazard management. Cosmides and her associates, notably Laurence Fiddick, have reported several studies aimed at confirming this possibility. Fiddick et al. (2000) go into detail about the distinction between social contract and hazard management schemas, emphasising that the latter is, for them, 'a separate system . . . with its own distinct architecture, representational format, and licensed inferential procedures' (p. 15). The hazard schema is not, for a start, concerned with social behaviour, but with your response to any kind of threat to your wellbeing. They report two experiments showing that people do indeed draw different inferences depending on whether a rule is given a social contract or a hazard management framing. You can see how this could be done with the Cheng and Holyoak immigration rule. It could be set up as a social contract permission, about the requirement you have to meet (inoculation) so as to obtain the benefit of entering the country. Or it could be set up as a precaution rule, emphasising the danger of the disease (Fiddick et al. used their own materials, not this).

Fiddick (2004) went on to explore several other aspects of the hazard management schema. In one experiment, he tested people's choices of emotional reactions to cases of violation of social contract and precaution rules, using pictures of facial expressions of emotion. He hypothesised that the most likely responses would be anger in the first case and fear in the second, and he found just this. In another ingenious experiment, he tested people's responses to accidental rather than intentional violations. This should affect the social contract rule (you will readily forgive someone if they simply forget to pay you back) but not the precaution rule (you are in just as great a danger if you break it whether you meant to or not). Again, this prediction was confirmed. One other notable feature of this work is that it moves research away from reliance on the selection task, hitherto the bedrock of evidence for the social contract theory.

Decision-theoretic approaches

The second response to non-social-contract facilitation is to look for another kind of theory that might explain both these results and the other findings with the deontic selection task; in particular, to look for a more domain-general explanation. That was the path taken by Manktelow and Over (1991). Their approach was based on decision theory, which we shall return to in detail in Chapters 8 and 9. They followed up two aspects of Cosmides' work: her emphasis on costs and benefits (a social contract exists when rationed goods are made available once some condition has been fulfilled) and her striking finding with the 'switched' rule (where people selected the previously unheard of *not-p, q* combination).

Costs and benefits are technically known as *utilities*, and decision-making research is concerned with the degree to which people make choices that maximise their expected utility. Manktelow and Over set out to see whether the social contract experiments might be tapping into something more general: people's ability to detect when someone has done the wrong thing, in decision-theory terms (i.e. where someone's maximising choice has been denied). Consider cheating. If someone cheats on a social contract with you, they either gain something from you that they should not have, or you fail to gain something from them that you should have. In the case of hazards, someone who breaks a precaution rule risks a loss of utility by exposing themselves to danger.

Note that in the case of permission (a social contract), two parties are involved: an *agent*, who lays down the rule, and an *actor*, who is the rule's target. Both parties have preferences (i.e. differing utilities) among all the possible outcomes. In fact, some reliable assumptions have to be made about both sides' utilities, otherwise the rule might not be uttered in the first place, or might not work if it were. Here is an example of the kind of rule in question, from Manktelow and Over (1991):

If you tidy up your room, then you may go out to play.

It was said to have been uttered by a parent to a child. The parent would never say this unless she preferred the room to be tidy rather than untidy; and the rule would not work for her unless she was right that the child prefers going out to staying in. Two aspects of deontic thought emerge from this analysis: (i) that there can be more than one kind of rule violation; and (ii) both parties can violate the rule (Cosmides & Tooby, 1989, produced a similar analysis but did not directly test it). Putting these aspects together, the following potential violations occur:

1   The agent sees that *p* is true but does not do *q* (the child tidies the room but the parent does not let him out to play) – this should lead to the choice of the *p, not-q* cards in a selection task.

2   The agent sees that *p* is not true but still does *q* (the parent lets the child out even though he has not tidied his room) – *not-p, q*.

3   The actor sees that *p* is true but does not do *q* (the child does not go out even though he has tidied his room) – *p, not-q*.

4   The actor sees that *p* is not true but does *q* (the child goes out without having tidied his room) – *not-p, q*.

Manktelow and Over found that all of these cases of violation were recognised by participants in selection tasks. Similar results were reported by Politzer and Nguyen-Xuan (1992) and Gigerenzer and Hug (1992), although they only tested for cases 1 and 4, which are the cases of cheating proposed by social contract theorists (see Cosmides & Tooby, 1989). Gigerenzer and Hug gave the effect the name by which it is generally known: the *social perspective effect*. It became one of the strongest pieces of evidence that there might be a qualitative distinction to be made between deontic reasoning and indicative reasoning, of which the standard non-deontic versions of the selection task and all the kinds of reasoning reviewed in Chapters 2 and 3 are examples.

As with social contract theory, several follow-up studies have been reported in which predictions of the decision-based approach have been tested. For instance, remember that decision theory talks about maximising expected utility. 'Expected' is a key word: it refers to probability (i.e. how likely you think something is). Manipulating subjective probability should therefore affect deontic inference. This was confirmed by Kirby (1994), who adapted the drinking-age task (see above) by adding two more under-19 customers, a 12-year-old and a 4-year-old. They also might be drinking beer but, as he predicted, Kirby's participants thought this unlikely and tended not to select their cards for further examination. Similarly, Manktelow, Sutherland and Over (1995) adapted the immigration task by adding probabilistic information: that cholera was particularly common in the tropics, and that passengers were travelling from tropical or European countries. People were less likely to select the European passengers. Finally, Kilpatrick, Manktelow and Over (2007) confirmed that rules laid down by more powerful agents were more likely to be adhered to.

This is not the only domain-general approach that has been applied to deontic reasoning. All the major theories that were introduced in Chapter 2 – mental logic, mental models and the probabilistic theory – have been applied to it. These will be reviewed in detail in the next two chapters. In addition, Sperber, Cara and Girotto (1995) use a psycholinguistic theory – relevance theory (Sperber & Wilson, 1995) – to explain not just the deontic results but the entire selection task literature. Indeed, they arrive at the conclusion that the task should be abandoned as a reasoning research paradigm. This is because, they say, the task is so strongly influenced by relevance-guided comprehension mechanisms that it does not usefully engage people's reasoning at all. Relevance varies according to the extent that a task has cognitive effects, balanced by cognitive effort: the more something is worth knowing and easy to find out about, the more relevant it is, in this sense. Sperber et al. argue that the deontic selection task makes the *p* and *not-q* items easy to represent (e.g. the under age drinker) and worth finding out about (owing to the background story and task demands). They show that it is possible to produce non-deontic facilitation by following this 'recipe', which undermines the social contract theorists' case for an evolved domain-specific schema. Not surprisingly, the latter have criticised Sperber et al. (see Fiddick et al., 2000), who have responded (Sperber & Girotto, 2002). The domain-specific/domain-general debate looks set to run and run.

One final point about deontic reasoning, and especially the perspective effect: several authors, including the evolutionary theorists (both Cosmides and Cummins and their associates) and the decision-based theorists, have argued for the distinctive nature of deontic reasoning, and the perspective effect has often been invoked in support. But what if it were possible to produce non-deontic perspective effects? That would be a blow against this argument, and in favour of more general views of reasoning.

As sometimes happens in science, several demonstrations of just this appeared from different researchers around the same time. Two of them appealed to the *condition relations* inherent in the use of conditional sentences. These relations are those of *necessity* and *sufficiency*. We can see how these work with 'ordinary' conditionals using the example from Chapter 3: *If Alex is a Christian (p) then he is a believer (q)*. Assuming that this claim is true, knowing that Alex is a Christian is all we need to know to enable us to conclude that he believes in God; it is not possible for him to be a Christian (*p*) and not a believer (*not-q*). However, it is not necessary for him to be a Christian to be a believer: he could subscribe to another religion, and the original claim would not be false. *Not-p and q* does not falsify *If p then q*. So we can say that *p* is sufficient (but not necessary) for *q*. We can also say that *q* is necessary (but not sufficient) for *p*, because although we know that *p* without *q* makes the sentence false, we cannot definitely conclude *p* from *q* (see Chapter 3).

Valerie Thompson (1994, 1995, 2000) argued that people have these condition relations in mind in their thinking about conditional rules, especially deontic rules, and Fairley, Manktelow and Over (1999) made use of this argument when testing for non-deontic perspective effects. They used causal rules. Causal conditionals state the claim that *If cause then effect*; for instance, *If you turn the ignition key then the car starts*. Condition relations work differently with causal conditionals compared to ordinary descriptive conditionals. With a causal conditional, it is possible for *p* (the cause) to be necessary but not sufficient for *q* (the effect), as well as the usual sufficient but not necessary. Consider the ignition key rule. You know that you also need fuel in the tank, a charged battery, absence of damp, and so on, before the car will start; turning the key is not enough by itself.

These other factors are therefore additional conditions that need to be satisfied before you can be fully confident about the relation between cause and effect. Fairley et al. used the rule *If you study hard, then you do well on tests*, and induced people's doubts about sufficiency by getting them to think about disabling conditions. These are factors that might stop you doing well even though you studied hard, such as feeling nervous in an exam. They also induced doubt about necessity, by having people think about alternative causes for exam success, such as cheating. In a selection task, casting doubt on sufficiency led to a high frequency of *p, not-q* responses, while casting doubt on necessity led to *not-p, q* responses. A very similar theoretical argument and results were published simultaneously and independently by Ahn and Graham (1999).

Thus it is possible to produce 'perspective' effects in non-deontic contexts, without a social perspective being invoked. Both sets of researchers, Ahn and Graham and Fairley et al., used the necessity/sufficiency argument to explain the existing deontic results as well. Take the mother–son rule above: it could be that the mother sees tidying up the room as a necessary but not sufficient precondition for letting her son out to play (he has to tidy up properly, say), whereas for the son, tidying is sufficient but not necessary (he might do something else worthwhile and claim his playing rights for that).

This approach was extended by Bonnefon and Hilton (2005), who pointed out the pragmatic use of deontic conditionals as what they called *conditional directives*. That is, when you say something like the blood rule above, you are directing someone to do something. As the decision theory approaches presume, this use occurs when the speaker (the agent) and the hearer (the actor) have goals. Bonnefon and Hilton go much further than previous authors, however, in specifying what these goals might be, and how conditional directives are used in achieving them. For instance, they use military rules such as:

If you see an unusual radar blip, then launch depth charges.

said to have been spoken by a commander to a sailor. There are several possible goals here: not only to destroy the enemy craft, but also to avoid errors such as failing to launch when there is a blip (a 'miss') or launching when the craft is friendly (a 'false alarm'). They found that these pragmatic considerations affected the conclusions that people would draw: in a selection task, they would choose the *p, not-q* cases in a context where misses were emphasised, and choose the *not-p, q* cases in false alarm contexts. Bonnefon and Hilton also found that different conditional phrasings were favoured depending on these contexts: *If p then q* when the goal was to avoid misses; *q only if p* when it was to avoid false alarms. As with the decision theorists, the authors also regard schema theories as inadequate to explain such findings.

We have seen in this section how it is important to study the ways people think about causal as well as deontic claims. A lot of attention has been directed at this area of human inference, so we shall now turn to it.

Causal reasoning: thinking about how the world works

Ben had had a hard day at the office, with problems to solve and deadlines to meet, and now he had to field a phone call from his wife, who was fussing about when he would be home. They had been arguing a lot lately, and the call worried him. He ran to his car and jumped in. On the way out of the city, he decided he needed a drink, and stopped at the next bar he saw. The first beer felt so good, he decided to have another. Realising he was going to be even later, and that he should not be drinking beer anyway, he got back into the car. After a short distance, he decided to try a short-cut down some unfamiliar streets. He was just over the speed limit when he came up to some traffic lights. They changed as he got to them, but he kept going.

As he crossed the junction, he heard the screech of brakes from his left. Ben turned; the sight of a van driver holding his cellphone in one hand and the steering wheel with the other was the last thing he ever saw, as the van smashed into his car.

What caused Ben's death?

Causal thinking is a vast topic with a long history, so I shall have to limit discussion of it here. This chapter will not be the only place where it features. We shall come back to it in the next chapter in the section on mental models, and in later chapters too, when dealing with inductive inference, hypothesis testing and judgment. It is a tricky topic, in at least two senses. Firstly, it has proved quite difficult to explain not only how we do it, but what it is we are actually doing; we do not have a universally agreed psychological account. Secondly, causality is quite a slippery notion in itself. This is important because causality is important: as Buehner and Cheng (2005) argue, echoing a sentiment that is centuries old, 'without causal reasoning, we would be unable to learn from the past and incapable of manipulating our surroundings to achieve our goals' (p. 143).

We can start by making a division between causal thinking about classes of events and causal reasoning about single events. Both are operating in the Ben story.

Causal reasoning about general events

Here is some text from a poster I saw on a local bus:

> FACT: Cigarettes and alcohol are the biggest cause of death by fire in the home.

What is the causal claim being made here? It is not easy to pin down. In what sense do cigarettes and alcohol *cause* deaths by fire? Does the sentence imply, through using 'cause' in the singular, that this happens especially when they are used together, or that each is separately but similarly causal? The text was superimposed on a picture of a person's hand resting on the arm of a sofa, a lit cigarette held loosely between the fingers and a beer bottle in the background. The message seems to be that there is a danger that people (in general) tend to fall asleep, let cigarettes fall to the floor and set fire to houses, and that if they have been drinking they are more likely to do this, and to die if they do. You clearly need a lot of background knowledge, in addition to the stated FACT, to make these causal inferences (they certainly livened up my bus journey), and you can see why causality is slippery. Cigarettes and alcohol don't in themselves cause death by fire, or even cause the fires that cause the deaths – you also need to do something to turn cigarettes into house fires, and to hinder people escaping them.

Below, we shall see how you might arrive at a causal model that makes the intended connections. Note that in the Ben story we might also think about general causes, such as the effect of alcohol, distracting thoughts or the use of mobile phones on driving performance, when reasoning about why and how he died. So bear in mind that, although reasoning about general and particular causes can be separated, in the real world they are often linked.

The covariational approach to causal thinking

As with many other forms of thinking, we have philosophical precedents to guide us, in this case the British empiricists David Hume, in the 18th century (Hume, 1739/1978), and John Stuart Mill, in the 19th (Mill, 1843/1973). Hume argued that we come to infer cause through *contiguity*, that is, when two events tend to occur together. Contiguity can be spatial or temporal: two events that occur close together in space tend to be seen as causally connected (Michotte, 1963; Rips, 2008), as do two events close together in time, provided that one always follows the other. Let's call them C and E, for (candidate) Cause and Effect. To the extent that we observe that C occurs and then E occurs, and also that E tends not to occur without C, we can say that they *covary* (they vary with each other). Mill argued that the more closely they covary, the more we believe that C causes E.

This is called the *covariational theory* of causal inference, and has been developed in greatest detail by Patricia Cheng and her colleagues. Cheng and Novick (1990, 1991, 1992) introduced the *probabilistic contrast model* (PCM), based on the idea of inferring causality from covariation. The basic idea was around before this, such as in social psychological work on causal attribution, where you try to judge whether someone's actions resulted from their character or the context they were in (Kelley, 1973). Now, suppose you are wondering whether mobile phones cause car crashes. Someone clearly has thought about this, as in many countries laws have been passed banning talking on hand-held phones while driving. There are four possible relations between mobile phones (candidate C) and car crashes (candidate E), which we can set out in a 2 × 2 table:

	E present	E absent
C present	a	b
C absent	c	d

This is a *contingency table*, so called because it shows a pattern, if there is one, of events that are contingent on other events. You may have come across these tables in statistics classes. The table will record the frequencies with which drivers were using a phone and they crashed (a), using a phone and didn't crash (b), not using a phone and crashing (c) and not using a phone and not crashing (d). The probabilistic contrast refers to the comparison between the proportions of occurrence of E with and without C. This is formalised using the Δp statistic (pronounced delta-p):

$$\Delta p = p(E|C) - p(E|\neg C)$$

where p is probability, | means given and $\neg$ means not. The probability of E given C, $p(E|C)$, is calculated as a/a + b: the proportion of times that E was present out of the total number of times when C occurred. The probability of E given not-C,

$p(E|\neg C)$, is c/c + d. The Δp statistic can vary between 0, when there is no contingency between C and E, and ±1, when C always produces E (+) or always prevents E (–). The PCM assumes that you will compute Δp only across a *focal set* of events (i.e. those that you see as relevant to the judgment problem in question). You think about a candidate cause, C, and hold the values of all other possibilities constant. Wasserman, Elek, Chatlosh and Baker (1993), using a causal learning task involving controlling a light, found a close fit between changes in Δp and changes in people's causal judgments when $p(E|C)$ and $p(E|\neg C)$ were varied.

To say that one thing covaries with another is to say that the two things are correlated to some degree, and another rule you may recall from statistics classes is that you cannot necessarily infer cause from correlation. All causal relations produce correlations, sure, but not all correlations indicate causes. For instance, where I live, traffic lights go in the following sequence: red / red + amber / green / amber / red, etc. Thus red and red + amber are perfectly correlated, and if we call red C and red + amber E, we will get a Δp value of 1 from a contingency table recording occurrences of C and not-C with and without E. So do we infer that the red light *causes* the red + amber combination? No. Rather, each has the same separate cause, to do with electricity, a switching mechanism and an algorithm that controls it.

One of the advantages of the Δp approach to causal inference is that, under certain conditions (such as repeated learning trials), its predictions closely match those of models of conditioned learning in animals. This parallel has been pursued by David Shanks and colleagues (e.g. Lober & Shanks, 2000; Shanks & Dickinson, 1987). However, there are problems with Δp as a model of human causal inference. Anderson and Sheu (1995) refer to two of them: sample size and differential cell weighting. The Δp statistic is not affected by sample size, that is, by how many observations of C, not-C, E and not-E we make; it simply reflects the proportions of each. However, imagine that there are just single-figure numbers in a contingency table. Now imagine that there are three-figure numbers (i.e. hundreds of observations) but in the same proportions. We would be much more confident of a causal relation in the latter case, but Δp would be the same. Differential cell weighting refers to the common finding that people are liable to attach more weight to the a and b cells of the table than to the c and d cells; they often ignore the d cell altogether (Wasserman, Dorner & Kao, 1990). The c and d cells are the ones you get from using a control condition in an experiment, but students have to be taught this, which shows that it is not something that comes naturally. Anderson and Sheu argue that it is in fact rational to underweight the c and d cells in the real world because $p(E|C)$, given by a/a + b remember, will be high if C does cause E, while $p(E|\neg C)$, given by c/c + d, will be low whether or not C causes E (Over & Green, 2001, show that this only applies when C and E are rare events). The point to note here is that Δp takes no account of these different weightings.

Thus causal inference must involve something more than the perception of covariation; but the problem is that this 'something more' cannot itself be directly perceived. Cheng (1997) extended the PCM to address this problem, and give an account of phenomena not explained by her earlier theory. The new version is called the *power PC theory*, an abbreviation of 'the causal power theory of the probabilistic contrast model' and a pun on the name of a desktop computer that was current at the time. Its aim was to account for the power of a cause to bring about an effect when it is present. The PCM, as we have seen, is only concerned with the covariation between occurrences of C and E, and says nothing about the power of C to produce E.

The sample size problem above is an example of the kind of judgment that the PCM cannot explain. Cheng gives others: for example, an apparently personal story where a doctor tested for food allergies (E) by making a grid of skin scratches and applying a range of food samples (C) to them. There was an allergic reaction to all of them: $p(E|C) = 1$ in each case. Was she allergic to all the foods? We also need to know $p(E|\neg C)$ to compute Δp. It turned out that there was a reaction to all skin scratches, even without food samples, so $p(E|\neg C)$ was also 1. These observations give a Δp of $1 - 1 = 0$, but the doctor did not conclude that the patient was not allergic to any of the foods. It is more likely that the doctor would conclude that the test was simply uninformative: it told her nothing about the power of the foods to cause an allergic reaction. She needed a different test.

Cheng (1997) modifies the PCM to include causal power by weighting Δp by the proportion of occurrences of E that are due to alternative causes apart from the candidate cause C. These must be included in the set of events that are ¬C: all possible causes apart from the candidate cause C. Using this factor, we can compute the generative power of C to produce E, which is otherwise unobservable. Cheng uses the expression q_c for generative (as opposed to preventative) power, and the equation relating this to Δp is:

$$q_c = \frac{\Delta p}{1 - p(E|\neg C)}$$

This enables an estimate of an unobservable entity (i.e. power) from observable events, just as scientists do when they propose a theory to account for their findings (Cheng, 1997). We can, of course, manipulate the world to vary the relation between C and its possible alternatives, again as scientists do, when they design experiments. More on the role of interventions of this kind below. Cheng reviews a range of findings and applies the power PC model to them, and in later work extends it to cover cases where two or more causes interact to produce an effect (Novick & Cheng, 2004). It explains the doctor's response in the allergy test: when $p(E|\neg C)$ is 1, the bottom line of the q_c equation above becomes zero and so q_c cannot be computed. The test that gives rise to this result is therefore uninformative. Where there are no other possible alternative causes, so that $p(E|\neg C)$ is zero, q_c is equivalent to Δp.

The power PC theory has been criticised on both empirical and theoretical grounds: see Lober and Shanks (2000), Luhmann and Ahn (2005, 2007) and White (2005), along with Cheng and Novick's (2005) response, for detailed examples. I shall briefly mention one particular objection, which White sets out and which addresses a different possible meaning of the phrase 'causal power'.

If you do perceive a covariation, such as repeated reports of drivers using phones in records of car crashes, you might start to look for some connection – some *mechanism* – that could account for it. Evidence that we do this comes from work by Woo-kyoung Ahn and his colleagues (Ahn & Bailenson, 1996; Ahn & Kalish, 2000; Ahn, Kalish, Medin & Gelman, 1995). For instance, Ahn et al. (1995) asked people to search for information to elucidate possible causal relations, or provide explanations for situations presented to them. In both cases, they were more likely to appeal to mechanism information rather than statistical (covariation) information. A mechanism is a system of connected parts that have causal force in producing effects.

According to White (2005; see also White, 1995), these parts are understood to be one of three types. All of them are necessary to produce the effect, but none is sufficient by itself. Take a well-known food intolerance, such as nut allergy. This can be deadly. The nuts have the causal power to do harm: the *capacity* to do so. If you are allergic to nuts, then you are *liable* to be harmed by them. Of course, the mere coincidence of you and some nuts will not result (thankfully) in your inevitable death: there needs to be a *releasing condition* as well, such as your eating the nuts. The power PC theory, indeed any based on covariation, ignores such factors. In reply, Cheng and Novick (2005) point to something that may already have occurred to you: that the aspects of causality being referred to by their approach and White's are different. We have been concerned up to this point with covariation, that is, patterns of events; White's causal powers approach is more concerned with accounting for single events. We shall return to this aspect in the final part of this chapter, when we consider the relation between causal inference and counterfactual thinking.

Prior knowledge and causal models

I mentioned above that Cheng's PCM assumes that people reason about the focal set of candidate causes (one C at a time) and effects. Something must be guiding the selection of C from all the possible Cs that are out there. That something must be either direct perception, where causality is seen automatically (the classic work of Michotte, 1963, has examples of this), or prior knowledge. Knowledge is clearly vital: you scarcely ever encounter a situation that is utterly new to you, where you can bring no existing knowledge to bear at all.

The role of knowledge was explored in studies of reasoning with causal conditionals by Cummins and colleagues (Cummins, 1995; Cummins, Lubart, Alksnis & Rist, 1991; see also Thompson, 1994, and Weidenfeld, Oberauer & Hörnig, 2005, for similar studies). We have already met the ideas she employed, in the section on non-deontic perspective effects. Cummins firstly produced a series of causal conditional sentences in *If C then E* form, such as *If Jenny turns on the air conditioner then she will feel cool*, and asked people to generate two kinds of possible factors: those that would stop the effect occurring even though the cause did occur, and those that would make the effect possible even without the cause. The former are called disabling conditions (DCs) and the latter alternative causes (ACs). Sentences varied in the number of DCs and ACs that people could generate. Cummins picked out those which were high or low in each kind, and gave them to separate groups of participants in conditional inference tasks (see Chapter 3). As predicted, these participants were less prepared to draw conclusions dependent on the *sufficiency* of C for E from sentences that had been rated as high in DCs compared with those rated as low: they could easily think of ways in which E might not occur. Similarly, they were reluctant to draw conclusions about the *necessity* of C for E when the sentence was the kind that had been rated as high in ACs: they could think of other ways that E might come about. ACs correspond to the ¬C set in the power PC theory: the more of them there are, the less is the causal power rating for C itself. Strangely, Cummins' work is not cited by Cheng (1997).

We still need an account of why some factors are invoked as ACs or DCs and some are not: what determines the boundaries of the focal set? One possibility is that all these conditions, C, ¬C, DCs and so on, are part of a more elaborate representation involving higher-order knowledge. For instance, Manktelow and Fairley (2000) proposed that in causal conditionals the stated C was part of a more general set of conditions that they called SuperP, after the *p* part of the *If p then q* conditional. So anything that satisfies SuperP, whether or not it is the stated C, will lead to the inference that E occurred, whereas DCs suppress this inference because they are seen as factors that prevent SuperP from being satisfied, even when C has occurred. These predictions were confirmed in experiments. For example, given the causal statement *If you study hard, then you do well on tests*, people will have confidence that you will do well even though you have not studied hard if another way of doing well (such as sneaking a look at the paper beforehand) is mentioned. And a DC such as exam nerves will lower confidence that you will do well, even though you studied hard. The analysis was also applied to deontic conditionals, extending the parallels between these forms that Fairley et al. (1999) had earlier promoted.

A more detailed analysis along similar lines is given by Politzer (2001; Politzer & Bourmaud, 2002). He points out that the idea that causal conditionals carry with them information not explicitly stated has a long history, and invokes the idea of the *causal field* proposed by Mackie (1974). A causal field is the set of all relevant possible factors and conditions that play a role in bringing about an event, some of which, although necessary, are not themselves usually seen as causes. Politzer uses the term *complementary necessary conditions* (CNCs) to describe this information. These CNCs can be classified: they can be strong or weak; and causal conditions can be distinguished from enabling conditions. For instance, turning the ignition key is a causal condition in starting a car engine, whereas a charged battery is an enabling condition, as is oxygen in the fuel–air mix that is ignited in a car engine's cylinders. The latter two would be weak and strong CNCs, respectively, in Politzer's terms, since cars can be started with flat batteries but not without oxygen. We return to the distinction between causes and enabling conditions, and to causal conditionals, in the next chapter, since they have played an important part in contemporary debates about general theories of reasoning.

All of this adds to the stack of evidence that causal reasoning is concerned with a focal set of relevant factors and what determines which factors are relevant. White (1989) proposed that one of the two kinds of causal information we have outlined so far, mechanism knowledge, influences the scope of the focal set that is appealed to when we appraise the other, covariation information.

This suggestion was tested and confirmed by Fugelsang and Thompson (2003). They gave people information about a candidate C (such as 'substance X') for an E (such as 'slippery roads') in both mechanism and covariation form. For instance, substance X was said either to be a chemical that raised the freezing point of water (mechanism), or to be correlated with slipperiness (covariation). Candidate Cs were designed to vary in their believability, and participants gave initial ratings of the likelihood that C caused E. They were then presented with all the information needed for them to be able to compute Δp, and asked to give a second rating, along with a judgment of the degree to which they thought they had been influenced by covariation and mechanism knowledge. The results showed that these two forms of knowledge were distinct in people's thinking, and that while people seemed to have an accurate assessment of how they used covariation, their assessments of the influence of mechanism knowledge were unrelated to its actual use: it seems to have been used intuitively. In further research, Fugelsang, Thompson and Dunbar (2006) found evidence that the role of mechanism knowledge in causal inference is influenced by factors such as imageability and familiarity. If you have come across a causal mechanism before, or can easily picture how it might work, you will use it.

Causal models theory

In the final part of this section on general causal inference, we shall consider a new approach that explains how we think about causality using knowledge and information: the *causal models* theory of Steven Sloman (2005; see Lagnado & Sloman, 2004, and Sloman & Lagnado, 2005a, for experimental studies). We shall then consider how people reason about the causes of single events, which will lead us to the final part of this chapter: counterfactual thinking.

Causal models theory, like covariation theory, makes use of statistical patterns in the world: what goes with what. However, we have seen that covariation models stumble over the fact that not all covariation relations are due to causal processes. Causal models have a central role for an aspect of inference that has so far been mentioned only in passing: action, or *intervention*. One powerful way in which we can judge whether C causes E is to manipulate C and note what happens to E. Scientists do this formally, using the structured conventional techniques taught in experimental design classes, but these are just refinements of the things the ordinary people do when figuring out how the world works. As Sloman argues, 'how the world works' is another way of saying cause and effect, because while particular Cs and Es may change, the relations between them are constant: ingesting poison – any poison – will harm a person – any person. Once we have figured causal relations out, we are in a position to predict and hence control the world we live in.

Causal models are structured according to a method known as Bayesian networks. You will recall from Chapter 1 that the term 'Bayesian' refers to how we update our beliefs, in this case causal beliefs, in the face of evidence. We observe a relation in which A and B covary, and look for evidence that they might be causally linked. These links can be represented graphically. There are three possible representations, given this covariation:

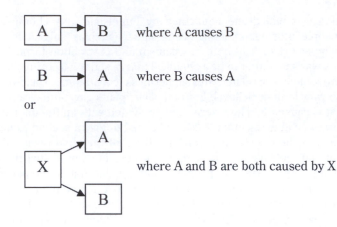

These are simple causal models. To find out which is the right one, we *intervene* by varying A or B. In causal models theory, this is done using the *Do* operator, introduced by Pearl (2000). *Do* sets a variable, such as A, B or X, to a value, such as *yes* or *no, up* or *down*. If we vary B and A changes, we can eliminate the first model, because effects must follow causes. Likewise, if we vary A and B changes, we can eliminate the second model. But if we vary A and there is no change in B, either the second or the third model could apply. That is when our ability to recall or imagine possible mechanisms will come in handy, so that we can look for an X.

Here is an example, adapted from Sloman (2005), partly imaginary and partly based on real life. We know that stomach ulcers cause abdominal pain, but what causes stomach ulcers? It used to be thought that stress was the cause, but an alternative possibility is that it is bacterial. A candidate causal model relating these factors might look like this:

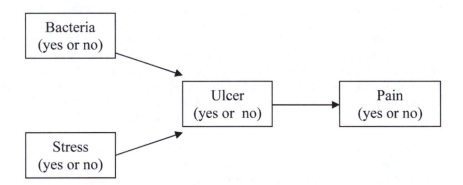

You could intervene to remove the pain by treating the ulcer directly, or by removing either of the candidate causes, stress or bacteria. Suppose we go for the first option and treat the ulcer directly; Sloman uses an imaginary medicine called 'Grandma's Special Formula' (GS Formula) to illustrate this. We know it acts directly on the ulcer, and so we get a new causal model that looks like this:

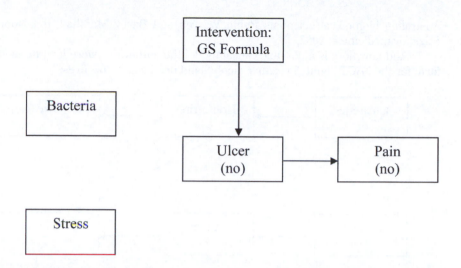

The intervention has, through the *do* operator, set the *Ulcer* variable to *no*. This leads us to expect that the pain will also go. But another thing has happened too: the variable *Ulcer* has been disconnected from its possible causes – this is because the intervention has happened at a later stage along the pathway, after the causes could have acted. Now suppose we intervene at a different stage and give patients antibiotics, which destroy the bacteria. The following causal model results:

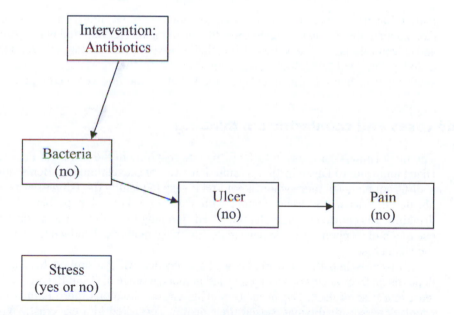

When the bacteria were destroyed, the patients' ulcers disappeared, whether or not they were stressed: ulcers are caused by bacteria, not stress. The involvement of the bacterium *Helicobacter pylori* in gut ulcers earned its discoverers, the

Australian biomedical scientists Robin Warren and Barry Marshall, the Nobel Prize for medicine in 2005.

And now here is a possible causal model the authorities were inviting us to form for the FACT about cigarettes, alcohol and deaths in house fires:

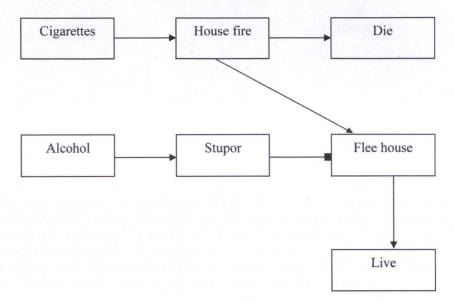

Rather than draw separate diagrams for the various yes/no settings, I have used the block next to the *Flee house* box to show that drinking blocks your ability to escape, and so you will stay on the pathway to death, initiated by your smoking. Without the drinking, you would stay awake, escape and live; without the cigarettes, you wouldn't set fire to your house in the first place. I think that's what they were getting at.

Single cases and counterfactual thinking

The most famous car crash in history, the one resulting in the deaths of Princess Diana and Dodi Al Fayed in 1997, resulted in a riot of causal thinking. Ben's story is different but even there you will not find it easy to identify the (single) cause of his death. Was it his preoccupation with work or relationship problems? His drinking? His choice of route? His speed? His jumping the lights? The van driver's use of a mobile phone? Courts have to decide these matters, as indeed they did in the Diana case.

In cases like this, covariation-based inference will be limited because it depends on frequencies of occurrence and non-occurrence of C and E: you need at least one case of each. But in many real-life causal situations there is only one event. A person died; what caused their death? They died in a car crash. What caused the crash? What caused them to die in the crash?

When thinking about the cause of a single event such as a fatal car crash, we usually have a sequence of preceding events and background conditions to consider. There are several different ways in which we can think about these things, depending on the kinds of question we want to ask – and there are several of them, too. For instance, we could ask *why* someone died in a car crash, or *how*: these are not the same thing, as we shall see.

David Mandel (2003, 2005), reviewing a wide range of previous research, systematically unpicks three basic ways in which we can ask causal questions: *covariational*, *causal* and *counterfactual*. The covariational approach to causal inferences about single events was set out by Spellman (1997), and adapts the Δp approach from general to single causal inference. You will recall that this approach is based on two conditional probabilities: the probabilities of E given C and given not-C. In the single case, we have an E (effect, or event) and a series of possible contributory causal events, C_1, C_2, etc. We start with the prior probability of E happening, and then look at C_1 and compute an updated probability estimate: how much more likely is E given C_1? We then consider C_2, and update our beliefs accordingly. Whichever C makes the greatest change in the probability of E is credited as the principal cause of E; Spellman's theory is called the *crediting causality model*, or CCM.

Spellman uses an example that appears in several authors' writings on this topic. Consider a game in which two people toss coins, and they win a prize if they both toss heads or both toss tails. Peter's coin comes up tails; Paul tosses next and his coin comes up heads, so they lose. Who feels worse, Peter or Paul? Most people say Paul. The CCM explains why. The prior chance of winning, before the game starts, is .5 and there are four possible combinations of two coin tosses: head-head, tail-tail, head-tail and tail-head. You win on two of the four. After Peter has tossed his coin, the odds are still 50/50, because they will win if Paul tosses tails and lose if he tosses heads; Peter makes no difference to the odds. But Paul's toss shifts the probability of winning to 1(tails) or 0 (heads). Spellman reports further experimental evidence for her model.

However, Mandel (2003) found that the CCM did not predict causal judgments in several experiments. For instance:

> Imagine a man, John, is given the option by his employer to stay where
> he is or to relocate, and he decides to move. In the new location he is
> unwittingly exposed to toxins and develops a lethal disease. At the hospital,
> a nurse accidentally gives him the wrong medicine and, although attempts
> are made to resuscitate him, he dies.

When people were asked directly what caused his death, 95% of them cited the drug error, 66% the disease and 38% the job relocation (they were allowed to list more than one possible cause). However, when asked to estimate the probability of John's dying prematurely depending on the various possible factors, they focussed on different ones: the greatest increase, 45%, was judged to be jointly due to the new location and exposure to toxins. John's decision to move accounted for an increase of 11%, and the drug error – judged the principal cause with a direct causal question – accounted for only 3%. Thus covariation and cause are not the same.

What about counterfactual questions? These are typically asked by giving people the sentence frame 'If only . . .' and asking them to complete it. In Mandel's

John experiment, the most frequent conditions focussed on were his decision to switch jobs and the nurse's mistake. There had been some earlier clues that such counterfactual thinking was open to biases. For instance, Girotto, Legrenzi and Rizzo (1991) found that people prefer to 'undo' controllable events in the set of possible causal factors (i.e. those that could be changed by personal action) – Ben's stopping at the bar would be an example. But this is only one possible factor, and some of them, such as the lights changing as Ben approached them, are not controllable, although just as necessary to the final outcome. Hilton and Slugoski (1986) found that people tend to undo 'abnormal' events in a sequence leading up to an effect E. Mandel and Lehman (1996) found that counterfactual judgments tended to be 'prevention-focussed': people focus on ways in which E might not have happened, rather than alternative ways in which it might have.

Thus, as Mandel puts it, causal, covariational and counterfactual judgments are *dissociated*. Judgment dissociation theory points to other respects in which these judgments differ. For instance, direct causal questions tend to focus on factors that were sufficient (but not necessary) for the effect E. A speeding van driven by an inattentive driver that jumps the lights and hits your car is sufficient to wreck it, but not necessary: there are other ways. So what *caused* Ben's death? The van and its driver crashing into his car. Counterfactual and covariational questions, on the other hand, tend to focus on factors that are necessary (but not sufficient) for E – without them, E would not have occurred. *If only:* Ben had not been preoccupied, had not drunk beer, had not taken an unfamiliar route, had not raced the lights ... Mandel also points out that causal questions tend to be about the actual event in question, and so address *why* it happened, whereas counterfactual and covariational questions tend to be about E or something like it, and so are more concerned with *how* it happened.

Thus the kind of question people are asked influences the kind of causal inference that people make. Hilton, McClure and Slugoski (2005) also describe how the *structure* of the events in a causal sequence can have a major effect on the kinds of causal inferences that are made. In doing so, they distinguish between distal, proximal and immediate events in the chain; these terms refer to how early they were, with distal being earliest. Five kinds of causal chain are identified:

1   *Temporal*. In a temporal chain such as Peter and Paul's coin-tossing game (see above), Peter's coin toss is the distal event and Paul's coin toss is the proximal event. Here, their order does not matter and the first does not influence the second.

2   *Coincidental*. This is a sequence of events like Ben's fatal journey in which, for instance, he is delayed not by stopping for a beer but by a flat tyre and other inadvertent snags. The distal event constrains the proximal because if he had not got a flat tyre, he would have arrived at the lights earlier than he did, and earlier than the van.

3   *Unfolding*. These are cases where a causal mechanism can be derived: for example, owing to sub-zero temperatures, ice forms on the road, leading to Ben skidding when braking at the lights and ploughing into the traffic. The distal event thus strongly constrains the proximal; there is almost a sense of inevitability about these chains.

4   *Opportunity*. The distal event enables the proximal event to bring about E. For instance, dry grass is set smouldering by a discarded cigarette (distal), and a breeze springs up (proximal) that fans the flames into a bush fire.

5   *Pre-emptive*. The distal event *precedes* the proximal, and the two are independent of each other. For instance, a criminal is pursued by two assassins. One puts poison in his drink, which will kill him in half an hour, but during that time the second shoots him dead (Mandel, 2003).

Concentrating on unfolding and opportunity chains, Hilton et al. show how these structures, along with other factors such as whether the events are controllable or not (e.g. a discarded cigarette versus a lightning strike), predict different causal inferences. These could be important factors in real-life causal judgment situations such as courts of law, where the causal question concerns the responsibility (blame) of a defendant. Hilton et al. refer to several real-life cases, such as Diana's, but here is one that will show what I mean:

> A plane was climbing after take-off when one of its engines developed a fault. The plane started to vibrate strongly and smoke filled the cabin. The flight crew needed to shut down the damaged engine, but they shut down the good engine instead. The vibration and smoke reduced. The plane was diverted to a nearby airport, but when the crew tried to power up for landing they did so using the damaged engine, which failed completely and the plane crashed, resulting in dozens of deaths. A subsequent investigation showed that the engine had failed because a fan blade had sheared off; this engine had not been fully flight tested before. The plane was a new model with a different instrument design on which the crew had had no prior training (the engine vibration indicators were much smaller than on the older model) and which used both engines to feed the air conditioning, instead of the one that in the event failed, which meant that their construal of the reduction in the smoke level was now wrong. The pilots, who survived the crash, were blamed for the accident and sacked.

As the aviation psychologist Earl Wiener later testified, 'There is a tendency to blame accidents solely on the last person in the chain of events, usually the captain' (Gavanagh, 1990; this article contains a reference to the full government report into this air crash). The crew's decision to shut down the good engine was the immediate cause, and the investigating tribunal seems to have viewed the events as an opportunity chain, where the initial engine problem enabled, but did not make inevitable, the subsequent crash: the pilots could, after all, have shut down the damaged engine. However, if you were defending the crew, you might have invited the tribunal to construe the events as an unfolding chain instead, where the foregoing conditions (e.g. the pilots' lack of training with the new aircraft and its instrumentation, faulty engine design, manufacture and testing and its failure) made their error all but inevitable, and reduced their culpability. Spellman and Kincannon (2001) look in detail at the legal implications of these kinds of issues, in particular the differences between causal and counterfactual thinking, and what they imply for legal codes that treat them as if they were the same. Some of the US laws they focus on have been changed in the light of such problems.

This is not the end of our consideration of counterfactual or causal thinking. We shall look more closely at counterfactuals in particular in the next chapter, and come back to causality in Chapter 7.

Summary

1   Much recent research on reasoning has moved away from abstract problems and used problem types and materials designed to approximate more closely to the kinds of thinking that people do in real life.

2   Two broad categories of effect of realistic materials can be identified: facilitation, where their use leads people to more logical responding, and bias, where they lead to less logical responding.

3   An important body of this work has involved the Wason selection task. Early claims that its solution could be facilitated just by realism were replaced by the finding that this influence usually depended on the use of deontic content, where the task concerns a rule of obligation or permission and the detection of transgressions.

4   The deontic facilitation effect has been explained in terms of pragmatic reasoning schemas, mental models, evolutionarily derived social contract algorithms and decision-making constructs. Social perspective effects show that the deontic task is logically distinct from the standard task.

5   Causal thinking has been studied by considering the covariation between classes of causes and effects, and by modelling the actions of single causes on single effects. Causal models theory emphasises the role of intervention in this process.

6   Causal thinking is closely related to counterfactual thinking: reasoning about things that could have happened but did not. However, different responses occur when people are asked causal versus counterfactual questions about events.

Explaining reasoning: the classic approaches

In this chapter, we bring together the themes that have appeared in the previous three, and begin to consider how human reasoning has been explained in general terms. While theorising about the nature of reason has been going on for as long as people have been thinking – Chapter 2 referred to Aristotle's writing from 2400 years ago – recent research has brought about both fundamental changes and enormous progress in our understanding. The period we are living through is something of a golden age for this work. This is reflected in a genuine paradigm shift in our understanding, from logic-based approaches, on which we will focus in this chapter, to a view that takes probability as its starting point, which will be the focus of the next one.

At several points in previous chapters we have seen how there are two ways in which we can view human reason. The first is the *normative* view. Normative systems are those that set out the judgments and conclusions that you should, objectively, arrive at. Logic is a normative system – logical validity is not a matter of personal opinion – and so are the rules of mathematics that are used to derive the statistical formulae that you have come to love. The second view is the *descriptive* view. A descriptive theory does what its name says: it describes what people actually do when they think and reason. You could have a descriptive theory of statistics: it would describe what people actually do when they think about statistical matters. In fact, we looked at just such a research area in Chapter 1.

If what people actually did when reasoning was to keep constantly to the laws of logic, we could stop this chapter right here. Chapters 2–4 have shown that they don't, though, and any descriptive theory of human reason has to account for the patterns in our thinking that do not fit the objective norms. There is a second, more subtle problem to confront as well: the question of which norms should be appealed to if we want to judge reasoning against some standard. This question has occupied theorists to an increasing extent in recent times, and we shall address it here, and later. We shall consider a third question, concerning what all these other debates and results imply for human rationality, in Chapter 10.

The two approaches we shall now review have already been outlined, especially in Chapter 2: the mental logic and mental models perspectives. We shall explore these in more detail now and then go on to consider others, the probabilistic and dual system theories, in the next chapter, since they form the basis of what has been called the new paradigm in reasoning theory. Central to our consideration in both will be conditional reasoning: conditionals are the battleground on which most of the main disputes have taken place.

Mental logic

All logic is mental in some sense, of course: logic had to come from somewhere, and that somewhere is the human mind. At its base, logic is purely a refinement of people's agreed-on intuitions of soundness and validity: there is no higher court than this (Cohen, 1981). Perhaps, then, what untutored people have is an unrefined set of logical rules in their minds. This argument has a long history in philosophy, as we saw in Chapter 2. In psychology, it forms the basis of Piaget's account of the growth of intelligence, set out over 50 years ago by Inhelder and Piaget (1958). In more modern times, several theorists have reworked the idea into *inference rule theories* of reasoning. We begin with an inference rule account of conditionals.

Braine and O'Brien's theory of If

Martin Braine and David O'Brien (1991, 1998; see also O'Brien, 1993, 1995) presented an influential theory of the conditional, based on natural deduction rather than formal logic (see Chapter 3). The BO'B theory (they just call it 'the model', so we need another name) has three major components: a set of *inference schemas*, a *reasoning program* that implements these rules and a set of *pragmatic principles* (a comprehension component that constrains their application in various contexts). Although the theory has been most fully worked out in the area of conditional reasoning (Braine & O'Brien, 1991), general accounts are also available (e.g. Braine, 1990) and it has been applied to text comprehension as well as reasoning (Lea, O'Brien, Noveck, Fisch & Braine, 1990). The theory's main components, the inference rules and the reasoning program, are set out in detail in the last two references and in Braine, O'Brien, Noveck, Samuels, Lea, Fisch & Yang (1995).

The inference rules take the form of reasoning schemas, which are not simply mental versions of the rules of textbook logic. These schemas are further subdivided into *core* schemas and *feeder* schemas. The core schemas 'describe a set of inferences that people make routinely and without apparent effort' (O'Brien, 1993, p. 115), including modus ponens and *Or*-elimination (the disjunctive denial inference: see Chapter 3); there are also 'incompatibility' rules that are used in detecting contradictions, such as when an argument leads to the inference of both *x* and *not-x*. Feeder schemas are auxiliary to the core schemas: they are only applied when their output provides propositions that are included in further inferences using the core schemas; *And*-elimination and *And*-introduction are among this set. *And*-introduction is where you conclude that there is a cat and a dog in the garden when it has been proved that there is a cat and that there is a dog; *And*-elimination is where you conclude there is a cat when it has been proved that there is a cat and a dog.

The reasoning program controls when these inference rules will be applied in a line of reasoning. There is a direct-reasoning routine and an indirect-reasoning routine, along with an inference procedure (for deriving conclusions from premises) and an evaluation procedure (for assessing the validity of given conclusions). The direct-reasoning routine is held to be common to all people (Braine et al., 1995). It applies the core and feeder schemas automatically when appropriate propositions are considered together: for instance, when *p or q* and *not-p* are jointly held in working memory, the conclusion '*q*' is supplied. This aspect of reasoning is therefore considered basic to human deductive competence: tasks that require the exercise of these processes should be carried out easily and accurately.

The indirect-reasoning routine contains strategies that may be subject to individual differences. It applies to problems that cannot be solved using the direct-reasoning routine. The BO'B theory allows that people may acquire complex schemas through learning, or that the application of such schemas may be facilitated (or inhibited) by certain contexts or problem domains. Problems that demand these more complex schemas for their solution will be less likely to be solved accurately.

The pragmatic principles help to determine which routines are called for. These principles can come from the natural-language meanings of connectives such as *If* and *Or*. According to Braine and O'Brien (1991), the basic meaning of a connective is supplied by its basic inference schemas. This is known as its *lexical entry*. In the case of *If*, the basic meaning is given by two schemas: modus ponens and a schema for conditional proof. The latter is a kind of *If*-introduction rule: you observe that p tends to be accompanied by q, and so you assert *If p then q*. In addition, however, a reasoner may be invited by context to infer that *If p then q* also implies *If not p then not q*, for instance in the case of a conditional promise, such as *If you mow the lawn I will give you $5*; see Chapter 4 and Geis and Zwicky (1971). Inferences of a non-logical kind are also allowed, such as from 'scripts', which are schemas for stereotyped social situations (Lea et al., 1990). O'Brien (1995) also includes the Gricean implicatures (see Chapter 2) among the list of pragmatic principles. Braine et al. (1995) found that almost a quarter of people's responses were attributable to these kinds of pragmatic schemas.

Evidence for the BO'B theory comes from direct tests by its advocates along with accounts of other observed findings in the literature, including the data on the selection task (see Chapter 3). In addition, the theory has been tested in distinctly different ways. The main sets of such data were provided by Braine, Reiser and Rumain (1984) and by Braine et al. (1995).

With the selection task, O'Brien (1993, 1995) argues that the abstract task simply falls outside the range of normal human deductive competence. He gives the lines of reasoning that the BO'B theory dictates would be needed to solve the task: not only is there more than one possible line for each card, but they are long and complex, ranging from 9 to 16 steps. Facilitation effects are put down to deontic problems being categorically different from standard, non-deontic problems, and logically simpler. Thus they may fall within people's natural reasoning range. Manktelow and Over (1991, 1995) made a similar point in their research on deontic reasoning: the deontic selection task asks for judgments of possible violations of regulations whose truth status is not in question, as opposed to the standard selection task, which asks for judgments of cases that could potentially falsify descriptive statements whose truth status is uncertain. Stenning and van Lambalgen (2004a, 2004b; 2008a, 2008b) take a similar position. O'Brien thus contends that there has been no reliably observed facilitation of the non-deontic selection task, as the BO'B theory would predict; hence, selection task research does not call the theory into question. However, this is a contentious claim now, in view of Sperber, Cara and Girotto's (1995) 'recipe' for such facilitation (see also Oaksford & Chater, 1995a, 2007) and other findings of non-deontic effects, such as in the causal versions used by Fairley, Manktelow and Over (1999).

Two different sorts of tests to which the BO'B theory has been subjected involve intermediate inferences and text comprehension. Intermediate inferences are those made while you work your way to a solution of a reasoning problem. O'Brien (1995) gives this example. Supply the conclusion to this set of premises:

n or p; not n; if p then h; if h then z; not both z and q; ?

From the point of view of the BO'B theory, this is a simple problem that is solved by direct reasoning as follows: the first two premises yield p by *Or*-elimination; p together with the third premise yields h by modus ponens; this in turn yields z by modus ponens; and *not-q* is then concluded by a schema that eliminates 'not both'. When people were given such problems and asked to write down everything that occurred to them while they did so, most wrote down the intermediate inferences in the predicted order – even when the premises were presented the opposite way round (see also Braine et al., 1995). The BO'B theory predicts that they will do this because of the way in which the inference schemas must be applied to solve the problem: this is independent of the order of presentation of the premises.

The theory has also been applied to text comprehension, by Lea et al. (1990, p. 368). They presented participants with story vignettes such as the following:

> The Borofskys were planning a dinner party.
> "Alice and Sarah are vegetarians," Mrs Borofsky said, "so if we invite either one of them, we can't serve meat."
> "Well, if we invite Harry, we have to invite Alice," Mr Borofsky said.
> "And if we invite George, we have to invite Sarah."
> "We already made up our minds to invite either Harry or George, or maybe both of them," said Mrs Borofsky.

These were the premises of the problem. You should be able to see where inference rules are called for. The last line of the story was the conclusion, and the participants had to judge whether it made sense. They were given one of two forms:

> "That's right," Mr Borofsky replied, "so we can't serve meat." [valid]
> "That's right," Mr Borofsky replied, "so we can serve meat." [invalid]

After the experiment, the participants were given a recognition test involving judging whether sentences had occurred in the story: the test sentences were either paraphrases of actually appearing sentences, sentences inferrable according to the BO'B theory or sentences inferrable only by standard logic but not by BO'B.

People were overwhelmingly accurate on the validity judgments, and they were also good at recognising the paraphrases as paraphrases. However, they also thought that the BO'B recognition items were paraphrases (i.e. rewordings of sentences that had actually appeared); this did not happen with the non-BO'B inference items. Thus the inferences made according to mental logic theory, but not standard logic, were so straightforward that people were unaware of having made them: they thought they were actual items from the text.

Rips' Psycop theory

In Chapter 2 we saw how this theory dealt with syllogisms, and it may help if you re-read that section. It is a technically complex and wide-ranging theory that aims to do more than just explain the results of reasoning experiments, but we shall keep to what it says about conditionals.

Here is the basis of the theory as set out by Lance Rips (1994, p. x):

> According to [Psycop], a person faced with a task involving deduction attempts to carry it out through a series of steps that take him or her from an initial description of the problem to its solution. These intermediate steps are licensed by mental inference rules, such as modus ponens, whose output people find intuitively obvious. The resulting structure thus provides a conceptual bridge between the problem's 'givens' and its solution.

These inference rules, in other words, are used to construct and verify a *mental proof*. Rips argues not that such attempts at proof are always successful – otherwise he would predict that reasoning would be logically infallible – but that such an attempt is always made. Factors that might cause an error would be those that hinder the application of an appropriate inference rule, such as working memory restrictions, the lack of an appropriate rule or possession of a non-standard rule.

The inference rules are said to construct mental proofs in working memory. In the case of an argument that a person has to evaluate according to whether it follows or not, the person tries to prove that the conclusion follows from the premises. The argument is entered into working memory and the premises are scanned to see if any inferences are possible from the battery of rules. If so, any new sentences are added to memory, the updated set is scanned for further inferences, and so on, until a proof is constructed or until no more rules can be applied, in which case the answer is that the conclusion does not follow.

There are two types of inference rules: forward and backward. Forward rules draw implications from premises; an example is the rule for modus ponens, with which you should be familiar (see Chapter 3 if you need reminding). Modus ponens is known as the rule for forward *If*-elimination in Psycop: the rule results in the disappearance of *If* from the conclusion. Forward rules thus generate sets of new sentences, or assertions. Backward rules work on conclusions, working back to find assertions that are necessary for the argument that the reasoner is trying to prove. Psycop's backward rules contain the family of introduction rules, such as the *And*-introduction cat-and-dog rule we met earlier. Backward *If*-introduction involves proving a conditional sentence by seeing whether, when p is assumed, q is also present, and so it resembles Braine and O'Brien's schema for conditional proof.

The system makes use of a principle derived from problem-solving theory: subgoals. This means that in trying to find a proof of the argument as a whole, the system will set up intermediate goals for proof that are necessary for the argument. Table 5.1 gives an adapted version of an example from Rips (1994, Ch. 4) to show how the following rules are applied to prove a deductive argument: forward *And*-elimination, backward *And*-introduction and backward *If*-introduction. This example also shows how one of the basic control assumptions of the theory is applied: Psycop applies its forward rules first and, if these are not enough to secure a proof, goes on to apply the backward rules.

Table 5.1 Proving a conditional deductive argument using Psycop's inference rules

---

IF Betty is in Little Rock THEN Ellen is in Hammond
Phoebe is in Tucson AND Sandra is in Memphis
Therefore, IF Betty is in Little Rock THEN (Ellen is in Hammond and Sandra is in Memphis)

The conclusion is the goal to be proved.

1 Psycop notices that the second sentence is a conjunction and applies forward *And*-elimination, generating two new sentences that are entered into working memory
2 Phoebe is in Tucson. Sandra is in Memphis
3 No other forward rules apply
4 Because the conclusion (i.e. goal) is a conditional, then backward *If*-introduction can be applied

Subgoal: prove Ellen is in Hammond AND Sandra is in Memphis
Make the supposition: Betty is in Little Rock
Assume: IF Betty is in Little Rock THEN Ellen is in Hammond
Conclude: Ellen is in Hammond [by forward *If*-elimination]

5 Ellen is in Hammond AND Sandra is in Memphis [by backward *And*-introduction from 4 and 2]
6 IF Betty is in Little Rock THEN Ellen is in Hammond AND Sandra is in Memphis [by backward *If*-introduction]

The Psycop theory can be evaluated both against the tests that Rips designed for it and against research data from elsewhere. Rips (1994, Ch. 5) gives as an example of the former, an experiment using materials similar to those in Table 5.1, along with some about imaginary machines. People were given whole arguments and asked to judge whether the conclusion was necessarily true or not. Thirty-two such problems were presented involving various rules, and predictions were made as to their respective difficulty using assumptions about the likely availability of rules to participants, plus a guessing factor. The predicted and observed perform-ance correlated closely; other possible factors such as number of premises in the argument or number of atomic (i.e. component) sentences – the conclusion in the argument in Table 5.1 has three, for instance – did not predict performance at all. Note, however, that Braine et al. (1995) raise a number of problems when Psycop was applied to their own data, because it cannot predict responses when these require their 'feeder' schemas, inferences that enable other inferences. Psycop does not distinguish between core and feeder schemas, only between forward and backward rules. Thus although, as Braine et al. acknowledge, Psycop and the BO'B theory are related, they are not identical.

As an example of the second type of test, Rips (1994, Chs. 5, 9) outlines Psycop's explanation for the observed behaviour on Wason's selection task. On the abstract task (see Chapter 3), the theory predicts that people should elect to examine only the *p* card, which is what about a third of participants do. This is because there is no conclusion to evaluate, so Psycop can only use its forward rules, and in this case the only one applicable is forward *If*-elimination (i.e. modus ponens), which can only be applied to the *p* card. However, an equally common response is to select both the *p* and *q* cards; Rips argues that this will happen when people assume that the target conditional can be read as a biconditional (i.e. implying *If q then p* as well as *If p then q*); forward *If*-elimination can then also be applied to the *q* card as well. In the case of people who get the task right, the explanation is in terms of their being able to project possible values on to the hidden sides of the cards.

On the question of the facilitation effects (see Chapter 4), Rips uses a memory-cueing argument in both deontic and non-deontic contexts. This and the other explanations for selection task performance cannot be taken as powerful evidence for Psycop, however, since they have all been advanced before: in the case of the abstract task, by Wason in the earliest days of selection task research. None of them is a novel explanation particular to Psycop. The theory is clearly on weak ground here, although whether the selection task could give it, or any other theory, a fair test in the first place is a question many have asked (e.g. Sperber et al., 1995).

The theory of mental models

The theory of mental models was devised by Philip Johnson-Laird and his colleagues initially to explain syllogistic reasoning, as we saw in Chapter 2, and has subsequently been extended to cover propositional reasoning, both conditional and disjunctive, including the selection task. It has been applied much more widely than this and has become much more than a theory of reasoning: there are mental models accounts of text comprehension and probability judgment, for instance. Whole books could be written about it, as indeed they have been: see in particular Johnson-Laird (1983) and Johnson-Laird and Byrne (1991); Johnson-Laird (2006) gives the full range of the theory's applications, written for the non-specialist. The set of chapters and papers where it is reviewed is literally too numerous to mention, but I will pick out three recent ones by Johnson-Laird himself. Johnson-Laird (2005) and Johnson-Laird (2008) give compact summaries of the theory's main components, while Johnson-Laird (2004) gives an interesting account of its histor- ical background and development. One of his closest colleagues, Ruth Byrne, runs a website devoted to the theory and the research conducted under its flag.[1] Many of the important books and papers to do with it are listed there. It has been the dominant theory in the psychology of reasoning, although that is not to say that it has crushed all opposition. On the contrary, alternative perspectives have been gaining ground, as we shall see later on.

In view of the scope of the theory and the amount of research it has spawned, I am going to have to be selective here, and keep largely to the themes that have concerned earlier chapters. We have already seen its account of syllogistic reasoning (Chapter 2), so we shall deal here with its account of conditional reasoning and the Wason selection task, look at how it deals with content effects, in particular deontic reasoning, and then review its take on causal and counter- factual reasoning and illusory inferences.

Mental models and conditionals

Johnson-Laird has always regarded the models theory as fundamentally distinct from inference rule (mental logic) theories, although not all theorists agree, as we shall see. The basis of Johnson-Laird's contention is that inference rules describe syntactic processes, whereas mental models are semantic. Syntax is the set of rules concerning the form of expressions: the grammar of a language is an example, as is logic. Semantics, on the other hand, concerns the relation between, for instance, the terms in a language and what they relate to outside the language: the real, or even the fictional, world. Thus in the case of a logical argument, syntax can tell you whether the argument is valid but not whether it is true: you need semantics for that. Mental models are fundamentally semantic, as the items that make them up and the relations between the items are derived directly from the world outside the models.

Let us see how this works when it comes to reasoning with conditionals. Remember that the models theory proposes that when you encounter a reasoning problem, there are several stages that you go through before drawing a conclusion (see Chapter 2). First, there is the *comprehension* stage, where you use your interpretation of the problem's contents, derived from current experience and background knowledge, to understand its premises. That process gives you a set of mental models of the problem's elements. From this, you pass to the *description* stage, where you attempt to draw a conclusion; a conclusion is something that is not explicitly stated in the premises. Then, having done so, you *validate* it by searching for alternative models that defeat it. If you fail to find one, you say that your conclusion follows validly; if you do find one, you go back to the description stage and see if you can formulate a conclusion that is true in all of the models that have emerged.

The 'classic' formulation of the theory's treatment of conditionals is in Johnson-Laird and Byrne (1991), although there have been modifications since. We have to be careful what we mean by 'conditional' as well because of the different kinds of conditional: indicative, causal, deontic, counterfactual, and so on. We shall deal here with what Johnson-Laird and Byrne (2002) call the basic conditional: a purely descriptive *If* sentence. Even there, we have to address the two possible readings, implication and equivalence or biconditional (see Chapter 3), and they make a further distinction as well (see below).

To recap, with an *If p then q* sentence, such as *If Alex is an archbishop then he is a Christian*, we have two parts: the antecedent (p) and the consequent (q). According to the models theory, mental models represent possibilities and what is true in those possibilities. So the antecedent in this case represents the possibility that Alex is an archbishop, while the consequent refers to what is true given that he is: he is a Christian. The mental model for this situation looks like this:

a   c

That cannot be all there is to it, however, because this would also be the model for 'Alex is an archbishop and a Christian', a conjunction, and you know that conditionals are not the same as conjunctions. That is, you know that there are other possibilities when this conditional is uttered. But what are they? You might not be able to say straight away. And this hesitation reveals another principle of the models theory: the *principle of implicit models*. The need for this rests on another, one that is common across cognitive theory: the *principle of cognitive economy*. This basically means that the mind will not do any more work than it has to. Johnson-Laird and Byrne represent these aspects of the conditional in this way:

[a]   c

. . .

You may remember these two bits of notation from Chapter 3. The three dots are an implicit model: a marker that there are additional possibilities (i.e. additional models) that are not represented explicitly. The square brackets indicate that *a* is, as Johnson-Laird and Byrne put it, exhaustively represented with respect to *c*: that is, any alternative possibility cannot have *a* in it. The brackets are not used in recent formulations by model theorists, but others continue to use them (Oaksford & Chater, 2009, is an example). They will not appear again.

We are now in a position to see how the theory deals with conditional inferences. You will recall from Chapter 3 that there are four standard inferences, and that the central empirical fact that any theory needs to account for is the difficulty of modus tollens, which is valid under both implication and equivalence readings but is often not made. First, the one that everyone agrees on, modus ponens:

If a then c

a
_____

?

The answer is *c*, of course. Look at the mental models of the conditional above and you can see why this is easy: you can simply read off *c* from the first model. Modus tollens is another matter, however:

If a then c

Not c
_____

?

You cannot read anything off the initial models given above to derive the conclusion, because *not-c* does not occur in them. Indeed, because of this, a reasoner may stop and say that no conclusion follows. To go further, you need to access the implicit possibilities indicated by the additional model, marked by the three dots. Johnson-Laird and Byrne call this the process of *fleshing out* the implicit possibilities, to make them explicit. These cannot include *a* because it has been exhaustively represented, so must be the two models containing *not-a*, written ¬a:

¬a   c

¬a   ¬c

The truth of the *not-c* premise eliminates the first of these models and leaves the second, so you can conclude, reading from it, *not-a*, and that is the modus tollens inference. The model theory thus predicts that modus tollens will be more difficult than modus ponens, and explains why: it depends on more work. It also depends on some skill, so its use should develop with age and be related to general intelligence. There is research evidence for both of these predictions: see Barrouillet, Grosset and Lecas (2000) and Barrouillet and Gauffroy (2010) for developmental work. In Chapter 10 there will be more on reasoning and intelligence.

As for the biconditional, *If and only if p then q*, Johnson-Laird and Byrne explain that while it has the same initial representation, fleshing out the implicit model only leads to one further explicit model: ¬p,¬q. This is because the ¬p,q case is excluded, owing to the biconditional being reversible (i.e. it can also be read as *If q then p*). A psychological prediction follows: modus tollens should be easier with biconditionals than with implication conditionals, because people only have one extra model to consider instead of two. And it is easier (Johnson-Laird, Byrne & Schaeken, 1992).

You may be thinking that there is one model that has not been mentioned yet:

a   ¬c

This has not been mentioned because mental models only represent what is true in possibilities: a, ¬c is therefore an *impossibility*, given the truth of *If a then c*. But suppose Archbishop Alex actually turns out not to be a Christian (perhaps he has lost his faith but kept his post, or is a member of some non-Christian sect that uses the title archbishop). Then the *If a then c* conditional would itself be false. The full set of models for the conditional therefore matches the truth table for implication (which was shown in Chapter 3): a conditional is true in all cases except *p, not-q*.

We can now go on to other aspects of reasoning introduced in earlier chapters and see how the theory deals with them.

The selection task

As we saw in Chapters 3 and 4, the selection task is a mysterious beast, and many people have spent much time stalking it. Let's remind ourselves once again of the known empirical facts about it that any self-respecting theory of reasoning must be able to accommodate. The first is that in the standard abstract task, with an *If p then q* rule, people nearly always select the *p* card, often select the *q* card along with it and hardly ever select the *not-q* or *not-p* cards. Standard logic tells us that the second and third of these choices are mistakes: since a conditional is only false in the *p, not-q* case, you should pick the *p* and *not-q* cards, in case they have *not-q* and *p* on their backs respectively, and ignore the *q* card, since it could not be a *p, not-q* item.

The mental models theory explains the behaviour of experimental participants in the following way. Bear in mind the initial models of the conditional, above.
These represent explicitly only that *p, q* is a true possibility given *If p then q*.
Johnson-Laird and Byrne (1991, 2002) have slightly different accounts of why this
may lead to selection of the *p* card alone. In the earlier version, they say that people
will consider both the *p* and *q* cards, but choose only *p* since that is the only one
that has a possible value (*not-q*, of course) that could bear on the truth or falsity of
the conditional. In the later version, they say that neglect of the *q* card comes about
when a person represents *not-p, q* explicitly (they cite evidence that some people
regard this as a falsifying item). Both versions of the theory attribute selection of
the *p* and *q* cards as a pair to the conditional being read as a biconditional, and
hence as reversible. Rips' Psycop theory has a similar explanation, as we saw, and
the idea featured in the first published theory of the selection task (Johnson-Laird
& Wason, 1970).

A second empirical fact, which has not been mentioned so far, is a crucial
finding by Evans and Lynch (1973). They presented people with selection tasks
whose conditionals contained negatives. For instance, the target sentence might
read *If p then not q*. An important logical thing happens when you do this: a *p, q*
item is now the *falsifying* case. This is because *q* is not *not-q*! So with a selection task
showing the usual *p, not-p, q* and *not-q* cards, whose target sentence is negated like
this one, standard logic now tells us that the *p* and *q* cards are the right ones. What
do people do? They select *p* and *q* both when the rule is negated and when it is not.
So they get the task *right* with an *If p then not q* rule but wrong with an *If p then q*
rule. The models theory explains this *matching bias*, as Evans calls it (Evans, 1972,
1998; Evans & Lynch, 1973), by proposing that a negation always leads to the
explicit representation of the positive item being negated, so that the *If p then not q*
sentence still leads to explicit models for *p* and *q*. People are getting the negated
task right by accident. We shall return to Evans' invention of the method of negatives in the next chapter, since it led to one of the most important theoretical developments in the whole field.

According to the models theory, then, the main reason why people go wrong
on the selection task is that they find it difficult to construct counterexamples to
the target sentence, because this requires the fleshing out of implicit models. It
follows that anything that makes it easier to do this should lead to improved
performance on the selection task. We have seen already, in Chapter 4 and in this
one, that Sperber et al. (1995) have a 'recipe' for doing this, which is consistent with
the models theory's proposal, and Johnson-Laird and Byrne cite other independent
evidence. One very powerful way of changing selection task performance is to use
realistic content, particularly deontic content. So let us see how the models theory
deals with content and context effects on reasoning.

Content and context

For most psychologists studying human thinking, the central challenge is to
explain how thinking is affected by the content and context of problems. Chapter 4
was devoted to this question, and much of the rest of this chapter will be too,

starting now. Note that the models theory is not the only one that acknowledges the central role of content, indeed in some theorists' hands, as we shall see later, content is all-important.

Early inference rule theories ran into difficulties over the role of content, since a theory that proposes that the mind contains a system of content-free rules (topic-neutral is the technical term) is going to have a problem dealing with content effects. Even the great Piaget (1972) had to make a late concession to his otherwise rigidly logical system in the face of such evidence, and the latter-day inference rule theories reviewed earlier have detailed components in them so that they can deal with content. The theory of mental models might seem immune at the outset to similar traps because of its fundamental semantic basis: the models are tokens representing real objects or events and the relations between them, after all. However, the machinery of the models theory is content-independent: any basic conditional concerning anything at all should be processed in the ways described above.

Mental models theorists are not, of course, oblivious to these issues, and in a major theoretical statement Johnson-Laird and Byrne (2002) set out a content-based mental models theory of conditionals. Some of its components you already know about: the principle of truth, implicit models and mental footnotes. The new elements are as follows. Firstly, the *principle of core meanings* relates to what Johnson-Laird and Byrne call the basic conditional, or rather conditionals: there are two of them, *If p then q* and *If p then possibly q*. In each case, p is a description of a possibility, and q is a description of something that can occur in this possibility. The mental models of these two basic conditionals differ both in terms of their initial representation (where some possibilities are left implicit) and their fully explicit forms:

	If p then q		*If p then possibly q*	
Initial models	p	q	p	q
	...		p	¬q
			...	
Fully explicit	p	q	p	q
models	¬p	q	p	¬q
	¬p	¬q	¬p	q
			¬p	¬q

As you can see, in the case of *If p then possibly q*, the p, *not-q* instance has appeared as a possibility; it is an impossibility with *If p then q*. Thus Johnson-Laird and Byrne say that *If p then possibly q* has a *tautological* meaning: it cannot be falsified, since all instances are possible.

These are two of ten possible model sets, depending on which combinations are allowed as possibilities. The other eight are generated by two further principles that give rise to the *modulation* (i.e. change or variation) of the meanings of conditionals: *semantic* and *pragmatic* modulation.

According to the principle of semantic modulation, the meanings of the p and q terms and the links between them act during the comprehension phase to add information to models, inhibit the formation of models or facilitate the explicit representation of models. Thus, for instance, time information can be added if the sentence is understood as causal, since the cause can never go after the effect.

Pragmatic modulation involves the contribution of general knowledge from long-term memory, or knowledge of the specific circumstances in which the sentence is uttered. We have already seen examples of pragmatic modulation in other forms of reasoning, such as the Gricean interpretation of 'some' in syllogistic reasoning to mean 'some but not all' (see Chapter 2). Here is a conditional example. We know that the modus tollens inference can be difficult to draw, but there is an interpretation that makes it trivially easy, sometimes known as the 'monkey's uncle' interpretation:

If war was the last resort then I'm a monkey's uncle.

You say this to someone secure in the joint knowledge that you do not, in fact, have a sibling who has spawned a monkey, and so your hearer readily infers what you intended to convey: that war was not the last resort. Johnson-Laird and Byrne call this the tollens interpretation, and specify that it comes with only one explicit possibility: *not-p, not-q*. This explains why modus tollens is easy here: you can read the desired conclusion straight off from this single model.

The full set of ten interpretations of the conditional is given in Table 4 on p. 663 of the Johnson-Laird and Byrne (2002) paper. In this table, they give two parallel sets of example conditionals: one indicative, and one deontic. For instance, under the conditional interpretation, the examples given are *If the patient has malaria then she has a fever* (indicative) and *If he promised then he must take the kids to the zoo* (deontic). This is because they acknowledge that there has to be a distinction between two kinds of possibility: factual possibilities and deontic possibilities. Both function differently: a deontic possibility is not one that can or does happen but one that *ought* to happen, either because it is permitted or obligated; a deontic 'impossibility', such as not going to the zoo despite promising to, or driving at 40 when the sign says 30, violates a rule but does not falsify it.

We shall not go through all these interpretations (Johnson-Laird, 2006, 2010, now regards the possible number as indefinite, rather than 10), but will shortly focus on some in particular: causal and counterfactual. Before we do, here is a phenomenon that is perhaps the most startling to be thrown up by the models theory: it is a genuine discovery.

Illusory inferences

You are playing a game of cards with your friend Mr Sharp. You have two clues about what he has in his hand. You know that one of these clues is true and the other is false, but you don't know which is which. The two clues are:

1   If there is a king in his hand, then there is an ace.
2   If there is not a king in his hand, then there is an ace.

What do you conclude? That there *is* an ace in Mr Sharp's hand; that there *may be* an ace; or that there is *not* an ace? Think about it and satisfy yourself as to what the answer must be.

You conclude that Mr Sharp must or may have an ace in his hand, don't you? Wrong: it is *impossible* for there to be an ace in his hand. Here's why. Consider the truth conditions of the basic conditional: it is only false when there is *p* with *not-q*. Now look at the two sentences above. Only one is true, the other is false. When sentence 1 is true, 2 must be false, and 2 is false when there is no king and no ace. When sentence 2 is true, 1 must be false, and 1 is false when there is a king and no ace. So either way, there can be no ace.

This is one of a family of such illusions, and they are highly compelling. They were discovered by Johnson-Laird through a computer implementation of the models theory, and in several accounts of them he relates how he thought there was a bug in the program, until he realised the program was right (so perhaps only a program would ever have led to the discovery). Our difficulty, according to the models theory, stems from the principle of truth. In the inference described here, we have a *disjunction of conditionals*: 1 *or* 2 is true. Inferences like this require us to think about what is false, and this requires extra mental work, in the shape of fleshing out implicit models, combining them and understanding the meta-principle of truth and falsity. Models only represent what is true in a possibility. People who fall for the illusion – that's everyone from you and me to Johnson-Laird himself – have responded to the above problem as if it said 1 *and* 2 are true. Finally, remember the THOG problem in Chapter 3? That is another case of illusory inference involving exclusive disjunction and problems in thinking about falsity.

Causal and counterfactual reasoning

I promised at the end of the last chapter that there would be more on these topics, and here it is. The reason for the delay is that so much of the recent work on counterfactuals has been done by people wearing the colours of the mental models theory, especially Ruth Byrne and her colleagues. A comprehensive account of this work is given by Byrne (2005; see also the summary and associated commentaries in Byrne, 2007).

The models theory of counterfactuals contains an additional principle: the *principle of subjunctive meanings*. 'Subjunctive' is a linguistic term for the mood of a verb, when what is being expressed is something wished for or hypothesised. In English, auxiliary verbs such as *have, had, would* and *might* are used to convey this sense: *war was the last resort* is indicative, while *war would have been the last resort* is subjunctive. So the principle of subjunctive meanings is a modification of the principle of core meanings to allow for the representation of possibilities that have not (yet) occurred.

This principle allows the models theory to deal with the various different kinds of factual possibility. There are actual facts such as *A man won the US presidency*, real possibilities such as *A woman wins the US presidency*, impossibilities such as *A Briton wins the US presidency* and counterfactual possibilities such as

A woman won the 2008 presidential election (Johnson-Laird & Byrne, 1991). Counterfactual possibilities therefore refer to situations that were possible but did not actually occur.

Here is an example of a subjunctive counterfactual conditional:

If a woman had won the US presidency, then the First Lady would have been a man.

This has the usual *If p then q* form, and you know that the models theory specifies an initial explicit representation of just the *p, q* case, plus an implicit model for the *not-p* cases. However, in this case we know, explicitly, that what is expressed here did not happen: a woman did not win, and the USA did not have a ticklish titular puzzle to solve. The models theory therefore proposes that with counterfactual conditionals two models are explicitly represented:

$$\neg p \quad \neg q$$

$$p \quad q$$

$$\ldots$$

The first one represents the facts: a woman did not win and the First Lady is not male; the second one represents the counterfactual possibilities expressed in the sentence.

Several testable predictions flow from this theory. One might have struck you straight away: this representation resembles the one for the biconditional, and since we know that modus tollens is made more readily from a biconditional than a conditional (see above), we would expect the same to be true of counterfactual conditionals. That prediction was tested and confirmed by Byrne and Tasso (1999; see also Thompson & Byrne, 2002): modus tollens was made 80% of the time with subjunctive conditionals, compared with 40% with indicatives. Exactly the same figures were found for the fallacious denial of the antecedent inference too (*not-p* therefore *not-q*), which is also consistent with the predictions of mental models theory: it should also be facilitated by the explicit representation of *not-p, not-q*. Byrne and Tasso also asked their participants to list the possibilities that best fitted conditional sentences. They listed the *not-p, not-q* item more often when given counterfactuals than indicatives, which again is consistent with its explicit representation in the initial models.

That is far from being the end of it, as far as the mental models account of counterfactual thinking is concerned. One of the hallmarks of this research is the ingenuity and energy of the researchers. I can give only a flavour of this work here, and urge you to go to Byrne's (2005) book or the Byrne (2007) summary for the full story.

The core of the mental models explanation of counterfactual reasoning is, as we have seen, the proposal that people represent explicitly two possibilities when thinking counterfactually: the world as it would have been were the counterfactual statement true (*p, q*) and the world as it actually is, where the statement is not true (*not-p, not-q*). With indicatives, we only represent the single possibility, the factual claim *p, q*. In addition to the conditional inference evidence just cited, there is support for this two-model hypothesis from studies that have shown there to be an asymmetry in the ways people think about actions versus inactions: people tend to regret their actions more than their inactions.

Probably the best known case of this is the series of studies of *omission bias* by Ilana Ritov and Jonathan Baron (e.g. 1990, 1999), although the effect was discovered by Kahneman and Tversky (1982b). People are reluctant to have their young children vaccinated: they want there to be a lower risk of harm from the vaccination than there is from the disease, and experimental participants judge that a person who has their child vaccinated and harmed will experience more regret than will a person who declines the vaccine and sees their child contract the disease. Why should this be? According to Byrne (2005), it is because when we represent actions, we readily think of the alternative to the action – not having done it – and so have two explicit possibilities in mind and can say, regretfully, *if only* I hadn't done that. But when we think of not having acted, we are less likely to think of the alternative, the action. This is because when you think about taking an action, you can readily think about the pre-action state, to which your action brings about a change. You think about two mental models of two states of the world: the post-action state and the pre-action state. However, when you think about an inaction, the two states of the world, before and after you failed to act, are the same (Byrne & McEleney, 2000). There is more discussion of regret in Chapter 9.

You may be wondering at this point whether it is really true that we don't think about alternatives to inactions. Don't we ever say, if only I *had* done this or that? Yes, we do. When people look back over their past lives (i.e. over the long term) they tend to do just that: regret the things they did not do – the opportunities they missed – as much as their misdeeds. Byrne explains this by proposing that in these cases we have available in memory the *consequences* of both our inactions and our actions, and that those become the second model. You had a good reason to act and yet you didn't (that person you were too shy to ask out and who married someone else . . .). Those reasons can operate in the short term too. For instance, consider two sports coaches whose teams are on losing runs. One changes the team, the other doesn't and both teams lose the next game. Which coach experiences greater regret? Most people say it is the one who made no changes: there was a good reason to make the change, but he didn't. At least the other one tried (Zeelenberg, van der Bos, van Dijk & Pieters, 2002). Thus when people think about the reasons for acting or the consequences of not acting, they switch from representing one possibility to two, which opens up counterfactual thinking.

A particularly intriguing aspect of counterfactual thinking that has also been addressed by mental models researchers is called *semifactual* reasoning. This is where you link a counterfactual antecedent – something that didn't happen – to a factual consequent – something that did. It is often expressed using the construction *Even if*, as in *Even if the coach had changed the team, they would still have lost*. The coach could have changed the team, but actually did not; the team did actually lose.

According to the models theory, semifactual *Even if p then still q* conditionals like this result in the representation of two explicit models:

p   q

¬p   q

. . .

The first model represents a conjecture: the team actually lost (*q*) and would, you claim, have done so if the coach had changed the team (*p*). The second model represents the facts: the team lost and the coach didn't change the team. This theory of semifactuals generates some novel psychological predictions, which have been confirmed by Byrne and her colleagues. One is that they should lead to fewer affirmations of the consequent inferences (*q*, therefore *p*) compared with *If p then q* conditionals: and they do (Moreno-Rios, Garcia-Madruga & Byrne, 2004). Another even more novel prediction is that there should be some *not-p*, therefore *q* inferences with *Even if* sentences, which is something never seen with ordinary *If* conditionals. Moreno-Rios et al. confirmed this too: about one-third of their participants made this inference.

Something interesting emerges when you compare semifactuals with counterfactuals:

> Even if the coach had changed the team, they would still have lost (semifactual).

> If the coach had changed the team, they would have won (counterfactual).

In both cases, the facts are that the coach did not change the team and that the team lost. But with the semifactual, the consequent is true (they did lose) while with the counterfactual it is false (they did not win). This has an effect on causal inference. Counterfactual statements are closely linked to causal claims (see Chapter 4): the one above leads to a strengthening of belief that changing the team causes the team to win. Semifactuals have the opposite effect: they reduce belief in the causal relation between *p* and *q*. You can imagine how this might work in legal contexts, for instance in investigations apportioning blame for disasters such as air crashes, as in the example at the end of Chapter 4:

> Even if the pilots had shut down the damaged engine, the plane would still have crashed.

> If only the pilots had shut down the damaged engine, the plane would not have crashed.

A lawyer who utters the first sentence, the semifactual, is aiming to absolve the pilots from blame. One who utters the second, the counterfactual, is directing blame squarely at them by highlighting the supposed causal role of their mistake.

A mental models theory of causal reasoning was put forward by Goldvarg and Johnson-Laird (2001), and Byrne (2005) uses this theory as the basis of her treatment of the subject. It offers a different perspective from the approaches described in Chapter 4: it argues that the way people think about causality is not based on frequency or probability, and does not depend on causal powers or mechanisms. Rather, naïve causality is based on what people regard as possible or impossible in the circumstances. In general, there are four mental models of the possibilities when a candidate Cause (C) occurs with or without a candidate Effect (E):

C	E	Cause is followed by Effect
C	¬E	Cause is followed by no Effect
¬C	E	No Cause, Effect occurs
¬C	¬E	No Cause, no Effect

There is a universal constraint when representing these models: that C cannot follow E. The different models that people consider to be possible determine the kind of causal relation they infer, and so they can be used to distinguish causes from *enabling conditions*. This is important, because this distinction has been troublesome for both philosophers and psychologists for a long time (Cheng & Novick, 1991, referred to in the last chapter, offer an explanation for the difference, which Goldvarg and Johnson-Laird reject).

Returning to the air crash example, here are the models for *Pilot error* **caused** *the accident to happen:*

C	E
¬C	E
¬C	¬E

The second and third models reflect people's sense that without the error the accident might still have happened, but might not have. Now here is the set for *Pilot error* **enabled** *the accident to happen:*

C	E
C	¬E
¬C	¬E

Notice that the second model is different here: with an enabling relation, the effect may or may not occur when the cause occurs. You need something else to bring about the effect, for instance the catastrophic failure of the damaged engine.

In an experiment, Goldvarg and Johnson-Laird found that there were differences in the possibilities that people listed for *cause* and *enable* that followed their predictions. For instance, 45% of participants listed the C, ¬E model as impossible for *cause*, but none did so for *enable*, while 25% listed ¬C, E as impossible for *enable* while none did for *cause*. You can see how these are the models excluded from the model sets for the two relations above, so they are exactly the ones that should be listed as impossible. This is one of five experiments reported in the paper, all of which corroborate the mental models account, and there is also a wide-ranging theoretical review of which I can only convey the gist here. It is well worth reading in full.

According to Byrne (2005), 'counterfactual and causal assertions mean the same thing and are consistent with the same possibilities' (p. 127), and she confronts the problem described in the last chapter, where people focus on different events when they are asked about causes and when they are asked counterfactual questions. Both causal and counterfactual reasoning are said to access the initial model, the *p, q* (or C, E) case, but counterfactual *If only* thinking makes use of a second explicit model, the ¬*p*, ¬*q* (¬C, ¬E) case. Only the first, she says, is represented explicitly in causal thinking, whereas, as we have seen, she proposes that both are explicit with counterfactuals. However, she emphasises that this parallel applies to *strong* causal assertions. A strong causal assertion is one where only two mental models are allowed as possible:

C   E

¬C   ¬E

which can be paraphrased as 'C and only C causes E' (Goldvarg & Johnson-Laird, 2001). Indeed, her argument requires her to make this stipulation, since these are the possibilities specified for counterfactuals. However, Goldvarg and Johnson-Laird do not make the same restriction, as we have seen. Byrne's claim is therefore itself too strong, from their point of view.

There is another problem for the mental models view of counterfactuals as well. Some counterfactual states are closer to the actual state than others, which means that counterfactual thinking must be to some extent probabilistic after all. For instance, when you say something like *A woman almost won the US presidential election*, you are signalling, by the use of *almost*, that the counterfactual situation (she won) was close to the facts (she lost, but not by much). English has a number of words that convey closeness: almost, nearly, disappointed, surprised, relieved, and so on (Kahneman & Varey, 1990). Who is more disappointed, the silver medallist or the bronze medallist? The silver medallist: even though this is objectively a better result, the counterfactual situation (winning the gold) is closer to the facts than it is for the bronze medallist (Boninger, Gleicher & Strathman, 1994; Medvec, Madley & Gilovich, 1995). When thinking about what nearly happened to them, people think about a strongly contrasting event rather than one close to the facts (Teigen, Kanten & Terum, 2011). For the silver medallist, this is winning the gold; for the bronze, it is winning no medal at all. Counterfactual closeness is acknowledged by Byrne (2005), but the models theory seems to have no way of accommodating it.

There is no denying the mental models theory's brilliant success in generating all these interesting hypotheses and findings. It is wide-ranging, much more so than the mental logic theory; indeed, it offers the prospect of a unifying account of many aspects of human thought, and Johnson-Laird (2006) attempts just that. However, we cannot close the book on the explanation of reasoning quite yet. In the next chapter, we encounter a fundamentally different way of explaining reasoning, one that also offers a wide-scope account of human inference and has locked horns with the models theory in recent years.

Summary

1   The two main classic approaches both have logical foundations: the theory of mental logic and the theory of mental models.

2   Braine and O'Brien's mental logic theory is entirely concerned with *If*. It proposes a lexical entry for *If*, a set of reasoning schemas and pragmatic principles that govern their application. It predicts the patterns of intermediate inferences in the course of reasoning.

3   Rips' mental logic theory, Psycop, is based on the idea of reasoning a mental proof of an argument. It contains forward and backward inference rules, and can be applied to both propositional and syllogistic reasoning.

4   Johnson-Laird's mental models theory started as an explanation of syllogistic performance, but has developed into a wide-ranging account of human reasoning.

5   It is based on semantic tokens as opposed to inference rules. There is a comprehension stage, where the problem's interpretation produces the elements to be reasoned with, a description stage, where a candidate conclusion is produced, and a validation stage, which involves searching for alternative models that may defeat it.

6   An important component is the idea of implicit models: those whose presence is noted, but whose contents are not fully represented unless the problem cues it. This aspect of the theory is motivated by the restricted capacity of working memory.

7   Johnson-Laird and Byrne have proposed a mental models theory of *If* in which the comprehension stage is controlled by semantic and pragmatic modulation, so that different model sets are derived.

8   The models theory drew attention to illusory inferences, which are compelling but illogical. They are explained by the theory's principle of truth.

9   A major research programme on counterfactual thinking has been motivated by the models theory.

Explaining reasoning: the 'new paradigm'

The probabilistic approach to reasoning was introduced in Chapter 2, in the shape of Nick Chater and Mike Oaksford's (1999) probability heuristics model of syllogistic reasoning (PHM), which I described as revolutionary. In fact, the first shots in this revolution were fired earlier, with the appearance of a radical reappraisal of behaviour on the Wason selection task by Oaksford and Chater (1994a). Since this paper, these authors have applied their general approach not just to syllogisms, but to conditional inference as well, and have become the leading advocates of a wide-ranging paradigm of research into cognition based on probability (see Chater & Oaksford, 2008).

In parallel with these developments, a group of researchers headed by Jonathan Evans and David Over have also developed a probability-based account of reasoning. These latter theorists have combined it with an aspect of cognitive theory that will figure prominently from here on: the dual process theory. Together, these ideas make up what Over (2009; Manktelow, Over & Elqayam, 2010a) has described as a 'new paradigm' in the explanation of reasoning and thinking. In this chapter, we shall start to see what this paradigm consists of.

Oaksford and Chater's Bayesian theory

The central insight upon which the Oaksford and Chater theory is founded is that in real life few things can be taken as certain. This is a problem for a conception of reasoning based on logic, because logic is the calculus of certainty: a valid conclusion is one that is necessarily (certainly) true, given that the premises are (certainly) true. You cannot have a deductively valid conclusion from premises that are to any degree uncertain. Oaksford and Chater therefore turn to the calculus of uncertainty – probability theory – and ask whether, when people engage in 'logical' reasoning, they might actually be doing something else: using information to update their beliefs. Let's see how this question is assessed when it comes to the selection task and conditional inference.

Rational analysis

The title of Oaksford and Chater's (1994a) original paper on the selection task is *A rational analysis of the selection task as optimal data selection*, and there you have the main elements of the argument. Firstly, rational analysis. This term refers to a technique developed by John Anderson (1990, 1991) and first applied to other areas of cognition such as memory and categorisation. Rational analysis assumes that human cognition is adapted (i.e. responds effectively) to its environment, and so is concerned with describing the problem the cognitive system is faced with, on the assumption that the mind is dealing well with it, within its processing constraints. It has a series of steps:

1   Specify precisely the goals of the cognitive system.
2   Develop a formal model of the environment to which the system is adapted.
3   Make minimal assumptions about cognitive constraints.

4   Derive the optimal behaviour function given steps 1–3.
5   Test the behaviour function against the research evidence.
6   Repeat, refining the theory as you go.

Step 4 is a formal step requiring the use of a normative system such as logic or probability theory. It was the latter that was used by Oaksford and Chater in their explanation of the selection task. This is because they conceive of the task as analogous to the problem that scientists face when trying to decide on the best experiment to conduct, given the research question they are dealing with. Students face exactly this problem in their project work.

So for Oaksford and Chater, the participants in a selection task experiment are faced with the task of judging what would be the best test to decide between two competing hypotheses: (i) that the target *If p then q* sentence is true, so that *p* is always accompanied by *q*; (ii) that *p* and *q* are not associated in any way and may occur with or without each other. These are called the dependence hypothesis (H_D) and the independence hypothesis (H_I), respectively. Oaksford and Chater assume that participants go into the task with the belief that each hypothesis is equally likely (i.e. has a prior probability of .5).

In the selection task, you have to think about which of four cards to choose so as to decide on the status of the target sentence (i.e. to decide between H_D and H_I). The standard logical answer to this challenge, you will remember, is that you should look for the combination of *p* with *not-q*, since only this instance could decisively settle the question, by showing that the *If* claim is false. But hardly anyone does this; most pick just the *p* card, or the *p* and *q* cards. Oaksford and Chater argue that this is rational behaviour if the participant's task is seen as one of *information gain* rather than logical proof. Instead of asking themselves about the logical consequences of what might be on the hidden sides of each card, perhaps what people are asking themselves is which cards might convey the most information: that is, which ones would most reduce their uncertainty about the sentence from the prob = .5 they started with?

Several components go into the rational analysis of this information gain task. Firstly, information means reduction in uncertainty, and so the best cards to choose are the ones that move you most from your prior belief state of prob = .5. Secondly, people don't actually turn the cards over in the selection task: they have to nominate which cards they would like to turn over. This means that we are not dealing with actual information gain but with *expected* information gain. Thirdly, there is the possibility of genuine error. Fourthly, selections are competitive, because of the demand characteristics of the task: people tend to avoid picking all or none of the cards, and so each card they do pick affects another card's chances of being picked. Fifthly, and importantly, there is the *rarity assumption* (this was referred to in Chapter 2 when considering the PHM). Most objects, events and properties in the world are rare with respect to their complements – the things they are not: people are rare in the world compared to things (even animals) that are not people; students are rare compared to all people; and so on. Evidence that conditionals are naturally used to refer to rare events has been independently provided by McKenzie, Ferreira, Mikkelson, McDermott and Skrable (2001).

All of these components are put into a formal mathematical analysis, which you can see in detail in the original paper and in revisions that have appeared since: see Oaksford and Chater (1994a, 2003, 2007, 2009). The analysis uses the Bayesian formula for belief revision in the face of some new knowledge, which we looked at in detail in Chapter 1, so I shall only describe it in outline here.

We start off with some algebra expressing the probabilities of the *p* and *q* items in the *If p then q* statement. Only three terms are needed for all the calculations. The probability of *p*, known as its marginal probability, is called *c*. Since this is a conditional, we also need an expression for the probability of *q* given *p*, prob(q|p), and this is called *a*. The marginal probability of *not-q* is called *b*. From these, you can derive probability expressions for all the combinations: *p,q*; ¬*p,q*; *p*,¬*q*; and ¬*p*,¬*q*. This can be done using a contingency table:

	q	*not q*
p	ac	(1−a)c
not p	1−b−ac	b−(1−a)c

For instance, the probability of *p,q* is shown in the top left cell: prob(q|p) × prob(p), or a × c.

Now we can assess the chances of finding a *q* value on the back of the *p* card. If the dependence hypothesis H_D is true, this is clearly *a*, whereas if the independence hypothesis H_I is true it is *c*. The probability that H_D is true given that you turn over a *p* card and find *q* on the back is $a/a + c$ (this is a version of the Bayesian formula, which appeared in Chapter 1), and the probability that H_D is true given the same is simply this result subtracted from 1. Information gain is then the difference between your prior belief in the two hypotheses and your revised belief after receiving this information. But since in the selection task you don't actually turn cards, we need to compute the *expected* information gained by choosing the *p* card. For that, you have to work out all the possible outcomes: for the *p* card, this involves not just the above, but a similar calculation for what would happen if you were to find *not-q* on the back, under both hypotheses. Here is the formula for prob(q|p):

$$prob(q|p) = prob(H_D)prob(q|p, H_D) + prob(H_I)prob(q|p, H_I)$$

The expected information (EI) from the *p* card is therefore:

$$EI(p) = prob(q|p)I_g(p_q) + prob(\neg q|p)I_g(p_{\neg q})$$

Which, translated into words, reads as: the expected information from the *p* card equals the probability of *q* given *p* weighted by the information gain associated with turning over the *p* card to reveal *q*, plus the probability of *not-q* given *p* weighted by the information gain associated with turning over the *p* card to reveal *not-q*. Take this result from the prior belief in the two hypotheses H_D and H_I, add up the outcomes and you have the expected information gain from the *p* card. The same kind of thing can be done for the other three cards as well.

There is something missing from all this: actual numbers instead of the algebraic variables *a*, *b* and *c*. This is where the rarity assumption comes back into play. Oaksford and Chater argue that for most objects and properties the marginal probabilities of *p* and *q* will be small, since they are rare in the world. When you put small values into the information gain formulae, the expected information gain from the *q* card turns out to be significantly higher than it is for the *not-q* card; it is also high for the *p* card and low for the *not-p* card. As we know (see above and Chapter 3), the most common patterns of performance in the selection task are to select the *p* and *q* cards and ignore the *not-p* and *not-q* cards. Keeping to the assumption that belief in the two alternative hypotheses starts at .5, and adding the assumption that prior belief in prob(q|p) was at .9, Oaksford and Chater (1994a, 2003) fitted the predictions of the information gain theory to the known research results. The outcome of this meta-analysis is shown in Figure 6.1. As you can see, there is a very close fit between the predictions and the data.

This is just the start of the information gain analysis of conditionals. I shall not be able to go into the same amount of detail about each application, so what follows is an outline of the main areas of research to which it has been applied.

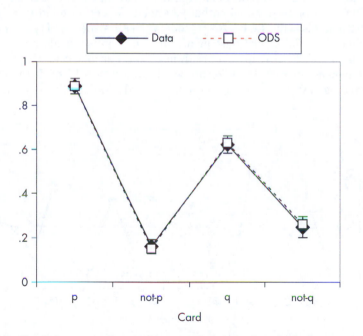

Figure 6.1 The fit between the predictions of Oaksford and Chater's optimal data selection model (ODS) and the published data from experiments on the indicative selection task

Source: Oaksford and Chater (2007), reproduced by permission of Oxford University Press

Matching bias

One of the earliest reliable empirical discoveries in the modern psychology of reasoning was made by Evans in 1972 and was outlined in the last chapter (see Evans, 1998, for a review): that people tended to concentrate on the items mentioned in the statement when reasoning about conditionals (i.e. they would concern themselves with *p* and *q* and not think about *not-p* and *not-q*). He discovered this by using conditionals containing negated components, such as *If p then not q* or *If not p then q*. Negation reverses the logical property of an item. However, people focussed on *p* and *q* come what may, ignoring their logical status. As we saw in the last chapter, this finding was extended to the selection task shortly afterwards (Evans & Lynch, 1973): for instance, given an *If p then not q* rule, people still selected the *p* and *q* cards most often.

The information gain theory was fitted to the relevant data on the negated selection task by Oaksford and Chater (2003). To find probability values they made a further assumption, based on previous research by Oaksford and Stenning (1992): that a negative statement brings with it a higher-probability *contrast class*. For instance, if you are told that Alex is not an archbishop, you are likely to think that he holds some other office in the Church, rather than that he is, say, a garage mechanic; 'some other office' is the contrast class, and is clearly more likely than 'archbishop'. The results of this model-fitting exercise are shown in Figure 6.2.

There is a piece of notation that you need to keep in mind when reading Figure 6.2 and this is the TA-FA-TC-FC code, where T stands for True, F for False, A for Antecedent and C for Consequent. This notation is needed because of the change in logical status that comes with negation. For instance, with a plain *If p then q* statement, the *p* card is a TA card and the *q* card is a TC card. But with an *If p then not q* statement, the *q* card is now an FC card. TA-FC is the logically correct

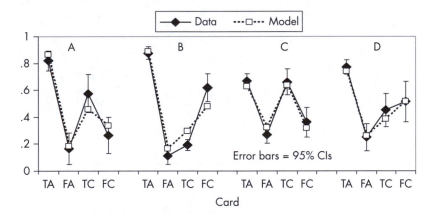

Figure 6.2 The ODS model fitted to the data from experiments using sentences with affirmative and negative components: *If p then q* (panel A), *If p then not q* (panel B), *If not p then q* (panel C), *If not p then not q* (panel D).

Source: Oaksford and Chater (2007), reproduced by permission of Oxford University Press

selection irrespective of negation. You can see the matching effect in the following way: the TA card, for instance, is picked more often when it matches, because the statement says *If p* . . ., than when it mismatches (when the statement says *If not p* . . .). The same effect applies to the other three: they are picked more often when they match the item named in the statement.

Again, you can see that the theory's predictions and the data are in close agreement (in these panels A–D, the note about CIs refers to confidence intervals: the range of scores that cover 95% of the participants' responses). Yama (2001) compared the information gain account against the matching heuristic and found support for both; in a follow-up, Oaksford and Moussakowski (2004) were able to make diverging predictions from the two approaches, and found that the experimental data supported information gain.

The deontic selection task

In Chapters 4 and 5 we considered the deontic selection task: the version that asks participants to look for violations of rules of permission or obligation, such as *If you are entering, then you must have 'cholera' on your immigration form*. People are reliably accurate on versions such as this, and tend to select the *p* and *not-q* cards, in stark contrast to the standard indicative task. These are the cards potentially showing the person entering without the required inoculation. People are also sensitive to perspective manipulations, and will select the *not-p* and *q* cards if they are cued to look at the rule from a different point of view (e.g. the passenger, in this case, rather than the immigration authorities). Manktelow and Over (1991, 1995) explained these findings in terms of decision theory: people were computing the expected utilities attached to each possible case (entering or not entering, inoculated or not) and responding to those with the highest utility in the circumstances: for the immigration officer, it is clearly most important to detect the person coming in who might be infected.

Oaksford and Chater (1994a; also Perham & Oaksford, 2005) put this theory on a more formal footing and provide mathematical formulae for working out the expected utilities for each card. Notice that this is not a pure information gain account, because now we are looking not at probability alone, but at probability (the 'expected' part) combined with utility. In the deontic task, people are no longer testing a rule, but are reasoning from it to detect transgressors. Therefore, there is no need for an alternative independence hypothesis, because we are not assessing the rule as such. The total expected utility of each card is calculated by adding the utility of each value that might be on its hidden side (e.g. for the *p* card, the *q* and *not-q* values) weighted by their respective probabilities.

The rarity assumption also has to be used more subtly in the deontic context because there are some circumstances in which we will have different expectations that cheating may occur. We saw in Chapter 4 two examples of this: Kirby's (1994) adaptation of the drinking-age problem, in which people were less likely to select very young customers, presumably because they thought it unlikely to begin with that they would be drinking beer; and Manktelow, Sutherland and Over's (1995) immigration task, where people on the lookout for incomers needing inoculations against a tropical disease were less likely to select passengers arriving from European countries. Oaksford and Chater (2007, Ch. 6) use their current expected utility theory to model the results of both these studies, and find very high correlations between the model's predictions and the data (better than .95 in both cases, for the statistically comfortable). They do not, however, address Bonnefon and Hilton's (2005) extension of this work.

Conditional inference

Although this area of reasoning is an equally important part of the Oaksford and Chater scheme, I shall not be able to go into it in as much detail as with the other two main areas: the selection task and the probability heuristics models of syllogistic reasoning (see Chapter 2). You learned in Chapter 3 that there are four basic conditional inferences: modus ponens, denial of the antecedent, affirmation of the consequent and modus tollens. The first and last are logically valid but the second and third are not, and so people should make MP and MT but not DA and AC. However, the patterns of actual inference are MP > MT > AC > DA. People do not make MT as frequently as they should, and they make DA and AC more than they should. Note also that there are asymmetries between MP and MT, and between AC and DA – in both pairs, frequencies should be equal, but they are not.

As with the selection task, the basic idea behind the rational analysis of conditional inference is that when thinking about *If*, people respond to the conditional probability, prob(q|p). Probability is, as always in this context, a subjective matter, and refers to a person's degree of belief. Your belief in a conditional is given by this conditional probability, and stems from a process known as the Ramsey test (after its inventor, the philosopher Frank Ramsey): add p to your beliefs, then assess your strength of belief that q follows. For instance, take a non-causal indicative conditional, such as the kind of identification rule beloved of birdwatchers: *If it has a heavy black bar on its breast, then it is a great tit*. You believe that the probability that it is a great tit, given that it has a black bar, is .9, say, which is very likely. So your belief that q follows from p being asserted (the MP inference) will be .9. To predict the frequencies of the other inferences, you need the marginal probabilities of p (birds in your area with black bars) and q (what proportion of birds are great tits); from them, you can work out the other conditional probabilities: p given q (AC), *not-q* given *not-p* (DA) and *not-p* given *not-q* (MT).

Using the existing research data, obtained from a meta-analysis reported by Schroyens and Schaeken (2003; see also Schroyens, Schaeken & d'Ydewalle, 2001), Oaksford and Chater found, yet again, close fits between their model and the evidence. This can be seen in Figure 6.3. Each panel shows the research data, the black diamonds. Panel A shows the predictions of standard logic against them. Panel B shows the predictions of standard logic, allowing that some people make a biconditional interpretation (see Chapter 3) and errors. Panel C shows the fit of the model just described: you can see that although it does well it underestimates the frequencies of MP and MT and overestimates DA and AC. Panel D shows the fit of a revised version of the model, to allow for the possibility that being told that the minor premise is true, rather than simply observing it, can alter your belief in

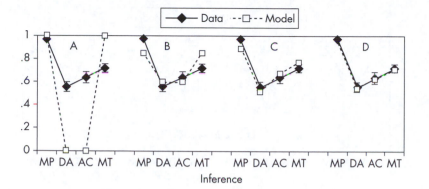

Figure 6.3 The data from experiments on conditional inferences fitted to four models: standard conditional logic (panel A), logic with biconditional interpretations and error (panel B), the probabilistic model of Oaksford et al. (2000) (panel C) and the revised model (panel D)

Source: Oaksford and Chater (2007), reproduced by permission of Oxford University Press

prob(q|p) – logically, this should not happen. For instance, if you are told that the car did not start, you might *not* conclude (by MT) that the key was not turned; more likely, you would infer that something had disabled the causal relation between key and starting, meaning that your belief in this relation, that *If the key is turned then the car starts*, has lessened. Allowing for change in belief in the *If* sentence in this way results in a much closer model fit.

So far, we have only been considering how well the theory fits the existing data, and the answer is, generally, very well. However, it has also been used to make novel predictions, which is the truest test of any theory. One clear prediction is that if the marginal probabilities of *p* and *q* are changed, then the frequencies of the conditional inferences, and card choices in the selection task, should change with them. Oaksford, Chater and Larkin (2000) did just that with conditional inferences. They used tasks with high-probability and low-probability *p* and *q* conditions. The fit between the predictions of the model and the data is shown in Figure 6.4.

Again, there is clearly a close fit between model and data. Oaksford, Chater, Grainger and Larkin (1997) used a reduced array version of the selection task, one where only the *q* and *not-q* items have to be considered, in sets of multiple items. This enables the probability of *not-q* versus *q* items to be varied: they simply changed the proportions of each. The results are shown in Figure 6.5, where you can see that, as predicted, selections of the *not-q* cards rose as prob(p) rose: as *p* becomes less rare, the information value of the *not-q* card rises. The opposite should happen for the *q* cards, and, as you can see from Figure 6.5, it did.

However, bear in mind that not everyone has found similar effects of probability. Examples of failure to do so are the work of Klaus Oberauer and colleagues (Oberauer, Weidenfeld & Hörnig, 2004; Oberauer, Wilhelm & Dias, 1999). Oaksford and Chater do not always have convincing explanations for these failures (see the critiques and reply that accompany Oaksford & Chater, 2009), but all that implies, I think, is that the course of revolutions never does run smooth. The

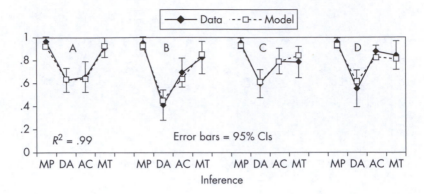

Figure 6.4 The fit between the model and the data of Oaksford et al. (2000), when low- and high-probability *p* and *q* items are used: (A) low prob(p), low prob(q); (B) high prob(p), high prob(q); (C) high prob(p), low prob(q); (D) high prob(p), high prob(q)

Source: Oaksford and Chater (2007), reproduced by permission of Oxford University Press

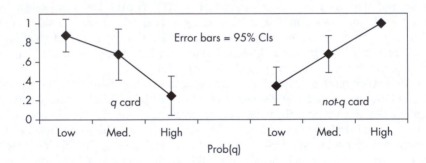

Figure 6.5 The effect of varying the probability of the *q* item (low, medium or high) on the probability of selections of *q* and *not-q* cards in a reduced array selection task

Source: Oaksford and Chater (2007), reproduced by permission of Oxford University Press

probabilistic revolution in reasoning theory is a real one. It is not the exclusive province of Oaksford and Chater either, as mentioned at the start.

Evans and Over's suppositional theory

Evans and Over's (2004) theory is more recent than Oaksford and Chater's, but in some respects its origins in previous work can be traced back further in time. The two approaches share many common features, but also have distinct differences.

Both are centrally concerned with uncertainty in reasoning, focus on the conditional probability of *q* given *p* and make reference to the Ramsey test in explaining how it is that people draw conclusions using *If*. Evans and Over reach back to a long-neglected book chapter by Rips and Marcus (1977) as the starting point of their analysis. These authors emphasised the role of *suppositions* in conditional inference: we suppose *p*, and then decide how confidently to infer *q*. People are said to do this by computing prob(q|p), which means comparing the relative likelihoods of *p,q* and *p,¬q* under the supposition of *p*. (See Wason & Johnson-Laird, 1972, Chapter 8, for an outline of a suppositional argument that goes back even further.)

Thus, as Evans and Over put it, we commonly use *If* to express hypothetical thought. Conditional sentences therefore express uncertainty: when we say *If it has a black bar then it is a great tit,* we mean that it is a great tit with some probability that may or may not equal 1. We can also have different degrees of belief in the conditional itself, depending on the context in which it is uttered. For instance, when this bird sentence is used by someone looking at the feeders in their garden, we will be inclined to believe it; perhaps not with certainty, but with a high degree of confidence. We add the antecedent (the black marking) to our beliefs along with knowledge about the context (the garden) and, say, the speaker's knowledge of birds (look at all those bird books on their shelves), and judge that the consequent (it is a great tit) is probably true. But what if the same sentence is uttered by a child, at a waterfowl reserve, looking at all the ducks and waders? We now think it is unlikely that *q* fits with *p*, and so we judge that the conditional is (probably) untrue.

This aspect of thinking, assessing the probability of the conditional, is central to the Evans and Over theory. They point out, along with Oaksford and Chater, that the Ramsey test states that the probability of the conditional is equivalent to the conditional probability of *q* given *p*, or, to put it in technical terms, prob(If p then q) = prob(q|p). The importance of this equation lies in the fact that it can be used as a testable prediction and lined up against alternative predictions from other theories. The major alternative theory is the theory of mental models. Evans and Over have pitted their theory and mental models theory against each other in direct competition, to see how each describes the data obtained from experiments in which people are asked to evaluate their belief in conditional statements, so in what follows I shall refer to their critique of the models theory alongside their own (this critique is set out in detail in Evans & Over, 2004; Evans, Over & Handley, 2005; Handley, Evans & Thompson, 2006; and Over, Hadjichristidis, Evans, Handley & Sloman, 2007). They give conceptual arguments against the models theory of conditionals as well as experimental data.

First, a bit of earlier evidence. Flip back to Chapter 3 and the section on truth-table tasks. Long ago, it was found that when people were asked to generate or evaluate instances that made a conditional true or false, they tended to ignore, or regard as irrelevant, instances where *p* was false; in the bird example, these would be birds without black bars (Johnson-Laird & Tagart, 1969). Wason and Johnson-Laird (1972) called this the 'defective truth table'. It is consistent with the suppositional theory, because there is no place for the *not-p* items in the conditional probability formula. This observation is important when we make the comparison between the suppositional theory and mental models theory, because the *not-p* items do play an important role in the models theory. In the previous chapter, it was explained that the models theory proposes that *If p then q* has an initial representation of *p,q* together with an implicit model, signified by three dots. This implicit model takes us to the *not-p* items when we need them, for instance when attempting the MT inference. Thus, for mental models theory, the conditional is true when *not-p* or *q* is true, and false in the case of *p* and *not-q*. This, say Evans and Over, means that the basic conditional in mental models theory is the material implication conditional of formal logic (see Chapter 3).

So let us see what happens when people are asked directly to judge the probability of the conditional, and how the two theories deal with the data. This was first reported by Evans, Handley and Over (2003a) and, in one of those strange scientific coincidences, simultaneously and independently in the same journal by Oberauer and Wilhelm (2003). In one experiment, Evans et al. gave people a problem about packs of cards, like this:

> A pack contains cards that are either yellow or red, and have either a circle or a diamond printed on them. In total there are:
>
> 1 yellow circle
>
> 4 yellow diamonds
>
> 16 red circles
>
> 16 red diamonds
>
> How likely is the following claim to be true of a card drawn at random from the pack?
>
> If the card is yellow then it has a circle printed on it:
>
> Very unlikely   1 2 3 4 5   Very likely

The proportions of cards specified contain the information you need to compute prob(If p then q). Three ways of doing this have already been outlined, and can be summarised as: the defective truth-table model (DTT), where you only consider *p,q*; the material conditional/mental models model (MC), where you consider *p,q and ¬p,q and ¬p,¬q*; and the conditional probability model (CP), where you consider the relative proportions of *p,q* and *p,¬q*. Stated formally:

$$\text{prob(DTT)} = \text{prob(pq)}$$

$$\text{prob(MC)} = \text{prob(pq)} + \text{prob(¬pq)} + \text{prob(¬p¬q)}$$

$$\text{prob(CP)} = \text{prob(pq)} \div [\text{prob(pq)} + \text{prob(p¬q)}]$$

Now we can relate these formulae to the numbers of coloured cards, and predict from each one whether the target conditional, *If the card is yellow then it has a circle printed on it*, should be judged as likely or unlikely. There are 37 cards mentioned, of which only 1 is a *p,q* item, so prob(pq) = 1/37. For prob(MC), you add up the yellow circle and all the red items, so prob(pq) + prob(¬pq) + prob(¬p¬q) = 1 + 16 + 16 = 33/37. For prob(CP), the *not-p* items (the red ones) are ignored, so prob(CP) = 1/[1 + 4] = 1/5. The defective truth table, prob(DTT), therefore predicts that the conditional should be judged as very unlikely; mental models, prob(MC), predicts that it should be judged as very likely, and the suppositional theory, prob(CP), makes a prediction between these extremes.

Using a variety of manipulations – varying the card numbers (which changes the computations in the formulae and the resulting probability predictions) – Evans et al. (and Oberauer & Wilhelm) found no evidence for prob(MC) at all. Overall, responses tended to be split almost evenly between CP (about 50% of people) and DTT (43%). This latter response might be explainable by the mental models theory, recalling its proposal that people initially represent just the *p,q* case explicitly (Girotto & Johnson-Laird, 2004). However, the theory states that they also represent the implicit model (the three dots), so that should have had some effect on probability judgment, but it did not. And the models theory has no way to predict the prob(CP) responses (see Evans & Over, 2004, and Evans et al., 2005, for more on this argument about the model theory; also Oberauer, Geiger, Fischer & Weidenfeld, 2007, who confirm the two response patterns).

The prob(pq) responses initially puzzled Evans and Over, with its implication that these people – university students – were apparently incapable of hypothetical thought. However, there is another important aspect of the suppositional theory. It relies on knowledge to feed the assessments people make of the likelihood of *q* or *not-q* given *p*. In a later study, they moved away from abstract tasks such as the one we have just been looking at; in that case, the 'knowledge' consisted of frequency information (1, 4, 16 and 16) and the task called for some mental arithmetic. Over et al. (2007) studied people's judgments of the probability of realistic causal conditionals, such as *If the cost of petrol increases then traffic congestion will improve*, using an adaptation of the truth-table task. This was described in Chapter 3: it involves listing all the possible logical cases of this sentence, and asking people to assign truth values to them. In the adaptation used by Over et al., people assigned the cases *probability* values, in percentages, with the requirement that they add up to 100. No explicit frequency information is used for this, only real-world knowledge and beliefs. So for instance, given the above sentence, participants would see:

Petrol price increases	Congestion improves	. . . .%
Petrol price increases	Congestion does not improve	. . . .%
Petrol price does not increase	Congestion improves	. . . .%
Petrol price does not increase	Congestion does not improve	. . . .%
		100%

These cases (*p,q*; *p,¬q*; *¬p,q*; *¬p,¬q*) can be used to derive conditional probability estimates. People can then be asked directly for their belief in the truth of the conditional sentence, and the two sorts of estimates can be compared. Once again, we can line up the predictions of the suppositional theory against its alternatives. This is done in a similar way to the original experiment with coloured cards. If people are judging the probability of the conditional by the conditional probability of q given p, then the former judgment should be predicted by $\text{prob}(q|p) = \text{prob}(pq) \div [\text{prob}(pq) + \text{prob}(p\neg q)]$. Mental models makes the MC prediction again: $\text{prob}(MC) = \text{prob}(pq) + \text{prob}(\neg pq) + \text{prob}(\neg p\neg q)$. In addition, as these were causal conditionals, Over et al. were able to assess whether people were using the Δp statistic (see Chapter 4), which is given by $\text{prob}(q|p) - \text{prob}(q|\neg p)$; if p causes q, then q should be more likely when p occurs than when it does not. Thus in this case, $\text{prob}(\text{If p then q})$ should be negatively related to $\neg p,q$, as well as positively related to p,q.

Once again, there was strong support for the conditional probability hypothesis and no support for the MC (mental models) hypothesis. There were some extra interesting features of this study as well. Firstly, there was much less evidence of people just using the conjunctive probability, (p,q), this time – so it does seem that this response was due to the abstract materials in the previous experiment, and that we can be reassured about students' ability to use hypothetical thinking. Secondly, in one experiment, direct judgments of the causal strength of the conditional were asked for. These turned out to be predicted by $\text{prob}(q|p)$ alone, just as the judgments of the probability of the conditional were: they were not related to $\text{prob}(q|\neg p)$ at all. So it seems that people in this experiment were not using Δp to judge causality. Thirdly, Over et al. also used counterfactual versions of these sentences (e.g. *If the cost of petrol had increased then traffic congestion would have improved*), asking people to think back to a past time. As we saw in Chapters 4 and 5, there is a close relation between causal and counterfactual thinking. The results were very similar to those for the causal and probability judgments: again, $\text{prob}(q|p)$ was a good predictor, while $\text{prob}(q|\neg p)$ was not. In this experiment, counterfactuals were thus treated in a similar way to other kinds of conditional, rather than in a different way, as Byrne (see Chapter 5) proposed.

Finally, the suppositional theory offers a way out of those pesky illusory inferences, described in the previous chapter. Here are the two sentences again:

1   If there is a king in his hand, then there is an ace.
2   If there is not a king in his hand, then there is an ace.

One is true and one is false; can there be an ace in the hand? You felt strongly that there had to be an ace in the hand, and yet this is a logical impossibility. It is not a probabilistic impossibility though. Firstly, consider that under the suppositional theory a false conditional is one where q is not likely when p is assumed, so you believe *If p then not q* instead. Also, remember that *not-p* cases are thought irrelevant when assessing a conditional's truth. Now, suppose there is a king and an ace in the hand: then sentence 1 is true and sentence 2 (which states *not-p*) does not apply. And if there is not a king and there is an ace, the position is reversed: sentence 2 is true and sentence 1 does not apply. In the two possible hands where there is no ace, one rule is false and the other does not apply. So suppositional reasoners should say either that there is an ace or that you cannot tell. This is what most people do. Characterising these conclusions as illusory thus depends on assuming that the conditionals are logical, material conditionals (see Handley et al., 2006). Moreover, if you reason suppositionally, there is no way you can believe the original instruction: that one sentence is true while the other is false.

It may seem from all this that suppositional theorists oppose the whole idea of reasoning by mental models, but this is not the case, as you will see if you read the references cited in this section. Evans and Over and their colleagues do believe in mental models, but not the two-valued, true/false mental models in the Johnson-Laird theory. The problem, as they see it, is that there is nothing in between true and false in formal logic or the Johnson-Laird models (the law of excluded middle), and so the models theory struggles to deal with models that are more or less likely (recall the problem of counterfactual closeness, raised in Chapter 5). Mental models theorists do have an account of people's probability judgments (see Johnson-Laird, Legrenzi, Girotto, Legrenzi & Caverni, 1999), but it depends on proportions of models that are either there or not there. The models themselves are not graded in terms of likelihood.

You would not expect the mental models theorists to take this criticism lying down, and of course they have not. Johnson-Laird (2010) mounts a robust defence of his theory, using a range of arguments and examples. Most importantly, given the centrality of the point in Evans and Over's critique, he rejects the equivalence between the mental models conditional and the material conditional that they attribute to it. This is because of modulation: semantic and pragmatic. Both were dealt with in the previous chapter; semantic modulation is the more important one in this case, because it adds information to even basic, abstract conditionals, such as temporal information (e.g. *If p happens then q happens next*) or spatial information (e.g. *If p goes here then q goes there*), both of which mean that the conditional is not necessarily true just because *p* and *q* are true. For instance, *If you play rugby then you have a broken nose* is not necessarily true just because you play rugby and you have a broken nose; it could have been broken some other way. Secondly, Johnson-Laird does not reject the idea that people reason using suppositions or the Ramsey test; instead he proposes that this is but one reasoning strategy among many. And as we saw, there is evidence in Evans and Over's experimental results for different reasoning patterns.

Other attempts have been made to reconcile the two accounts. Pierre Barrouillet, a mental models theorist, and his colleagues (Barrouillet & Gauffroy, 2010; Barrouillet, Gauffroy & Lecas, 2008) point to the difference between reasoning *from* a sentence assumed to be true about the possibilities that are consistent with that sentence, and reasoning *about* the truth of a sentence from stated possibilities. Mental models researchers tend to study the former, while suppositional theorists concern themselves with the latter. Barrouillet admits that mental models theory does not handle judgments about the probability of the conditional well, and suggests that this situation would be improved if the theory acknowledged that only a possibility that *makes* the conditional true will be represented explicitly. This is the *p,q* case, and that alone will be considered, using the Ramsey test, when evaluating the truth of the sentence. The *not-p* cases are *compatible* with the sentence, and tend to be listed as such, but do not make it true. Therefore, this revised mental models theory proposes that people will compute prob(q|p) and not prob(MC) when evaluating the conditional. However, there still remains the fundamental difference between the two approaches, emphasised by Evans and Over and restated by Oberauer and Oaksford (2008), that probabilistic explanations allow that mental models can have probability values in between complete certainty and uncertainty, whereas the models theory cannot.

The suppositional theory is part of a wider theoretical structure developed by Evans since the 1970s, in which there is a difference between people's initial responses to a problem and the kinds of thinking that they do when they have to work a problem out. For the final part of this chapter, we therefore turn to the proposal that we use two kinds of thought processes when we engage in thinking and reasoning. This is a deep proposal about the way the mind works, and we shall come across it again and again in the rest of the book.

The dual process theory

Much of the research on conditional reasoning reviewed in this chapter and the two previous ones shows that when we think about *If*, we are very strongly influenced by the meaning of the terms in the sentence, plus the connection between them (its content), and by the circumstances in which it is used (its context). Linguists call the latter aspect of language use *pragmatics*, and you have seen this term used by psychologists, such as the mental models theorists. The pragmatics of a reasoning problem seem to be computed by the mind directly and effortlessly (Stenning & van Lambalgen, 2008a, 2008b). Thus when you encounter a conditional in an ordinary piece of speech or writing, you are hardly aware of the properties and processes set out above.

Using a conditional to reason with is something else again, however. This can seem much more like hard work, to the extent that sometimes, as we have seen, people can simply give up. Sometimes, however, an inference seems effortless. Take the modus tollens inference. We have seen that this is not made as often as it logically should be, when you have to reason about letters and numbers or other such unrelated items. But the monkey's uncle conditional makes the inference not just easy but obvious. The difference is in the pragmatics: the consequent is patently absurd and so you are led to infer the falsity of the antecedent; that this is the clear goal of the conversation is what makes it obvious.

However, pragmatics can lead us into illogical temptation. For instance, suppose I tell you about my lovely classic convertible sports car, which you know I have to look after carefully and keep out of the weather as much as possible. I tell you that *If it's summertime, then I take the E-type out* (I wish). You will readily infer that at other times of the year I keep it garaged. But that, of course, is an invalid DA inference. Pragmatically, though, it is quite all right: why would I state the conditional in the first place if it were true that I took the car out all year round? However, in reasoning experiments, people do not accept the DA inference as readily as this. This is similar to the Gricean use of 'some' in everyday language to imply 'but not all', in contrast to its logical use where it includes 'all' as a possibility (see Chapter 2).

Such observations imply that there are two kinds of process going on here: an effortless pragmatic process and a harder reasoning process. We don't just have to rely on intuitive examples, however: there has been an increasing accumulation of evidence for these dual processes for well over 30 years. The name of Jonathan Evans once again features prominently in this research, so I shall first focus on two areas with which he has been associated: conditional reasoning and syllogistic reasoning. Other theorists have also been active in developing the theory, and I shall introduce their ideas and the more recent versions of the theory as we go along.

Dual processes in the selection task

In the last two chapters, a phenomenon called *matching bias* was referred to: the tendency to focus just on the items mentioned in the conditional statement. In the selection task, this was used to explain why it was that people tended to select the *p* and *q* cards and ignore the *not-p* and *not-q* cards. They do so when the target sentence reads *If p then not q* as well. In this case, they are getting the task logically right, whereas with an ordinary *If p then q* sentence it is logically wrong.

Do people really have logical insight when a negative is used but no insight without it? How could we tell? Why not ask them? That was the strategy used by Wason and Evans (1975). In earlier research, Wason had used people's verbal reports to confirm the idea that there were different states of insight into the selection task, and that choosing the *p, not-q* combination was the result of complete logical insight (Goodwin & Wason, 1972). The matching bias findings spell trouble for this idea, as Wason immediately conceded (Evans, 2004): they imply that logical insight can be turned on and off like a tap, simply by wielding negatives.

Wason and Evans gave people the abstract version of the selection task with *If p then q* and *If p then not q* sentences, and asked them to explain their choices. Half had the affirmative rule first and half had the negative rule first (so it was a nicely counterbalanced within-subject design). As matching bias would predict, people tended to select the *p* and *q* cards with both forms of the conditional. Their testimonies were very revealing. If a person selected *p* and *q* with the affirmative sentence, they tended to say that they had made this choice so as to prove it true. If they made the same choice with the negative sentence, they tended to say it was because they were seeking to prove it false. This was often the same person, remember – that was the advantage of using the within-subject design. A further blow against the insight theory came from the fact that the people who got the negative version first, and got it right, were no better at the affirmative version than the people who got the affirmative version first. If the negative task promoted insight, it should have helped with the simpler sentence, surely.

Wason and Evans therefore proposed that people's choices and the explanations they provided for them derived from two fundamentally different cognitive processes. The choices were determined by linguistic cues to relevance: the *If*-heuristic (an *If* sentence is primarily concerned with *p*) and the *Not*-heuristic (negations are still primarily concerned with what is being negated, e.g. *not-q* is still about *q*), later renamed the matching-heuristic. The explanations, on the other hand, were post hoc rationalisations: it was as if people had observed their own behaviour and thought to themselves, 'Why must I have done that?' Note, by the way, that these explanations are actually logically accurate: the *p,q* instance does verify a conditional, and the $p, \neg q$ instance does falsify it. Evans (1984, 2006) went on to develop a detailed account of these processes, called the *heuristic–analytic theory*. We shall consider it in more detail after the next case, which Evans (2007a, 2010; Evans & Over, 2004) still regards as giving some of the strongest evidence for dual processes.

Belief bias in syllogistic reasoning

If you want to refresh your memory about syllogisms, go back to Chapter 2. Then look at these arguments, and in each case note down whether you judge it valid or invalid:

1   All the athletes are healthy
    Some healthy people are wealthy
    Therefore, some of the athletes are wealthy
2   All the monks are men
    No monks are married
    Therefore, some men are not married
3   All the men are healthy
    Some healthy people are women
    Therefore, some of the men are women
4   All the monks are men
    No monks are women
    Therefore, some men are not women

You are quite likely to think that 1 and 2 are valid, while 3 and 4 are not. If so, you have fallen prey to belief bias. Both 1 and 2 have conclusions that you probably agree with: it is factually true that some athletes are healthy and that some men are unmarried. Arguments 3 and 4 are different: their conclusions seem either absurd (3) or strange (4). However, there is a trick here: 1 and 3 have the same structure, as do 2 and 4. You know that the logical validity of an argument is to do with structure, not content, and of course when an argument is valid, true premises must lead to a true conclusion. So if 1 is valid, then 3 should be too; ditto 2 and 4. In fact 1 and 3 are invalid, while 2 and 4 are valid (see Chapter 2 for how to verify this).

Research on belief bias in syllogistic reasoning goes back a very long time, to Wilkins (1928), a paper that is still often cited. However, many of the older studies were not soundly designed. It was not until the 1980s that experiments that meet the proper standards of experimental design were reported. The classic pattern of data, which has been replicated many times (see Klauer, Musch & Naumer, 2000), was provided by Evans, Barston and Pollard (1983) and is given in Table 6.1. They gave people sets of arguments of the same structure (No ..., Some ...; Therefore some ... are not), with contents designed to produce believable and unbelievable conclusions, such as *Some addictive things are not cigarettes* (believable) and *Some cigarettes are not addictive* (unbelievable). In Table 6.1, you can see what happened. Firstly, the valid conclusions were accepted more than the invalid conclusions; secondly, the believable conclusions were accepted more than the unbelievable. However, thirdly, the effect of believability was much stronger on the invalids: belief and logic interacted.

Table 6.1 The belief bias effect in syllogistic reasoning, with data from three experiments in Evans et al. (1983)

	Valid	*Invalid*	*Overall*
Believable	89	71	80
Unbelievable	56	10	33
Overall	73	41	

Note: Data show the percentage of arguments accepted

Several explanations for these effects have been put forward in the literature (see the reviews by Klauer et al., 2000, and Morley, Evans & Handley, 2004). I shall not go through them in detail, but focus on the development of the one that relates to the dual process theory. This explanation was introduced by Evans et al. (1983) and was called the *selective scrutiny* theory. It proposes that, when asked to evaluate a complete argument such as the examples above, people zero-in on the conclusion, accepting the argument if it is believable and only going on to do some actual reasoning if it is unbelievable.

However, although this makes intuitive sense, there are problems. First, of course, is the fact that there is an effect of logic with believable conclusions: the valid arguments are accepted more than the invalid arguments. So clearly there must be some reasoning going on here as well. Secondly, the selective scrutiny theory makes a prediction about response time. It suggests that there are two processes operating, belief and reason, and that only one is used with believable arguments but both are used with unbelievable arguments. This in turn implies that responses to the believables will be quicker. However, when this prediction has been tested in experiments, it has not been confirmed (Ball, Phillips, Wade & Quayle, 2006).

To accommodate these and other belief bias findings, the theory was updated by Evans, Handley and Harper (2001; see also Evans, 2007a) to the *selective processing* theory. The theory put forward by Klauer et al. (2000), based on the Johnson-Laird mental models theory, is similar to this; both refer to mental models. Figure 6.6 shows the structure of the updated theory. The two processes operating in belief bias experiments are the *default* response (a response that happens unless something stops it) and the *analytic* (reasoning) response. So if someone is confronted with a believable conclusion, they will accept it unless they do some thinking; with an unbelievable conclusion, they will reject it. However, they might detect the conflict between belief and logic (the effect of logic on believable conclusions shows that they do, at least sometimes), and think about it. This thinking, importantly, is also influenced by belief: if you are dealing with a believable conclusion, you will search for a mental model that supports it, whereas if you are dealing with an unbelievable conclusion, you will try to find a model that refutes it; either way, you are seeking to confirm the conclusion that belief has already supplied you with. Since valid conclusions only have one possible model, there is not much room for belief to have any further influence, but invalid conclusions have models that both support and refute them, and so belief will have more of an effect

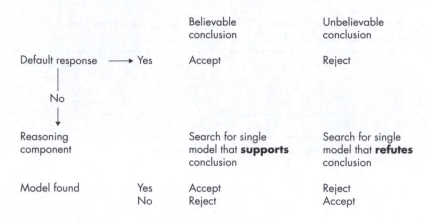

Figure 6.6 The selective processing theory of belief bias
Source: Adapted from Evans et al. (2001)

here – hence the belief by logic interaction, with the greatest effect on invalid unbelievable arguments. The lack of effects on response time is explained by the proposal that people only look for a single model in each case.

Heuristic and analytic processes

Faced with these kinds of data from his own experiments, Evans (1984, 1989, 2006) introduced the *heuristic–analytic theory*. It was designed to account for what happened in studies of reasoning, but it turns out that dual process ideas have been introduced in a wide range of psychological areas of study and can be traced back over the centuries, to the ancient Greek philosophers. This has only been realised quite recently. I shall spare you a blow-by-blow account of the development of dual process theories in all these eras and areas, and instead go from the original outline to the current state of play.

The general dual process theory is a very current aspect of psychology and is evolving all the time. For recent reviews from a reasoning perspective, go to: Evans (2003) for a nice short panorama; Evans (2004) for a first-person account of how the theory developed; Evans (2008) for a more detailed review and an extensive list of references to back it up; and Evans and Frankish (2009) for a wide-ranging survey of both psychological and philosophical aspects from 20 contributors. Evans (2010) has also written an account for a non-specialist readership. Evans has been strongly influenced by Keith Stanovich in his dual process theorising, and it will also be worth reading several works by Stanovich (1999, 2004, 2009a, 2009b; Stanovich & West, 2000; Stanovich, West & Toplak, 2010). We shall return to this theory in detail in Chapter 10, and at various points along the way.

The two forms of thinking were originally labelled Type 1 and Type 2 and referred, respectively, to non-logical and logical influences, competing to determine reasoning responses. The term 'dual process' was introduced in the Wason and Evans paper, and referred to non-logical factors such as matching bias competing in parallel with a logical rationalising process. In the heuristic–analytic theory, this structure was changed to a serial one: the heuristic processes were said to operate before the analytic. Heuristic processes select information as relevant to the problem, and this information is then operated on by the analytic processes. We have seen this idea applied to the selection task above: with the abstract task, there are the If- and matching-heuristics, both of which are linguistic cues to relevance. Heuristic processes can arise from personal knowledge as well as language, and so content can also influence reasoning. As Evans detailed in his 1989 book, a wide range of effects and biases can be explained in this way, since relevance cueing can overlook information that should, logically, be attended to (e.g. the *not-q* card in the selection task) and recruit information that is logically irrelevant, such as belief in a conclusion.

Some novel predictions were derived from the theory. For instance, Evans, Clibbens and Rood (1996) proposed that matching bias should be removed if the items in a reasoning problem used explicit rather than implicit negation, because all the items would match. This is because an explicit negation involves *not* attached to the item being denied, e.g. *If it has a black bar then it is not a blue tit. Great tit* would be an implicit negation of *blue tit*. Evans et al. (1996) used the abstract selection task, with items such as *not an A* and *not a 4* as negations of the items in sentences such as *If there is an A on one side then there is a 4 on the other side*, instead of, say, *B* and *5*. Matching bias completely disappeared.

However, Stahl, Klauer and Erdfelder (2008) found that matching bias was reduced but not eliminated in a replication study. They had vastly greater numbers of participants in their web-based study (group sizes of over 300) compared to Evans et al.'s 32, and concede that the effect of logic in the explicit condition, although still there, is very weak. They attribute the changes in responses between the implicit and explicit conditions to a change in participants' test strategies: they are reasoning, but differently. Thus they depart from Evans' dual process explanation. It is possible that there are individual differences here, with some people basing the responses on Type 1 processes whereas others, a minority, use their Type 2 and reason about the problem. Bear in mind that with a web-based study such differences are likely to be greater than they are with a typical student sample. We shall go further into the role of individual differences below and in Chapter 10.

In the same year, Evans (1996) used a novel task to test the heuristic–analytic theory. People were given selection tasks on a computer, and had to use the mouse to indicate which cards they chose. They were instructed to point the cursor at the cards as they thought about them, and then click on the ones they chose. Evans predicted that people would spend more time looking at cards they ended up selecting, owing to the involvement of the Type 2 rationalisation process only with them, and they did.

Following criticism of this method from Roberts (1998), the much more reliable method of eye-movement monitoring was used by Ball, Lucas, Miles and Gale (2003). Their results also confirmed Evans' predictions. Lucas and Ball (2005) went back to the Wason and Evans procedure of collecting participants' verbal reports, using a more detailed experimental design, and again confirmed the theory (they interpret their findings as also favouring Oaksford and Chater's information gain theory; see above).

Dual processes and dual systems

In the 1990s, dual process theory developed considerably, under the influence of other theorists as well as Evans. Evans and Over (1996) expanded the treatment of Type 1/heuristic and Type 2/analytic processes into the idea of *implicit* and *explicit* thinking processes. Implicit processes include all aspects of knowledge and perception that are relevant to the task at hand, and so would include, from the literature reviewed so far, aspects such as conclusion belief and Gricean implicatures in syllogistic reasoning, 'invited inferences' such as the DA and MT examples above in conditional reasoning, modulation of mental models (see Chapter 5) and the probabilistic effects on conditional reasoning and the selection task described by Oaksford and Chater.

Contemporary with this development was a paper by Sloman (1996), which reviewed a wide range of literature from within and outside the psychology of reasoning and put forward the idea that there were two *systems* of reasoning, which he called associative and rule-based; the resemblance to Evans' scheme, which Sloman cites, is clear. Sloman's theory proposes what Evans (2007b) calls a *parallel-competitive* structure: two processes competing for control of thought and response. An even more wide-ranging review was provided, however, by Stanovich (1999; Stanovich & West, 2000). Stanovich includes not only Evans' and Sloman's ideas, but dual process theories from across psychology, including from personality (e.g. Epstein, Pacini, Denes-Raj & Heier, 1996) and perception (e.g. Shiffrin & Schneider, 1977). Stanovich adopts Sloman's terminology and groups the various types of thought proposed by these theorists under two no-nonsense headings: System 1 and System 2.

Stanovich provides a table of attributes of these two systems, along with a list of the theories he reviewed in deriving it. An elaborated version of the attribute portion is given in Evans' (2008) recent review and contains many aspects that I shall not be talking about here, so Table 6.2 adapts the condensed versions given by Evans (2009) and Frankish and Evans (2009); similar tables can be found in most recent articles in this area. We can work through this table and discuss its features in turn. Some of them have already been dealt with and some overlap.

The first four rows show attributes that have already been mentioned, and the fifth (Intuitive–Reflective), uses terms that appear in various theories but not those mentioned so far. Intuition has become a hot research topic in the field of decision making recently, so we shall return to it, along with dual process ideas in that area, in Chapter 9. It is related to the Unconscious–Conscious distinction that comes next. System 1 processes tend to take place outside conscious awareness: we are often aware *that* we have responded in some way but not *how* we have done so (as the participants' verbal reports in the matching bias experiments show), but when we have to work something out deliberately we can report on the process. This relates to the next two rows (Automatic–Controlled; Fast, parallel–Slow, sequential): we can monitor and influence our deliberative reasoning, but not our intuitions. Thus we can use language only with System 2 processes, both as a means of thinking and to make verbal reports.

The next dimension, Contextualised–Abstract, is prominent in Stanovich's dual system theory and has become widely influential. It relates to the aspect of

Table 6.2 Typical properties of the two systems in dual system theories of thinking

System 1	System 2
Implicit knowledge	Explicit knowledge
Belief-based, pragmatic reasoning	Logical reasoning
Associative	Rule-based
Intuitive	Reflective
Unconscious/preconscious	Conscious
Automatic	Controlled
Fast, parallel	Slow, sequential
Not linked with language	Linked with language
Contextualised	Abstract
High capacity	Low capacity
Independent of working memory	Depends on working memory
Not correlated with intelligence	Correlated with intelligence
Evolutionarily old	Evolutionarily recent
Shared with animals	Distinctively human

Source: Evans (2009) and Frankish and Evans (2009)

System 1 that is to do with belief. According to Stanovich, we are prone to a *fundamental computational bias*: the tendency to see everything in its context, particularly in the light of our existing beliefs. However, in many situations, he argues, we need to decontextualise and reason according to the form of the problem in front of us, not just its content and context. This, of course, is what formal logic tells us to do. Decontextualisation is a prime System 2 activity. The belief bias effect discussed above is an obvious example of the bias, and there are many more in the areas of judging risks and making decisions, which we shall review in later chapters.

This override function makes the Stanovich theory an example of what Evans (2007b) calls a *default-interventionist* theory: we tend to respond according to System 1 until provoked to override this response, for instance by instructions to reason logically or the detection of a conflict between possible solutions. This had been shown in an early study by Epstein, Lipson, Holstein and Huh (1992). They studied counterfactual closeness (see Chapter 5). For instance, consider two people who each miss their flights because they wasted time on the way to the airport and were then held up through no fault of their own; one misses it by five minutes, one by half an hour. Who feels worse? Almost everyone says the near-misser. When Epstein, himself a pioneering dual process theorist, and colleagues told participants to set their feelings aside and think rationally, this effect was greatly reduced.

There is an aspect of this dimension that has been extensively researched by Stanovich and his colleagues: a link with cognitive ability (i.e. intelligence). Given that abstract, logical thinking depends on the cognitive resources that a person has available, we should find that people higher in intelligence are more likely to provide the logical answer to a problem when this answer depends on System 2. System 2 is the kind of thought that we acquire through education and effort, whereas System 1 is given to us through our evolutionary history or direct experience.

Stanovich (1999) reports a set of large-scale studies on various reasoning problems that confirm this link between System 2 and intelligence. For instance, people at the high end of the intelligence scale are more likely to select the *p, not-q* combination of cards with the abstract, indicative selection task. This response depends on System 2; System 1 is telling us to select *p, q*. Now, ask yourself what you would predict about the relation between intelligence and the *deontic* task. You will recall from Chapter 4 that this is the version that gives people rules to reason about, such as *If you drink beer then you must be over 18*. You will also recall that people usually get such tasks right: they look for the under-age drinker. This response is cued by both System 1 (your knowledge of the world) and System 2 (a logical understanding of the problem). So there should be no link with intelligence, and that is exactly what Stanovich's research showed. This differential prediction is powerful evidence for the two systems of thought.

The final two rows in Table 6.2 refer to an aspect that has not been mentioned so far but figures prominently in the writings of many dual system theorists: evolution. Few people these days would deny that animals have cognitive processes, but far fewer would accept that animals have all the cognitive processes that humans have. The ability to respond to problems on the basis of instinct and learning are System 1 abilities and we can share them with other animals. What is distinctively human about System 2, though, is that it enables us to engage in *hypothetical thinking* (Evans, 2007a, 2009): we can imagine alternative worlds, ones that may yet exist, that might have but did not come about (counterfactual thinking; see the previous two chapters) or that could never be (fantasy worlds), work through their implications and make decisions from what we infer. We can make predictions and propose explanations, test them and criticise them. No other animal can do this, or talk about it (Pinker, 1994).

Dual minds

Dual system theory has recently developed into 'two minds' theory: the proposal that we have a mind at war with itself (Stanovich, 2004) or two minds in one brain (Evans, 2003). Evans (2009, 2010) now refers to the old mind and the new mind, following the evolutionary argument, and cites neuroimaging research indicating that these functions are associated with different brain areas. For instance, it has long been known that the frontal lobes are involved in executive functions – those involved in controlling and planning (Norman & Shallice, 1986). Evans identifies these as 'new mind' functions (see Table 6.2). These brain areas are thought to be fairly recent, in evolutionary terms.

He has also reverted to talking about Type 1 and Type 2, rather than System 1 and System 2. This is a result of the huge wave of interest in this kind of theory, and the resulting fractionation in the systems' descriptions. The 'Systems' terminology implies something rather more integrated, and so Evans urges us to drop it. For the final section in this account of dual process theory, I shall outline these new developments.

They began with Stanovich (2004), who proposed that we replace the idea of System 1 with TASS: The Autonomous Set of Subsystems. We have already seen that there is a wide range of cognitive activities that can be tagged as System 1: instinctive responses, intuitions, belief biases, linguistic cueing, learned habits, skills, and so on. These all share features in common, such as not being dependent on working memory, running in parallel and operating unconsciously, but they seem (and indeed are) quite different in character. They also have different origins. For instance, we learn conditioned responses much as any organism does, by reinforcement (reward and punishment); acquiring a belief system, such as you are doing explicitly now in your studies and have done implicitly through your life experiences, is not the same thing. Belief is an interesting aspect of TASS, because it is not an aspect that we share with animals (such exceptions being another reason for steering away from a unitary System 1). Does your cat *believe* that metal cylinders contain food, or, when it goes crazy as you reach for the can opener, is it simply responding to the start of a sequence of events that tends to end in a filled bowl? You believe it, you can reflect on that belief and you can discuss it with others – as I am doing with you now.

'Autonomous' is a key word in TASS. It refers to the property that these subsystems have of being able to operate in a self-contained way, in two respects: they can be separate from other parts of TASS, and they can determine thought and behaviour without any System 2 involvement. TASS subsystems can therefore be *modular*, in the sense that evolutionary psychologists use the term (see Chapter 4). However, TASS does not seem to include the kinds of heuristic processes that originally started off the development of the dual process theory over 30 years ago. Because of this, Evans (2009) argues for a fundamental split in Type 1 processes between heuristic processes and TASS. This is shown in Figure 6.7. The difference between them is that TASS processes influence behaviour directly, whereas heuristic processes serve up information for working memory, where it can be operated on by System 2. Evans (2009) goes on to propose a Type 3 process for

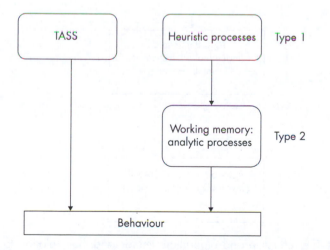

Figure 6.7 The two Type 1 processes and their route to control of behaviour
Source: Adapted from Evans (2009)

deciding whether to accept the output of TASS or whether to engage analytic reasoning.

Similar concerns motivate the proposal by Stanovich (2009a) to subdivide System 2 into two levels of processing, called the *algorithmic* and *reflective* minds. Stanovich reports research that shows two independent influences on people's ability to override TASS. We have already met one: intelligence. People high in cognitive ability are more likely to be able to override System 1/TASS and think analytically to a logical solution. However, Stanovich identified another factor that influences this, independent of intelligence: personality. Specifically, this is people's tendency towards actively open-minded thinking, or need for cognition. Stanovich calls these influences *thinking dispositions*. The reflective mind determines how likely you are to try to override TASS, while the algorithmic mind determines how efficiently you think once you have done so. This structure is shown in Figure 6.8. Note that Evans (2009), although accepting that there are these differences, does not accept that there needs to be a third-level 'mind'; rather, he regards them as aspects of System 2, the 'new mind'. We shall return to Stanovich's distinction in Chapter 10, since it raises a serious question about rationality.

If we have two minds in one brain, then you might expect to find evidence for them in how the brain actually works. To test that, we need to be able to look directly at the working brain. Fortunately, we have techniques available to us now,

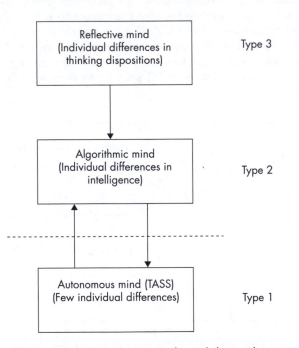

Figure 6.8 The reflective and algorithmic minds and their relation to the autonomous mind

Source: Stanovich (2009a), reproduced by permission of Oxford University Press

which simply did not exist until recently, that enable us to do this: brain scanning. It is possible to monitor the electrical and chemical action of the brain while a person is thinking. Since it has been known for at least 150 years that different parts of the brain are involved in different kinds of cognitive activity, we can look to brain research for evidence of different areas being involved in System 1 and System 2 thinking. Vinod Goel and his colleagues (De Neys & Goel, 2011; Goel, 2005; Goel, Buchel, Frith & Dolan, 2000; Goel & Dolan, 2003) provide us with just such evidence.

For instance, Goel et al. (2000) studied brain activity when people were given belief bias syllogisms (see above). You will remember that these can be divided into those where logic and belief are consistent (valid-believable, invalid-unbelievable) and those where they conflict (valid-unbelievable, invalid-believable). In several experiments, Goel et al. showed that, while the consistent problems produced activation in a left-hemisphere temporal area (at the side of the brain), the conflict problems produced activation in both left and right hemispheres, in an area known as the parietal system (at the top middle of the brain). They suggest therefore that System 1 responses are dealt with in the temporal area, while System 2 recruits activity from a different, and wider, area.

De Neys and Goel have gone on to show a very similar pattern with a different kind of thinking problem; judging probability using personality descriptions and base rates (see Chapter 1). Here, you can also have consistent and conflict forms, where the description and the base rates either both indicate the likely candidate, or point in different directions. This finding is important, since it shows that the earlier results were not just restricted to syllogistic problems, or even just to reasoning. It seems as if System 1 and System 2 are processed in different parts of the brain no matter which kind of thinking we are dealing with, just as the dual process theorists predict. It also shows that these two areas of thinking – deduction and probability judgment – may be closely related under the surface. Again, this is consistent with the message coming from recent research and theory. Vartanian and Mandel (2011) have collated a series of chapters on these and similar brain studies, of which De Neys and Goel's is one.

Just what triggers any switching from System 1 to System 2 is a topic of vigorous current research. Thompson (2009) argues for what she calls the *feeling of rightness* (FOR). The word 'feeling' is important here: it is an affective response, and we use the strength of that response in deciding whether or not to think more deeply about a problem. If the System 1 answer *feels* (not just seems) right to us, then we are unlikely to check it by System 2 thinking. The first belief bias syllogism above, about wealthy athletes, is an example of this: it just feels as if the conclusion must be right, and so we let it stand. But the conclusion is invalid.

The brain must be detecting conflicts in the output of the two systems somehow. Goel and Dolan (2003) found a 'conflict detection system' located in a precise area of the brain, the right dorsolateral prefrontal cortex. It is implicated not just in belief bias, the problem focused on here, but in a wide range of cognitive tasks where conflict detection is needed. People with damage to this brain area have trouble filtering out irrelevant information and are easily distracted (Purves et al., 2008). A nearby right-hemisphere area, the inferior frontal cortex, was also implicated in conflict detection in belief bias problems, by Tsuji and Watanabe

(2009, 2010). Tsuji and Watanabe used various manipulations to suppress the action of this brain area, and found that conflict detection was inhibited.

Such findings lend further strength to the 'two minds' perspective. However, Goel (2008) urges caution in interpreting theoretical claims made on the basis of neuroscience findings: they are complex and their implications are not always as clear-cut as they might seem. Despite this note of caution, these last sections show how active is the current development of the dual process theory of thought: it is one of the most exciting and appealing developments in recent cognitive psychology.

Not that the theory has carried all before it: critical voices have been heard. Prominent among them is Gerd Gigerenzer, whose work on probability we met in Chapter 1 and whose approach to decision making will be considered in later chapters. Kruglanski and Gigerenzer (2011) focus on one particular dimension often used to distinguish System 1 and System 2: the associative versus rule-based dimension. Continuing a line of critique opened by Gigerenzer and Regier (1996) in response to Sloman's dual process theory, they offer a range of evidence that this distinction cannot be maintained, because both System 1 and System 2 responses can be shown to depend on rules. However, Kruglanski and Gigerenzer do not cite Stanovich at all, and do not pay much attention to the other dimensions that dual process theorists appeal to. Gigerenzer is a firm advocate of the efficiency and effectiveness of simple, well-learned, intuitive rules in delivering judgments that can be at least as accurate as those produced by exhaustive System 2 thinking, and we shall return to this point of view in Chapter 9. It presents a serious challenge to the dual process perspective, and we shall return to the theory again, notably in Chapters 9 and 10. It presents a challenge to standard theories of decision making too, as we shall also see.

Summary

1   New paradigm theories of reasoning are those based on probability rather than two-valued logic.

2   Oaksford and Chater's Bayesian probabilistic theory of the Wason selection task recast it as a problem of information gain for belief revision rather than a logical hypothesis-testing task.

3   The theory has also been applied to conditional inference, and can explain most of the observed patterns of performance. To explain deontic reasoning, it adds the construct of utility alongside probability.

4   Evans and Over's suppositional theory explains conditional inference by proposing that people judge the probability of *If p then q* as being equivalent to the probability of *q* given *p*. From this, they compare judgments and find that they are better explained in these terms than by mental models.

5   The suppositional theory has also been used to explained causal reasoning and illusory inferences.

6   The dual process theory proposes that there are two types of thinking: Type 1, rapid and intuitive, and Type 2, slow and deliberative. It was originally developed to account for the reasons people gave for their responses in the selection task.

7   Belief bias in syllogistic reasoning is one of the central pieces of evidence for dual processes. People's belief in the truth of a syllogism's components can conflict with the logic of the problem. Responding according to belief is held to be a Type 1 process, while working out the logic is Type 2.

8   Dual process theories have been produced independently in a wide range of areas of psychology. Stanovich has proposed that propensity to use Type 2 thinking is linked to intelligence, and Evans argues that we have effectively two minds in one brain.

Hypothetical thinking: induction and testing

You decide to have a New Year break in Scotland, and find yourself in an agreeable hotel on the shores of Loch Ness. Heading out for an early-morning walk you peer through the mist, in the pre-dawn light, across the black waters of the lake, and there . . . Wait! What's that strange pattern of ripples disappearing round the headland? Could it be – the Monster? There's only one way to find out: you dash up the hill and look into the inlet. That's where the creature will be . . .

Many of the forms of thought that have already been dealt with in this book contribute towards the kinds of thinking that you would do in situations like this. You wonder what *caused* those ripples, you assess the *probabilities* of candidate causes, you engage in *conditional inference* to make predictions (If it's a monster, then it will be in the inlet). In this chapter we look at research that has studied other aspects of this set of cognitive activities. Producing a hypothesis to account for your observations (it's the Monster) is a facet of *induction*. Hypothesis testing, which we shall consider later in this chapter, is where you assess how well such conclusions stand up.

Induction

Induction and deduction

Induction is a very wide-ranging property of human thought, and probably of animal thought too (Holland, Holyoak, Nisbett & Thagard, 1986). We have seen some detailed accounts of how it operates in earlier chapters. Causal inference is usually inductive, as in the monster example above, or in accident investigations and other kinds of forensic work described in Chapter 4. Probability judgment is also inductive; indeed, it is one of the aspects of induction that has been most intensely studied. Other kinds of inference that have been reviewed are usually thought of as deductive. A deductive argument is one where the conclusion necessarily follows from the premises. An inductive argument leads to a conclusion that is plausible but not necessary (i.e. not certain), as in the monster story above: it could be a monster, but it might be something else. Let us look more closely at this contrast.

There are two possibilities when we compare the two forms of thought. One is that they are fundamentally different, and the other is that they are two aspects of essentially the same process. Logically and philosophically speaking, the differences between them are stark. Firstly, there is the question of certainty versus uncertainty when we draw conclusions. A deductively valid conclusion is by definition certain, as we have seen. Given true premises and a sound argument structure, you can be sure that the conclusion follows. For instance, suppose that we assume that these two premises are true (and plenty of people do assume this, if the websites are to be believed):

If there are unexplained patterns of ripples in Loch Ness, then there is a monster.
There are unexplained patterns of ripples in Loch Ness.

then we can be sure of the conclusion, because this is a modus ponens argument (see Chapter 3):

Therefore, there is a monster.

Such an argument does not prove the factual truth of the Loch Ness monster, of course: you cannot just assert a couple of premises and have done with it, case closed. Valid conclusions are not necessarily true. You have to *assume* the truth of the premises at the outset, and then the conclusion follows (see Evans, 2002, for a detailed analysis of the problems that this restriction poses for the study of reasoning, and the previous chapter for how new paradigm reasoning theory escapes from them). Assessing the likelihood that a premise such as the conditional above is factually true is a matter for inductive thinking. Monster fans might think inductively along these lines:

There are occasional unexplained ripple patterns in the waters of Loch Ness.
Not only that, but there are witness testimonies of strange apparitions.
Then there was that old picture of a neck and head appearing out of the water.
And what about that underwater photo of what looked a lot like a plesiosaur flipper?

Therefore, there is a monster in Loch Ness.

How sure can we be of this conclusion? This is what the 18th century Scottish philosopher David Hume called the *problem of induction*: the answer is that we can never be sure (see Sloman & Lagnado, 2005b). Hume held that causality was at the basis of all induction (see Chapter 4 for more on causality) and that causal knowledge was based on experience, not abstract reasoning. But experience alone cannot guarantee that the future will look like the past – it is perfectly possible for similar causes to have different effects – and so no inductive conclusion can be drawn with certainty. We shall return to causality below.

Induction is useful because it takes us from the known (the observations) to the unknown (the conclusion, or hypothesis), and so increases our knowledge and enables us to make predictions. The better we are at this, the more we have things under control. But it does so at a price: doubt. Deduction, by comparison, takes us from the known, or rather what we assume is known, to something else that can be known, the conclusion. It does not, therefore, increase our knowledge; a sound argument only makes explicit something that was implicit in the premises. That is where the conclusion's certainty comes from.

Johnson-Laird (1994) states this relation more formally, defining induction as 'any process of thought that increases the semantic information in its initial observations or premises' (p. 11). We have met the notion of semantic information before, in the sections on information gain approaches to syllogistic and conditional reasoning in Chapters 2, 4 and 6. A statement is informative to the extent that it is surprising; surprising statements have the greatest effect on reducing uncertainty. Another way of saying this is that informative statements rule out more possibilities as false. So if you conclude, on your walk along the shores of Loch Ness, that what you have seen was caused by a monster, you have ruled out all the alternative possibilities, such as that the ripples were caused by a fish, a submerged log or a scuba-diving prankster. Deductive conclusions, by contrast, do not rule out any more possibilities than the premises do, and hence deduction does not increase our knowledge.

It is for this reason that the contemporary American philosopher Gilbert Harman (1999) regards 'reasoning' as a term that should be reserved for induction, since only induction has the power to change belief; for Harman, there is no such thing as 'deductive reasoning', since no new knowledge comes from deduction. Induction is absolutely necessary to us and any animal with a stake in understanding the world and predicting future events, and it is difficult to see how we could do without it. But you get nothing for nothing, and our projections from the known to the not yet known come with a cautionary note attached: your inductive conclusions, about monsters, murder suspects, air crashes or anything else, are only ever provisional.

Hypothesis production clearly has elements of creativity about it: you produce a new idea, or at least adapt an old one, to account for some observations or statements. Creativity is still slightly mysterious when looked at directly, but psychologists always have indirect methods at their disposal when they come to study mysterious bits of mentality. When you produce a hypothesis, you scarcely ever do so in a psychological vacuum: you always operate against a background of constraints and conditions. Discovering what these are gets us closer to an understanding of the process.

The main constraint is *knowledge*. This is another way in which induction can be separated from deduction. It is possible to construct perfectly abstract deductive arguments, as we have seen in previous chapters. Indeed, one of the essential properties of a deductively valid argument is that the assessment of validity is independent of the content of the argument. However, there is no such thing as an abstract inductive argument. Induction is always about something. Much of the research effort that has gone into induction has been devoted to exploring how we use knowledge to derive conclusions. An important question about induction concerns which conclusions are produced: there is an infinite range of possibilities, since all inductive conclusions are probabilistic. But we usually hit on only a few, sometimes just one; if you are a true believer in the Monster, those ripples can mean only one thing. So a fruitful way into the riddle of induction is to consider the constraints that operate on it when knowledge is deployed.

This area was given its greatest impetus by a paper by Lance Rips in 1975. As with so many agenda-setting pieces of science, its impact was not immediate – it was only properly followed up in the 1990s, but the following up is still going on. In the next section, we shall outline the area that this paper kicked off, and then trace the findings that have resulted from the explosion of subsequent research.

Category-based induction

Most of our knowledge does not consist of single items or facts, but is organised into structured systems of concepts, categories and schemas. When reasoning inductively, we are therefore often concerned with *projecting* an attribute from one such schema to another: if an attribute is true of this item, will it also be true of that one? Rips (1975) recognised this central aspect of induction, and the research that followed up his work now dominates the area, as any recent survey will confirm (see Adler & Rips, 2008, section 4; Feeney & Heit, 2007; Heit, 2000; Sloman & Lagnado, 2005b). Thagard (2007) regards this aspect of induction as 'esoteric' (p. 230), but there is no doubt that it features in our real-world thinking, as in a nice example given by Feeney, Coley and Crisp (2010). Suppose there are two political parties in two different countries that you think stand for the same kinds of thing. If one party takes a certain position on taxation, say, how confident are you that the other party will adopt a similar stance?

In Rips' pioneering study, participants in two experiments were told about an imaginary island in which there were several species of bird (Expt. 1) or mammal (Expt. 2). They were told that all the members of one of these species were infected with a new kind of disease. They were then given the name of another of the species, and asked to estimate the proportions of each of the remaining species that they thought would contract the disease, on a percentage scale from 0 to 100. This is a measure of *argument strength*: a person's score tells you how confident they are in projecting the disease onto the unknown (the target species), given the known evidence (the given species). Subsequent papers have usually presented these arguments in this way:

1   Sparrows have disease X

   Robins have disease X

The really ingenious aspect of these experiments, the one that led to such an upsurge in research, was that Rips had previously rated the *similarity* of each species to each other, and to its superordinate category, bird or mammal. Sparrows and robins are quite similar, sparrows and ducks less so, and if you have to come up with examples of 'bird' you will think of sparrow and robin before you think of duck or hawk. Sparrows and robins are therefore more *typical* birds than are ducks and hawks.

Rips found that both these factors, similarity and typicality, influenced judgments of argument strength. The more similar were the premise item (above the line) and the conclusion item (below the line), as in the example above, the stronger the argument was judged to be. So when the conclusion above said Ducks instead of Robins, people judged that fewer of them would contract the disease: ducks are less similar to sparrows than robins are. Secondly, the more typical the premise item, the stronger the argument: people are more willing to project from sparrows than they are from hawks, say. Thirdly, a negative finding: typicality of *conclusion* item had no effect – people are as happy with Duck as with Robin as a conclusion category, at any given level of premise–conclusion similarity.

These, then, are the first constraints on the use of knowledge in induction: premise–conclusion similarity and premise typicality. More have been uncovered in further experimental research and theoretical development, as we shall now see.

Extensions and explanations

The Rips (1975) paper was the basis for the next most influential contribution to research and theory in this area: that of Osherson, Smith, Wilkie, Lopez and Shafir (1990). They built on and expanded Rips' work in several important ways, and introduced a formal theory that generated a range of novel predictions, 13 in all, for which they provided empirical evidence. The theory is called the *similarity-coverage theory*. Let us see firstly how it predicts and explains Rips' initial findings and then look at some new phenomena that it predicts.

We have already seen from Rips' work that an important influence on confidence in drawing inductive conclusions is similarity. The 'coverage' part of the Osherson theory comes from Rips' second finding: typicality. This referred to a superordinate category, which is birds in the above examples. A category such as this has some essential features and some peripheral features, an idea that goes back to Rosch (1973, 1978). Birds fly, build nests in trees, perch on branches, have high-pitched melodious songs, eat worms, and so on. A typical instance is one that shares many or all of these central features. For Osherson et al., argument strength is determined by the total amount of similarity between the lowest-level superordinate category of which both the premise and conclusion terms are members and the items themselves. This explains the typicality effect. Here is a simple additional factor that will give a further illustration of how the coverage principle works.

Rips (1975) used single-premise arguments, as we have seen with those involving birds above. Now see what happens when you add an extra premise, as Osherson et al. did:

2 Sparrows have disease X
Blackbirds have disease X

Robins have disease X

An extra premise increases the amount of coverage of the features in the super-ordinate category, and so people should rate this argument as being stronger than the original single-premise argument, and they do; perhaps you did too. This manipulation can be made more powerful by changing the typicality of the premises, as in:

3 Sparrows have disease X
Ducks have disease X

Robins have disease X

This argument tends to be rated as even stronger than the previous one. Osherson et al. called this the *premise diversity effect*: sparrows and ducks are relatively more diverse in their features than are sparrows and blackbirds, which are more similar to each other. So the sparrow–duck pair increases coverage. You can relate this principle to other aspects of inductive reasoning, such as the monster story we began with, or detective work: if all you have are witness reports about weird scenes or suspects from the same kinds of people – slightly strange men with woolly hats and binoculars, say – you will probably remain sceptical about monsters. But occasionally you hear of different kinds of people, such as police officers or military personnel, making such reports. Your degree of belief in the monster hypothesis is strengthened by a more diverse set of witnesses.

Diversity has limits in increasing argument strength, however: pushed too far, and it goes into reverse. Consider these two arguments, both from Osherson et al. (1990):

4 Crows secrete uric acid crystals
   Peacocks secrete uric acid crystals
   _____

   Birds secrete uric acid crystals

5 Crows secrete uric acid crystals
   Peacocks secrete uric acid crystals
   Rabbits secrete uric acid crystals
   _____

   Birds secrete uric acid crystals

The second set of premises is clearly more diverse than the first, and yet the first argument seems stronger than the second. According to Osherson et al., this is because the introduction of 'rabbits' has led to the argument becoming a 'mixed' argument, where it traverses the usual category boundaries that come with concepts such as 'birds'. This is a case of what they call a *non-monotonicity effect*; there are several. Monotonicity is where an extra premise from the same category is introduced, such as sparrows and blackbirds or ducks; non-monotonicity is where you veer off the track by having to think about a premise from another category, such as rabbits in the context of birds. The first increases argument strength, but the second reduces it.

There is a second aspect to this effect, which Osherson et al. also point out. Arguments with general conclusion categories, such as 'bird', tend to be less strong than arguments with more specific categories, such as 'garden bird': this is called the *conclusion specificity effect*. As Heit (2000) notes, this makes logical sense, since more general conclusions need more evidence to support them. More general categories also have a feature that had previously been found to affect induction: *variability*. 'Birds' is a more varied class of creatures than is 'garden birds': I never see peacocks, penguins or pelicans in my garden.

Nisbett, Krantz, Jepson and Kunda (1983) explored this factor using a different method from the one used by Rips and Osherson et al. Their participants imagined an expedition to an exotic island, where new minerals, birds and people had been discovered. Two properties of each were given, and the participants had to estimate which proportion of the total population of each item would possess these properties, depending on a sample of 1, 3 or 20 cases. Overall, people were as happy to project from 1 mineral sample as they were from 3 or 20, but they were less happy with birds. We know, of course, that one sample of a given mineral will be very much like another, but that birds may vary more (e.g. in terms of their plumage or behaviour). Most striking, however, were the results with the island tribe, called the Barratos. People's confidence in generalising from a given sample size depended on the feature in question. Participants were told that the Barratos people encountered (1, 3 or 20 of them) had brown skins, or were obese. How many of the rest of the population would be brown-skinned or obese? Skin colour was seen as a predictor that was almost as reliable as the properties of minerals, and it is easy to see why members of a single tribe on a small island would be thought to be fairly uniform in complexion. But obesity was treated very differently: in this case, sample size played a crucial role, so that people were reluctant to generalise from 1 large person, were more confident with 3 and were more confident still with 20 obese Barratos.

This chimes with what you learn in methodology courses: larger samples are more statistically reliable – and projecting from a sample to a population is exactly what you are doing when collecting and analysing research data. There is also an interesting social parallel, pointed out by Thagard and Nisbett (1982): people tend to generalise more readily about out-groups, of which they are not members, than in-groups, to which they belong. You know more about your in-group than you do about an out-group, and so the latter is less variable than the former: they're all the same, aren't they?

This set of effects does not exhaust all of those explored by Osherson and colleagues, and by successive later studies, but it will exhaust you if we carry on through the whole list. Refer to the recent survey by Feeney and Heit (2007), and to the original research papers, if you need more details. At this point, we shall go on to those phenomena that have a bearing on alternative explanations of induction.

Category-based induction without categories

Categories are central to our ability to think efficiently about the world, as we have seen: they enable us to treat different things as if they are the same, and that cuts down on the amount of work the mind has to do at any one time. But do we need categories for category-based induction? This paradoxical-sounding question was addressed by Steven Sloman (1993). He noted that by basing induction on categories, Osherson and his colleagues had to propose that whenever we attempt to generalise we are invoking, or creating from new, extra categories. Look at arguments 2 and 3 above: the lowest-level common category seems to shift when ducks come into view, and this process was explicitly specified by Osherson et al. with the non-monotonicity effects.

According to Sloman, this step is unnecessary: 'argument strength is, roughly, the proportion of features in the conclusion category that are also in the premises categories' (1993, p. 242). What he is proposing is that feature overlap is sufficient to determine argument strength, without the intervention of some common superordinate category. Sloman explains and extends the conclusion specificity effect on this basis: conclusion categories with fewer features should lead to stronger arguments than those with more features, since the fewer there are, the more likely it is that they will all be shared with the premise categories. Here is an illustration from Sloman. Consider these two arguments and see which you think is the stronger:

6 All collies produce phagocytes[1]

All Persian cats produce phagocytes

7 All collies produce phagocytes

All horses produce phagocytes

Argument 6 should seem stronger than argument 7. This is because people know more about horses than they do about Persian cats, and so there is less featural overlap with horses. This prediction was confirmed in an experiment.

In later work, Sloman (1998) demonstrated that feature-sharing could override categorical knowledge altogether, which is a strong refutation of the involvement of extra categories in inductive generalisation. Again, here is an example from his materials; judge for yourself which argument seems stronger:

8 Every individual body of water has a high number of seiches[2]

Every individual lake has a high number of seiches

9 Every individual body of water has a high number of seiches

Every individual reservoir has a high number of seiches

Sloman's participants made two interesting judgments here. Firstly, they judged argument 8 as stronger than argument 9. This is a typicality/feature-sharing effect: lakes are more typical examples of bodies of water than reservoirs are, and they share more features. Note that this is a conclusion typicality effect, which Rips originally found did not exist. Secondly, they did not always judge either argument to be perfectly strong. They should have, because they readily accepted that both lakes and reservoirs were bodies of water, and so what is true of bodies of water should be true of both lakes and reservoirs. This kind of argument, where there is a hidden premise, has a technical name: *enthymeme*. If you take the hidden premise and make it explicit, you turn an enthymeme into a syllogism (see Chapter 2) and the inference is then deductive:

10 All lakes are bodies of water

All bodies of water have a large number of seiches

All lakes have a large number of seiches

When Sloman did this, all his participants judged the argument to be perfectly strong, as indeed true deductions are. So similarity influenced judgments only when the argument's second premise, which specified category membership, remained implicit, which implies that category membership was not being used in the inductive form of the argument.

Findings such as this show that there is more than one way of going about inductive reasoning, and that the strategies people use may depend on the kind of material they are dealing with. This possibility has been noted since quite early on in the modern phase of induction research that began with Osherson et al. (1990).

For instance, Heit and Rubinstein (1994) looked more closely at the construct of similarity, which played such a prominent role in the research of Osherson et al. and of Rips before them: they asked, similarity with respect to what? Consider animals, the most popular characters in these studies. Animals can be similar to, and different from, each other on a number of dimensions: appearance, size, species, anatomy, behaviour, for instance. In an experiment, they asked people to project either an anatomical property (has a two-chambered liver) or a behavioural property (travels in a zigzag path) from bears to whales or from tuna fish to whales. With the anatomical property, the argument from bears to whales was stronger than the argument from tuna to whales. With the behavioural property, the opposite was found: now people were happier projecting from tuna to whales. Whales and bears are more similar biologically (they are both mammals, whereas tuna are not), but whales and tuna are more similar ecologically (they live in the sea, but bears do not).

Continuing this theme, Sloman (1994) gave people statements such as the following:

Many ex-cons/war veterans are hired as bodyguards.

Many ex-cons/war veterans are unemployed.

Participants rated the probability that these statements, by themselves, were true. The statements were then presented in arguments, like this:

11 Many ex-cons are hired as bodyguards

Many war veterans are hired as bodyguards

12 Many ex-cons are unemployed

Many war veterans are unemployed

He predicted, and found, that belief in the conclusion given the premise would be higher than its initial, unconditional degree of belief with arguments such as 11 but lower with arguments such as 12. Why? Because with argument 11 it is easy to think of a reason why both types of people might end up as bodyguards: they are tough men with experience of fighting. However, with argument 12, the reasons why an ex-con and a war veteran might be unable to find work are likely to be quite different. When explanations clash like this, degree of belief is weakened – an effect Sloman calls *explanation discounting*. Or, to put it another way, coherent explanations promote induction.

Reasoning inductively about explanations is what you would be doing if you found yourself in the story at the opening to this chapter. Producing explanatory hypotheses has a particular name, derived from the philosopher C.S. Peirce: *abduction*. And you can see from the two cases just given that abduction is, as Hume proposed over 200 years ago, inseparable from causal inference (which was previously reviewed in Chapter 4). As Johnson-Laird (2006, p. 182) puts it, 'people have a propensity for explanation'. We can't stop ourselves looking for them. This is another constraint on induction: we will search for, and reason with, explanations where they are available, and we will use causal reasoning when we can. Both of these observations imply that when we reason inductively we are not just using the kinds of similarity relations described by Osherson and his colleagues. Perhaps we only use similarity as a strategy when it is appropriate to the task, which, in the case of the kinds of research outlined above, was to project largely meaningless properties (known as 'blank' properties in the trade) between items and levels in a taxonomy such as birds.

Abduction: finding explanations and causes

There has been an accumulation of evidence about abduction in recent times, which means that Thagard's (2007) remark that it is a much less familiar term than induction or deduction is likely to have less force in future. Thagard sketches the philosophical underpinnings of this central aspect of mental life, as he aptly describes it, and also outlines the conceptual basis for a complete theory of it. He points to an aspect of inductive explanation that has received little recent research attention, although you can find it in classic Gestalt studies of problem solving: emotion. Emotion can trigger an effort to reason abductively, and when you derive what seems like a viable hypothesis, that can give you an emotional charge too. But, as I say, little research has looked at these experiences in any detail. Gopnik (1998, 2000) provides an arresting exception and an explanation for our 'propensity for explanation': she proposes that finding explanations is essential to human success, both personal and genetic. It is therefore no accident that finding explanations can be thrilling: it motivates us to look for them all the more. Her attention-getting device is to make an analogy between this process and sexual fulfilment, which encourages us to have more sex and hence more babies.

Douglas Medin, John Coley and their colleagues have conducted a series of studies of the cognitive factors that throw the contrast between category-based induction and abduction into sharp relief. They have assessed a range of different kinds of people, not just the usual student populations so beloved of experimental psychologists. Among these groups have been indigenous Maya people from Guatemala, Central America, and experts in the USA, as well as university students from around the world. Their research is collected in a book by Atran and Medin (2008). In one of their first studies, Lopez, Atran, Coley, Medin and Smith (1997) found that the premise diversity effect (see above), which is one of the most reliable patterns in projecting blank properties from one category to another, was almost entirely absent from the responses of Maya people when thinking about animals but was present in American university students. This finding was repeated by Bailenson, Shum, Atran, Medin and Coley (2002) and extended, in that American bird experts (the problems were about birds) also failed to show not just the diversity effect, but the premise typicality effect as well. We shall come back to the relation between culture and thought in Chapter 10.

Medin, Coley and colleagues attribute the non-appearance of what had previously been considered to be standard response patterns to that familiar constraint, knowledge. Remember that much of the work reviewed above, such as the classic studies of Rips and Osherson et al., had used blank properties, ones that would be largely devoid of prior knowledge by the participants. This was a deliberate research strategy, to enable a clear test of the nature of category-based induction. However, it does open up the possibility that the resulting effects that this research strategy uncovers, such as similarity, typicality and diversity, might themselves be particular strategies that participants use for the task in hand: reasoning about blank properties. Other contexts may call for other strategies.

In knowledge-rich areas, where we are thinking about meaningful properties, people tend to use causal knowledge and reason abductively when asked to project these properties. We then have to ask which aspects of causal knowledge are involved when we think in this way. Medin, Coley, Storms and Hayes (2003) base their answer to this question on Sperber and Wilson's (1995) relevance theory, which we have met before in Chapter 4. Relevance, in the terms of this theory, is determined by two factors: effect (e.g. the amount by which some information changes belief) and effort. The more effect some information has, and the less effort needed to acquire it, the greater the relevance. Medin et al. use the following story from their research to illustrate the influence of relevance in abduction. They gave American tree experts statements such as:

> River birches get disease X
> White oaks get disease Y
> Ginkgos get disease Z

and asked them which disease was likely to affect all trees. One man thought that disease X was more likely to spread to all trees than disease Y, because birches are notoriously disease-prone. However, he thought that disease Z was more likely than disease Y, for exactly the opposite reason: that ginkgos are highly disease-resistant. He thought himself that he was being contradictory, but Medin et al. excuse him on the grounds that he was thinking about different possible causal mechanisms, because of his knowledge of trees (the premises) and their properties (disease proneness, in this instance). He was using the most relevant information in each case. The students in classic category-based induction research, thinking about blank properties, focus on relevant aspects of the premise categories: similarity, typicality and diversity.

Medin et al. went on to test their relevance theory in experiments that were designed to see whether the effects of causality that come from rich knowledge, such as is possessed by indigenous peoples or by educated experts, could be predicted in non-expert populations such as university students. Would general causal knowledge override the classic factors of similarity, typicality and diversity? They tested five phenomena predicted by their relevance-based theory, in each case basing the prediction on the increased effort that causal thinking would bring. The simplest of these effects was what they called *causal asymmetry*. Consider these two arguments:

13 Rabbits have property X
———————————————
Carrots have property X

14 Carrots have property X
    _____
    Rabbits have property X

All that has happened here is that the same categories occur in different places, as premise and as conclusion. However, Medin et al. predicted, and found, that people judged argument 14 as stronger than 13: with argument 14 it is easier to see a causal link between carrots and rabbits, through the fact that rabbits eat carrots. And here is an argument where relevance trumps diversity:

15 Cats have property X
    Rhinos have property X
    _____
    Lizards have property X

16 Cats have property X
    Sparrows have property X
    _____
    Lizards have property X

Here, the categories in argument 16 are more diverse than they are in 15, and so 16 should, according to the similarity-coverage model, be stronger. But Medin et al. predicted, and observed, that argument 15 would be judged to be stronger. This is because of a salient (i.e. relevant) causal relation between cats and sparrows (ingestion again), which should make people doubt the connection between them and lizards. The items in argument 15, on the other hand, lead you to suspect that property X might be something to do with all animals, and so it seems likely that lizards share it.

Rehder (2006, 2007) reports related work in which causality is played off against similarity, and also found that causal knowledge, either from participants' background beliefs or provided experimentally, can override the classic factors when it is available. I say 'can' because, interestingly, he found evidence of individual differences: some people used causality to judge argument strength, whereas some used similarity. This confirms the idea that these are strategies that people can opt into or out of.

Abduction is not always successful. Johnson-Laird (2006) quotes the case of the *Mary Celeste*, the ship found in mid-ocean in the 19th century, seaworthy but abandoned. No ready explanation suggests itself: we are simply baffled. Or we come up with fanciful 'explanations' invoking supernatural processes for which there is no evidence; put the ship's name into your favourite internet search engine and you will see what I mean.

Induction and deduction revisited

We have seen in this part of the chapter, along with related material in previous chapters, that induction is a vast, complex and vital component of human mentality, and it is perhaps surprising that there has been less research attention paid to it in recent times than there has been to deductive reasoning. Indeed, Feeney and Heit

(2007), in their preface, note that their book is the first on the psychology of induction to have appeared in over 20 years, since Holland et al. (1986). However, this is only true of general induction, and then only if you confine that term mainly to category-based induction. There have been, as we have seen in the present book, numerous publications about areas of inductive thinking such as probability judgment and causal inference.

Whatever terms you use for these aspects of thinking, we are still left with the question of whether the formal distinction between induction and deduction, outlined at the start of this chapter, stands up psychologically. The first way we can address this question is to see whether the kinds of theories of deduction that were reviewed in Chapter 5 can or cannot be applied also to induction. Mental logic theories such as those of Braine and O'Brien (1991) and Rips (1994) cannot, by definition: they apply only to particular forms of argument (in the former case, only conditionals) that are stated in language. And there is no reason to restrict induction solely to language – that would be to deny induction to young children or non-human animals.

However, its chief rival until quite recently, the theory of mental models, has been applied to induction by Johnson-Laird (1994, 2006) and to its sub-category, probability, by Johnson-Laird, Legrenzi, Girotto, Legrenzi and Caverni (1999). A mental model is a mental representation of a state of affairs that is not necessarily in verbal form – it could be an image or an abstract thought. Thus in situations where several observations are made, each is turned into a mental model. We can then formulate another model to account for all of them, like this:

Cats have property X
Mice have property X
Whales have property X
. . .
_____

All mammals have property X

In deductive reasoning by mental models, a valid conclusion is one where there is no possible model that is inconsistent with it. Allowing for the hidden premise that all the above animals are mammals, the conclusion is true of all the premises; but it is not deductively valid. The reason lies in the three dots: a mental footnote that there may be other cases as yet unobserved with or without property X. Duck-billed platypuses, for instance, are mammals but they don't give birth to live young like the others do (they lay eggs), so an inductive conclusion, although plausible, is not necessarily true. The particular kind of conclusion, according to Johnson-Laird, depends on knowledge and on constraints such as those detailed in this chapter. In general, we will produce the most informative conclusion that is consistent with the premises – the one that explains the most in the most economical way – the most relevant, in other words. That process enables abductive reasoning and deductive hypothesis testing.

More recent developments in theories of reasoning have also served to blur the psychological distinction between deduction and induction. A deductively valid conclusion is one that necessarily follows from the premises, whereas an inductive conclusion is one that is drawn with less than complete certainty. We saw in Chapter 6 that two recent theories of conditional inference, which from a logical point of view is a deductive activity, are based on probability: those of Oaksford and Chater (e.g. 1994a, 1998, 2007, 2009) and Evans and Over (2004). Each asks the question of how much deduction there is in our lives, and comes up with the answer: not much, outside the technical domains of logic and mathematics.

Consider, for instance, Evans and Over's suppositional theory of the conditional. They propose, and have evidence, that people judge the probability of a conditional *If p then q* sentence as the conditional probability of its consequent *q*, given its antecedent *p*. Category-based induction can be seen as a conditional probability problem as well: when judging argument strength, we are judging the probability of the conclusion (e.g. rabbits have property X, given the premise that carrots have it). Over (2009; see also Manktelow, Over & Elqayam, 2010a) argues for the *new paradigm* in reasoning theory, based on probability, because so few of the propositions we reason with are held with certainty, and so most reasoning must be probabilistic. This new paradigm would therefore include induction and deduction as two sides of the same coin.

At the heart of these probabilistic approaches to reasoning is Bayesian theory (see Chapters 1, 2 and 6). Bayes' rule, as we saw, enables a precise mathematical account of belief change in response to new information. Induction is about something very similar. Heit (1998) used this parallel to develop a Bayesian account of category-based induction. He takes this form of induction to be one of using the information in the premises to estimate the range of the property concerned (i.e. that it extends to the conclusion category). Take one of Sloman's examples above: given that ex-cons are often hired as bodyguards, how likely is it that this attribute will also extend to war veterans? Heit argues that you have prior knowledge of these categories – ex-cons, war veterans and bodyguards – and that this knowledge is revised in the light of the premises (in this case, just the single premise). So there we have the two components required to apply Bayes' rule to compute belief change: prior belief and new information. The posterior belief is your confidence in the projection of the property 'bodyguard' to the new category 'war veteran'.

More formally, Bayes' rule is a formula that allows us to compute change in belief in a set of hypotheses, H_i, as a result of encountering some information, D (data). We have a prior degree of belief in each hypothesis, expressed as prob(H). After the new data, we have a posterior degree of belief, written as prob(H|D), which is the probability of the hypothesis given the data. Now let us see how Heit applies this process to category-based induction, using Sloman's bodyguard example.

There are four possible ranges of the property *often hired as bodyguards* with respect to ex-cons and war veterans: that it is true (i.e. we believe it to some degree) of both, true of ex-cons but not of war veterans, true of war veterans but not of ex-cons and not true of either. These are the four possible hypotheses in this context. You have some prior beliefs about the premise categories, and about how any new property will relate to them. Table 7.1 shows some possible figures for these; since I don't know what your beliefs are, they are imaginary. The figures mean that you believe: what is true of ex-cons will be true of war veterans with probability .70 (i.e. very likely); what is true of ex-cons will not be true of war veterans with probability .05; what is true of war veterans will not be true of ex-cons with probability .05; and what is false of ex-cons will also not apply to war veterans with probability .20. Your prior degree of belief that ex-cons have the property is therefore .75: the sum of the first two hypotheses.

Now we have the new information (D), that ex-cons are often hired as body-guards. This can be used along with the prior probabilities to update belief in the conclusion, that war veterans are also hired as bodyguards. Table 7.1 shows how this is done using the Bayesian formula. Each of the four hypotheses is revised in the light of the new information. All you do is read off the values given for prob(H$_i$) and prob(D| H$_i$) and plug them into the formula. Since you are told that ex-cons have the property, the latter expression is zero for Hypotheses 3 and 4, where this is denied, and so posterior degree of belief in them vanishes. But prob(D|H) is 1 for Hypotheses 1 and 2 since the argument states that the property is true for ex-cons,

Table 7.1 A Bayesian analysis of category-based induction

The argument:

Ex-cons are hired as bodyguards (C)

War veterans are hired as bodyguards (V)

Hypotheses		Range	Prior degree of belief: prob(H$_i$)	Data: prob (D| H$_i$)	Posterior degree of belief: prob(H$_i$ |D)
1	C:	True	.70	1	.93
	V:	True			
2	C:	True	.05	1	.07
	V:	False			
3	C:	False	.05	0	0
	V:	True			
4	C:	False	.20	0	0
	V:	False			

The Bayesian formula:

$$\text{prob(H|D)} = \frac{\text{prob(D|H)} \times \text{prob(H)}}{[\text{prob(D|H)} \times \text{prob(H)}] + [\text{prob(D|¬H)} \times \text{prob(¬H)}]}$$

To compute belief revision for Hypothesis 1 (the argument):

$$\text{prob(H|D)} = \frac{1 \times .70}{[1 \times .70] + [1 \times .05]} = \frac{.70}{.75} = \textbf{.93}$$

Note that ¬H is the set of all alternative hypotheses to H1 (i.e. H2, H3 and H4) but we do not have expressions for H3 and H4 in the bottom line because they reduce to zero.

Source: Based on Heit (1998)

so belief in Hypothesis 1, the one in question in the target argument, is strengthened, from .70 to .93. That makes intuitive as well as mathematical sense: you started out believing that the two premise categories had quite a lot in common, and so having learned a fact about one you think it very likely that it is shared by the other. The argument seems like a strong one.

Heit successfully applies this analysis to various phenomena of category-based induction, such as the similarity and diversity effects. However, it is less successful in accounting for non-monotonicity effects (Sloman & Lagnado, 2005b), and it suffers from the Achilles heel of so many theories of reasoning: accounting for knowledge. Heit invokes the availability heuristic (see Chapter 1) in saying where the prior probabilities come from, but more recently Joshua Tenenbaum and his colleagues (e.g. Kemp & Tenenbaum, 2003; Sanjana & Tenenbaum, 2003; Tenenbaum, Kemp & Shafto, 2007) offer an alternative, theory-based Bayesian explanation.

In doing so, Tenenbaum et al. converge with other researchers on a crucial attribute of human thinking. We develop *theories* of how the world works from an early age – Susan Carey (1985), the first researcher to follow up Rips (1975), produced a wealth of evidence about what she called conceptual change in childhood, showing how these concepts undergo radical, structural change as knowledge accumulates, just as real scientific theories do. The papers by Gopnik, cited earlier, were also concerned with the child's theory-formation system, as she calls it.

Tenenbaum et al. refer in detail to the area of knowledge that has occupied induction researchers the most: the living world. They propose two kinds of theories of the living world that ordinary people have: biological properties and causal properties. We have already met these in looking at the research of Medin and colleagues above. Tenenbaum et al. propose in both cases that we have a *theory structure* and what they call a *mutation principle*. Take the biological properties. The theory structure consists of a taxonomy. This seems to be a universal way of thinking about the living world – all cultures seem to have some notion of a tree of life. A taxonomy consists of several layers of increasing generality (in one direction) or precision (in the other), as in an imaginary one for a person's knowledge of birds, shown in Figure 7.1.

The mutation principle allows for an attribute to be turned on or off at some point in the hierarchy. This is what limits the projectability of a property, such as 'flies': in Figure 7.1, the setting for this attribute is 'off' at the branch that leads to ostrich, emu and penguin, and 'on' for the other main branch. For the causal properties, Tenenbaum et al. propose a theory structure based on 'food web' relations, so that a property can be projected more confidently from prey to predator than from predator to prey, because the predator ingests the prey and so may absorb the property. This theory-based approach to induction credits abduction as having a more general role than previously thought: our prior probabilities, on this argument, are bound up with the ways we explain the world to ourselves.

Although the probabilistic 'new paradigm' approaches as well as the mental models-based approaches to reasoning seem to favour an integration between induction and deduction, the father of category-based induction research, Rips (2001), comes down in favour of there being a qualitative distinction. He allows that

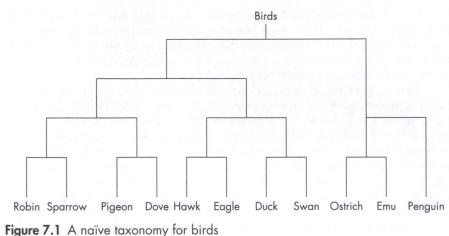

Figure 7.1 A naïve taxonomy for birds

inductive and deductive argument strength can be thought of as positions on the 0–1 probability scale, with deductive strength at the 1 end. If reason were a unitary matter, asking people to judge deductive correctness and inductive argument strength should lead to the same kinds of responses.

Rips tested this hypothesis by giving people arguments that varied in causal consistency (i.e. the extent to which they match causal knowledge). For instance, if you learn that a car hits a wall, you know it is more likely to stop than speed up. These elements can be put into inductive or deductive arguments like this:

Inductive	*Deductive (modus ponens)*
	If a car hits a wall, it stops/speeds up
A car hits a wall	A car hits a wall
It stops/speeds up	It stops/speeds up

The interesting cases are the ones where the argument is causally inconsistent but deductively correct (where the major premise and the conclusion of the MP argument both say 'speeds up'), and where the argument is causally consistent but deductively incorrect, as in the inductive argument where the conclusion is 'stops' (it is deductively incorrect because the conclusion does not necessarily follow). When people judged deductive correctness, their belief in the first was greater than the second: they were sensitive to the logic of the problem. However, when they had to judge argument strength, the difference went the other way. This, says Rips, implies that two forms of reasoning were going on; if the unitary view were right, and all reasoning was about argument strength, then the patterns should have been the same. Rips also calls in evidence neuroimaging research that shows different areas of the brain becoming active when people reason about validity and plausibility: examples are the work of Goel, Gold, Kapur and Houle (1997) and Osherson, Perani, Cappa, Schnur, Grassi and Fazio (1998).

Feeney (2007) offers a dual-process view of Rips' results (see Chapters 6, 9 and 10 for more detail on the dual process theory). He argues that judging validity is an activity that requires use of System 2 (analytic) thought, whereas judging plausibility can be done in a System 1 (intuitive) manner. Dual processes can be applied in both inductive and deductive thinking. To back up this argument, he reports experimental data where people higher in cognitive ability perform better on inductive tasks, based on Rips (2001), with high System 2 involvement (see Chapters 6 and 10 for more on the use of this kind of evidence by Stanovich and colleagues).

Sloman (2007; also Sloman & Lagnado, 2005b), surveying the range of research and theory on category-based induction, extends this argument further and espouses the strategy idea mentioned above: we have, he says, a 'bag of tricks' (Sloman & Lagnado, 2005b, p. 111) available to us when thinking, and it is a mistake to assume that there is just one way we could, or should, go about it. There are numerous kinds of judgment we can make, and numerous sources of information on which we can base these judgments. In the second part of this chapter we look at another one, which is closely related to induction, especially in scientific thinking.

Hypothesis testing

We begin with a fascinating piece of history, which Johnson-Laird (2006) uses to illustrate the kinds of thinking that we are concerned with at the moment. In the mid-19th century there was an outbreak of cholera (a horrible, lethal and contagious disease) in England. John Snow was a doctor working in London, who set about trying to explain its transmission so that it could be contained and prevented. Looking at the observed facts about cholera, he was able to infer that it was a single disease and that it spread from person to person: the appearance of one infected person would invariably be followed by a cluster of cases. These are inductive conclusions. But *how* was it spread? Now he needed to test hypotheses as well as come up with new ones.

Snow ruled out transmission through the air, because of what he knew about the fluid dynamics of gases; there was little relation between physical closeness to an infected person and likelihood of catching cholera. Snow thought about how other diseases were spread by ingestion. Perhaps people took in some kind of particle that multiplied inside them (this was before the germ theory of disease had been developed); its effect on the body would account for the physical symptoms. This was a piece of category-based induction. But how did the particles get from one person to another? By abduction, using his existing knowledge, Snow narrowed down the possibilities. Infected people could contaminate clothing and bedlinen, which others then touched; or sewage could contaminate the water supply and spread the disease over distance. Snow eventually put this idea to a famous test, in Soho in London. He collected statistics of cholera cases that he suspected were linked to a water pump, and then had the pump disabled. No further cases were recorded after this.

We can see, in this rather compressed account (Johnson-Laird's is far more detailed), features of inductive reasoning that have been dealt with earlier in this chapter. But now we can add another: John Snow also went about gathering evidence to *test* the old theories of disease transmission and his new one. His the any prevailed in the end, although he did not live to enjoy the triumph.[3] For the rest of this chapter, then, let us look at how people test hypotheses once they have them.

Two broad lines of attack to this question have been used. The first is to study core aspects in the laboratory, as is done in most of the psychology of thinking. The second is to study hypothesis testing in the field, using observational techniques. We shall take them in order. The first strategy returns us to a familiar name, that of Peter Wason. Modern experimental research can be traced directly back to his work half a century ago.

Wason's 2 4 6 task and its descendants

Wason was inspired by classic studies of concept formation (a form of inductive reasoning) such as that of Bruner, Goodnow and Austin (1956), and brought his genius for devising tasks to bear on the question of hypothesis generation and testing. The 2 4 6 task was the result (Wason, 1960, 1968b) and research based on it continues to appear to the present day. Here it is:

> You are presented by the experimenter with the following set of numbers, known as a triple: 2 4 6. You are told that this triple conforms to a rule that the experimenter has in mind, and your task is to discover what that rule is. To do so, you have to generate more triples. For each one, the experimenter either says yes, that is an instance of my rule, or no, it is not. Once you think you have discovered the rule, you announce it and the experimenter tells you whether you are right or not. If you are not, you go on generating triples and receiving feedback until you are in a position to venture another rule, and so on until you succeed or give up.

In case you think this is a silly artificial puzzle, it is easy to think of real-world examples. Say you are working for a health authority and your job is to set up a publicity campaign aimed at reducing smoking in teenagers. You form a hypothesis based on your knowledge of young people that 'viral' advertising campaigns that get a lot of hits on internet sites such as YouTube will be most effective. Are you right? This is a formally identical problem to the 2 4 6 task: your observations lead to a hypothesis, and you then have to figure out how to test it. You generate ads in different media rather than numbers, and they either work (yes) or not (no).

Back to the 2 4 6 task. Ask yourself what you would give as the next triple, after 2 4 6. It's a fair bet that it would be something like 8 10 12 or 3 5 7, and that you are beginning to home in on a hypothesis such as 'increasing regular numbers' or 'numbers increasing by 2'. The sting in the tail of the 2 4 6 task is this: the experimenter's rule is much more general than the kinds that are invited by the regular pattern in the opening triple. It is just *increasing numbers*. Leading participants to form more restricted hypotheses than the real one in this way was a deliberate strategy on Wason's part, of course. With the parallel health campaign, the same situation would exist if it turned out that ad-type messages in any medium – TV, radio, internet, etc. – were equally effective. You don't know this at the beginning, of course, but have to discover it by generating and testing hypotheses. It is an analogue of scientific reasoning.

So say you give 8 10 12 as your next triple, and the experimenter says yes. You give 3 5 7 as the next one: yes again. It's looking a lot like 'numbers increasing by two' as the experimenter's rule. If you carry on doing this kind of thing, you will carry on getting confirmations of this initial hypothesis, and your belief in it is strengthened. When you announce it, and the experimenter says no, you get a shock. Now what? The triples you produce and the rules you announce provide a rich record of your hypothesis testing behaviour, made even richer in Wason's research because he asked people to comment on the triples they generated as well. While your success, or otherwise, in hitting on the right rule is interesting, what is really interesting are the steps you take in getting there.

In the first reported experiment on the 2 4 6 task, Wason (1960; see also Wason, 1968b and Wason & Johnson-Laird, 1972, Ch. 16) found that only 21% of his participants announced the correct rule – increasing numbers – first time. Over half made at least one incorrect announcement before getting it right, while the rest, some 28%, never found it at all, even after wrestling with it for an hour in some cases. Now we can look at the different routes to the solution. Two examples of protocols from this study are shown in Table 7.2. The first is from someone who succeeded first time; the second is from someone who got there eventually, after the shock of being wrong.

Wason described three testing strategies, and you can see them in the two protocols of Table 7.2:

1 *Verification*. Generate confirming instances of your hypothesis and announce it as the rule. This is the process described above, and it is visible in both protocols in Table 7.2: in protocol (a) it happens towards the end of the sequence, while in protocol (b) it is clearest in the first set of triples.

2 *Falsification*. Generate an instance inconsistent with your current hypothesis. Protocol (a) has this half-way along, with the descending triple, while in protocol (b) it appears only at the very end, where the participant produces a triple that is unequally spaced.

3 *Vary the hypothesis*. Protocol (a) shows this happening almost from the start, while in protocol (b) it only occurs later. The second, third and fourth rule announcements for this person are especially interesting: they are simply rewordings of each other, not actually different hypotheses. This person, who was far from unique, kept a tight grip on her original idea.

These patterns of generated triples, hypotheses and rule announcements are typical of what happens in this task (see Kareev, Halberstadt & Shafir, 1993, for a more recent example): people follow where the given triple leads them, and fix on numbers evenly spaced. Vallée-Tourangeau, Austin and Rankin (1995) found that success was predicted by the number of triples a person generates that do not conform to this pattern, and you can see that happening in the two examples. We shall look at further factors that promote success below.

Table 7.2 Two protocols from Wason's study of the 2 4 6 task

(a) Correct first announcement

Triples		Hypotheses
2 4 6	Given	
3 6 9	Yes	Three goes into the second figure twice and into the third figure three times
2 4 8	Yes	Perhaps the figures have to have an LCD
2 4 10	Yes	Same reason
2 5 10	Yes	The second number does not have to be decided by the first one
10 6 4	No	The highest number must go last
4 6 10	Yes	The first number must be the lowest
2 3 5	Yes	It is only the order that counts
4 5 6	Yes	Same reason
1 7 13	Yes	Same reason

'The rule is that the three figures must be in numerical order.' Correct: 16 minutes.

(b) Four incorrect announcements

Triples		Hypotheses
2 4 6	Given	
8 10 12	Yes	Two added each time
14 16 18	Yes	Even numbers in order of magnitude
20 22 24	Yes	Same reason
1 3 5	Yes	Two added to preceding number

'The rule is that by starting with any number, two is added each time to form the next number.' Incorrect.

2 6 10	Yes	The middle number is the arithmetic mean of the other two
1 50 99	Yes	Same reason

'The rule is that the middle number is the arithmetic mean of the other two.' Incorrect.

3 10 17	Yes	Same number, seven added each time
0 3 6	Yes	Three added each time

'The rule is that the difference between two numbers next to each other is the same.' Incorrect.

12 8 4	No	The same number is subtracted each time to form the next number

'The rule is adding a number, always the same one, to form the next number.' Incorrect.

1 4 9	Yes	Any three numbers in order of magnitude

'The rule is any three numbers in order of magnitude.' Correct: 17 minutes.

Source: Based on Wason and Johnson-Laird (1972)

Confirmation bias

Wason was intrigued by the behaviour of those people who did not crack the 2 4 6 task easily, and introduced the idea of *confirmation bias* to label it (although he called it verification bias): people seemed to seek out information that would only confirm their ideas. You may recall from Chapter 3 that this was also his initial take on selection task performance; he started running this task in 1962 (Wason & Johnson-Laird, 1972), shortly after the appearance of the 2 4 6. Evans (1989) goes into further detail in comparing the two tasks, and Joshua Klayman (1995) gives a wider-ranging review of confirmation bias.

Almost immediately, an objection was raised to this interpretation, by Wetherick (1962). He pointed to a subtle but vital distinction between confirmation and positivity. For instance, suppose you generate 3 5 7 as your first triple after 2 4 6. This is a positive instance of a likely initial hypothesis of 'numbers ascending by two'; but are you confirming? Only if you expect it to get the answer 'yes', to show that it conforms to the hidden target rule. If your confidence in your initial hypothesis is low, perhaps because you suspect the rule may only apply to even numbers, you might expect a 'no', in which case your positive test would be expected to disconfirm it. Similarly, if you perform a negative test expecting a 'no', you are actually confirming (you can see this happening in both protocols in Table 7.2 when descending triples are produced). Wason's account ignores such expectations, which are an essential part of hypothesis testing.

This insight was extended by Klayman and Ha (1987), who conducted what was effectively a rational analysis of this task (cf. Oaksford & Chater's treatment of the selection task; see Chapter 6), in that they took into account the environment in which testing is done. Think about how the participant's hypothesis might relate to the hidden rule, which you will remember was deliberately designed to be more general than the 2 4 6 triple implies. There are five possibilities:

1   Your hypothesis (H) and the target rule (T) are *the same*: H is 'increasing by 2' (or only viral ads work) and so is T. All triples that are instances of H are instances of T, and vice versa.
2   H is *more specific* than T: H is 'increasing by 2' but T is 'ascending numbers'. All triples that are in the H set are in the T set, but some in T are not in H.
3   H is *more general* than T: H is 'increasing by 2' but T is 'even numbers increasing by 2'. All T triples are in H, but some H triples are not in T.
4   H and T *overlap*: your H is 'increasing by 2' but T is 'three even numbers'. Some triples in H will also be in T, but each set contains triples that are not in the other.
5   H and T are *disjoint*: your H is 'increasing by 2' but T is 'descending numbers'. No H triple is in the T set.

These relations are illustrated in Figure 7.2. The 2 4 6 task is an example of relation 2. Positive testing – generating triples that are in the H set – can never lead to the discovery of T because you will always get a 'yes' even though H is false. There are no H items that are not also T items. You must use negative testing. The triple 3 6 9 would be a negative test of the 'ascending by 2' hypothesis: they ascend by 3.

Relation 1: H and T are the same

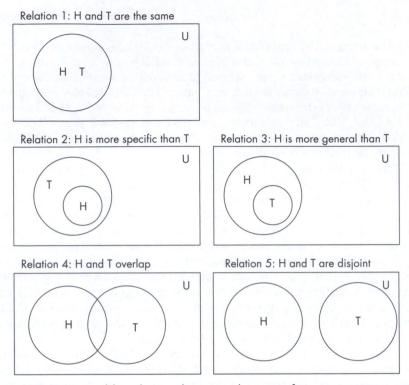

Relation 2: H is more specific than T

Relation 3: H is more general than T

Relation 4: H and T overlap

Relation 5: H and T are disjoint

Figure 7.2 Five possible relations between the sets of items consistent with a hypothesis and a target rule

Note: H, the participant's hypothesis; T, the target made; U, all possible instances

So it will be outside your H set but inside the T set, and so will get a 'yes'. You might have expected just such an outcome, in which case both of these tests would be confirmatory tests. Seeking confirmation can thus be done by both positive and negative testing: confirmation bias is not the same as positivity bias.

However, what happens if people really do have a positivity bias, which they carry with them whatever the relation between H and T? Consider relation 3, where T is less general than H, the mirror image of the classic 2 4 6 situation. This would be the case if the target rule T was something like 'even numbers increasing by 2' or, in the smoking campaign, that only funny viral ads work but not scary ones. When you produce a triple such as 3 5 7, which is a positive instance of your H, it gets a 'no' response: instant falsification! You immediately see that you have to find another H.

In this situation, then, a bias towards positive testing will lead to rapid falsification, hypothesis change and rule discovery. This is the same bias but a completely different outcome from the classic 2 4 6 situation. On the basis of their analysis, Klayman and Ha argue that positive testing is generally rational. They make two reasonable assumptions in arguing this. The first is that the probability of an instance's being in T is about the same as its being in H; in real life, hypotheses are unlikely to be perfectly accurate or wildly off-beam – they will be somewhere in between. The second is that the probability of an instance's *not* being in T is greater than its being in T. This is because in the real world, with all its complications, the T set of instances is rare: most number sequences are not ascending, and most sick people do not have cholera. This *rarity assumption* was also central to Oaksford and Chater's analyses of reasoning (see Chapters 2 and 6).

The link between confirmation, falsification and rule discovery was further explored by Klayman and Ha (1989). They used the rule–hypothesis relations 2 (the one in the original 2 4 6 experiments) 3 and 4 (see Figure 7.2). Although positive testers received more falsifications with relation 3 (where T is more specific than H) than with relation 2, they did not hit on the rule more often than they did with the other relations. How come? Fenna Poletiek (1996, 2001) points to another relation, that between the nature of the target rule and the participant's belief in their hypothesis. When a rule is hard to find, your belief in your hypothesis will be low, and so falsifications will be likely and rather off-putting; although they tell you to reject the H you are working with, they may inhibit the formation of alternatives.

Poletiek (2001) is the place to go for detailed information about all aspects of hypothesis testing: philosophical, logical and psychological. She links the kinds of research we have been considering here to the philosophy of science, especially the highly influential perspective of Karl Popper. Popper (1959b) argued that the proper attitude of a scientist is to offer bold conjectures (hypotheses) and subject them to severe tests – those that are likely to result in refutations. Although widely criticised as an unrealistic portrayal of actual human behaviour – does anyone really set out to prove themselves wrong? – Poletiek seizes on the H–T relation to argue that such an attitude is in any case unnecessary. If you do what Popper says, and subject your ideas to severe tests, you must be expecting falsification. That is what a severe test is. So when you get it, you have not learned much: you expected your hypothesis to fail to account for the test's results, and it did. Only if your H survives such a test will you learn anything: the more unexpected an occurrence, the more informative it is. Similarly, soft testing, where you expect confirmation, only tells you something if you receive unexpected falsification. Confirmatory and falsificatory strategies turn out to be equivalent. What matters is the relation between H and T.

Better hypothesis testing

As with Wason's other great problem, the selection task, a number of manipulations of the 2 4 6 task were tried with the aim of facilitating performance, before a sure-fire way of doing so was discovered. Among the less successful adaptations were to engineer more falsifications (i.e. instructions to search for falsifications) and the use of more realistic materials; as we saw in Chapter 3, similar manoeuvres were performed with the selection task, with similar outcomes: uneven results (see Poletiek, 2001, for more details on these). With the 2 4 6 task, the sure-fire method is to give people more than one hypothesis to test.

This has become known as the *dual goal* method. It was first used by Tweney, Doherty, Worner, Pliske, Mynatt, Gross and Arkkelin (1980), although it had origi-nally been suggested by Wetherick (1962). The idea is actually quite simple. Instead of instances being given yes/no feedback, they were classified as being consistent with one hypothesis or another. These were given nonsense-word labels: Dax (for instances consistent with the target rule) and Med (for any other kind of instance). If you were taking part in a Dax–Med 2 4 6 experiment, your task would be to figure out which rule, Dax or Med, the experimenter had in mind, with 2 4 6 being given as a Dax triple. Tweney et al. found that 12 out of 20 participants (60%) announced the correct rule first time with this form of the task, which is a far higher success rate than with other forms. The effect has been replicated many times.

There followed a series of studies aimed at finding out why the dual goal method was so successful. Initially, it was proposed that *goal complementarity* was the important feature: in the Tweney et al. experiment, Dax and Med cover all the possibilities, because Med is merely the complement of Dax: anything that is not a Dax instance is a Med. A goal complementarity theory was put forward by Wharton, Cheng and Wickens (1993). They made use of the features identified by previous researchers such as Wetherick, and Klayman and Ha: that people's initial hypoth-eses will be led to be more specific than the target rule, and that they have a posi-tivity bias. To this they added complementarity, so that people alternate between positive tests of Dax and Med. They get unexpected Med feedback in the first place, leading to the realisation that their H for Dax is too narrow, and they get unexpected Dax feedback in the second, leading to their narrowing their H for Med. The upshot is rapid zeroing-in on the true Dax rule.

This theory was called into question by Vallée-Tourangeau et al. (1995). They used a version of the dual goal task in which people were told that triples could be Dax, Med or neither – the extra 'neither' category means that Dax and Med are no longer perfectly complementary. In this version of the task the success rates were still high, which the authors interpret as evidence against complementarity. However, Gale and Ball (2006, 2009) point out that Vallée-Tourangeau and colleagues never actually gave 'neither' feedback; it was always Dax or Med. So in reality, Dax and Med were still complementary.

Gale and Ball put forward an account of dual goal facilitation in terms of *contrast classes* (cf. Oaksford and Stenning's account of the negated conditional in Chapter 3). A contrast class is your idea of what something isn't, compared to what it is. When thinking about pets, the contrast class for 'dog' is 'cat', rather than 'all other animals', for instance. Gale and Ball (2006) found evidence for this account in the fact that it was the production of descending triples (e.g. 6 4 2) rather than vari-able positive triples such as 2 4 8 (where the numbers increase by unequal amounts) that predicted success. This is true in both the dual goal and the classic single-goal version of the task; it is just that the dual goal version leads to the earlier produc-tion of descending triples. In their later paper, Gale and Ball (2009) found that both complementary and non-complementary dual goal tasks led to high levels of successful rule announcements. The great majority of successful participants produced descending triples, while few of the non-solvers did.

Gale and Ball's contrast class theory is more specific than a rival explanation in terms of variety of triples (Vallée-Tourangeau et al., 1995). It is true that successful solvers produce more varied triples and that the dual goal task promotes this. It is also true that graphical representations of the task do so as well, as recently found by Vallée-Tourangeau and Krüsi Penney (2005; see also Vallée-Tourangeau & Payton, 2008). But what is important is the particular kind of triple that is produced among the set: descending.

Do people test alternative hypotheses without being placed in a Dax–Med type of context deliberately? Klayman and Ha (1989) found that successful testers mentioned explicit alternative hypotheses three times more often than unsuccessful testers did. Farris and Revlin (1989) proposed that successful testers use a *counterfactual* strategy: they start with a hypothesis based on the given triple 2 4 6, such as 'numbers increasing by two', then generate an alternative, complementary hypothesis and test that using a positive test. The problem with this idea, as Oaksford and Chater (1994b) pointed out, is that the alternative H must be false at the outset, since it is the complement of one that is consistent with the given triple, and so there is no reason for it to be generated. Oaksford and Chater instead argue that successful testers use what they call an *iterative counterfactual* strategy: they start with their first plausible hypothesis and then generate what they suspect may be an inconsistent instance. If this gets a 'yes' response, they revise their initial hypothesis on the basis of the information this feedback provides about what the two instances have in common. In effect, what people are doing is testing the limits of their hypotheses. Then they do the same again, and so on, until further revisions to H are met with 'no' responses and the rule is discovered. Thus people use successive tests to refine the scope of H and its alternatives.

You can see from the dates against many of the papers above that, as mentioned earlier, research inspired by Wason's inventiveness over 50 years ago is still appearing. However, psychologists have also studied hypothesis testing in more realistic settings, outside the laboratory.

Hypothesis testing in the wild

Although hypothesis testing is something that everybody does, many of the psychological studies of it in the real world have involved science and scientists. It is easy to see why: hypothesis testing is their business, and its outcomes can affect us all. When looking at the psychology of science, researchers have three basic strategies open to them: go back into history and reconstruct the processes from the records left by past scientists; conduct 'field' research among contemporary scientists; or replicate the scientific process in the laboratory. The third of these is largely what the 2 4 6 task was about, of course, although it is not the only experimental approach that has been tried. We shall look at some representative cases of each of these strategies that continue the themes of this chapter. You should be aware, though, that the psychology of science ranges further and wider than I can portray here; Dunbar and Fugelsang (2005) give a good overview of this range and will direct you to rich sources of further information.

Two psychologists who take the historical approach are worth picking out: Ryan Tweney for his extensive work on the great British physicist of the early 19th century, Michael Faraday (he discovered electromagnetic induction and colloids), and Michael Gorman, who studied the records of the prolific American scientist/inventors Alexander Graham Bell and Thomas Edison. Both have spent decades on this work (see Gorman, 1992; Tweney, 1985; Tweney, Doherty & Mynatt, 1981). Tweney recently rediscovered a set of Faraday's microscope slides and is currently busy writing about what these artefacts tell us about his thinking.[4] This is exciting, because usually we have just the written records to go on, not the actual research materials. In this case, these materials can still be used for research purposes, even though they are over 150 years old. Faraday conducted a huge number of studies, many of which threw up results that were contrary to his beliefs. He seems to have been quite dismissive of such disconfirmations. But wasn't he a great scientist? Surely he cannot have suffered from chronic confirmation bias. In fact, he did not, and Gorman's study of Bell will show us how this apparent conflict can be resolved (Gorman, 1992, 1995; see also Carlson & Gorman, 1990).

Bell's records are extensive, because they were often used in patent applications and court cases. He also wrote a lot of letters, many of which survive. In the mid-1870s, he was working on the development of the first telephone. He knew about the mechanics of the human ear, and used this knowledge as his starting point. The ear has a membrane, the eardrum, connected by a series of tiny bones to another membrane on the cochlea, the snail-shaped organ of the inner ear that sends neural signals to the brain. The lever action of the bones amplifies the vibrations from the eardrum and sends a wave pattern through the fluid in the cochlea.

Bell's aim was to construct a mechanical device that would do the same thing – convert sound into a fluctuating electrical current – and he ran a series of experiments on the most effective way of doing this. He went through each component of his device, changing features one by one and noting any effects on its efficiency. Some of these changes were predictions derived from previous experiments, and can be seen as positive and negative tests of them. After a series of such studies, he thought he had the basis for a telephone (this is like the rule announcement stage of a 2 4 6 task), and filed for a patent. Shortly after, he learned of a similar patent with a different design, using a liquid rather than an electromagnet to vary electrical resistance: an alternative hypothesis. He started a series of experiments on the electrical properties of liquids, culminating in the world's first intelligible phone call, from Bell to his assistant Watson on 10 March 1876.

Despite this powerful confirmation of the alternative hypothesis, Bell did not give up his earlier ideas about electromagnetic devices and their efficiency in regulating current. He abandoned liquid devices, went back to experiments with electromagnets and filed for another patent the following year. He seems to have regarded his success with the liquid resistor not as a disconfirmation of his electromagnet hypothesis, but as confirmation of his wider theories of undulating electrical currents. He was concerned with the science of telecommunication devices; Edison was the practical genius who brought us the telephone as we came to know it.

This sequence of events, along with Faraday's and those in other historical records, reveals a consistent pattern in studies of real science: scientists seem to confirm early and disconfirm late. When a scientist's inductive reasoning produces a working hypothesis for a set of observations, he or she looks to see what its range is: scientists conduct positive tests that look like confirmations when they work. But when they get a disconfirmation, they do not immediately abandon their theory, and may not even change it. First, they wonder about the experiment, especially if the refutation comes from someone else. Was the right method used, were the statistics done properly? This is not irrational behaviour: if we revised our view of the world every time there was an event that did not quite fit it, we would be in a permanent state of doubt; and remember, doubt is always attached to inductive conclusions. However, it is no use clinging to discredited theories either: we need to be open to contrary results once we think we know what is going on. It is always possible that we may be wrong.

This confirm-early/disconfirm-late sequence was also observed in studies of contemporary scientists conducted by Kevin Dunbar and Jonathan Fugelsang (e.g. Dunbar, 1995, 2001; Dunbar & Fugelsang, 2005; Fugelsang, Stein, Green & Dunbar, 2004). Dunbar spent a year in four biology laboratories at a US university in the early 1990s, recording the scientists' discussions as well as their experiments, results and theories. Fugelsang et al. (2004) report 12 such meetings, concerning 165 experiments and yielding 417 results. Of these, fewer than half were consistent with the scientists' predictions. These consistent results were used in the planning of further research. Inconsistent findings – the majority – resulted in a lot of abductive reasoning: the scientists devoted much effort to coming up with causal explanations for these disconfirmations. These explanations tended to break down into two types: experimental or theoretical. Fully 88% of them were experimental: the scientists blamed the method for the failed predictions. The 12% remaining resulted in the scientists taking a critical look at the theory. However, when a disconfirming result was repeated, their response was very different: 60% of the explanations for these – five times as many – were now theoretical. Once you have a theory that you have confirmed early, you need a good reason to change it. Repeated refutation is just that, and these scientists responded to it rationally.

Fugelsang et al. went on to conduct an experimental test of the processes they had observed in the field, with university students instead of professional scientists as participants. Using a scenario involving the possible effects of two drugs on happiness, they varied the Δp statistic, which you may recall from Chapter 4: it is an expression of the degree of covariation between cause and effect. It takes into account the instances of the effect with and without the supposed cause. This was set to either high or low, indicating a strong or weak cause–effect relationship. They also varied the number of observations from which Δp was derived, and presented the participants with plausible and implausible causal theories for the results. There was an interaction between plausibility and Δp: with a plausible theory, people attached more weight to the strong evidence; it seemed to confirm this theory. With the implausible theory, where no effect was expected, even the strong causal evidence was discounted. However, this interaction disappeared with the largest number of samples: just as with the biological scientists, repeated inconsistencies between theory and data were taken notice of, eventually. These students, too, confirmed early and disconfirmed later.

Hypothetical thinking theory

For the final part of this chapter, we shall look at a recent integrative theory put forward by Jonathan Evans. Evans (2007a; Evans, Over & Handley, 2003b) surveys a wide range of reasoning research (not just that reviewed in this chapter) within a dual process framework. He regards hypothetical thinking as one of the hallmarks of human mentality and includes many facets of reasoning under this heading, from conditional inference to probability judgment.

The theory has three principles that, according to Evans, we can see operating in various forms of reasoning:

1   The *singularity* principle: people consider a single hypothetical possibility at one time.
2   The *relevance* principle: people consider the possibility that is most relevant in the current context.
3   The *satisficing* principle: possibilities are evaluated with respect to the current goal and are accepted as long as they are satisfactory.

Evans and his colleagues accept the general idea of mental models when describing the mental representation of these possibilities, deriving from Johnson-Laird's theory (see Chapters 2–5), although they reject his specific proposals. We saw that the Johnson-Laird mental models theory also usually incorporates a singularity component, in that it allows for only minimal representation of explicit models, usually one, along with mental footnotes for alternative models. There is also evidence for this idea from the hypothesis testing literature, not only above, in the findings where people tend to conduct positive tests of existing hypotheses, but also in an effect we have not yet encountered: *pseudodiagnosticity*.

This elephantine term was coined by Doherty, Mynatt, Tweney and Schiavo (1979; Mynatt, Doherty & Dragan, 1993; Tweney, Doherty & Kleiter, 2010). They asked people to say where they would look for the evidence they would need to decide between two hypotheses. Information that enables you to do this is *diagnostic* information. Suppose you know that a relative of yours has a new car, and that it is a Honda or a VW but you don't know which. All you have to go on is information about Hondas and VWs. You know that the car in question is economical to run and is in the top half for reliability ratings and that 65% of Hondas are also in this reliability bracket. Which further piece of information would you seek out?

1   The percentage of VWs that are in the top half of the reliability range.
2   The percentage of Hondas that are economical to run.
3   The percentage of VWs that are economical to run.

Think about this for a minute and then read on.

Pooling across a number of problems like this, Doherty et al. (1979) found that 28% of people chose (1), 59% chose (2) and 13% chose (3). So most people wanted to find out more about Hondas, or their equivalent. However, this is not the diagnostic choice; it is pseudodiagnostic. The reason is that when faced with two hypotheses, you need information about both when deciding between them (this is a feature of Bayesian theory, which we met in previous chapters). You should look at the reliability figures for VWs, since you know what they are for Hondas. Mynatt et al. (1993) put forward a singularity explanation for their participants' error: they were only able to consider one hypothesis (it's a Honda) at a time. They interpret the success of the Dax–Med version of the 2 4 6 task in this way too: it succeeds because it forces people to think of alternative hypotheses, first one, then the other. The fact that this version has such an effect shows that, in the main, people do not readily shift from their first hypothesis without a prod.

The relevance principle is where the dual process aspect of hypothetical thinking theory comes in, because Evans holds that this is an implicit process (System 1 in the terms of standard dual process theory; see Chapter 6): it takes place without awareness. Relevance is meant in the Sperber and Wilson sense that we encountered earlier, in reviewing Medin's work on induction. Information is relevant to the extent that it has greater cognitive effects for less cognitive effort. What is relevant is thus bound up with the knowledge and goals of the person receiving and working with the information. Medin's research provides some good examples of this. It can also be applied to the pseudodiagnosticity effect, as Evans (2007a; Feeney, Evans & Venn, 2008) reports. If the focal property is a rare one such as 'has a top speed of 140 mph', rather than a common one such as 'is reliable', people are more likely to check the second make of car: the feature's rarity makes it more relevant and hence more diagnostic. This seems to be a System 1 tendency, because it also happens when both kinds of cars are fast cars, which makes top speed less diagnostic. It is the nature of the feature itself that makes it psychologically relevant.

The satisficing principle introduces a processing constraint on the explicit, or System 2, aspect of hypothetical thinking, the aspect that is to do with inference-making. *Satisfice* is a word that we shall become much more familiar with in later chapters, when we deal with decision making and rationality. It is a blended word combining 'satisfy' and 'suffice', and embodies the idea that when you choose among options, or, in the present context, formulate a conclusion or a hypothesis, you settle on an option that is good enough but not necessarily the one that is the absolute best. The reason why we often need to do this is that it is hard, indeed sometimes impossible, to find the best option. This is especially true in situations where there is uncertainty, which, as the 'new paradigm' reasoning theorists mentioned above contend, means pretty much any real-world reasoning context, because few things in life are certain. Evans is one of these theorists (see Manktelow, Over & Elqayam, 2010a, 2010b). In hypothetical thinking theory, then, the satisficing principle states that you form a (single) mental model that captures the essence of the problem (in induction) or use the one delivered to you by the implicit system (in deductive reasoning) and stick with it until you have a reason to change or reject it. This fits the confirm-early/disconfirm-late pattern in hypothesis testing.

The attraction of the hypothetical thinking theory is that it uses a small number of components – the three principles, some sub-principles and the dual process structure – and applies them to a wide range of reasoning contexts: Evans (2007a) uses it to interpret most of the major findings that have appeared in this book so far, such as belief biases in syllogistic reasoning, biases and suppositional

185

effects in conditional inference, judgment fallacies and pseudodiagnosticity. He has also extended it to decision making. In the next chapter, we go into that field ourselves.

Summary

1   Hypothetical thinking has two stages: the formation of hypotheses, and their testing.
2   Hypothesis formation comes under the heading of inductive reasoning. Induction leads to conclusions that are plausible but not necessary, and so it extends knowledge, but at the price of uncertainty.
3   Most recent research on induction has focussed on category-based induction, in which people project attributes from one category to another and assess their confidence in doing so.
4   The major theory in the area, the similarity-coverage model of Osherson et al., predicts and explains a range of phenomena resulting from differences in the overlap between problems' terms and common superordinate categories. The necessity of superordinates has been questioned.
5   Abductive thinking (i.e. reasoning with explanations) has been explained in these terms. Bayesian accounts of these forms of induction have been proposed.
6   Hypothesis testing research has been dominated by Wason's 2 4 6 rule-induction task. It gave rise to observations of confirmation bias, where people fail to test their own hypotheses. This idea was later modified to a bias towards a positive test strategy.
7   Research on hypothesis testing in field settings has shown a typical pattern of behaviour in which people initially seek to confirm their hypotheses, only later moving to potentially disconfirming testing.
8   Evans' hypothetical thinking theory, based on dual processes, proposes that people consider only a single hypothesis at one time, consider only the most relevant hypothesis and accept candidate explanatory models as long as they are satisfactory.

Decision making: preference and prospects

One of the most popular programmes on TV worldwide is *Who wants to be a million-aire?* I am going to assume that you are reasonably familiar with its format, and ask you to imagine that you have found yourself in the hot seat. If everything goes your way, you could wind up $1,000,000[1] richer. But things have not been going as well as you hoped. You have answered the first few questions with some difficulty and have won $4000, but have used up two of your lifelines, 'ask the audience' and 'phone a friend', in the process. Now you are on the $8000 question, and it is the worst yet: you have absolutely no idea which of the four possible answers is the right one.

So you use the last lifeline, '50–50'. This takes two of the four options away, leaving the right one and a wrong one. You have a decision to make. You can quit now and leave with the $4000 or you can answer the question – it will be a pure guess in this case. If you guess right, you can take home $8000 and possibly go on to higher prizes still; if you guess wrong, you go home with just $1000. On a January evening a few years ago, I watched a man faced with this choice and he decided to take the $4000 and run. Did he do the right thing?

If you feel like a challenge, you can try to answer this question by working out the figures that will tell us. We need to assess what the likely gains would be from quitting and from gambling by attempting the question; you should go with whichever is the higher. You have all the information available to enable you to arrive at an objective solution. It is a vivid real-world case of the kinds of decision making that we shall look at in this chapter, and shortly I shall show you how you can do the necessary calculation, if you are stumped at this point. First, we need to set out the basic building blocks of this central part of mental life.

Subjective expected utility

We have already dealt with one of the major components of decision making in Chapter 1: judging probability. Although judging probabilities may be interesting in itself, in the main we do it in order to help us decide what to do. In the Diesel and Roscoe example in Chapter 1, the two gumshoes had to decide whether to raid the pub in order to seize Dick. Being good Bayesians, they figured out that he was more likely to be in there than not. But they will not charge in just on this basis; they will also assess the risks of going in, and what they stand to gain if they do. When you watch the weather forecast you don't just want to know how likely it is to rain tomorrow, you want to know whether you should take a coat, cancel the picnic or water the garden.

Decision making thus involves taking information about probability and combining it with information about your goals and interests. As with the other forms of thinking that we have looked at in previous chapters, there are formal, normative accounts of what we should ideally do in the situations just described. These can be compared with research data about what people actually do when they make decisions. We will need a psychological, descriptive theory if human behaviour deviates from what normative decision theory prescribes.

Probability gives us the 'expected' part of the term 'expected utility theory'. The goal and interest aspect is what is referred to by the word 'utility'. *Utility* is an important word: something has utility to you if it is useful in taking you nearer a goal, or is in your interests. It is not the same thing as pleasure or even money value. You may decide to have some dental treatment: it won't be much fun, but it is in your interest to have it, and so it has positive utility for you if your goals are to have healthy teeth and freedom from toothache. An option can have negative utility: it takes you away from a goal, or is not in your interests. We shall go further into these matters when we look at decision dilemmas in the next chapter.

The example from *Millionaire* is of a decision about a gamble for money. Subjective expected utility (SEU) theory, as we have come to know it, is based on the idea that all decisions can be seen in this light: essentially as gambles. This tradition began in the modern era with von Neumann and Morgenstern (1944). Modern decision theory, deriving from this approach, states that when people make decisions, they trade off the utility of possible outcomes against their probability. Let us take a simple form of gambling and see how this is done, and then we can unlock the *Millionaire* case.

We saw in Chapter 1 that dice-rolling has figured large in historical studies of probability judgment, so let's consider a simple dice-rolling game. You pay me $1 for a roll of my dice. I will pay you a prize every time a pair comes up, as follows: $2 if you throw a pair of 2s, 3s, 4s or 5s; $5 if you throw a pairs of 6s; and $10 if you get 'snake eyes', a pair of 1s. I keep the $1 stake money if you throw anything other than a pair. Your decision is whether to play.

We can work out the expected value of each outcome, using these prize figures and our knowledge of the odds. Notice the phrase 'expected value': it is not the same as subjective expected utility. With SEU, your judgment of probability might not correspond to mathematical probability, and your assignment of utility might not be the same as money value. The difference between expected value and SEU has generated mountains of research, but at this point we shall park it for a while, for the sake of simplicity. We shall, of course, come back to it, because people make their decisions on the basis of utility, not value, when these are different.

The odds in the snake-eyes game are given by the number of faces of the two dice (6) and the number of possible combinations of these two sets of six faces: $6 \times 6 = 36$. Each pair only has one chance of coming up, so the probability of each is $1/36 = .028$. This is a logical possibility (see Chapter 1). The top prize, snake eyes, gets you $10, but as there is only a .028 probability of this happening the expected value of this option is $10 \times .028 = .28$. The logical possibility therefore delivers the long-run outcome that for every $1 staked, $0.28 comes back as winnings from snake eyes.

We can do the same for the other prizes. The odds are the same for each one, of course, so you simply multiply the prize amount by this figure. For a pair of 6s this is $5 \times .028 = .14$, and for the other pairs it is $2 \times .028 = .056$ each. Now, the decision question was: do you play the game? There is a general formula that can be used to decide this:

$$SEU = \sum_i p_i U_i$$

The symbols on the right are: i, each outcome; p, probability; U, utility; and Σ, add. We are assuming that expected value and SEU are the same in this case, to keep things simple. So, in words, the formula means that to find the expected utility in this situation, we take each outcome, multiply its utility by its probability and add all these results up. If we do this for the dice game, we get .28 + .14 + (4 × .056) = .64. This means that in the long run I pay out about $0.64 for every $1 stake I receive. Compare that with the expected utility for you of not playing, which is zero. You should not play, because the expected utility for playing is lower than that for not playing: you stand to lose. If enough people play, or you play often, however, I will make a lot of money. This is how all gambling works: there are more losers than winners, and the bookmakers laugh all the way to the bank. Which may make you wonder why anyone ever plays. We shall return to this question.

We can now apply this system to our man in the *Millionaire* hot seat. Should he have quit, or would he have been better advised to have a go at answering the question? Those are his two options, so we need to work out the expected utility of each. Decision theory assumes that he should opt for the one with the highest expected value. For quitting, this is straightforward: the rules of the game are that you can take whatever prize you currently hold. He has answered the $4000 question correctly, so the expected value of this option is $4000 × 1 = $4000.

We therefore need to know whether the expected value for the gamble is higher or lower than this. Here is one way to work it out.[2] Remember that if he guesses right he wins $8000, but if he guesses wrong he leaves with just $1000. He is guessing between only *two* possible answers, having played 50–50. So he has $1000 for sure plus either an extra $7000 with probability .5 = $3500, or nothing extra also with probability .5 = 0. He can therefore expect $1000 + $3500 + 0 = $4500 if he gambles. This is more than $4000, so our man should have gambled.[3] But he did not. Was he just being irrational? This situation has cropped up since then, and people have sometimes gambled; bear in mind that the expected value of the gamble is in fact higher than this, because if you guess right it also opens the way to even higher prizes, all the way up to $1,000,000. My own feeling, though, is that his action was perfectly understandable; indeed, I might have done the same. We shall look at possible reasons why he quit, and should not necessarily be pilloried for doing so, later. Points like this illustrate how expected value and SEU can diverge.

Principles and problems

The basic idea that people try to maximise expected utility, which is at the base of decision theory and, as we shall see in the next two chapters, is assumed by economists, makes immediate intuitive sense. Why would anyone do anything else? Several further principles flow out of this first principle, once you accept it. The first is known as *weak ordering*. This states that there is always some preference order between the options open to you, which you are trying to decide between. You might prefer Option 1 to Option 2, or Option 2 to Option 1, or rate them equally (economists call this indifference); but there will be some kind of preference relation. From this principle, there flows another: *transitivity of preferences*. If you prefer Option 1 to Option 2, and Option 2 to Option 3, you must prefer Option 1 to Option 3. From which we can safely conclude that Option 1 has the highest utility for you.

Another principle integral to SEU is the *independence axiom*. This has to do with the features of the options. If a feature is common to all the options open to you, then it cannot be used to decide between them. Suppose Diesel and Roscoe are after two fugitives, and each is an armed robber. They cannot justify pursuing desperate Dick instead of villainous Vic just because Dick is an armed robber, because Vic is too. Dick's lawyer will want to know what was the real reason they went after his client. As before, this principle leads logically to another, identified by another of the architects of modern decision theory, Savage (1954), who called it the *sure thing principle*. This relates to the situation you find yourself in when having to make a decision. If you prefer Option 1 to Option 2 when you are in situation A and in situation B, then you should prefer Option 1 when you do not know which situation you are in. Suppose Diesel and Roscoe have decided that they will raid the pub if Dick is in there and they will also raid the pub if he is not. They should decide to raid it if they don't know where he is.

Once again, all of these four principles make intuitive sense, on the face of it, and it begins to seem that the normative theory of decision making, SEU, might also serve as a reasonable descriptive theory of how people actually think. Not so fast. You may already harbour two suspicions about this possibility: firstly, the copious evidence from previous chapters that when people are measured against normative standards they tend to deviate from them. Much of this evidence concerned probability judgment, and probability is a central component of decision making, so we should be wary straight away. Secondly, there is the sneaking feeling that *Millionaire* man, who chose the non-maximising option, might not have been completely crazy.

As it happens, we can point to some problems with SEU before we even start running experiments. Some have been known for a long time, such as the paradox described by the 18th century mathematician Daniel Bernoulli. He was one of the first to describe a behavioural effect that has since become a law of economics: *diminishing marginal utility* (also known as diminishing returns). It is one of the basic observations which show that utility is not the same as money value. Suppose that you are earning $20,000 a year and you get a pay rise of $1000: nice. Then you get another $1000 pay rise: this is also nice, but not quite as nice as the first one, and subsequent increments of the same amount mean less and less to you. This is curious, because each $1000 is worth exactly the same in the shops. But the *utility* of each unit of wealth decreases as total wealth increases, although it never disappears completely, of course. As Hardman (2009) notes, this function, which is shown in Figure 8.1, is common in psychology: it describes our response to a wide range of stimuli. It is also the shape of the 'learning curve' when we acquire new skills. Extra increments of anything have diminishing effects on us.

The paradox in question is known as the *St Petersburg paradox*, after the journal in which Bernoulli described it. You have the opportunity to play a game where you toss a coin and win money when it comes up heads. If it comes up heads on the first toss, you win $1; heads on the second toss wins you $2, on the third toss $4, on the fourth, $8, on the fifth $16, and so on. How much could I offer you to buy you out of the game? Bernoulli thought that what he called a fairly reasonable man

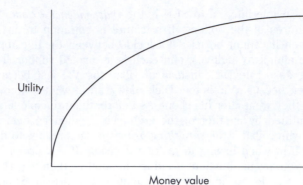

Figure 8.1 Diminishing marginal utility

would sell for about $20, but Baron (2008) reports the figure to be around $3–4 when he actually asked people. The paradox is that the expected value of the game is infinite: there is no telling when heads will come up. According to Bernoulli, while the expected value may be infinite, the expected utility diminishes, so that after some point there are no additions to utility. This may be the case, but it seems just as likely that people are sensitive to the diminishing probabilities as the sequence of tails before heads lengthens.

A second paradox is due to the Nobel Prize-winning French economist (and part-time physicist) Maurice Allais[4] (1953), and involves the independence axiom. Imagine you have bought a scratchcard, which requires you to choose between two ways of receiving your winnings:

1a $1000 with probability 1

    or

1b $1000 with probability .90

    $5000 with probability .09

    $0 with probability .01

Which would you choose? You are faced with a certain gain in 1a and a smaller probability of a higher gain, plus a slight risk of no gain at all, in 1b. Make a note of your choice.

This must be your lucky day, because you now have a second winning card, which again asks you to choose between two options for your winnings, as follows:

2a $1000 with probability .10

    $0 with probability .90

    or

2b $5000 with probability .09

      $0 with probability .91

Now you are faced with two less than certain outcomes. Once again, note down which you would choose.

If you did what people usually do when presented with these two choices, you chose 1a over 1b, and 2b over 2a. If you did so, you have been inconsistent from a normative point of view: you should have chosen 1a and 2a, or 1b and 2b (actually, you should really have chosen the latter, as we shall shortly see). Why? Because of the independence axiom: features common to both options should not be used to determine choices. In this case, the *a* and *b* options are in essence the same, and so preferences between them should have been the same. To see why they are the same, we can convert them from probabilities to frequencies.

This can be seen in Table 8.1, where probabilities and frequencies are compared (cf. Chapter 1 on probability as frequency). Instead of thinking about a single scratchcard, think of 100 in each situation: 1a/1b and 2a/2b. The probabilities result in the 100 cards being divided up in the proportions shown. In situation 1a all 100 tickets result in the $1000 prize, whereas in situation 1b ticket number 1 shows zero, tickets 2–10 show $5000 and tickets 11–100 show $1000. In situation 2a tickets numbered 1 and 2–10 show $1000 and tickets 11–100 show zero, whereas in situation 2b tickets 2–10 show $5000 and tickets 1 and 11–100 show zero. Now cover up the right-hand column, for probability .90 (tickets 11–100), and look at the figures you can still see. The choices between 1a and 1b and between 2a and 2b, involving tickets 1–10, are *exactly the same*. All that is different between situations 1 and 2 is that in the case of 1 the remaining chances deliver you $1000 whereas in 2 they deliver you nothing, and since these features are the same for either choice, *a* or *b*, they should not influence your decision. But they did.

Looking at expected utility can help explain this inconsistency. The expected value of the gamble in the *b* forms of these options is higher than it is in the *a* forms. In 1a it is $1000, while in 1b it is $1350; in 2a it is $100 while in 2b it is $450 (this helps you see the relation between them: just take 900 – the expected value of tickets 11–100 – from *both* options in 1 and you get the figures in 2). So, just like

Table 8.1 Probabilities and frequencies in the Allais paradox

Options	Probabilities		
	.01	.09	.90
	Frequencies (ticket numbers)		
	1	2–10	11–100
1a	$1000	$1000	$1000
1b	$0	$5000	$1000
2a	$1000	$1000	$0
2b	$0	$5000	$0

Source: Allais (1953): reproduced by permission of Psychology Press

Millionaire man, people strongly prefer the certain gain to a less certain gain of higher expected value, in situation 1. The difference between the two uncertain gains in situation 2 is proportionately much greater, which, together with the lack of a certain option, pulls people's preferences in the normative direction. Certainty clearly exerts a very powerful effect on people's choices, biasing them against what are normatively better options. This is further evidence that SEU theory will not do as a complete descriptive theory. We shall return to psychological explanations for choices in the Allais paradox in the next chapter.

More recent research throws up problems for other apparently unassailable principles of utility theory. The weak ordering principle gives rise to the norm of transitivity of preferences, as we saw. Do people always conform to this? Amos Tversky (1969) found that they do not. Imagine that you are a university admissions tutor, selecting among applicants. Each person has been given a score on three dimensions: intelligence, emotional stability and social facility; intelligence is clearly the most important when it comes to student admissions, but the other factors are important too. In front of you are the scores for five applicants; these are shown in Table 8.2.

Ask yourself which of the five candidates you would put at the top of your list to admit. Is it candidate E? Compare this person with candidate A: Tversky found that most people did indeed prefer E to A. The interesting part of this experiment was that Tversky used another way of assessing preferences: people were also asked to compare A with B, then B with C, C with D and D with E. They tended to prefer the candidates in that order: A > B, and so on. This should have meant that A was preferred to E, but, as we have seen, preference reversed when A and E were compared directly. In interviews after giving their choices, the participants were unaware that they had violated transitivity. It appears that the differences in intelligence between A–B, B–C and so on were so small that, even though this was the most important aspect of the candidates, it was discounted, and people focussed on the ones where differences were wide, which can be used to discriminate clearly between the options. But with the direct A–E comparison, the difference in intelligence score is now wide, and so it comes back into focus.

The same effect was strikingly demonstrated by Eldar Shafir (1993). People were asked to imagine they were deciding between two parents in a messy

Table 8.2 Some results from Tversky's university admissions experiment

| Candidates | Attributes | | |
	Intelligence	Emotional stability	Social facility
A	69	84	75
B	72	78	65
C	75	72	55
D	78	66	45
E	81	60	35

Source: Adapted from Table 7 in Tversky (1969)

divorce case involving custody of their child. The parents were described in the following ways:

Parent A	Parent B
Average income	Above average income
Average health	Minor health problems
Average working hours	Lots of work-related travel
Relatively stable social life	Extremely active social life
Reasonable rapport with child	Very close relationship with child

When participants were asked which parent they would award custody to, their choices were:

Parent A: 36%   Parent B: 64%

Participants who had to choose who to *deny* custody to made the following choices:

Parent A: 45%   Parent B: 55%

This is strange, from a normative point of view, because Parent B is the majority choice in both cases. Awarding and denying should have been perfectly complementary: the majority choice for one should have been the minority choice for the other. People seem to have focussed on different aspects, depending on the task. Parent A sounds a rather colourless character, but Parent B is much more interesting, with stand-out features that are both positive and negative. When looking for aspects on which to base the choice, people focus on the strong positives in the award condition and on the strong negatives in the deny condition.

The *sure thing principle* (see above) can also be undermined by changing how a decision problem is presented, even though Savage himself regarded it as the most compelling non-logical intuition in decision making. This was demonstrated in some research conducted by the two authors whose work we have just been considering, Tversky and Shafir (1992; see also Shafir & Tversky, 1992). They presented US students with the following kind of scenario:

> Imagine that you have just taken a tough qualifying examination. It is the end of the fall quarter, you feel tired and run-down, and you are not sure that you passed the exam. In case you failed you have to take the exam in a couple of months – after the Christmas holidays. You now have the opportunity to buy a very attractive 5-day Christmas vacation package to Hawaii at an exceptionally low price. The special offer expires tomorrow, but the exam grade will not be available until the following day.

There were three decision options: to buy the holiday, not buy the holiday, or pay a $5 fee for the right to buy it at the special offer price after the exam result was known. Nearly twice as many people (61%) chose this third option compared to those who chose to buy (32%). That this is a clear violation of the *sure thing principle* was confirmed by a second condition in which participants were told that they had either passed or failed. In both cases, the majority elected to buy the holiday straight away. Tversky and Shafir call this the *disjunction effect*: people are faced with an either–or situation, which introduces uncertainty, and it seems that people are reluctant to think through uncertainty in such circumstances, or perhaps are unable. The task is reminiscent of the kinds of problem described by Evans (2007a) in his account of hypothetical thinking theory (see Chapter 7). One of the principles of this theory is that people generally only consider one hypothesis at a time; Tversky and Shafir's task requires them to hold two in mind and it seems that people will pay money to escape from this burden.

Tversky and Shafir argue that knowing the result gives you a reason to make the choice: to celebrate passing or to cheer yourself up after failing. It may well be true that we do engage in this kind of justification, and if so it could be seen as reflecting the System 2 part of hypothetical thinking, where we monitor the conclusions we arrive at and accept them if they fit our goals.

Note that the award/deny experiment above is also interpretable in terms of Evans' theory: here, it would be the relevance principle that is in operation, causing people to change focus between the attributes of the warring couple.

Complex decisions

One of the most famous, indeed infamous, documented pieces of personal decision making is to be found in Charles Darwin's journal, where he sets out the pros and cons of getting married. He lists both positive and negative reasons for and against marriage.[5] Among the points against marriage, he includes:

> Freedom to go where one liked
>
> Choice of society
>
> Conversation of clever men at clubs
>
> The expense and anxiety of children
>
> Not forced to visit relatives

and among the advantages of marriage, he considered:

> Children (if it please God)
>
> Constant companion (and friend in old age)
>
> Home, and someone to take care of house
>
> It is intolerable to think of spending one's whole life. . . working, working. . .
>
> Better than a dog anyhow

'Marry – Marry – Marry – QED' was his conclusion.

This was in 1838, the year of Darwin's 29th birthday, and clearly a long time before political correctness came to the fore. Later that year, he proposed to his cousin, Emma Wedgwood. To his delight, she accepted, and they were married the following January. Perhaps his prayer for children was heard: they had ten.

Whether or not to get married is a decision – a gamble, even – but it does not look much like the kinds of decision we have been considering so far. It is much more complex. The same can be said for many other major decisions we might be faced with in our lives: whether to go to university (which one, which course), which job to apply for, whether to buy a house (which one), whether to relocate (where to), and so on. One obvious source of complexity is the sheer number of factors that have to be considered, along with the relative importance of each. A formal technique has been developed to try to put such decisions on an objective footing: *multi-attribute utility theory*, or MAUT (Keeney, 1992: Keeney & Raiffa, 1976). More psychological approaches propose how we might reduce this complexity, and we shall consider them later.

MAUT is a development of SEU, and incorporates its basic assumption that decisions are made according to the maximisation of utility. We can see how it works using an everyday example of complex decision making: choosing a mobile phone contract. These contracts have lots of attributes: price, free minutes, texts, camera, monthly tariff or pay as you go, and so on. If you are in the market for a mobile, you can put these attributes in order, deleting any that you don't care about; you can also do more than this, and attach a weight to each one according to how important it is to you – these weights are purely subjective, of course. Then you can look at the contracts you are thinking about and score them on each attribute; we actually use everyday expressions such as 'weighing up the options' to describe this process.

In MAUT, this scaling can be done mathematically, using a technique called conjoint measurement. An attribute is a scale on some dimension, such as price: a contract might be cheap, reasonable, pricey or outrageous on this scale. We can use a centigrade scale, 0–100, for this, where a higher score means a cheaper contract. Take two such points, say reasonable (70) and pricey (40), and then think of another dimension, such as free minutes. You prefer more free minutes. Your candidate contracts will vary along this scale too, say from 10 (few) to 90 (hundreds). You are prepared to pay the reasonable price of $30 a month for a contract that scores 40 on minutes. What would the price of a contract that scored 20 have to be, such that you would be indifferent between them? Cheaper, of course, given that you prefer more minutes. You can establish scales for any attribute using this technique.

Now let us see how it could be used in a situation in which you are trying to choose between five contracts on four attributes. In Table 8.3, you can see some imaginary data. Take the score of each contract on each attribute and multiply it by its weight, and you can derive an aggregate utility score. The weights have to sum to 1, since they are assigned to all and only the aspects that you are considering. The option with the highest aggregate utility wins. These are given on the right in the table. For instance, the aggregate score for Contract 1 is $(80 \times .40) + (20 \times .30) + (50 \times .20) + (60 \times .10) = 54$.

Table 8.3 Choosing phone contracts the MAUT way: weights, attribute scores and aggregate utilities

	Attributes				
	Price	Free minutes	Texts	Camera	
Weights	.40	.30	.20	.10	
	Scores				
Options					Aggregate
Contract 1	80	20	50	60	54
Contract 2	70	60	50	50	61
Contract 3	30	80	20	30	43
Contract 4	80	40	30	40	54
Contract 5	50	50	40	70	50

You can see that there is a clear winner: Contract 2 gets the highest aggregate score. It is not the outright best on any aspect, but it scores highest overall because you are trading off each aspect against the others in terms of their importance to you.

Can people really be expected to engage in this kind of process when making choices? Not even Darwin assigned weights to the various properties of marriage that he listed, and many of us might not even go so far as to write down lists for something like that. Using a technique such as MAUT obviously requires a lot of effort and expertise, and in real life we might run short on both. Most of the time, we must therefore be simplifying the process in some way. We shall go more into this simplifying process in the next chapter, but at this point we can look at two possibilities.

The first was introduced by Tversky (1972), and is called *elimination by aspects*. You choose the most important aspect, find which options are the best on that and reject the rest. If there is no clear winner, go to the next most important aspect and repeat the process, and so on, until you are left with the one winning option. Looking at the contracts in Table 8.3, price was the most important aspect (it has the highest weighting to reflect this). Two contracts, 1 and 4, come out on top, so we have to look at free minutes: Contract 4 scores higher on that, and so you choose Contract 4. This is certainly much easier than all that multiplication and addition, but its disadvantages are also clear. It leads to the rejection of what was our all-round winner on the basis of the MAUT analysis. In fact, it led us to the two worst options (Contracts 1 and 4) on the second most important aspect, minutes. The danger, then, is that using this heuristic can lead to lack of consideration of relevant aspects and an unsatisfactory conclusion; indeed, one that is objectively irrational, since it is not the best on offer.

Baron (2008) points to a related technique with a related problem: the use of *lexical rules*. Lexical rules are 'rules of life' such as *be honest, keep your word* or *do no harm*. People sometimes use these rules because there are some aspects that they feel should not be traded off against anything. One is human life: people are often uncomfortable with putting a value on it, which is what you have to do if you are making life-or-death decisions, as, for instance, people in the medical profession do. This is an extreme form of elimination by aspects: decide that human life is paramount and that's that.

However, using these rules inflexibly leads to two problems. The first is that they can fly in the face of another norm of decision making, that of *consequentialism*. You can see this norm implicitly in the previous discussion: decisions should be taken on the basis of their consequences. You look at the options before you and go for the one that will have the best outcome. Forget the past, or you will find yourself falling prey to the gambler's fallacy and other such horrors (see Baron, 1994). The second is that lexical rules can lead to intractable dilemmas. You cannot be completely honest without hurting people's feelings more than you would with the occasional little lie; and allotting unlimited resources to the saving of a single life will put other lives at risk. In practice, most of us tend to place high but not absolute values on these aspects. We shall consider dilemmas in more detail in the next chapter.

Preference

At the core of decision making, such as the cases we have been considering so far, is the concept of preference. In the mobile phone example, you may prefer camera phones to phones without cameras, for instance: a phone camera carries utility for you. Where do these utilities come from? For decision theorists, the question is circular: we infer people's utilities from the preferences that are reflected in their choices. Psychologists want to know more.

We already have some clues as to the psychology of preference and utility, in the shape of the disconnect between utility, pleasure and money value, in the Bernoulli and Allais paradoxes and in the preference reversal phenomenon. In this section, we shall look at three further aspects of the psychology of preference that go beyond these observations: different definitions of utility, the influence of competing options and the effects of how the decision problem is described. They all lead to the conclusion that for real decision makers, preferences are not so much revealed in the choices we make, as *constructed*, in Slovic's apt term (Slovic, 1995), when we think about them.

Different utilities

Saying that utility is not the same as pleasure is not to say that the two are completely divorced. Pleasure can certainly contribute to utility. Indeed, utility and pleasure were combined in the Utilitarian philosophy of Jeremy Bentham in the late 18th century. Bentham popularised a moral philosophy based on the idea of right action being that which delivers the greatest pleasure and least pain to the greatest number of people. We thus have two conceptions of utility, a distinction that has recently been revived and focussed on by Daniel Kahneman (Kahneman, 2000a,

2000b; see also Read, 2007): *decision utility* and *experienced utility*. Decision utility is the kind that we have mainly been dealing with up to now: it is revealed in people's choices. We have already seen that there are problems with inconsistency even in these apparently sober contexts. When we look more closely at experienced utility, and some of the research that has been done on it, further complications emerge.

The first thing we have to do is to note that experienced utility can itself be subdivided into *remembered* utility and *predicted* utility. The two are related, of course: how you evaluate a past experience can affect whether you choose to repeat or avoid it in future, as we shall see. But they can be distinguished. Kahneman's studies have produced evidence that when both evaluating and predicting their experiences, people focus on what he calls *moments* that represent the experience, rather than on the whole experience. This tendency is most strongly reflected in the neglect of duration in remembered utility. Moment utility is the sign (positive or negative) and intensity (from high to low) of your hedonic experience at a point in time (Kahneman, 2000b). The word *hedonic* refers to the feelings, say pleasure or pain, that accompany an experience. From this comes a utility profile: each experience contains a series of moments with associated utilities, and you can describe them or even draw them on a graph. The whole set can then be evaluated.

Kahneman and his colleagues have reported a series of striking empirical studies of both fictitious and real episodes; interestingly, he reports little difference between the two kinds in terms of their findings (Kahneman, 2000b; see also Mellers, 2000). We shall begin with two examples of the real ones. Redelmeier and Kahneman (1996) studied people undergoing colonoscopy, which is a very uncomfortable invasive procedure used to diagnose conditions such as bowel cancer. Every 60 seconds, these patients graded the intensity of the pain they were experiencing on a 10-point scale. Afterwards, they evaluated the whole experience in various ways: for instance, by giving a global pain rating for the whole procedure, or by scaling it against other nasty experiences. The procedure took different times to conduct, from a few minutes to over an hour.

You would expect that people's global evaluations of its pleasantness, or rather unpleasantness, would depend on this factor. You would be wrong: there was no correlation between duration and remembered utility. What actually determines remembered utility in this and similar situations is an average of the utility at two representative moments: the moment when pleasure or displeasure is most extreme (the peak) and the moment at the end of the episode (the end). Consequently, this has become known as the *peak–end rule* (Kahneman, 2000a, 2000b).

The peak–end rule leads to some very surprising predictions, observations and implications. For instance, in a follow-up to the colonoscopy study, Katz, Redelmeier and Kahneman (1997) assigned patients randomly to two groups. One group had the usual procedure and the other group had the probe left in place, without being moved, for one minute at the end of the procedure. Patients find this mildly uncomfortable compared to the procedure itself, but still unpleasant. These people reported significantly higher remembered utility (i.e. the experience was less awful) compared to those who did not have the extra period of discomfort, just as the peak–end rule predicts.

In this case, then, people seem to prefer an experience with *more* total pain in it – as long as the pain is declining at the end. This preference had been observed in an earlier, non-clinical study by Kahneman, Fredrickson, Schreiber and Redelmeier (1993). They had people immerse a hand in cold (14°C) water for one minute, which hurts; and for one minute followed by 30 seconds in which the temperature was raised, without the participant being told, by one degree. This still hurts, but less. Later, they were asked to choose which trial to repeat, the short one or the one with the extra 30 seconds of pain. Most chose the longer one. Again, they preferred more pain to less, as long as the pain was declining at the end.

When you make a choice, of any kind, part of your task is to predict the utilities of the outcomes. That is what consequentialism requires of you. You can see in the two cases of experienced utility just cited that remembered utility can feed into this process of prediction: you will choose between options depending on what you remember of similar experiences in the past. Kahneman's work shows that experienced utility introduces complications that decision utility ignores, because there is a clear difference, described by the peak–end rule, between subjective utility and objective utility. Utility considered in purely decision-theoretic terms prescribes that people should choose the utility-maximising option, which objectively must be the experience with the least amount of pain. But they don't: people actually prefer experiences with greater total amounts of pain in them, as long as that pain is decreasing, and their decisions follow this hedonic preference.

Notice some ethical problems that this research raises, to do with informed consent (see Kahneman, 1993; Slovic, 1995). Should doctors recommend a treatment that they know will cause more pain at the time, but which will be remembered as better than one that causes less pain? Should they add an extra dose of diminishing pain to bring about this effect? Should they do so in order to make it more likely that patients will come back for more (painful) treatments?

The moment approach advocated by Kahneman can also be applied to predicted utility in situations where we do not have memories of past experiences to go on. Something everyone likes to ponder and discuss is how our lives might be different if we were on the receiving end of a life-changing event such as winning millions in a lottery (or a TV game show). How do you think you would feel if you were rich? Wonderful, surely! We also do this with negative events, such as having a terrible accident that leaves us disabled in some way. There has even been a rising trend for 'living wills', in which people leave instructions not to be resuscitated if they survive an accident that leaves them paralysed, say. They would rather die than live like that, they think. Really? This is a testable question about *predicted utility*: we can compare it with the actual experience of people who win millions, or who become disabled.

This was done many years ago in a classic study by Brickman, Coates and Janoff-Bulman (1978). They questioned groups of both lottery winners and accident victims; the latter had suffered very serious injuries and were left either paraplegic or quadriplegic. The lottery winners' happiness was no different from that of similar people who had not won the lottery, in terms of their ratings of past, present or future happiness. The accident victims' rating of past and present happiness was lower than it was for the controls, but there was no difference in ratings of future happiness. In short, there was far less difference in actual happiness between these two groups and ordinary people who had not experienced either event than might be expected.

Brickman et al. attribute this surprising finding to two processes. First of all, people's evaluations of everyday events and memories change after a life-changing event. But, more importantly, there is the effect of adaptation. Brickman et al. studied people some time (about a year) after the event in question. Quite simply, you get used to your changed circumstances. But when projecting forward to the changed state before it happens, people forget about adaptation and focus on a moment: the transition between the pre- and post-change states. The lottery winners in the Brickman et al. study did indeed find winning a positive experience and the accident victims found their injury a negative experience (by about the same degree relative to neutral), but this effect wore off.

The adaptation effect was confirmed in an ingenious study conducted by an undergraduate student, Beruria Cohn, which Kahneman (2000b) reports. She managed to find participants who actually knew someone who had won the lottery or become paraplegic, along with those who did not know such people. Each group was asked to estimate the proportions of time fictional characters, including lottery winners and paraplegics, would be in a good or a bad mood. Some were told that the events had occurred one month before, whereas some were told one year before. The people who did not know any winners or paraplegics gave similar ratings for both time intervals, but people who were personally acquainted with them were much more sensitive to the time factor: they rated the difference between good and bad mood as much less after one year. This is just what happens if you adapt to your situation. Unless you know this, your rating will be governed by the transition event.

There is a large literature on how we predict future feelings, a field known as *affective forecasting* ('affect' is the noun that psychologists use when they talk about feelings). It is brilliantly reviewed by Daniel Gilbert (2006) in a book written for the non-specialist audience. Gilbert describes in detail the trends and biases that occur when we try to imagine how we might feel about something we have not yet experienced. If we acknowledge that such predictions feed into our judgment of the utility of the options we are considering, then these biases are a serious matter for the explanation of decision making, and theories that ignore them are missing something essential about the process; see also Ayton, Pott and Elwakiri (2007) and Hsee and Hastie (2006) for more on the problems of affective forecasting,

Competing options

A principle that follows logically from expected utility theory is that of *invariance*: values and probabilities are expressed as numbers, and a number does not change from one context to another. A probability of .20, or a value of $500, should be the same however they are derived (*procedure invariance*) or described (*description invariance*). We have already seen that there are numerous reasons to doubt that people keep to these sub-principles. In this section and the next we shall pile more doubt on our ability to think objectively about the figures in decision problems.

In this section, we shall be mainly concerned with aspects of procedure invariance, or rather of its violation, that arise when decisions are lined up against each other. There are two basic ways of indicating value when you make a decision, nicely captured in an example given by Hsee (2000): the shop and the auction room. If you are buying an item from a dealer, such as a picture, a piano or a piece of furniture, you will be able to assess it alongside a lot of alternatives, and choose among them. However, in the auction room, the item in question might be the only one of its kind in the sale. You then have to put a value on it without reference to any alternatives. Objectively, choosing and valuing should reflect one another. But in some situations they become detached, resulting in preference reversals, where the favoured and rejected options in one situation change places in another.

Many of the demonstrations of such effects are due to Paul Slovic and his colleagues over a long period of time; Lichtenstein and Slovic (2006) have edited a compendium of them, conducted by themselves and other researchers. In an early example, Lichtenstein and Slovic (1971) gave people a choice between two bets: one with a high probability of low winnings (called the P bet) and one with a low probability of high winnings (the $ bet). People usually preferred the P bet. Other people were asked to place a value on the P bet and the $ bet (e.g. by stating what sum of money they regarded as being of equal value to the bet). They tended to give a higher rating to the $ bet this time, which is a clear reversal of preference. Tversky, Slovic and Kahneman (1990) showed that this effect was mainly due to overvaluing the $ bet. This in turn can be seen as a kind of response compatibility effect: the valuation task makes you think about money, and so you focus on the money aspect of the $ bet. Lotteries seem to have this property: in thinking about whether to buy a ticket, you focus on the size of the prize and lose sight of the infinitesimally small chance of actually winning it. This helps to explain why people buy lottery tickets in the first place.

Choosing can be compared in a similar way to valuation by *matching*. Once again, we find that two ways of eliciting values, which should objectively reach the same result, give rise to psychological differences. For instance, here is an example of an imaginary job selection procedure, from Tversky, Sattath and Slovic (1988). Participants in an experiment were given two candidates' scores on two attributes, with technical knowledge specified as the most important, as follows:

	Technical knowledge	*Human relations*
Candidate X	86	76
Candidate Y	78	91

When asked to choose between the two candidates, X was preferred by about two-thirds of the participants.

Another group was given the same information, except that one of the values was missing, for instance, the 78 in the bottom left cell. They were asked to fill in a value such that the two candidates were equally rated. This was the matching task. Now, call the number of people who favour X over Y in the choice task C, and the number who do the same in the matching task M. Objectively, C should equal M. However, C was 65% in the experiment reported by Tversky et al., while M varied between 26% and 44%, depending on which cell had the missing value, so they were significantly different. This pattern was repeated using a number of different contents. What seems to be happening here is something that Tversky et al. call the *prominence effect*. When you have all the information available to you, as in the choice task, you choose on the basis of the most prominent attribute. That was what happened in Shafir's award/deny child custody problem described earlier. But the matching task requires a different kind of thinking, where you have to do some calculation, and prominence counts for less then.

A similar but distinct context effect is found when *separate* and *joint* evaluations are made. Unlike with the choice versus matching studies, in this case we don't have incomplete information, but a comparison of situations in which you either have or don't have whole alternative options to consider. Thus we are not dealing with an effect of using different evaluation scales. Hsee's example of the auction room and the shop fits this framework. Consider an example from Lowenthal (1993). People chose between two political candidates: one with an unblemished personal history who could bring 1000 jobs to the area, and one who could bring 5000 jobs but had a minor conviction. They preferred the latter. But when other people had to evaluate each candidate separately, the blameless person was given a higher evaluation than the slightly dodgy character – another preference reversal.

Of course, in real elections we are always making joint evaluations. Hsee (2000; see Hsee, Loewenstein, Blount & Bazerman, 1999, for a more detailed treatment) reports research in which rather more realistic contents were used, and where any joint–separate effects could be precisely quantified, using the index of *willingness to pay*. Table 8.4 gives details of two music dictionaries that participants were asked to judge; they played the role of music students in a second-hand book store, with between $10 and $50 to spend. Below the descriptions, you can see the amounts that participants were willing to pay when they judged each dictionary by itself, and when they judged them together. Dictionary A was valued more highly

Table 8.4 Choosing music dictionaries: attributes of two options and willingness-to-pay (WTP) values when they are considered separately and jointly

	Dictionary A	Dictionary B
Year of publication	1993	1993
Number of entries	10,000	20,000
Defects	None; like new	Torn cover, otherwise like new
WTP values		
Separate	$24	$20
Joint	$19	$27

Source: Based on Hsee (2000)

when each was considered separately, but Dictionary B was the preferred option when they were compared.

Hsee explains separate–joint preference reversal using the *evaluability hypothesis*. Some attributes are hard to evaluate in isolation: number of entries in a dictionary, for instance, or technical specifications for complex items such as cars or computers. Is 10,000 a good number for dictionary entries? What about 100 bhp in a car, or 1.5 gigabytes in a computer? On the other hand, some are easy to evaluate, such as whether a book has any defects or whether a car costs over $10,000. Knowledge is the difference. In separate evaluation, values are determined by the attributes that are easy to assess because we already know how to scale them. However, joint evaluation gives us a basis on which to assess hard-to-evaluate attributes: set against a dictionary with 20,000 entries, one with 10,000 now sounds distinctly unattractive, never mind the condition of its cover. You can see how this explains the political candidate finding above. People have also been found to offer different starting salaries to job candidates depending on whether they give separate or joint evaluations (Hsee, 2000), something to bear in mind the next time you are job-hunting.

Evaluability is a heuristic (cf. Chapter 1) and so contains the drawback that dogs all heuristics: while generally useful, it sometimes leads to choosing the less-than-ideal option. This is because, in separate evaluation, the easy dimension may be less important than the hard one, and you will tend to choose according to the easy one, as we have seen. Hsee (1998) demonstrated this using. . . ice cream. Different groups of people were asked what they would be willing to pay for 7 oz (200 g) of ice cream in a 5 oz (140 g) cup or 8 oz (225 g) in a 10 oz (280 g) cup. They were willing to pay *more* for the smaller amount! The reason seems to have been that in the first option a small cup was overfilled, so it looked like a generous portion, whereas in the second case a big cup was underfilled. Naturally, when evaluating them jointly, people chose the larger amount because they could see that it *was* larger. The overfill cue was easy to use, and the portion size hard, when the options were considered separately, but when they were seen together it was easier to scale the portions against each other.

Framing: the effects of description

Description invariance entails that figures should not be affected by the way they are described: a number is a number is a number. But when it comes to making judgments and decisions, they are affected. The two paradoxes mentioned earlier gave some early evidence that this is so. Thaler (1980) pointed to a classic case of the influence of description in the real world: people are more inclined to shop at stores that offer a discount for cash than a credit card surcharge, even when the relation between these prices is the same in each shop (e.g. you pay $10 cash or $10.10 by credit card). It sounds as if you are making a gain in the first case and sustaining a loss in the second, and, as we shall see in greater detail later, money amounts change their values when they are framed as losses and gains.

The paradigm case of framing comes from the research of Tversky and Kahneman (1981): the disease problem. Jack and Meg are health service officials making plans for dealing with a new disease that is expected to strike their district soon. They expect the disease to kill 600 people unless something is done. Jack's scientific advisers tell him about two treatment programmes: Programme A will definitely save 200 lives, while Programme B has a one-third (.33) chance of saving 600 lives. Which programme does Jack approve? Meg's advisers tell her about two other treatment programmes: Programme C will certainly result in 400 deaths, while Programme D has a two-thirds (.67) chance that 600 people will die. Which programme does Meg approve?

Most people given Jack's problem chose Programme A; most people given Meg's problem chose Programme D. All four situations are identical: the expected result is 200 lives saved versus 400 lives lost. So people should have been indifferent between them. However, the description brought about a bias, once again depending on whether the outcomes were framed as gains or losses.

Similar effects have been observed in the field of insurance by Johnson, Hershey, Meszaros and Kunreuther (1993). They found that 68% of people were prepared to buy an insurance policy that gave a $600 no-claims rebate on premiums of $1600. However, when exactly the same deal was presented in terms of a $600 policy excess (deductible, in US terminology) on premiums of $1000, only 44% said they would buy. The $600 feels like a gain in the first case and a loss in the second; in both cases, customers pay $1000 in premiums if they do not make a claim and $1600 if they do.

These authors also report an interesting effect of availability and subadditivity in insurance (see Chapter 1 to refresh your memory about these effects). They asked people to price insurance premiums for policies that paid out stated amounts on risks such as accident or disease. People asked to price *accident* alone, or *disease* alone, were prepared to pay significantly higher premiums than were people who were asked to price coverage for *accident or disease*, or for *any reason*. Johnson et al. explain this in terms of availability: when given 'accident' or 'disease' to think about, you can readily recall instances. It is not so easy to generate examples of 'any reason'. Note that insurance companies could use this effect to make money out of you. Accident is clearly, and logically, less likely than accident or disease, and less likely still than any reason. People are therefore prepared to pay more to insure against a less likely event, for purely psychological reasons: availability. Now you know about this, you can be on your guard next time you take out accident, health or travel insurance. Don't be dazzled by the mention of specific risks.

As we saw in Chapter 1, one of the ways availability can affect judgments of probability is by vividness. Johnson et al. report a striking real-world case of this in their work on insurance. In 1990, there was a lot of publicity about a predicted earthquake in the USA. In the two months prior to the predicted quake, over 650,000 clients of just one insurer added earthquake cover to their home insurance policies. The quake never happened.

Prospect theory: a descriptive theory of decision making

We have seen in the course of this chapter that what initially seemed like an open-and-shut case for human rationality, that people will always seek to maximise their expected utility, is left with a lot of explaining to do when faced with the vagaries of actual human thought and behaviour. The call for such an explanation – a new theory – was answered by Daniel Kahneman and Amos Tversky (1979b), in the shape of *prospect theory*. You have seen a parade of effects and biases in human choice. Prospect theory has become the dominant means to account for them under one roof, as it were. The theory's impact cannot be overstated: according to Wu, Zhang and Gonzalez (2004), Kahneman and Tversky's (1979b) paper was the second most cited in economics in the last quarter of the 20th century. It and related work contributed to the award of the Nobel Prize for economics to Kahneman in 2002. Tversky missed out because he died in 1996, and the prize is not awarded posthumously.

Prospect theory is not a total departure from SEU theory, but an adaptation of it. It retains the basic structure of decision making as a combination of the assessment of utility with the judgment of probability. However, it takes into account the systematic deviations from normative prescriptions that have been observed since at least the time of Bernoulli, and integrates them into this structure. The result is a descriptive theory (i.e. an account of what people actually do) that explains the kinds of effects that have been outlined above, makes some surprising novel predictions and does so using quite a small number of components.

We start with prospect theory's treatment of utility. This differs from the classical treatment of utility as money value in several ways. The first is to adopt the principle of diminishing returns: as wealth increases, each extra increment of wealth means less and less to us, as Bernoulli described. The second is to ask what happens to negative utility. As we saw in the cases of the Allais paradox and the framing effects, the introduction of negative utility changes people's preferences: we place a higher negative value on a given level of loss than we place a positive value on the same level of gain: you feel the hurt of losing $10 more than you enjoy a gain of $10. This implies that the diminishing utility curve for losses will have a different shape than for gains: it will be steeper.

These two curves were integrated into a single function by Kahneman and Tversky, as you can see in Figure 8.2, which shows what they call the *value function*. The two axes of the value function show money value (horizontal) and subjective value (vertical). Both loss and gain segments flatten out, with increasing losses and gains showing diminishing utility, but the loss curve is steeper than the gain curve.

There is another property of this function that marks a radical shift from SEU: the point where the loss and gain curves cross. Kahneman and Tversky call this the *reference point*. This is the state of your current wealth. Any change is either a gain or a loss with respect to what you already have; once there has been a change, your reference point shifts to this new level. SEU does not have this property: logically, any increment should be considered in terms of its proportion of your total wealth, not as a move one way or the other.

Here is a little thought experiment to illustrate how the reference point works. Suppose you have been playing the lottery, the top prize is $5 million and you have the six winning numbers. How do you feel? I think we can guess. Now suppose it's the following day, and the lottery company rings you up: 100 people

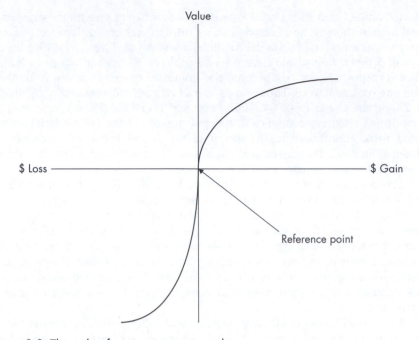

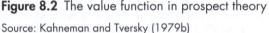

Figure 8.2 The value function in prospect theory

Source: Kahneman and Tversky (1979b)

had those six numbers, so your prize is actually $50,000. How do you feel now? It seems likely that you will feel disappointment, perhaps slight, perhaps bitter – almost as if you had lost $4.95 million. Psychologically, you *have* lost it: your reference point when you found out that you had won shifted from your measly state of current wealth to that plus $5 million, and you have had to come down from it. It feels like a loss, and it hurts. But objectively, you are still worth $50,000 more than you were yesterday, and if you had been the sole winner of a top prize of $50,000 you would be smiling now instead of kicking the cat.

An actual illustration of this effect comes from Ali (1977), who found a curious pattern in the behaviour of punters at horse race meetings. If they had had a bad day, they tended to bet on longer-odds horses in the final race of the meeting than they did earlier – thus making it more likely that they would lose again, since outsiders are less likely to win. The prospect theory explanation would be that the bettors had a reference point in terms of an aspiration to make a gain, or at least break even, at the end of the day. They therefore feel the loss they have sustained keenly, and engage in risk-seeking behaviour in an attempt to recover their position (Hardman, 2009).

This is a novel prediction of prospect theory: that people will engage in risk-seeking behaviour when losses are in prospect, but be risk-averse when gains are in prospect. It offers us a way to explain the decision of *Millionaire* man, which we began with. He has $4000 for sure if he quits: that is his reference point. He has a .5 probability of $8000 plus a .5 probability of $1000 if he gambles. If the possible loss of $3000 from his reference point of $4000 is felt more acutely than the possible gain of $4000, he will quit, and that is what he did. People are risk-averse when gains are in prospect. The idea of the reference point opens up an intriguing possibility in this situation, because of the two ways of working out the expected utilities (see above). Starting from the point of $4000 that you will take home if you quit means that one of the outcomes from the gamble will be framed as a loss, and loss aversion leads you to quit. But you could start from the point of the $1000 you are guaranteed to take home whatever happens, and then you might think only in terms of different possible gains: zero, $3000 or $7000. Perhaps the people who gamble when in this situation are doing this.

The classic framing effects can also be explained in this way. In the disease problem, Jack's situation starts with a reference point of 600 deaths, and the A and B options are framed in terms of gains: lives saved. Meg's reference point, however, is different: it is the current state, and the outcomes of the C and D options are framed in terms of losses. Because people are risk-averse for gains, they choose the certain gain of 200 saved in Jack's case; and because they are risk-seeking for losses, they choose the uncertain prospect of 600 saved, and avoid the certain loss of 400 lives, in Meg's case.

Prospect theory also has a distinctive treatment of probability, based on the kinds of findings reviewed in Chapter 1. There, we saw that people tend to over-weight very low probabilities and underweight medium-range probabilities; they are, though, quite clear on what the probabilities of 0 and 1 imply. In Figure 8.3, prospect theory's *weighting function* is shown, which reflects these departures from objective probability. The straight diagonal line shows what the relation between subjective judgment and objective probability would be if we were calibrated exactly as mathematical probability theory dictates. The curved line is the weighting function, expressed in the theory as π (pi). As you can see, it veers above

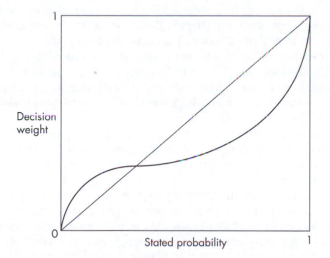

Figure 8.3 The weighting function in prospect theory

the diagonal at low values, showing their overweighting, and dips below it at higher ranges. It converges on the 0 and 1 points. This function, like the value function in Figure 8.2, is idealised: the precise shape of each will vary according to context.

Together with the value function, the weighting function enables us to account for the kinds of decisions we see in the Allais paradox, as well as *Millionaire* man and the framing effects. Because of the rapidly decelerating shape of the gains curve, and the convergence of π on the value of 1, there will be a certainty effect: people will tend to opt for a certain gain rather than an uncertain gain of the same, or even greater, expected value. They do not want to risk gaining nothing. But because of the steeper curve for losses, reflecting people's aversion to loss, they will tend to avoid a certain loss and take a chance on a larger loss. Doing this leaves them with some hope, albeit small, of avoiding loss altogether. The weighting function also helps to explain why people gamble, or buy insurance, when in each case the outcome is highly unlikely. They do so at least partly because they overestimate very low probabilities (and in addition, may think of them as $ bets anyway, as we saw above).

Mental accounting

Prospect theory predicts and explains a number of observed phenomena that occur when people make real-world choices, and which might otherwise be regarded as inconvenient anomalies. They can be grouped under the general heading of *mental accounting*, a term coined by Richard Thaler (1999). Mental accounting is what you do when you think about your personal finances.

A signal instance of mental accounting was reported by Kahneman, Knetsch and Thaler (1990, 1991; see also Knetsch, 1989; Thaler, 1999): the *endowment effect*. Thaler originally observed it when a friend would rather keep wine that was worth much more than he paid for it than sell it or buy more of it at the high price. Kahneman et al. replicated this effect in the laboratory, with university students. These people were presented with coffee mugs and money prices. One group was asked whether they would be willing to buy a mug at one of the set prices. The average price at which they agreed to buy was $2.87. People in a second group were given mugs and asked whether they would sell them at various price levels. They wanted more than double the money, $7.12, to part with their recently acquired endowment. Both students and wine buffs – and many other people in many other settings – are reluctant to part with what they hold, even when they stand to make a gain by doing so. If you have ever declined to move from your reserved seat in a rowdy train carriage, say, to a quieter carriage, you have fallen prey to the endowment effect.

This reluctance is predicted by prospect theory's value function: giving up a possession is a loss, and losses have higher negative values than gains have positive values. As Schwartz (2004) notes, this is one reason why firms that offer no-quibble money-back guarantees are not taking much of a risk: the higher value that people place on an item once they have it prevents them returning it for its money price.

In mental accounting, we often subdivide the areas of our personal finances, which is another kind of framing. Doing this can have implications for the decisions we make, which again can be made sense of using prospect theory. Here is an example, from Tversky and Kahneman (1981). Suppose you are about to buy a calculator for $15 when the sales assistant tells you that the other branch of the shop, on the other side of town, has it for $10. Would you make the trip? Tversky and Kahneman found that most people said they would. Now what about the same question regarding a jacket that you are about to buy for $125: it is on sale at the other branch for $120. Would you make the trip? This time, most people turned it down. But the saving is the same in each case: $5. The difference is in the reference point: $5 seems fairly massive from a $15 start but is hardly worth anything from $125. Tversky and Kahneman also showed that people would be more prepared to pay twice over for a theatre ticket when they had lost the money for the ticket than when they had lost the ticket itself. In the latter case the price is already in the 'ticket account', which makes the double price seem unreasonable; in the former it is not.

Thaler (1980) reported similar instances. People can be easily induced to add quite large sums to a purchase they are already committed to making, such as fancy wheels to a car or an extra function to a desk computer. Another $500 when you are already about to spend $10,000 does not seem like much. Here, salespeople encourage you to *integrate* the extra loss with the existing commitment. This takes you only a little way further along the value function, and so the loss hardly hurts at all. However, they can also get you to *segregate* values as well, for instance when introducing 'cashback' offers rather than simple price reductions. You buy a car for $10,500 and get $500 cashback: $500 in lovely crisp banknotes feels like much more than the numerical difference between $10,500 and $10,000.

Tversky and Simonson (1993) showed that valuation is also, as they put it, context-dependent. That is, preferences can be influenced by what should be irrelevant alternatives. Suppose that you prefer Option x to Option y. That preference should not, logically, change if a further option, z, is added to the set. And yet there is a lot of evidence that it can. Tversky and Simonson use a political illustration to show how this is possible. Candidate X, the liberal candidate, beats Candidate Y, a conservative, in a two-choice poll: X is the preferred option. A second liberal candidate, Z, enters the race. It is now possible for Y to win, because X and Z split the liberal vote, which makes it look as if Y is now preferred to X: a preference reversal.

They provide experimental evidence in the familiar shape of consumer choices. They argue that loss aversion in prospect theory can be extended to predict *extremeness aversion* in a set of options. This aversion leads in turn to two effects on choices: *compromise* and *polarisation*. Polarisation happens when an additional option focuses attention on just one attribute, such as price or quality: choices shift against the option that falls down on that attribute. Compromise happens when two options, x and z, have significant positive and negative attributes with respect to each other, while a third option, y, lies in between them and has minor plus and minus points with respect to each. Even though x and z may both be preferred to y in pairwise comparisons, extremeness aversion predicts that y will be preferred in a three-way choice.

211

This should happen when a second extreme option, z, is introduced to a set that consists of x and y. Tversky and Simonson report an experiment in which people were asked to choose between Minolta cameras:

Model	Level	Price
X-370	Basic	$170
3000i	Mid-range	$240
7000i	High-end	$470

A group of participants who had to choose just between the X-370 and the 3000i were evenly split between them. A second group made the three-way choice. Now, 57% chose the 3000i, the middle option, while the rest were split evenly between the other two (i.e. just over 20% each). The middle option has *increased* its market share through the introduction of the third option, which should not happen. Faced with two extremes, people choose the middle way. The journalist Aditya Chakrabortty appealed to this effect to explain the surge in popularity of the third party candidate after the live TV debates between the party leaders prior to the British general election of May 2010 (*The Guardian*, 20 April 2010). Note, though, that this did not translate into greater success in the election itself: the third party actually lost seats. Rated feelings, or stated intentions, are not necessarily the same thing as choices, as the dual process theory (see Chapters 6 and 10) would predict.

Prospect theory has been enormously successful in explaining decision behaviour and its apparent anomalies, and in predicting new phenomena, but it is not the last word on the psychology of decision making. For instance, the theory concerns decision under risk. *Risk* in this context has a technical meaning: it means probability when the odds are known, as they are in dice games. Each point on the weighting curve represents a subjective probability for the prospect in question. When the odds are not known, we are said to be deciding under conditions of *uncertainty*. Tversky and Kahneman (1992) extended prospect theory to deal with this important aspect of judgment: they developed *cumulative prospect theory*. It is called cumulative because under uncertainty people tend to think of the probabilities of various prospects relative to each other: you might think of outcome x as being no more likely than, at least as likely as or a safer bet than outcome y. Cumulative prospect theory includes the construct of subadditivity from support theory (see Chapter 1): people assign higher cumulative probabilities to explicitly named prospects than they do to a higher-level category that includes them. For example, football supporters would tend to rate the chances of Celtic or Rangers winning the Europa Cup as higher than the chances of 'a team from the Scottish Premier League', even though Celtic and Rangers are just two of twelve SPL teams (see Fox & Tversky, 1998, for experimental evidence for this factor). There are several other examples of rank-dependent utility theories where outcomes are thought of relative to each other: see Quiggin (1982), Lopes (1996) and Birnbaum and Chavez (1997).

In the next chapter we shall look at further explorations of how people think about their choices. To conclude this one, it is worth pointing out that there is something else missing from prospect theory as a psychological theory: an account of cognitive processes. Several authors have made this point recently (see Baron, 2008, and Hardman, 2009, for examples in the textbook literature).

Prospect theory developed out of SEU theory, and therefore out of economics, and adapted the earlier theory in the light of what was known about human behaviour. An alternative approach would be to take the reverse route: start from psychology and predict economics. Like its ancestor SEU, prospect theory contains the assumption that when you make a choice you think about probability and utility and the trade-offs between them. In the next chapter, we shall consider an increasingly influential approach developed by Gerd Gigerenzer that rejects this assumption in favour of what he calls a one-reason decision process.

To conclude this one, here is an example of a cognitively based account of decision making, given by Stewart, Chater and Brown (2006) in their *decision by sampling* theory. It makes use of constructs that will be familiar to you from previous chapters. Stewart et al. ask the question of how cognitive processes might give rise to the value and weighting functions. They propose that people use their memories when assessing value and probability in a decision situation. You do not come to any such situation cold, but have knowledge of previous similar options, values and chances. You assess current values by making simple, binary, ordinal comparisons to a sample of such values drawn from memory. You ask yourself, in other words, do I prefer x or y? You also ask yourself where the attribute's value lies in the range of the sample: is it high, medium or low?

They further assume that our memories are tuned to the distributions of values in the real world, an assumption that is part of the rational analysis approach to reasoning that Chater was instrumental in developing (see Chapters 2 and 6), and with Gigerenzer's natural sampling approach to probability (see Chapter 1). Putting these elements together, Stewart et al. were able to derive the two components of the value function (see Figure 8.2) and the S-shape of the weighting function (see Figure 8.3). To do this for the value function, they first gathered data about real-world gains and losses: credits to and debits from accounts at a major high street bank. Think about the amounts you pay in to your bank account: they vary in size. Most will be small and some will be quite decent, but very few, alas, will be huge. The shape of this distribution was found by Stewart et al. to match closely the Bernoulli curve shown in Figure 8.1 and in the gains section of Figure 8.2 (the value function). When it came to debits, Stewart et al. found that there were far more small debits than there were small credits (how quickly you have to dice up your paycheque – the credit – into the chunks needed to pay various bills – the debits), and fewer large debits compared with large credits. This gives you the steeper curve for losses that appears in the value function. They conduct a similarly ingenious analysis of probability expressions (their numerical equivalents), and how they are used, and derive the S-shaped weighting function.

By assuming that people make simple comparisons from rational samples of the relevant parts of these distributions, Stewart et al.'s theory predicts risk aversion for gains, risk seeking for losses and also loss aversion. Stewart and Simpson (2008) extend the analysis to account for all the effects originally reported by Kahneman and Tversky (1979b) in their announcement of prospect theory, and others besides. This kind of work (Stewart's papers comprehensively review similar studies), along with Kahneman's recent explorations of experienced utility, helps to put more psychology into the psychology of decision making. In the next chapter, we shall look at other approaches to decision making that have the same objective.

Summary

1   The founding normative theory of decision making is subjective expected utility (SEU) theory, which derives from the economic principle of expected value: utilities of outcomes are weighted by their probability of occurrence.

2   Utility deviates from money value in the shape of diminishing returns, where the same amount is valued less with repeated increments.

3   SEU theory logically implies properties such as independence of common attributes, the *sure thing principle* and transitivity of preference, but these are violated under certain circumstances.

4   Multi-attribute utility theory was put forward to account for complex decisions. It makes use of conjoint measurement, where values of one attribute can be scaled against others.

5   The construct of utility can be unpacked into decision utility, reflected in people's expressed preferences, and experienced utility. Experienced utility can be predicted and remembered. These psychological processes lead to deviations from normative prescriptions.

6   Preferences are also influenced by joint or separate evaluation and by framing due to description, implying that they are constructed rather than revealed in the course of decision making.

7   The mismatch between SEU's prescriptions and actual human performance motivated Kahneman and Tversky's prospect theory, which proposes a reference point representing current wealth, a steeper utility curve for losses than for gains relative to this point and an S-shaped probability function where low probabilities are overweighted and medium-to-high probabilities are underweighted.

8   Later theories take a more psychological approach, and are rooted more in the cognitive processes that are supposedly activated when people make choices.

Decisions in context

In the last chapter, we saw how the study of human decision making had progressed from the idea, introduced by Bernoulli in the 18th century, that we think about how much we value each option before us and trade this off against how likely it is to come about: utility combined with probability. Bernoulli realised that utility was not the same thing as wealth, an idea that is still with us, while the 20th century innovators of subjective expected utility theory, such as von Neumann and Morgenstern and Savage, detached utility from emotion in favour of pure preference. This latter idea has lessened its grip recently, in the face of renewed research on experienced utility, which can deliver decisions that fly in the face of what decision utility would predict.

In this chapter, we shall go further into the complexities that the real world introduces into the process of decision making. We shall be particularly concerned with an aspect that was touched on in the previous chapter: affect, or feelings. In doing so, we shall revisit a large-scale theory that was previously reviewed in the context of reasoning: dual process theory. We begin by examining some ways in which decisions influence feelings. Later, we shall look at the relation the other way round: at how feelings are used in decisions.

Paradoxes of choice

Deciding means choosing and, as we have seen, that should mean thinking about the options before us, their likelihoods and consequences, and going for the one that best suits our interests. There may be problems when we put this general principle into operation, but the principle is fine; isn't it? We make choices to further our goals, and the best choices are the ones that do this best (Baron, 2008). Not only that, but the economic and political culture in which most of us are steeped is one in which individual choice has been raised to an eleventh commandment. Thou shalt choose. Choice means freedom, and everyone wants to be free, so the more choice we have, the freer and happier we will be. Won't we? That is a psychological prediction: that you and I will be happier the more choice we have. Naturally, you would not expect things to be that straightforward when you look at choice from a psychological viewpoint. We shall examine two *paradoxes of choice*, both of which give us pause for thought should we blithely assume that more choice is always better.

Too much of a good thing?

The first of these paradoxes is the one that gave rise to the expression, in the title of a book on the subject by Barry Schwartz (2004). The paradox of choice in Schwartz's terms is as follows. We (he refers exclusively to America and Americans, but we can generalise to the rest of the industrialised world) live in times of almost limitless decision options and yet we are no happier. Indeed, in some respects, we are less happy than people in these same societies used to be when there were fewer choices available. Here are some examples of the range of options Schwartz found at his local shops:

	Varieties
Cookies (cakes or biscuits)	285
Shampoo	360
Toothpaste	40
Pasta sauces	120
Cereals	275
Tea bags	175
Televisions	110
Integrated stereo systems	63
Hi-fi components sufficient for	6,512,000 possible configurations

And of course, there is the uncountable number of possible mobile phone contracts, which we looked at in the last chapter, not to mention the handsets you can enjoy them on.

Truly, you might think, we are blessed to be living in such a world; it sounds almost too good to be true. It is. This degree of choice is overwhelming, and can have adverse consequences for the chooser. You have been round supermarkets and been faced with hundreds of shampoos; you have tried to decide on the right phone contract. It was not always fun; but is the experience of *choice overload* any more than not fun?

A classic experimental test of this question comes from Sheena Iyengar and Michael Lepper (2000). This famous study is notable not just for its findings but for its methods. It was conducted in the real world, not in a laboratory, and people were faced with real choices, not imaginary ones. Not many studies of thinking and reasoning have these features. They conducted three experiments, the first being the best known: it involved what the authors intriguingly call 'exotic jams'. They set up a tasting stall in a store that was noted for the wide variety of goods that it stocked. Every hour, they changed the numbers of jams on display: there were either 6 or 24 varieties. As you might expect, more people stopped at the booth when there were 24 jams on display. However, there was no difference in the number of jams people sampled: in each condition, they sampled just one or two. The big surprise came when the customers' actual purchases of jam were examined: ten times as many people went on to buy some jam if they had been in the limited, 6-choice booth than in the extensive, 24-choice booth (30% vs. 3%).

In two follow-up studies Iyengar and Lepper varied a number of aspects of this basic situation. They gave students an optional essay assignment; some had 6 topics to choose from, some had 30. More students in the 6-choice condition wrote essays, and their essays were of higher quality than were those written by students in the 30-choice condition. Lastly, they looked at mood and affect ratings in a third experiment, where students had to choose among chocolates. Again, there were either 6 or 30 to consider. The participants rated the experience of the chocolates along various dimensions, including how difficult and enjoyable choosing among

217

them had been, and they also rated the chocolates. There were three groups: one chose from 6 chocolates and one chose from 30, and they were allowed to sample the ones they had chosen and then rate them; the third group had no sampling choice at all and just had to rate the chocolates they were given. At the end of all this, they were given a choice of payments: either $5 cash or a $5 box of chocolates.

As with the jams, where people were attracted to the wide-choice display, participants in the chocolate study enjoyed the experience of choosing more when they had a lot of options to choose from. However, they also found the process more difficult and frustrating than did people given the narrower range of options. There was no correlation between these two kinds of ratings: they were quite separate. When it came to satisfaction with the chocolates they actually tasted, the 6-choice group reported more enjoyment than the 30-choice group did; and both groups enjoyed their chocolates more than did the people in the no-choice group. Payment decisions were also influenced: narrow-choice people were more likely to choose chocolate over cash than were wide-choice people, whose choices were the same as those of no-choice people. Iyengar (2010) goes much further into the issues raised by studies such as this, in a book written for a non-specialist readership.

Here, then, is a first powerful paradox of choice: people seemed to like being in a situation where there was lots to choose from, but when it came to thinking about what they had chosen they were more satisfied when choice was limited. No choice at all was worst, not surprisingly. So some choice is better than none, but there really is such a thing as too much choice.

In seeking to account for this strange state of affairs, we can consider four factors. The first is cognitive: the work that goes into choosing. The second is emotional: the feelings that choosing produces. Thirdly, there are personality factors, to do with the kind of person making the choice. Lastly, there are social factors, to do with comparing our decisions against those made by other people. They are all interlinked, but can be separated.

Having said that, we can treat *effort* and *emotion* together, because one has a profound influence on the other. Wide choices obviously require more effort from the chooser: if you think back to the last chapter, deciding among options ideally means assessing each one in terms of *how likely* it is to deliver *how much* utility to you. This might be fairly straightforward with only two or three options (assuming you can be accurate about each factor – which as we saw cannot be taken for granted), but for 30? In fact, as we shall see in more detail in the next chapter, there are good grounds for regarding this demand as not just difficult, but impossible. However, there is another factor altogether that the effort of choosing among many options brings with it: the greater scope for experiencing *regret*.

Regret can operate in two directions: backward and forward. Have you ever chosen something in the shops and then, when you got home, wished you had bought the one you rejected, not paid so much or not bought it at all? This kind of backward regret is linked to the economic construct of *opportunity cost*. Whenever you lay your money down for item A, you are passing up the opportunity to buy B, C or D. The opportunity cost of the Bentley is the lack of the Ferrari you might otherwise have bought. This is sometimes known as buyer's remorse. Bear in mind the idea of loss aversion, which is central to prospect theory's description of decision making (see Chapter 8): if you regard not having a Ferrari as a loss, even though you now have a Bentley, then you will experience negative feelings. The same goes for anything else you might buy, from a house to a chocolate bar. And if you feel bad when contemplating the ruins of your bank account, this will partly be down to the visions of all those other things that you can no longer buy. Opportunity costs often come from trade-offs: even in the unlikely context, for most of us, of luxury cars, one will score more strongly on some features and the other more strongly on others. The more options there are to choose among, the greater the number of trade-offs that have to be considered, the more opportunity costs there are and hence the greater the scope for regret once the choice is made (see Chapter 8 for more on trade-offs).

Remember the example of the contestant on *Who wants to be a millionaire*, described in the last chapter? Viewers are often entertained by seeing the looks on the faces of quitters who are made to say which answer they would have chosen if they had gambled and it turns out that they would have chosen the right one. We also saw the likely influence of forward regret in that case, when our man chose to quit even though quitting had a lower expected value than gambling. Forward-operating regret is known as *anticipated regret*, and is linked once again to loss aversion, although this time it concerns losses that you have not yet sustained but have predicted. If the regret you anticipate should you lose a bet is greater than the joy you expect to feel if you win, then you will not play, especially if the difference is large (Bell, 1982). Loomes and Sugden (1982) proposed a modification of prospect theory to include the anticipated regret associated with decision options alongside their utilities (and we saw in the last chapter how Kahneman, one of the parents of prospect theory, has also turned to the affective aspects of decision behaviour in his more recent research). They propose that anticipated emotion is over-weighted relative to value, again especially with large differences.

Obviously, the more options there are in front of us, the more chances there are that we will anticipate feeling regret over the losses we may experience through the ones we reject. This is clearly linked to counterfactual thinking, of the kind covered in Chapters 4 and 5: we ask ourselves *what if* I choose this and lose that? Or, retrospectively, we say *if only* I had chosen that and not this.

In Chapter 5, we saw that a particularly powerful contributor to anticipated regret was identified by Ilana Ritov and Jonathan Baron in their studies of *omission bias* (e.g. 1990, 1999; see also Baron & Ritov, 1994). They presented people with a decision over which all parents agonise: whether to have their child immunised. If you do not have your child immunised, there is a risk that she will catch the disease, say 10 in 10,000. However, the vaccination also carries a risk: some babies are harmed by it. When asked what level of risk they would accept in deciding to immunise, people typically report a figure around 5:10,000; any figure below 10 should clinch it, but clearly people want a much lower level of risk than this. The reason seems to be that they anticipate more regret from the things they do than from the things they don't do, at least in situations like this (see Chapter 5 for exceptions to this rule). In the case of immunisation, omission bias leads to a greater than necessary exposure of another person, the child, to danger, as a family

I knew found to their cost: both children contracted whooping cough, leading to permanent lung damage, after their parents had declined immunisation.

Personality factors play a part in this paradox of choice, and are one of the focal points of Schwartz's (2004) book – or rather one personality dimension in particular. Are you only satisfied with the best, and search high and low until you find it? If so, you are what Schwartz describes as a *maximiser*: you seek always to maximise utility. You can see straight away how the proliferation of options will cause trouble for such people: the more options are laid out before you, the more cognitive effort you will be confronted with, along with all those chances to feel regret. In today's world of choice, argues Schwartz, to be a maximiser is to consign yourself to a life of misery: if only the best is good enough, when there are infinite options it is always likely that there is a better one round the next corner. In the extreme, choice overload can cause such people to freeze, and avoid choosing altogether. We saw in the previous chapter that people will pay money to avoid choosing in some situations. This is also paradoxical, since decision theory tells us that we should be maximisers all the time.

It does not have to be this way: Schwartz contrasts maximisers with *satisficers*. We met 'satisfice' in Chapter 7: it is a blended word combining the constructs of satisfy and suffice. It was introduced into the economic and psychological lexicons by the Nobel Prize-winning cognitive scientist Herbert Simon in 1957. If you are a satisficer, you will be happy with something that is *good enough*. Once you find it, you stop searching, trading off and experiencing regret.

Does anyone need, asked Lou Reed (1989), a $60,000 car? This is a good psychological question. For many people, in many situations, the answer is yes, because of the last of the four factors introduced earlier: *social factors*. An awful lot of the utilities we experience in various aspects of our lives come from social comparison. Social comparison is important because it sets expectations, and expectations determine the reference points that prospect theory specifies are a central determinant of utility. Once you have a reference point, deviations from it are experienced as either gains or losses, and losses hurt more than gains cheer. If you get a B+ for your assignment, and you normally get straight Bs, you will feel good – until you discover that everyone else in the class got an A: what was a gain from your initial reference point becomes a loss when it shifts due to social comparison. It seems to be an unavoidable aspect of human life: if you ask yourself how well you are doing, on any scale at all, the answer is always with respect to how others are doing.

There is nothing new in this, of course: we have the common phrase 'keeping up with the Joneses' to describe status competition between neighbours; the expression dates from a comic strip in the New York *Globe* around 100 years ago. What is new, though, is that it has been possible to predict and observe a range of consequences, psychological, medical and societal, that stem from our need to compare ourselves with others. Who these others are is an interesting question in itself. They used to be just the people around you (the Joneses), but Schwartz (2004) points to the explosion of mass communication in the last 50 years, especially the rise of the internet in the last 20, in arguing that social comparison now has a much wider, perhaps global, scope; in July 2010 it was reported that there were 500 million subscribers to just one social networking site. Maximisers will clearly be more troubled by this kind of social comparison than satisficers will be: if you want to have the best, the best is a function of what other people have, and there are thousands of millions of people who may have better than you.

We can predict, therefore, that cultures that promote maximising should lead to more people experiencing more misery than cultures that do not. Schwartz argues that ever-expanding choice is likely to turn people into maximisers anyway, and so societies such as the USA and the UK should be particularly prone to misery-making on this score. Another prediction is that where there are wide inequalities between the wealthiest and least wealthy, there should be more observed misery because of the greater distance between aspiration and actuality. And this is not just among the poorest: you may recall from the last chapter that people adapt to the level of health, wealth and happiness they find themselves at. So although you may exult in your new $50,000 car, the effect quickly fades and, yes, you will soon think you need a $60,000 car (especially if Jones has one). This effect is known as the *hedonic treadmill*: we keep having to give ourselves extra shots of exultation to stay at the same overall level of satisfaction. Maximisers work harder to make their decisions and so will find adaptation harder to take.

Large-scale studies of this trap within and across societies have been conducted, for instance by the World Health Organization. Their findings are summarised in two recent books, one by Avner Offer (2006) and a more popular treatment by Oliver James (2007; James acknowledges Offer's influence). Inequality hurts, as Offer puts it (p. 270): as predicted, countries with wide income inequalities, such as the USA, UK and Australia, record much higher levels of emotional distress (depression, anxiety, substance abuse, impulsivity) than do countries with lower indices of inequality, such as Japan, Germany and Belgium. James gives the condition, which he notes is most prevalent in English-speaking countries, a snappy name: *affluenza*, 'the placing of a high value on money, possessions, appearances (physical and social) and fame' (p. xiii). There are clear implications of this state of affairs for how we might treat this distress: individualistic therapies that ignore the social and political context in which they operate risk doing their clients a disservice (Thatcher & Manktelow, 2007). Important though these wider issues are, I shall not go any further into them here, otherwise we shall stray too far from the psychology of thinking and reasoning. Instead, let us go on to the second paradox of choice.

Decision dilemmas

We return to one of the central points about decision making, which has been referred to several times, both here and in the previous chapter: good decisions are those that best enable us to achieve our goals. By now, you will be thinking that there must be a catch behind such an apparently unarguable sentiment. Here it is. What happens when you have multiple goals and, especially, when these clash? Life is a complicated business, and there are going to be times when we have to choose not just between outcomes but between goals: which one should we aim for? When you are in such a situation, you are faced with a *dilemma*. Let us be clear at the outset about how this term will be used here. A dilemma is not just any difficult choice, nor, as the dictionary definition would have it, only a choice between two unpalatable alternatives. You have a dilemma when you are faced with two different but equally valued goals, such that whichever choice you make takes you closer towards one but further from the other.

In this chapter, I shall set out the psychology of dilemmas before, in the next chapter, following up their implications for how we characterise human rationality. The first step in exploring a general class of problems is always to classify them. We can adopt a broad division, between *personal* and *social* types. A personal dilemma is one where the conflict is entirely to do with your own beliefs or desires. A social dilemma comes from the thoughts and actions of people considered in relation to others. The two often overlap, and many dilemmas contain elements of each: a social dilemma may play out over time, for instance. It is a useful division rather than a strict one. As we shall see, in both cases these dilemmas are not mere theoretical niceties, but can be profoundly serious for real people living real lives.

Personal dilemmas

One of the richest sources of personal dilemmas is *time*. When you look into the future and try to gauge utility and probability, you can take two general views: short-term and long-term. These two time perspectives can produce dilemmas. What might be in your interest in the short term might not be in the long term, and vice versa. Short-term gains, where utility is positive, can lead to long-term losses, where utility is negative; and short-term losses can lead to long-term gains.

These clashes have been debated for a long time: as far back as Plato and Aristotle, more than 2000 years ago (Over & Manktelow, 1993). Platt (1973) is a more recent, landmark treatment of the problem. He takes a Skinnerian (behaviouristic) stance and refers to what he calls sliding reinforcement. In behaviourist terminology, a reinforcer is anything that alters the probability of a response. Rewards and punishments are common everyday categories: rewards raise the probability of a response, whereas punishments lower it. Immediate reinforcement is more powerful than delayed reinforcement: if you do something and get something straight back as a result, your behaviour is much more likely to change than if you do something and the consequences only follow some time later. In human life, this delay can be over a period of years. The consequences may in fact never accrue at all, as in the cases of people who do things for posterity, such as plant forests, or sacrifice themselves for a cause.

Platt picks out the case of drug-taking as possibly the purest case of a short-term/long-term dilemma. Recreational drugs typically have an immediate, intense pleasurable effect – why else take them? – and yet the delayed consequences can be dire, not just for you but for the people close to you. So here is your dilemma when faced with the choice of whether or not to take a drug. In the short term, you will get high. In the long term, you may damage your health and, if the drug is one of the illegal ones, get a criminal record. Both routes can even lead to your death, medically or, in some countries, through the criminal justice system.

The dilemma then consists of choosing between goals to follow: to attain this moment's pleasure or avoid the future dangers. They are categorically different, and you might place no more value on one than the other. What, then, is the right choice in this situation? Note that there are other aspects of life that share this structure: sex (immediate pleasure versus possible disease, unwanted pregnancy or scandal); credit (immediate acquisition versus future debt and possible ruin) and food (immediate gratification versus obesity or disease). Note also that, while the immediate gain is certain, the long-term loss is uncertain; this makes the immediate gain even more alluring.

As mentioned above, this kind of dilemma also occurs when the values are reversed, so that a short-term loss of utility can lead to a long-term gain. Drug-taking serves as an example here too: addicts who have the goal of shaking off their addiction and returning to health have to abstain (i.e. forgo their immediate pleasure) in order to do so. The most ubiquitous dilemma in human life takes this form: whether to save or to spend. Saving incurs the opportunity costs of all those nice things you have to pass up in order to see your bank balance rise. Banks offer interest on savings in order to induce you not to spend your money now: the discount rate, as it is called, is the amount of interest that has to be offered to do this (Thaler & Shefrin, 1981). They do this because they want your savings; they want your savings so that they can lend them out to other people as loans, on which they charge much higher rates of interest than the savings rate. That is how high street banking makes money. Loan interest rates are a kind of fee for not waiting until you actually have the money to buy that shiny new thing.

The popularity of consumer credit shows that people will generally pay a large fee so that they can have what they want now; the opportunity cost of not having it for another year or so is evidently much higher (especially if Jones already has it). The value function in prospect theory would lead us to expect this effect: if the opportunity cost is seen as a loss, it will be given a stronger negative value than the money value of the item in question. Loan interest rates give us an index of just how much keener this 'loss' is felt to be: look at the final amount payable in adverts offering credit, such as those for cars in newspapers, and you will see that it can be a huge increase over the cash price. Hoch and Loewenstein (1991) argued that this sense of loss can come about because buyers sometimes regard themselves as owners of the product before they have actually bought it, so that not buying feels like losing it.

There are individual differences between people in terms of their propensity to favour the short term over the long term, and there are differences between items as well. For instance, Dittmar (2001) reviews her studies of impulse buying: buying things on the spur of the moment, without prior planning. She found that, while most people do this (and most regret having done so, at least sometimes), for some people it turned into almost an addictive behaviour, and they became compulsive shoppers. Items that had to do with people's self-presentation, such as clothes and jewellery, were more likely to be impulse-bought than were more functional goods. Personality variables helped to predict who would turn into a compulsive shopper: for example, a high level of materialist values (or as James, 2007, puts it, infection with the affluenza virus), and a wide discrepancy between a person's sense of their actual and ideal selves.

Not all time dilemmas involve short-term/long-term considerations: the *sunk cost dilemma*, which has attracted a lot of research attention, does not. You will be familiar with it – it is captured in the everyday phrase: throwing good money after bad. Its essence is continuing to invest in a failing project on the grounds of the investment already made. The most influential paper about it was by Arkes and Blumer (1985). They provide many illustrations, real and imaginary, and the Sydney Opera House planning disaster, described in Chapter 1, can be seen in this light. Here is an imaginary one, adapted from one of their examples. Suppose you have spent $40 on a non-refundable concert ticket, and as the day of the concert approaches you get an invitation to a party that clashes with it, from someone you want to get to know better. You would rather go to this party than the concert, but you have spent $40 on the concert that you cannot get back. Which do you go to?

Most people when given choices of this kind select the option into which they have already sunk their money, even when it is the less preferred option. It is an error, because of the norm of consequentialism in decision making: decisions should be taken on the basis of their consequences. Past investments are just that – past. They should not influence future decisions. And yet everyone will be familiar with this error, which shows that it is committed routinely. It does not need to involve money; investment of any resource will give rise to it. For instance, think of couples who stay together because they have been together for so long and for no other apparent reason. What a shame, we say, when they eventually split up, even though it is best for the two people concerned.

In the animal behaviour literature, the effect is known as the Concorde fallacy (Dawkins & Carlisle, 1976), after the decision by the British and French governments to continue investing in the development of the supersonic airliner long after it became apparent that it would never recoup anything like its costs, partly on the grounds of the millions already invested. Non-monetary factors such as prestige seem also to contribute to decisions like this (Staw & Ross, 1989). The human and animal sunk cost literatures made little contact with each other until the paper by Arkes and Ayton (1999). They found that there was no convincing evidence that animals do, in fact, commit the fallacy. The same goes for young children: they seem to be more rational, therefore, than adults are!

Arkes and Blumer appealed to prospect theory for an explanation of the sunk cost effect. The loss curve, which we are on when making investments, is steep, but each further loss (investment) hurts less and less; and people are risk-seeking for losses. So people will risk further losses in attempting to recover their costs, and may become trapped in an escalating commitment (Brockner & Rubin, 1985; Staw & Ross, 1989). Arkes and Ayton refer to a lexical rule such as those mentioned in the last chapter to explain children's apparent immunity: *do not waste*. They argue that children have not learned this rule to the extent that adults have, and so are less bothered by their investment history. Indeed, Arkes (1996) had previously found that people are more likely to discontinue an investment if what it had already bought could be re-used by someone else rather than merely scrapped, even when the financial compensation from re-use and scrapping was the same. Scrapping implies waste. So if you think of the $40 cost of the ticket as granting you the *option* of whether or not to go to the concert, and you decide not to go after all, the money was not wasted. You paid for freedom of choice, and exercised it.

Social dilemmas

The paper by Platt (1973) referred to above is entitled *Social traps*: it refers not just to the sliding reinforcers that come with time delays, but to those that come with other people. Consider his example of the *missing-hero trap*: there is a traffic jam caused by an obstruction in the road. All it needs is for one person to be a hero, get out of their car and move it, and then everyone is happy. But once you get to it, after waiting for ages in the queue, there is a strong incentive just to get past it, and once you have done so you are in the clear, with nothing more to gain by stopping to move it. So you don't play the hero, neither does anyone else and the jam gets worse. This case resembles the well-documented phenomenon of bystander apathy, which you can find in many social psychology texts. The more people there are in a situation where someone needs to be a hero, the less likely it is that any one of them will step forward – it is too easy to assume, or hope, that someone else will take the risk and do the right thing.

The essential tension in social dilemmas, then, is that between individual and group utility. In the missing-hero case, an individual needs to incur a cost in order to benefit the group. As with time dilemmas, social dilemmas also operate when the polarity is reversed: individuals seeking gains can bring about losses to the group – of which the individuals themselves are members. If you have ever sat in your car bemoaning the traffic, walked down Oxford Street or Fifth Avenue irritated by the crowds or lamented how your favourite holiday spot has been wrecked by tourism, you have confronted, and contributed to, this kind of social dilemma.

Perhaps the best-known case of social dilemmas, where individual utility maximisation brings about collective loss, is the *commons problem*, set out in a famous paper by Garrett Hardin (1968). He traces it back to a paper written by an amateur mathematician in the early 19th century. It is illustrated by a story about an imaginary agrarian community, where there is a set of farmers and some common pasture. It is in each farmer's interest to graze as many additional cows on the common pasture as he can. However, each additional animal will deplete the pasture by consuming grass that would otherwise have been available to the cows already there. The point is that while the gain is private – it goes to the individual farmer – the cost is public – it is shared among the community. So while each farmer has every incentive to maximise his use of the commons, the inevitable result, says Hardin, is collective ruin.

You can see how this comes about by looking at Table 9.1. Say there are six farmers, each with a cow weighing 500 kg (about 1000 lb; the exact numbers in the table do not matter, what is important is the relation between them). Each additional cow depletes the pasture so every animal's weight drops by 50 kg (100 lb). You put an additional cow on the land: you will now have two cows that each weigh 450 kg (900 lb), totalling 900 kg: you are 400 kg up, but everyone else is 50 kg down. Each farmer has the same incentive, and so adds a cow to the pasture. If they all do this, though, the result is that all six are left with two scrawny beasts each weighing just 200 kg (400 lb), which is less meat on the hoof than they started with – they have all lost. That may not be the end of it: each will surely attempt to recover his position by putting yet more cows on the land, leading to the ultimate destruction of the commons and the ruin of all those farmers striving to better themselves.

Table 9.1 The commons problem: what happens to six farmers who each start with a 500 kg cow and each adds an extra cow to the pasture; each additional cow reduces the weight of all cows by 50 kg

500	500	500	500	500	500
[450+450]	450	450	450	450	450
[400+400]	[400+400]	400	400	400	400
[350+350]	[350+350]	[350+350]	350	350	350
[300+300]	[300+300]	[300+300]	[300+300]	300	300
[250+250]	[250+250]	[250+250]	[250+250]	[250+250]	250
[200+200]	[200+200]	[200+200]	[200+200]	[200+200]	[200+200]

Source: Adapted from Hardin (1968)

Is this anything other than a neat little thought experiment? It may already remind you of situations you have experienced in real life. Take the case of short-ages of goods and panic buying. If people hear that some useful commodity, such as fuel or a foodstuff, is running short, they will dash to the filling station or the supermarket and fill up their tanks or trolleys as best they can. Each person has the incentive to look after themselves. The individual's incentive is strengthened by a factor sometimes known as the *voter's paradox*. Why should anyone vote, given that any one vote will never affect the outcome of an election? Voting is literally, for the individual, more trouble than it is worth. And yet people do vote. With resource depletion problems, the pull is the other way. Your single tank of fuel or trolley full of flour will not make any difference to the overall crisis (Dawes, 1988). But if everyone does this, they may actually bring about the shortage that by their own individual actions they were seeking to escape. They are the farmers, and the commodity is the commons.

You can see Hardin's tragedy looming on a global scale with some resources, such as the most valuable commodity of all: oil. Everyone wants to live a good life, which these days involves driving cars (better, faster), flying in planes (further, faster), living in fine houses (with lots of land), having plenty of food (from all over the world), buying nice things (such as the new Mac I am typing these words into), and so on. And in general, those that can, do; especially if they are maximisers. But oil underpins all these activities, and there is only so much oil. It is not possible for all 6–7 billion people in the world to live this way, or for those that do to do so for much longer. The exhaustion of oil is a truly terrifying prospect, all the more so for being certain.

Hardin (1968) regarded social dilemmas such as the commons problem as having 'no technical solution' (p. 1243). To see what he meant by this, let us look at a puzzle that has generated a huge amount of research and theory and has been used to model formally the kinds of dilemma of which the commons problem is merely a subset: the *prisoner's dilemma*. It is so called because when it was discovered, in the 1950s, it was presented as a toy problem involving two prisoners held incommunicado, facing a plea bargain and trying to decide what to do. In Table 9.2, I have presented a stripped-down version that applies to any situation at all where the incentives are arranged in this way. Once again, it is the relation between the incentives that is crucial; the exact numbers do not matter.

Table 9.2 The prisoner's dilemma

		B	
		Cooperates	*Competes*
A	Cooperates	**A: 3** *B: 3*	**A: 1** *B: 4*
	Competes	**A: 4** *B: 1*	**A: 2** *B: 2*

Note: Each cell shows the payoffs to A (bold) and B (italic)

The table shows the incentives, or payoffs, to two players, A and B, depending on whether they choose to cooperate or compete with each other. The payoffs are exactly the same for each – the game is symmetrical. Each player also has full knowledge of the game's structure, and cannot communicate with the other. They each have to figure out what they should do based on what they think the other might do. For this reason, this kind of thinking is sometimes known as *strategic interaction* (Colman, 2003).

Now we can work through the strategies and their outcomes to see how this situation leads to an insoluble dilemma, and how it models the commons problem. The two strategies are to cooperate or compete. A has to consider what will happen if B does one or the other. Suppose A thinks that B will cooperate. What should A do? Look at the two cells under *B cooperates*: if A cooperates he will get 3 units of payoff, but if he competes he gets 4. So he should compete. What if B competes? Under *B competes*, you can see that A gets 1 if he cooperates and 2 if he competes. So again, he should compete. In other words, it does not matter what B does, A should compete. By the same token, B should also compete, because she is better off doing so no matter what A does (see how the same relations between payoffs for B appear under *A cooperates* and *A competes*). Because this strategy is the one that delivers the best payoff whatever the other player does, it is called the *dominant* strategy.

But look what happens when you follow it: the players arrive at the bottom right cell, where each gets 2 units. However, if they had both cooperated they would have landed in the top left cell, with 3 each. There is a straightforward clash between individual and collective utility maximisation. Players in a prisoner's dilemma *must* compete: they are individually better off if they do. No one wants to risk being in the wrong '1, 4' cell, which is where you will be if you cooperate but the other player competes. But if everyone competes, all are worse off than they could have been.

As can be expected from some of the language used to describe it, the prisoner's dilemma is an example of the kinds of situation addressed by a very wide-ranging theoretical system known as *game theory*. It has been hugely influential in many fields, such as economics, political science and evolutionary biology. Game theory is extensively reviewed from a psychological point of view by Andrew Colman in a book (1995) and a major review paper (2003); see also Camerer (2003), Gächter (2004) and Binmore (2007) for what Binmore's book cover promises: a very short introduction. In the argot of game theory, the 2, 2 cell in the prisoner's dilemma game is known as an *equilibrium point*, or Nash equilibrium after the mathematician John Nash who defined it (and won the Nobel Prize and was later the subject of the Hollywood film *A beautiful mind*). It is the state of the game that is inevitable when the players maximise their individual utility.

Colman (2003) points out two problems with the prisoner's dilemma as a model of what people do in situations where there is a clash of individual and social utility. The first is that there is a difficulty in prescribing what actually is the rational choice just from common knowledge of the game's innards. Each player also needs to have well-founded expectations of what the other player's strategy will be, each time the game is played. More importantly, the fact is that the game does not predict very well what people actually do when they play it. There is what Colman calls 'rampant cooperation' (p. 147), when strictly speaking there should be all-out competition; compare the voter's paradox, above, where people also act socially rather than individually.

The prisoner's dilemma described above is the simplest possible form of the game: just two players and only one play. Even then, some people cooperate. In real life, there are many more players and many more plays: you have the chance to change your strategy in the light of experience, of other players' strategies and of the resulting payoffs. Suppose, for instance, that there is a bonus for acting kindly and a penalty for acting meanly, over and above the utilities set out in Table 9.2; social approval or disapproval might be an example. This acts as a *payoff transformation*. Over time, and repeated plays, the top left 3, 3 cell emerges as the new equilibrium point and everyone's a winner (Camerer, 1997). In short, Colman's message is that formal game theory will not work as a descriptive theory of strategic interaction without psychological components that enable us to account for the 'theory of mind' that you need to have of the other players in order to play.

Payoff transformations like this may have deep origins: Purves, Brannon, Cabeza, Huettel, LaBar, Platt and Woldorff (2008) report that, on repeated plays of the prisoner's dilemma game, people tend not only to cooperate more but the activity in their brains changes. The brain areas associated with the evaluation of rewards (the ventral striatum, anterior caudate and anterior cingulate cortex) become more active. This could mean that people find cooperation rewarding; or perhaps, since more cooperation will result in increased gains if both players do it, the brain areas are reacting to the rewards.

Elinor Ostrom (1990), in work that contributed to her receiving the Nobel Prize for economics in 2009, the first woman to do so, addressed the commons problem and how it might be solved. Remember that Hardin had noted that this form of dilemma had no technical (i.e. logical) solution; the prisoner's dilemma has helped to show us why. Commons problems, which Ostrom calls common pool resource (CPR) problems, are acute because their consequences are so potentially severe, and because they are so hard to solve: the temptation to be a free rider, taking the personal benefits of consumption without regard to the collective costs in producing or maintaining the resource, is just too strong for everyone to resist all of the time (see Chapter 4 for studies of the free-rider problem by reasoning researchers). That being so, how do we protect a CPR from the ravages of its users?

Hardin's solution was coercion, or what he called 'mutual coercion mutually agreed upon by the majority of the people affected' (1968, p. 1247). He was careful not to equate coercion with physical force. Taxes, charges and rules are forms of coercion from this point of view, as when an elected local authority institutes no-parking zones or charges so as to alleviate the congestion that would result from car drivers parking where they please (and, who knows, raise a little revenue). Ostrom calls this kind of solution a Leviathan solution, after the overarching authority argued for by the 17th century English philosopher Thomas Hobbes as the basis of civil society. We agree to cede power to an authority and then to abide by its orders. Later writers, including Hardin himself (1978), have been rather less restrained, some even calling for military governments to ensure the survival of CPRs.

Ostrom points to some of the problems that stem from this apparently simple, albeit draconian, solution. The authority would need to have complete knowledge of the degree to which the resource could be sustainably exploited and about the consumers' intentions and behaviours (Colman's theory of mind point again), and would need to be able to enforce its will at no cost. None of this sounds plausible. What then of the alternatives? Hardin (1968) referred to the celebrated 'invisible hand' advocated by one of the founders of the science of economics, the 18th century Scottish philosopher Adam Smith: that people pursuing their own interests will be led as if by an invisible hand to further the public interest without even trying. The very existence of commons problems would seem to dispose of this idea – Hardin certainly thought so – but other theorists have argued for privatisation as a solution. Take the 'common' out of the common pool resource and have instead a resource to which an authority sells rights. Again, Ostrom points out the problems with this approach. It sounds plausible when thinking about parcels of land, but with resources such as marine fisheries it has proved impossible to define ownership rights, let alone price them or enforce them.

Ostrom (1990) suggests a third way, based on the insight that the crucial word in the term prisoner's dilemma is *prisoner*. What if people are not the prisoners of the game they find themselves playing, but can alter its rules? This is perfectly possible in the real world. What we need, she proposes, is a CPR game in which 'the [players] themselves can make a binding contract to submit themselves to a cooperative strategy that they themselves will work out' (p. 15). 'Binding' is a key word: the contract must be unfailingly enforced to guard against free-riding. The advantage of such an arrangement is that it will be adaptable to local conditions and changes. Pie in the sky? It might be, were it just an untested idea, but Ostrom reports detailed analyses of communities around the world dealing with local CPRs in just the way she outlines. She goes on to distil these observations, of their failures as well as successes, into a set of principles for the analysis of CPR problems. We had better hope that people in charge of energy, oil in particular, are listening.

Deciding without thinking

We have already seen an example of deciding without thinking in Chapter 8: the use of lexical rules, such as *keep your word*. We sometimes actually use the expression *unthinking* when people use this strategy. But even when we don't have strict rules to follow, we can still make choices without apparently doing any thinking at all. In previous chapters, especially Chapter 6, we have encountered dual process theory: the idea that there are two basic forms of thought, two minds even. There is the deliberate, conscious thought of the kind that seems to be required to follow the prescriptions of decision theory, where to be truly rational you need to work out all those trade-offs between utility and probability or, as we have just been considering, between goals. This is known as System 2 or Type 2 thinking. Then there is the more intuitive, unconscious kind of thought, where we form judgments and make choices but are not quite sure how. When we are aware of having decided something, we often ascribe it to *intuition*, without having much idea what we mean by the term. This is System 1 or Type 1 thinking.

The dual process theory of thought has been adopted not just by reasoning theorists, but in the psychology of decision making as well. We can make use of the general idea introduced by Stanovich (2004) with regard to System 1. He proposed that it is not a unified system at all, but rather a collection of modular subsystems to which he gave the acronym TASS: The Autonomous Set of Subsystems. The TASS construct seems to gel nicely with the findings of research into deciding without thinking. We shall now look at some representative cases. Myers (2002) is an excellent source of further examples.

Many decisions are arrived at by 'feelings', where we have little sense of doing any thinking at all. Sometimes these are emotional responses, sometimes not. We may even make a choice and be quite unaware of having done so; such influences on our choices are more like the pure heuristic components that Evans (2009) sought to separate from the TASS components of System 1 (see Chapter 6). There is a similarity between them and perceptual processes, as Kahneman (2002, 2003a, 2003b) notes. Both perceptual processes and System 1 processes are fast, automatic, unconscious and effortless; and there is an important additional property. In both cases, you can experience something and be completely oblivious of having done so.

Priming

The most startling demonstrations of this effect in research on thinking have come from John Bargh and his colleagues over a number of years. They have studied *priming*, and startling is not too strong a word for some of their findings. Bargh starts from the position that 'most moment-to-moment psychological life must occur through nonconscious means' (Bargh & Chartrand, 1999, p. 462). This is because there is simply too much psychological life going on for it all to be mediated by conscious, deliberate information processing. We know from other fields that many of our cognitive processes become automatic and unconscious: acquired skills are an obvious example. If you have learned to drive, cycle or play an instrument well, you will be able to recall how difficult it was in the early days, and how little effort it seems to take now. Skilled drivers may remember almost nothing of their actual driving at the end of a routine journey; a cyclist cannot tell you how they ride a bike, as anyone who has ever tried to teach this to a child will confirm. We know *that* we can do these things, but not *how*; this knowledge is no longer available to the conscious mind. But how widespread are these unconscious processes, and just how automatic and unconscious are they?

According to Bargh, the answer is 'very' to both questions. Here is a recent case reported by Ackerman, Nucera and Bargh (2010). They report a series of studies on how the sense of touch can influence decisions, even though touch has nothing directly to do with the decisions in question. In one study, they had participants rate job candidates' CVs on a range of dimensions while standing up. Some participants were given light clipboards to rest their forms on, while others were given heavy ones. Overall ratings were higher when the raters held heavy boards than when they held light ones. Not all categories showed this effect: for instance, while serious interest in the job was affected, likely ability to get on with colleagues was not. The same effect was found in a decision study, where people had to say whether public money should be given to various causes, serious or less serious. In this case, there was an interesting interaction: only the male participants showed the effect, allocating more money to the serious causes. The women were immune to clipboard weight.

Ackerman and colleagues point out that the weight effect only primed responses to the 'weighty' issues in both experiments. They argue that metaphors like this are an important mediator of priming. The metaphors themselves come from the sense of touch: touch primes concepts that are associated with it, such as weight. They back up this idea with tests of other touch-related primes. For instance, people were given a five-piece puzzle game, with the pieces feeling either smooth or rough to the touch. They then went on to take part in a strategic interaction game (see above) called the ultimatum game: you make an offer, such as dividing a set of tokens, which the other player either accepts or rejects. If the offer is accepted you both keep the payoffs, but if it is rejected you leave empty-handed. The 'rough' people made more generous offers than the 'smooth' people did. They appeared to be more cautious, trying to placate the opponent. Rough–smooth, say the authors, is a dimension that can be applied to social interactions, and so behaviour in a strategic interaction can be deflected by prior priming with actual tactile roughness or smoothness.

Finally, in a pricing experiment, people who sat on hard chairs revised their offers less than did people who sat on comfy cushions; we are familiar with the idea of driving a hard bargain! This is just one example of a stream of studies of this kind. For others, see Hassin, Uleman and Bargh (2005).

That people can be totally unaware of the influences on their choices had been reported much earlier, in a very well known paper by Nisbett and Wilson (1977; at the turn of the century, it was one of the ten most cited papers in the history of the journal in which it appeared, *Psychological Review*). Nisbett and Wilson mention the common experience of two people having the same thought at the same time. They may not be aware of the external cue that caused them both to have the thought, and may come up with more far-fetched explanations, such as telepathy. Nisbett and Wilson used a priming experiment to test this idea. Students were given a word-pair memory test, with some of the pairs designed to prime associations with commercial names. Twice as many students given *ocean–moon* to remember, later generated the brand name *Tide* when asked to name a washing powder than those who had not seen this pair. They were unaware of the connection.

The last observation is the rule. In all these experiments, the participants were questioned after their decisions as to whether they were aware of the associations the experimenters had designed into the tasks. Hardly anyone ever was.

Deciding through feeling

In another classic paper from the same era, Zajonc (1980) proposed that we have an affective information processing system (i.e. one devoted to feelings) distinct from our more purely cognitive processes. We can ascribe this system to TASS, and in their review of these unconscious processes Bargh and Chartrand (1999) agree that we seem to have an *automatic evaluation response* to just about any stimulus: we immediately tag it as good or bad, whether or not evaluation is part of the goal we have. This response can be primed. Given a reaction-time task involving positive words such as *music* or *friends*, people later reported themselves as being in a happier mood than were people who had to respond to negative words such as *cancer* or *cockroach*. Automatic evaluation like this affects not just mood but behaviour: Chen and Bargh (1999) found that people were faster at pulling a lever towards them when presented with positive words, and faster to push the lever away from them when the words were negative. Of course, you want to be nearer good things and to push bad things away, and Chen and Bargh's research shows that this happens even when you are not directly being asked to approach or avoid anything. Once again, when questioned, people had no idea that this influence was occurring.

Automatic good/bad evaluation as a decision process was called the *affect heuristic* by Slovic, Finucane, Peters and MacGregor (2002). They allow that the use of such feelings to make decisions can be either conscious or unconscious, and so this idea is not the same as Bargh's priming concept, although there is clearly some overlap. Slovic and colleagues use the affect heuristic to explain some of the findings we have seen before, as well as ones introduced in this chapter. Here are two examples of previous results, which were reported in the last chapter. Firstly, the case of preference reversals between P bets (high probability of low winnings) and $ bets (low probability of high winnings) when rating and pricing are used, which Slovic himself had discovered many years previously (e.g. Lichtenstein & Slovic, 1971). The P bet tends to be rated as more attractive, but people are prepared to pay more for the $ bet. It was argued that this was because pricing makes you think of money, and money makes you think of the winnings, whereas rating makes you think more of likelihoods. Slovic et al. reasoned that if they could change the affective status of the $ bet, they could disrupt the preference reversal.

They did this by adding a component that would make it clearer to people how attractive the winnings in the $ bet were: they added a small loss to it. The original gamble was a 7/36 chance of winning $9, which they argued was not easy to scale in terms of attractiveness. The revised version was for the same chance of the same win plus a 29/36 chance of losing 5 cents. Now there is a steep payoff ratio between the win and the loss, which should make the win look more attractive. It did: when this was the $ bet, almost twice as many people (61%) preferred it to the P bet, compared to the original without the loss component (33%). The second example involves Slovic et al. reinterpreting the evaluability results of Hsee, which were described in Chapter 8, also in terms of the affect heuristic. Thus we now have the same process accounting for different sets of findings.

They also offer it as an explanation of some forms of decision dilemmas, using the case of smoking as an example. Many people start smoking when they are young and most find it hard to give up, even though the great majority regret ever having started. Young, beginning smokers are enticed by feelings of excitement, of being at one with their friends and the sensations of smoking itself. They lack the experience of addiction and ill health, even though they have heard about them; it is only later that these aspects of smoking produce their own affective tone, leading to regret and the desire, if not the ability, to quit. So it is not just the reinforcers that slide (as Platt, 1973, had it) but the affect associated with them.

The findings reported in this section show that, far from emotion being in some way opposed to reason, the two faculties are intimately bound up: as Slovic et al. (2002) strikingly put it (p. 420), affect lubricates reason. It is possible to go further even than this. Damasio (1994) considers the relation between emotion and reason in great detail. He reports research by Bechara, Damasio, Damasio and Anderson (1994) on people with localised brain damage, whose ability to feel was impaired but not their ability to reason. You might expect them to turn into hyper-rational Mr Spocks, but they ended up making poor decisions and suffering as a result. They could easily be lured into disastrous gambles that the rest of us learn to avoid. This was not because they were insensitive to loss, but because the effects of sustaining a loss were only short-lived. They did not learn a new, stable affective response to loss that enabled them to avoid such losses in future, and so they kept suffering them. Feelings in real-world decision situations are not a luxury, nor even a lubricant, but a necessity. Bechara (2011) offers a recent review of this and related work.

Fast and frugal decision processes

Both Bargh and his colleagues and Slovic and his colleagues remark on the System 1 aspects of the non-thinking decision processes they studied: they are quick, effortless and useful in that they free up cognitive resources. The same aspects are at the heart of an approach to decision making studied extensively by the team headed by Gerd Gigerenzer, whom we met in Chapter 1 as the principal advocate of the natural sampling approach to probability judgment. They have conducted a major research programme on what he calls *fast and frugal* decision heuristics, a term popularised by Gigerenzer and Goldstein (1996). Probability judgment is a central part of decision making, and in Chapter 1 we briefly considered this relation from the natural sampling perspective, for instance in its implications for medical diagnosis and treatment prescriptions. In this chapter, we shall extend this consideration into more directly decision-making areas.

Gigerenzer's decision heuristics programme shares with his natural sampling project the presumption that human cognition is well adapted to its environment.

These heuristics are therefore proposed to be not only efficient but effective: they usually deliver us the right answers. There is thus a different emphasis in Gigerenzer's heuristics compared with those put forward by Kahneman and Tversky (see Chapter 1), as was made clear in a rather bad-tempered exchange between the two camps (see Gigerenzer, 1996; Kahneman & Tversky, 1996). Research on them is reported in a wide range of publications, not just academic papers but books as well. Brief reviews can be found in book chapters such as Gigerenzer (2004a) and Gigerenzer, Czerlinski and Martignon (2002). For detailed specialist accounts, go to Gigerenzer (2008), Gigerenzer and Todd (1999a, 1999b; also Todd & Gigerenzer, 2000) and Gigerenzer and Selten (2001); books for the non-specialist include Gigerenzer (2007). The latter's title fits into the theme of this part of the present chapter: *Gut feelings*.

The core idea behind Gigerenzer's account of intuitive decision making is that when we do this we do not necessarily take account of all the information potentially available to us; we take the best and leave the rest. Just because a situation needs a lot of complicated calculation to be solved normatively does not mean that humans perform such calculations when faced with it. For one thing, the formal calculi are, like percentages and probabilities, recent cultural developments, but we have been making these choices for millennia. For another, remember that intuitive judgments tend to be quick and easy, too much so for complicated calculation to be going on. We must be using some kind of heuristic, rather than formal algorithms, just as we can detect grammatical blunders without knowing explicitly the rules of grammar.

To see how take-the-best works, we can use the most familiar example from Gigerenzer's research: the city size question. Note that there are other cases to which take-the-best has been applied, as detailed in Gigerenzer and Todd (1999a), particularly in the chapter by Czerlinski, Gigerenzer and Goldstein, and his other books; the sometimes voiced criticism that this approach is only tested on this problem is misplaced. Think of two German cities, Duisburg and Mönchengladbach: which would you say has the biggest population? Take-the-best involves not using all the possible information you might have at your fingertips about these places (apart from in the situation we shall shortly come on to). Rather, what you do is find a cue that, on the basis of the knowledge you have, can be used to discriminate between the two candidates on the aspect in question. Once you find one, you use it, and that is that.

Do you think Mönchengladbach is the bigger? If you do, perhaps you used the football (soccer) team cue: Mönchengladbach has a team in the German premier league, the Bundesliga (Borussia Mönchengladbach), whereas Duisburg does not. Gigerenzer and Goldstein (1996) showed that this cue was a good one: for pairs of cities with populations over 100,000, the city with a team in the Bundesliga was the biggest 87% of the time. They call this the *cue validity*. How about these two cities: Herne and Heidelberg. You cannot use the Bundesliga cue this time, as neither city has a Bundesliga team. When I thought about this pair, I went for Heidelberg. I was using the most basic of the possible cues: the *recognition heuristic*: I had heard of Heidelberg, but never heard of Herne.

Gigerenzer proposes that if you recognise one item and not the other, you use that cue and, on the take-the-best principle, stop there, no matter what else you know. It will be useful when two conditions apply: (i) that you recognise one object but not the other; (ii) that there is a strong correlation between the object and the value in question, such as a city's population (Goldstein & Gigerenzer, 1999, 2002). So if you have heard of both cities, or neither, you cannot use recognition. Goldstein and Gigerenzer report an experiment in which 22 US students were given 25 or 30 names of the largest cities in Germany in pairs (resulting in 300 and 435 questions, respectively). They made the size judgment and also indicated, for each city, whether they recognised its name. Looking at the pairs where just one was recognised, around 90% of size judgments followed the recognition heuristic. This is the exception referred to earlier: if all you know is that you know one and not the other, then you use that.

This theory makes some surprising predictions, foremost among them being the *less-is-more* effect. It was first reported by Gigerenzer (1993). He gave German students city-size questions about German cities and American cities. Judgment accuracy was almost exactly the same, at around 76% in both cases. How is this possible? Clearly, German students will know more about German cities than US cities. It was results like this that gave rise to the take-the-best principle. Remember that the theory assumes that you will not use all the information you have about the items in question: you will find a cue that seems to work, use that and stop; Gigerenzer calls this one-reason decision making. The cue validity of recognition for city size in this sample was found to be. 90, which is about as high as it could be. The German students using recognition when thinking about US cities were therefore using a very useful cue. They could not use it for their own cities, since they recognised all of them. They therefore had to use other cues, and these were about as useful to them; no more useful than mere recognition was for less familiar items.

Goldstein and Gigerenzer (1999, 2002; see also Gigerenzer, 2007) point out that the less-is-more effect will be observed not just between classes of items, as described above, but between groups of people with different levels of knowledge about a particular class, and even within the same person at different stages of learning. As long as the two conditions above apply – differential recognition and good correlation – you will do well with only a little knowledge on questions like these.

The take-the-best principle is more than the recognition heuristic: this is just specified as the one to use if you can. When you cannot apply it, you go to the next cue, if there is one. Take-the-best, as its name implies, assumes you know something about the range of cue validities, so that you go to the one that has the highest and see whether you can discriminate between the candidates on this basis. The Bundesliga cue is an example, which you can use when you recognise both cities and know something about German football.

How good is take-the-best as a decision strategy? Gigerenzer and Goldstein (1996; see also Gigerenzer, Czerlinski & Martignon, 2002) conducted computer simulations of it along with statistical models that use more, sometimes all, of the information available. Take-the-best performed at a very similar level – it found about the same proportion of right answers – but it did so using fewer cues (between two and three on average) than did its more complex rivals (which averaged over seven), and was therefore more efficient. This, argues Gigerenzer, counts in favour of take-the-best, since humans tend to prefer to save themselves work (see Chater, Oaksford, Nakisa & Redington, 2003, for a critique of this assumption, among others).

Fast and frugal decision strategies have been applied in the real world. Gigerenzer quotes two instances of them being applied in the life-and-death situation of emergency hospital admission for patients who are suspected of having had a heart attack (see Gigerenzer, 2007; Gigerenzer & Todd, 1999b; Todd & Gigerenzer,

2000). When a patient is admitted, there is a huge amount of information available: the patient's medical history, lifestyle, presenting symptoms, test results, and so on. Doctors can be overwhelmed by this information, and respond conservatively by sending most patients to the cardiac intensive care unit, to be on the safe side as far as both the patient and themselves are concerned – they don't want to be sued by the relatives of a person sent to the regular ward who subsequently dies of a heart attack.

Gigerenzer (2007, Chapter 9) shows a three-step fast and frugal decision tree, developed by Green and Mehr (1997), which you can see in adapted form in Figure 9.1; Gigerenzer and Todd (1999b) refer to a similar system but with different

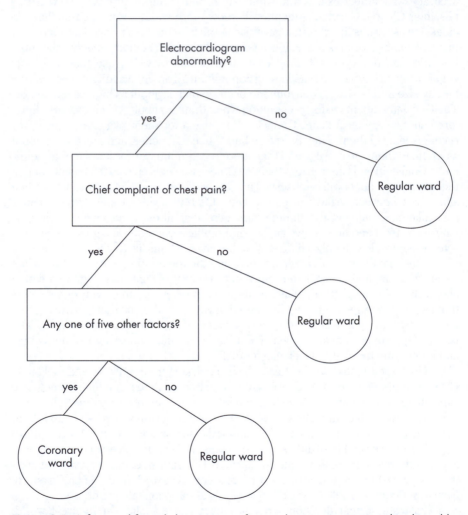

Figure 9.1 A fast and frugal decision tree for cardiac emergencies, developed by Green and Mehr (1997)

Source: Adapted from Gigerenzer (2007)

components developed earlier by Breiman, Friedman, Ohlson and Stone (1993). The three cues, in the oblongs, were found to be the cues that experienced doctors had memorised during their training and practice. They did not need to do any calculation once they had. Accuracy of clinical decisions improved significantly when this system was introduced at a Michigan hospital in the USA.

Heuristic-based fast and frugal strategies have been proposed for the kinds of decisions covered in detail in the last chapter, where the gambling framework was the basis on which they were considered, and the core of decision making was seen as the trade-off between utility and probability. Brandstätter, Gigerenzer and Hertwig (2006) propose that people use a *priority heuristic* in making these kinds of decisions. It is so called because it adopts the take-the-best principle of considering cues in order, and stopping when one is found that is good enough to decide the issue. In this case, the cues are reasons for choosing.

On the basis of a review of the empirical evidence, Brandstätter and colleagues propose that the priority rule contains three reasons, which people consider in order: the minimum gain, the probability of the minimum gain and the maximum gain. To judge when to stop going through these cues, the authors introduce a stopping rule: if the minimum gains of the gambles you are considering differ by at least 1/10 of the maximum gain, choose on this basis; otherwise, see whether the probabilities differ by at least .10 on the probability scale and choose on that basis; and if that does not decide it, choose according to the maximum gain. Lastly, choose the most attractive option: the one with the higher gain, or the lowest probability of the minimum gain. There is a similar set of rules for losses. The numbers (1/10) were chosen on the basis of their prominent cultural use: we have a base 10 number system and like to use multiples of 10 whenever possible, such as when celebrating anniversaries. The 1/10 maximum gain cue gives you an *aspiration level*: the amount that you judge to be large enough as a difference to enable you to decide.

Here is how the priority heuristic decides in a simple choice between two gambles: $200 with probability .5 versus $100 for sure (i.e. prob. = 1). The minimum gains are zero in the first case, because if there is a probability of .5 of $200, there must be a probability of .5 of getting nothing, and $100 in the second case; the aspiration level is $20 (1/10 of $200); the difference between minimum gains ($100–$0 = $100) exceeds this value; so stop and use this cue. Because the minimum gain is highest with the certain $100, choose that.

The heuristic can also explain the notorious Allais paradox, which we met in Chapter 8. So flip back to that, and then we can follow what happens. The first choice was between a certain $1000 (gamble 1a) or $1000 with prob. = .90, $5000 with prob. = .09 and zero with prob. = .01 (gamble 1b). Most people choose 1a. According to the priority heuristic, the maximum gain of $5000 gives us an aspiration level of $500; the minimum gains are $1000 (a) and zero (b), which is a difference of $1000; since $1000 is more than $500, use the minimum gain cue and go for the higher, which is gamble 1a.

With the second gamble, you were offered $1000 with prob. = .10 and zero with prob. = .90 (gamble 2a), or $5000 with prob. = .90 and zero with prob. = .91 (gamble 2b). Most people go for 2b, in violation of expected utility norms. The priority heuristic tells us that the minimum gains are the same in both cases (zero), so we cannot use that cue; the probabilities are .90 and .91, which is a difference of only .01 and less than the aspiration level difference of .10, so we cannot use that cue either; so we go with the maximum gain cue and choose the one with the highest – 2b, where it is $5000.

How about our *Who wants to be a millionaire* man? He was faced with the choice between $4000 if he quit versus $8000 with prob. = .5 and $1000 with prob. = .5 if he gambled. The maximum gain of $8000 gives an aspiration level of $800; the minimum gains are $4000 and $1000, which is a difference of $3000; this is more than the aspiration level, so stop and use this cue; since quitting has the higher minimum gain, choose that. The priority heuristic can thus explain his choice too.

As always with Gigerenzer's research group, the Brandstätter et al. paper goes through an impressive array of tests: the heuristic is employed to explain a range of the phenomena predicted by prospect theory, such as risk aversion for gambles and risk seeking for losses. However, Hardman (2009) sounds a note of caution. He regards the 1/10 stopping rule as rather arbitrary, and points out that there are some aspects of prospect theory that the priority heuristic does not explain, notably framing, and that it has no account of affective influences on decisions, such as the ones we were concerned with earlier in this chapter. Note also that people who do gamble in the *Millionaire* situation we have looked at are acting contrary to the heuristic.

These last remarks show that the fast and frugal approach, especially in its take-the-best guise, has not gone unchallenged. Apart from the particular issues addressed by Hardman, it does not seem to be applied by people generally; it is only applied when the costs of acquiring the information are high, for instance when there is a lot of information to be held in memory, as in the case of the doctors mentioned above (Bröder & Schiffer, 2003; Newell & Shanks, 2003). Its use also seems to be subject to wide individual differences (not everyone in the *Millionaire* case quits), so it may be best regarded as a strategy that some people use but others do not, and in some contexts but not in others (Newell & Shanks, 2003). It is also doubtful whether people actually use pure recognition; when you recognise something such as a city name, you usually do so for a reason, such as that it is a national capital or very large. Such information will also be employed in the decision process, which seems to imply that you are using two reasons for your choice – recognition plus this other factor – and not just one (Oppenheimer, 2003).

The 30 commentaries that follow the Todd and Gigerenzer (2000) paper have much more in this vein. A major dual process theorist, Evans (2010), is strongly critical of Gigerenzer's emphasis on gut feelings as decision procedures: in contrast to his 'two minds' theory, he calls this a 'no mind' theory. As we shall see in the next chapter, Gigerenzer has, in turn, a critique of dual process theory. This is clearly a particularly lively area of current controversy, and we can expect more exchanges between the two camps.

As for the two city questions earlier, if you used the Bundesliga cue for the first one, you would have got it wrong: Duisburg, at 513,000, is almost twice the size of Mönchengladbach. And I was wrong about Heidelberg: its population (140,000) is nearly 20% lower than Herne's (172,000). That's the trouble with heuristics: they are not just fast and frugal, but quick and dirty. Although they usually give you the right answer, they can lead you astray.

Intuition and expertise

The fast and frugal approach developed out of Gigerenzer's evolutionary stance: such processes are said to be part of our long history of developing successful adaptations to complex environments. But as we have already seen in the example of the heart doctors, he recognises an alternative route to intuitive judgment: it can develop out of individual learning and experience. In short, intuition can come with expertise. The doctors acquired their knowledge of cue validities from their learning as medical students and practitioners, and this knowledge could then be passed on to other doctors through the fast and frugal decision tree. It is not a gut feeling at all (Evans, 2010).

An extensive set of studies of the 'learning perspective' on intuition is collected in a recent volume by Plessner, Betsch and Betsch (2008). In his chapter, Hogarth (2008) describes the 'inventories of intuitions' that we all have as our 'cultural capital' (p. 93): we acquire them through a continuous process of largely implicit learning. This learning process is like a broadband connection: always on. People do not learn about everything at an even rate, and so tend to follow their interests and aptitudes and specialise. We therefore develop domain-specific areas of expertise in which our intuitive processes emerge. Because of biases in the ways we sample and reason about the objects and events we experience, many of which have been reviewed in earlier chapters, we will not necessarily build up inventories of good intuitions.

A particular case is that of the *illusion of validity*, which arises out of a sampling bias: we tend to sample only the cause-present/effect-present cell of the 2 × 2 contingency table that is necessary for accurate causal learning (see Chapter 4). Hogarth gives the example of a manager who interviews people for jobs, observes the people she appoints doing well in their work and so acquires an intuitive but illusory sense of the accuracy of interviews. (You need also to think about appointees who don't do so well, along with rejects who do and do not do well; but you will never come across the last two.)

The intuitive decision processes of experts have been studied in great detail by Gary Klein (1998, 2009; Klein, Orasanu, Calderwood & Zsambok, 1993), who has established the field of *naturalistic decision making* (NDM) in doing so. It is naturalistic mainly in terms of the people and contexts studied: Klein tends to conduct research on people in the field, doing the jobs where they bring their expertise to bear. NDM's theoretical approach builds on an insight that emerged from earlier studies of expertise in chess players (e.g. Chase & Simon, 1973): that the crucial ability that experts acquire, which can take them a decade or more of experience to acquire it, is the ability to recognise patterns. It is easy to see what these are in chess: the arrays of pieces and the ways they transform during games, which themselves take the courses they do through the applications of strategies and gambits.

Klein calls this *recognition-primed decision* (RPD). In his best-known study, conducted in the 1980s, his team explored the decision making of firefighters, especially chief officers present at the fire (known as fireground commanders). Their experience allows them to 'size up the situation to recognize which course of action makes sense' (Klein, 1998, p. 24) – that is, recognise a pattern. This is stage 1 of the RPD model. Note the use of the singular 'course'. Typically, they come up with just one option; they do not weigh up more, not even one more, and choose between them (this idea is consistent with Evans' theory of hypothetical thinking: see Chapter 7). Next (stage 2), they run a mental simulation to see if the course of action they are considering will work. If they decide against it, only then do they consider an alternative. And bear in mind that they are doing this under intense pressure: these decisions need to be taken quickly, and are highly consequential. The commanders' expertise enables them to see instantly which cues are worth taking notice of, and the pattern they retrieve from memory supplies them, effortlessly, with a set of expectations about what will happen next and what are the typical ways of responding. Several other striking instances of this kind of intuitive judgment are recounted in Malcolm Gladwell's bestseller, *Blink* (2005); he also cites the jams experiment and the less-is-more effect (see above).

Not that RPD is an infallible process, of course. As noted above, the trouble with heuristics is that, while generally good, they can go wrong. Doctors can misdiagnose a patient; a firefighter can misjudge a fire. Klein (1998, Chapter 6) tells us about how the same processes that lead to firefighters saving lives led to tragedy when a US warship shot down an Iranian civil airliner in the Persian Gulf in 1988. The cues fitted the pattern of a hostile military aircraft, and a single mental simulation followed. It was the wrong pattern. The consequences are still being felt, and not just by the families of the people who died.

Recently, Klein and Kahneman have reviewed and compared their two approaches, NDM and the 'heuristics and biases' (HB) approach, which was covered in Chapter 1 (Kahneman & Klein, 2009). On the surface, they look quite different: NDM studies experts in their domain of expertise, while HB usually studies naïve participants such as university students in laboratories; HB researchers tend to be sceptical of people's ability to adhere to judgmental norms, while NDM researchers 'are more likely to adopt an admiring stance toward experts' (p. 518); and the criteria used to define expertise are normative for HB and practical or peer-judged for NDM. Nevertheless, the two authors, themselves about as expert in their fields as it is possible to be, identify more areas of commonality between their two approaches than areas of difference. Genuine skill in intuitive judgment is possible when it is acquired in environments that supply highly valid cues, such as the ones identified by Klein and Gigerenzer. In areas that do not have this feature, such as predicting the stock market, any apparent expertise will be illusory; Gigerenzer (2007) and Myers (2002) both report that you will be better off – substantially – following a naïve strategy such as recognition, or relying only on stocks mentioned in the FTSE 100 or S & P 500 indices, than tips from stock market 'experts' in deciding where to invest your money. As Kahneman and Klein (2009, p. 525) conclude: 'a psychology of judgment and decision making that ignores skill is seriously blinkered ... but a psychology of professional judgment that ignores errors cannot be adequate'.

Summary

1   Paradoxes of choice have been discovered, where people find too many options intimidating.

2   Personality factors play a part: some people are maximisers, always searching for the best, while some are satisficers, content with what is good enough. Satisficers tend to be happier than maximisers.

3   Social comparison processes also affect choice and happiness, and can lead to a hedonic treadmill, where people become trapped into escalating patterns of spending.

4   Decision dilemmas, where utility maximisation is impossible, arise because there are goals that are inconsistent. Thus a given action can take a person closer to one but further from another that is equally valued.

5   Major forms of decision dilemmas concern time (short-term gains versus long-term losses, and vice versa) and other people (acting in the interests of the individual or the group).

6   Decisions are often made with minimal thought. Examples are influences through priming and through feelings.

7   Gigerenzer's one-reason decision theory is a major competitor to earlier expected utility-based theories: he has evidence that simplified choice algorithms can deliver rational outcomes for little cognitive effort.

8   Intuitive decision making is partly a product of expertise: Klein's naturalistic decision-making theory proposes that expert decision makers recognise the patterns in an event, entertain only one candidate solution and change policy only if they have to.

Thinking, reasoning and you

Much of the discussion in the previous chapters has been in the terms that science often uses: general statements about average tendencies. At various points, though, we have paused to consider the ways in which people depart from the average, or where the average conceals a more interesting picture. This has been seen most in the previous two chapters, on decision making. In this one, we shall see how the field of reasoning research has also been changed by the study of individual differences. To do that, we need to stay with decisions for the moment and address a construct that always comes up when people discuss them, one that turns out to be at the centre of the relation between thinking and reasoning and you and me.

Rationality

People think they know what they mean when they describe a person, action or belief as rational or irrational, and systematic uses of this understanding can be found in more formal settings, such as medicine or the law: laws or verdicts can be overturned, and people committed for or refused medical treatment, on the grounds of irrationality. Aristotle, almost two and a half thousand years ago, claimed rationality as the distinguishing mark of the human species, sparking a philosophical debate that has rumbled on ever since. Lately, this debate has taken a more psychological turn. A detailed review of rationality from a psychological perspective is given by Nickerson (2008). As he argues, rationality is a complex business, and if you ignore these complexities you run the risk of making the wrong call about a person's beliefs or actions. If you are a high court judge or a medical consultant, this could have serious consequences. So let us start to unwrap the parcel of rationality and see what we find inside it.

Do you think of yourself as a rational person, who at least tries to do the right thing most of the time, and whose beliefs are pretty much on the right track about most things? Me too. But you make different choices from mine, and we believe different things as well; you will never meet anyone whose beliefs and preferences are exactly the same as yours. So if you are rational, must they be less rational? The rationality we claim as our own we find quite easy to deny to others, as when you find someone who hates something you love or disbelieves something you are convinced of. Some people, bigots, take this to an extreme and regard anyone who does not like or believe in something that they do with contempt, or worse. As The Doors (1967) so wisely remarked all those years ago, people are strange, and never more so than when we examine their beliefs and preferences.

This is an inconvenience in at least one very important practical respect: the economy. As Tetlock and Mellers (2002) pointed out in their review of Kahneman and Tversky's (2000) compendium of studies on decision making, the people who run governments and businesses disregard the strangeness of people and assume a kind of universal rationality: the rationality of expected utility maximisation. Economists call this *rational choice theory*. In the previous two chapters we have seen numerous reasons to be cautious about this assumption, compiled not just by Kahneman and Tversky but by a host of researchers round the world. A banker or a finance minister might object to all these findings: very interesting, they might say, but are they any more than the result of tricks and catches perpetrated on unsuspecting citizens by other-worldly academics? Surely no one can question the basic fact that people always and everywhere seek to choose what is best for themselves.

In fact we can. It is not just an empirical generalisation that, when put to the test, people wander from the true path of normative theories such as deductive logic, the probability calculus and decision theory. There is an in-principle objection too: that these formal systems ask too much of ordinary minds. It is not just that human thinking does not meet normative standards, but that it could not under any circumstances. If by rational thinking we mean thinking in accordance with normative systems, as rational choice theory entails, then we are condemned before the trial even begins. In the next section, we go further into this argument and its resolution.

Bounded rationality

What kind of mind would we have if we were all good children of *homo economicus*, the rational chooser? What operations would it have to perform? Think back to subjective expected utility theory, described in Chapter 8. Its foundational principle is that of *consequentialism*: you (must) choose on the basis of what will have the best consequences for you in the future. Now consider what you have to do in order to do this. You need to know what all the options are before you. You need to know what all the possible consequences will be of choosing each one. You need to know for each one what value you will place on it, should it come to pass, and how likely each one is to do so. And you have to know all of these with perfect accuracy, and to be able to compute, precisely, the trade-offs between them. You would be, as Gigerenzer and Todd (1999b; Todd & Gigerenzer, 2000) put it, a demon – or a god: something that knows everything.

Even setting aside the demonstrations of our shortcomings in all of these aspects of choice, which have been detailed in previous chapters, this is an impossible standard to hold people to. Impossible is a serious word, and needs a serious justification. The reason for using it is itself formal, and is to do with the *combinatorial explosion* of options that occurs once there are more than a very few possibilities to think about: that is, their number simply goes out of control. There is a similar problem in physics, called the *n*-body problem. With more than two bodies, such as the earth, sun and moon, their motions and relative positions become chaotic (increasingly unpredictable) owing to the exploding number of variables arising from the interactions of their gravitational fields as they move around each other.

Andrew Colman (1995) has a nice illustration of this combinatorial problem for psychology, using chess. It is a game with tightly structured rules and a finite number of elements, and so is much simpler than just about any real-life situation you find yourself faced with. Chess players need to maximise utility: you win the game, or at least avoid defeat, if you find the best move from whichever position you are in. There are on average about 30 moves available from a chess position, and an average game takes about 80 moves, 40 from each player. The number of possible chess games, taking into account these figures and all the possible combinations of moves, is therefore about 30^{80} (30 multiplied by itself 80 times). This figure exceeds the total number of particles in the universe (its upper estimate is about 10^{80}). A computer, or a mind, that assessed its options at a rate of 1 billion (10^9) per second would be stuck in thought over each move for billions of years (see also Gigerenzer, 2004b).

But lots of people play chess, some to a very high level, and there are chess-playing computer programs too. Both must be using something other than an unbounded ability to perform the complete set of utility-maximising calculations. We must have a *bounded rationality*. The term was introduced by Herbert Simon in 1957. He was a Nobel economics laureate in 1978, although he is better known to us as a cognitive scientist; his prize recognised his contribution to the understanding of decision making. We shall come back to Simon's ideas for bounded rationality shortly. To appreciate their force, we need to continue with the problems that unbounded rationality sets for us.

Playing chess is a problem that is *computationally intractable*: the logically necessary computations cannot be done in real time, because of the combinatorial explosion. Oaksford and Chater (1993, 1995b) follow through this phenomenon with respect to real-world human reasoning rather than games. There is a killer problem of cognition that has foxed generations of artificial intelligence researchers, who ran up against it as a practical problem, and more recently psychologists, who need to solve it in order to develop fully computational explanations of mentality. The clearest way to introduce it is with a thought experiment. I am going to ask you a quiz question. When you answer it, monitor the mental processes you go through to derive the answer. Here it is: who wrote *Macbeth*?

If you are from the English-speaking world,[1] where William Shakespeare hovers over the culture like a fine mist, the chances are that you found the answer instantly and effortlessly. So the introspection instruction was a trick: you have absolutely no idea how you found the answer; it was just there. This is as hard to explain as it is easy to do. Somehow, you sorted through all your factual knowledge, found the relevant area and zeroed in on the answer, in literally a fraction of a second, without any sense of having to do anything. Artificial intelligence (AI) researchers call this the *frame problem*; 'frame' is an AI expression for a package of knowledge. How does a computer, or a mind, find the *relevant* package from its vast store of knowledge, and do so quickly enough for it to be useful?

The problem that Oaksford and Chater raise in this context concerns the uncertain nature of the real world. Even apparently reliable statements such as *birds fly* have exceptions: that is, most statements about the world are *defeasible* – they can be defeated in the light of information. The bird you have in mind might be a kiwi or a cassowary, for instance. If we want to reason logically, we need statements that can be taken as certain. To be able to take a statement as certain, we must assess whether it has any exceptions. This, Oaksford and Chater argue, means we have to search our entire knowledge base, which simply cannot be done. Their solution, as we saw in Chapters 2 and 6, is to abandon logic, the calculus of certainty, as the basis for explaining human reasoning in favour of probability, the calculus of uncertainty. They describe their position as *Bayesian rationality* (Oaksford & Chater, 2007, 2009): reasoning as belief updating rather than deduction. But adopting this posture does not in itself free us from the frame problem: we still have to reach into our beliefs when reasoning and pull out the relevant ones.

As Chapter 6 showed, this has become a highly influential theoretical step, leading to what Over (2009) has described as a *new paradigm* in reasoning research, one with its foundations in probability rather than binary (true–false) logic. Some authors have resisted it, however, and urge the retention of logic in explaining how we think. Keith Stenning and Michiel van Lambalgen (2008a, 2008b) are the most prominent recent advocates of this view. They argue for the primacy of interpretation in reasoning: whenever we encounter a thinking problem, we instantly and unconsciously decode its properties, and reason from the knowledge that they entail. Different logics are applicable in different cases. For instance, we can reason from a *credulous* or *sceptical* stance. Credulous reasoning is where we expect that the situation will adhere to the Gricean principles of cooperation (see Chapters 2 and 4): arguments are being put forward, and all parties in the debate are being informative, relevant and well-mannered.

Things are not always so gentle. Sceptical reasoning, by contrast, might happen in a court of law, where a prosecuting or defending counsel may try to pick holes in a witness's testimony, inviting the jury to doubt it – and they will, using a different logic from the one they would use in ordinary social life. The witness had better not use the logic of conversation during the cross-examination. The same goes for business transactions. The salesperson is not really interested in the kind of day you've had; she just wants to sell you stuff.

For Stenning and van Lambalgen, human reasoning is *closed-world* reasoning: once interpretation has kicked in – which it always does – then a domain is established and its inherent logic is activated. They propose that you use default values: something like If p (and there is nothing funny going on) then conclude q. You might find yourself thinking about causes, explanations, obligations, beliefs, desires and so on, and do so credulously or sceptically. We have seen in earlier chapters how the thinking processes in such cases can be distinguished experimentally. A clear example, referred to by Stenning and van Lambalgen, is the difference between indicative and deontic versions of the Wason selection task, described in Chapter 5, where researchers have noted logical as well as behavioural distinctions. Is closed-world reasoning an answer to the frame problem? Stenning and van Lambalgen (2008a, p. 185) think so, but admit that it is only a partial one. We still have to figure out whether or not something funny *is* going on; we still don't really know how we answer such *Macbeth*-type questions so efficiently.

Satisficing

Along with the basic notion of bounded rationality, Simon (1957; see also 1978, 1983) was responsible for introducing the idea of *satisficing*, as we saw in Chapter 9. They are two sides of the same coin. If maximisation is impossible in principle, then we must be doing something else: we must be finding a solution that is good enough for our current goal, rather than the best one in all possible worlds. Simon gives us a picturesque metaphor in setting out where the bounds on our rationality are set. Think of the page of possibilities as being trimmed by a pair of scissors. The scissors have two blades. The first is the limited processing capacity of the mind (or computer). The second is the structure of the environment. Minds do not evolve or operate in a vacuum, and they are not blank slates (Pinker, 1997, 2002): they are adapted to their world.

These insights have recently been extended by Gigerenzer and his research group, as we saw in the previous chapter. Evans' theory of hypothetical thinking (see Chapter 7) is also a theory of bounded rationality through satisficing. Gigerenzer (2006; Gigerenzer & Todd, 1999b; Todd & Gigerenzer, 2000) helpfully sets out the possibilities for bounded and unbounded rationality. We have already seen one of them: the omniscient demon. As they acknowledge, few theorists actually argue for this; everyone recognises cognitive limitations.

There is another kind of demon, however, whose super-powers might slip by unnoticed if we were not careful. This is the demon who reasons by *optimisation under constraints*. The main constraint here is the cost of searching for information. We can all think of occasions when someone seems to be spending too much time agonising over a decision, poring over every possible aspect of a choice that will not actually make much difference one way or the other (I am told that men sometimes feel this way about the time women spend choosing what to wear, for instance. Women, on the other hand, are apparently irritated by men's obsessive researching of technical specifications when thinking about buying some new toy.) We are aware of the effort that making a choice demands, and we are aware that some choices are worth a lot of effort, while some are not. Perhaps, then, what we do is compute the costs and benefits of continuing search, and stop the process when the costs exceed any likely benefits. This sounds like a plausible way of limiting the mind's work. The trouble with it is that, once again, the mind needs unlimited resources to compute all these possible utilities, and this allows unbounded rationality to sneak back in.

We are therefore drawn inexorably to satisficing as a means of explaining how we think and reason about real problems in real time. Gigerenzer and Todd consider alternative kinds of satisficing and argue for a particular form: the adaptive toolbox of fast and frugal heuristics. *Adaptive* is the crucial word here: it brings back into play the second blade of Simon's scissors, the structure of the environment. The environment has worked in the past to shape the contents of the toolbox, through evolution, and it works in the present by telling us which of the tools to use. Examples were given in Chapter 9.

Several of the 30 commentaries to the Todd and Gigerenzer (2000) paper show that not all theorists are convinced by this approach (see also Over, 2003). For example, there are arguments about whether and where the adaptive toolbox meets its limits: do people really just use one-reason algorithms when thinking about highly consequential choices such as career moves or marriage? Some commentators are also worried about the adaptability of the toolbox to new and uncertain situations: the world we live in now is very different from the one in which the toolbox evolved, so how do we cope with all this novelty if we only have this old set of tools? Still others are concerned with the search problems within the toolbox itself: how does the mind decide which tool to take out? Todd and Gigerenzer give replies to these questions later in the article (see also Kruglanski & Gigerenzer, 2011). However, the debate about whether our rationality can be captured in purely fast and frugal terms, or whether we need, after all, to propose some form of general-purpose reasoning ability – for instance to account for our thinking in unfamiliar contexts – is still going on.

Dual rationality

Up to now, we have been discussing rationality as if it were a single construct, but there are important distinctions to be made between different types of rationality. Once again, the ancient Greeks have been here before us. Aristotle distinguished between *episteme*, correct reasoning about matters of fact, and *phronesis*, reasoning about the right action to perform (see an earlier book chapter of mine, Manktelow, 2004, if you want to be lowered gently into these ideas). These days, we would refer to theoretical or scientific reasoning and practical reasoning, respectively. In this book, the chapters on reasoning have mainly been concerned with episteme and those on decision making with phronesis; probability judgment is epistemic, while deontic reasoning is phronetic.

Theoretical and practical reasoning can both themselves be considered from two standpoints, and it is these that we shall focus on here, since this is where most of the argument has been. The argument started about two decades ago, when Anderson (1990, 1991) distinguished between *normative* and *adaptive* rationality; shortly afterwards, Gigerenzer and Hug (1992) opened their paper with this question: 'What counts as human rationality, reasoning processes that embody content-independent formal theories . . . or . . . that are well designed for solving important adaptive problems?' (p. 127). Evans (1993, 2007a; Evans & Over, 1996; Evans, Over & Manktelow, 1993b) further explored this distinction and argued that it has often been overlooked. Evans sets it out in these terms (Evans & Over, 1996, p. 8):

> Rationality$_1$: Personal rationality, or rationality of purpose. Thinking in a way that is generally reliable for achieving one's goals.

> Rationality$_2$: Impersonal rationality, or rationality of process. Thinking where there is a reason that is sanctioned by a normative theory.

For Evans, rationality$_1$ is axiomatic: it is possessed by everyone, because everyone is trying to attain their goals (other theorists, such as Baron, 2008, also take this position). This is not a restatement of rational choice theory, since psychologists acknowledge that this effort can be less than perfect, which is why the definition says *generally* (i.e. usually) reliable: it admits the possibility of error. Rationality$_2$ will generally be in the service of rationality$_1$: if we believe what is true and infer what is justified, we will tend to do better in the world. But that word *generally* has popped up again, indicating that there are exceptions. It is in these exceptions that we can see the difference between the two rationalities in a clear light.

Evans et al. (1993b) give the example of belief bias, which we met in Chapter 6. People tend to accept logically valid arguments more when they believe the conclusion, and reject invalid arguments more when they find the conclusion unbelievable; the latter effect is much the stronger. In doing so, they are being irrational$_2$: a reasoned argument should be judged on its soundness, not its palatability. However, Evans et al. argue that this bias could have a rational$_1$ justification. Numerous studies have shown that people tend to be more critical of arguments that go against their existing beliefs than of those that confirm them (confirmation bias: see Chapter 7). This can be rational$_1$ because it is not useful to revise your beliefs unless you have a good reason (i.e. powerful evidence) to do so. We would have no beliefs at all if they were continually buffeted by all the little bits of evidence flying around, and the processing demands involved would be overwhelming.

Consider also the 'new paradigm' research on reasoning, such as the initial demonstration by Oaksford and Chater (1994a) that responses on the Wason selection task could be accounted for in terms of Bayesian models (see Chapter 6). People do not select the cards that are prescribed by a logical analysis, and so appear to be irrational$_2$. However, their choices do fit the predictions of an analysis based on belief revision, and belief revision looks like a rational$_1$ process.

There is philosophical support for dual rationality in the work of Harman (1995, 1999) as well. His *rationality of belief* (theoretical rationality) and *rationality of action* (practical rationality) resemble Aristotle's classification. He gives two imaginary examples to help distinguish them. First there is Jane, who goes to a party, even though she knows she should stay in and revise for her exam. This is an example of weakness of the will, or *akrasia*, an idea that goes back to Plato: you know you should do one thing, but you do another. Jane's belief is rational, but her action is irrational, says Harman (but see below). Then there is Bob, who gets a bad grade and attributes it to prejudice against his ethnic group, even though the papers were anonymously marked. Now it is the belief that is irrational. Harman also shows how *arbitrariness* can highlight the theoretical–practical distinction. If you have no grounds to believe A or B (e.g. that one suspect or another is guilty), then you should withhold your judgment. However, you should not withhold action on the basis that you have no reason to do A rather than B (e.g. take one of two routes home). If you do, you won't get home. This was the fate of Buridan's ass: a donkey stuck between two bales of hay, who starved to death because it could not choose between them.

Harman also cautions us against taking a black-and-white view of dual rationalities. Sometimes, we can have practical reasons for holding particular beliefs, or for engaging in theoretical reasoning. Examples would be refusing to believe that a close friend did a bad thing, or holding a belief in something in order to be in with the in-crowd. Indeed, Harman argues that there is always a practical aspect to reasoning: 'the inferences it is reasonable for you to make depend on what questions you have reasons to answer, and [so] on your needs and goals' (1999, p. 21). You can, of course, have the eminently practical goal of being a good thinker and reasoner (see also Baron, 1985, on this point).

Dual rationality and dilemmas

Harman's imaginary Jane, above, did the wrong thing because she went to the party when she knew she should have been revising. Or did she? She found herself on the horns of a personal dilemma, of the kind described in the previous chapter.

It is formally equivalent to the one faced by the prospective drug-taker, spendthrift or adulterer: immediate pleasure versus longer-term pain. Jane's two conflicting goals were the short-term one of having fun and the longer-term one of being properly prepared for her exam. She had to choose one or the other: going for one meant forsaking the other. Dilemmas are decision situations where there are two (or more) different goals, which you value equally, and you know it. They have to be taken into account at the moment that the choice is made. Are dilemmas a problem for dual rationality? They are if two conditions apply: that the two clashing goals cannot be logically ranked in terms of utility, with one clearly judged as superior to the other; and if they are unexceptional.

I think that both conditions do apply, and so dilemmas *are* a problem for dual rationality. Take the first one. This is true by definition: you only have a dilemma when you have equally valued but inconsistent goals, such that by approaching one, you move away from the other. If one can clearly be ranked higher than the other, then you have no dilemma. As for the second condition: many of the examples you read about in the literature sound like exceptions, and Stanovich (1999) takes this line: 'At the extreme,' he says, 'there may be goals that are in conflict with other goals' (p. 17). There are two ways in which dilemmas could be at the extreme: in terms of probability and utility. That is, they could be extremely rare, or only involve extremely serious matters, such as the life-and-death situations described in Chapter 9.

Let's look at both of these aspects and see if we can come to a judgment. First, rarity. The only way to assess this is by enumeration: count how many dilemmas you come across in day-to-day life. Are they hard to find? I did this a few years ago, just making a note of all the dilemmas I recalled or noticed over a period of about a week. In Table 10.1, you can see a list of some of them (there were several pages in the end), arranged in a rough typology, along with the conflicting aspects that are common features of them (you might not have these as goals yourself, of course). You can readily add to them from your own experience, once you are tuned into them. They are not rare at all.

As for seriousness, there is a short-cut way to assess this: see if there are extremely trivial situations that have the structure of a dilemma. It turns out that there are. Here is one from personal experience, and I challenge you to find anything less important. But it is still a dilemma. It concerns my three favourite breakfast foods. Call them A, B and C. I prefer them in that order: A > B > C, and my preferences are transitive: A > C. So far so good. Which, then, should I have tomorrow? For a rational choice theorist, the question is a no-brainer. It must be A, every day: it is the utility-maximising option. But I don't do that, I have them in a regular order, following the proverb that variety is the spice of life.[2] So there are the conflicting goals: to have the best now, or defer it in search of a different form of pleasure. One or the other.

The important point to note is why examples such as this mean that dilemmas are a problem for dual rationality; it is *not* an attempt to prove that decision theory is wrong. We are talking about rationality$_1$ here, the one that dual rationality theorists such as Evans and Stanovich regard as axiomatic: rationality of purpose. Are Jane and I really being irrational in our choices? Dilemmas show that there is *no formal answer* to this question – no technical solution, as Hardin (1968) put it – because

Table 10.1 Some everyday dilemmas

Personal dilemmas

Foreign holidays
Pleasure of travel; adding to noise, pollution, resource depletion
Exotic foods from faraway places
Nice things to eat; environmental damage (e.g. through air freight)
Sweet or fattening foods
Pleasure of eating; adverse health consequences
Dentistry and medicine
Discomfort now; improved health later
Insurance or pensions
Less spending money; later benefits
Season tickets or multi-packs of goods
Higher initial outlay; less spent over time
Buying a drink for a friend who is driving
Doing a favour; risk to the friend and others
Eating meat or owning a carnivorous pet
Enjoyment; killing food animals

Social dilemmas

Over-claiming on insurance or expenses/under-declaring taxes
Personal gain; rates rise generally
Driving children to school
Protect them from traffic; increases traffic
Traffic calming, congestion charging, speed cameras
You are delayed; people are safer
Living and working in different towns
Nice living environment; transport costs, congestion, pollution
Powered transport (cars, planes, etc.)
Personal convenience; resource depletion and environmental degradation
Exotic pets
Enjoyment; threat to wild animals
Hardwood furniture
Desirable goods; tropical forest destruction
Patio heaters
You can sit outside when it's too cold to sit outside; environmental damage

Note: These are classified according to the typology in Chapter 9. In each case, possible conflicting goals are given in italics below the name

rationality$_1$ is measured against goals, and here we have conflicting goals in the same situation: whichever way you turn, you appear to be rational$_1$ from one angle and irrational$_1$ from the other. In other words, it is impossible to state norms for rationality$_1$; in which case, it can hardly be held to be axiomatic for people. Paradoxically, we can state norms for rationality$_2$, the one that is harder to acquire and is therefore not endowed to everyone to the same degree.

And yet we do make up our minds when faced with such apparently intractable choices – we are not bipedal Buridan's asses, paralysed by indecision. We have a number of strategies available, all purely psychological, not logical. You can set aside one of the goals, using a 'just this once' or 'because I'm worth it' heuristic: you can have that drink or take that flight or anything else that way. You can discharge the conflict between the goals by changing the way you value them: global warming is so important, you decide, that you will sell your car, or never fly again. Dilemmas disappear once one goal is valued more highly than the other. You can use a compensatory strategy, such as the carbon offset schemes that airlines offer: you can then tell yourself that you are actually doing the environment a favour by flying! Conflict-resolving cognition has been researched in other areas of psychology, such as social psychology, for decades (e.g. Heider's, 1958, balance theory). There is a mountain of good evidence that we do it, and Tavris and Aronson's (2008) review of this research, and the wonders of human self-justification it reveals, is highly recommended.

Remember that one of the labels used for rationality$_1$ is *personal* rationality (Evans & Over, 1996). This means that this form of rationality is, as Shira Elqayam (2010) points out, explicitly relative (p. 398). Rationality$_1$ depends on what a person's goals are; we have to know this before we can assess how good their thinking is in terms of achieving them. The goals themselves, however, are personal to them. This is a position that derives from the philosopher David Hume, who argued that 'Reason is or ought only to be the slave of the passions, and can never pretend to any other office than to serve and obey them' (1739/1978, p. 295). Taking this position means that, once again, we cannot then describe Jane as having been irrational in going to the party. What is important is the rationality of the action at the point at which it is chosen. Her passion then was to have a good time with her friends, and she successfully pursued it. Sure, she may, on the morning of the exam, reflect that she should not have gone after all but stayed in and revised; you may agree, after getting off the plane, that it would have been better if you had not taken the flight. But it's too late then: the damage is done. These evaluations after the fact are from rationality$_2$; you are reflecting not just on your actions but on the goals themselves. Rationality$_1$ offers us no prescription for rational goals.

These issues are important, and there is an ever-increasing popular literature on irrationality. An early survey was by Sutherland (1992); more recent examples include Dawes (2001) and Ariely (2008). The first two review the literature, while the third concentrates more on the research of the author and his colleagues, some of which is astonishingly ingenious. You will find a lot of the cases we have seen in the last chapter and this one in these books: endowment effects, sunk costs, priming and the effects of immediate personal values, for example. Bearing in mind the themes of this chapter, it can be a moot point whether they are actually dealing with irrationality in every case. As we have seen, the use of this term can be problematic.

Elqayam goes on to defend a relativist view of rationality$_2$ as well, giving it the neat label of *grounded rationality*. She notes that apparently objective norms have been subject to wide variation, both historically and geographically. Nickerson

(2008) is also sympathetic with this view. We shall look in detail at the role of geographical variation in thinking (i.e. culture) later in this chapter.

Rationality and personality

In this section we shall go further into the relation between thinking and the thinker. This has been a relatively recent concern in the field, pioneered by two researchers, Keith Stanovich and Richard West. Stanovich has written extensively about the implications of this work for our understanding of rationality, so we shall concentrate on his research and theorising before broadening our scope by looking at one particular kind of individual difference – delusional thinking – later.

Individual differences and their implications

Stanovich and West began their systematic study of individual differences in reasoning and judgment in the late 1990s. The first wave of this extensive research programme is summarised in Stanovich (1999) and Stanovich and West (2000). Stanovich has gone on to theorise more broadly about its implications in Stanovich (2004, 2009a, 2009b) and Stanovich, West and Toplak (2010). These books and articles will take you to the original research papers.

The starting point for this project was an observation that runs like a mineral vein all through research on thinking and reasoning – and through this book – the gap between the prescriptions of normative theories and tested human perform-ance. Stanovich calls this the *normative–descriptive gap*, and in his earlier publica-tions lists four possible responses to it.

First, the gap could be ascribed to *performance errors*: slips or lapses of memory, attention or skill. Theorists who argue strongly that this is the primary source of the gap (examples are Cohen, 1981, Stein, 1996, and economists who believe in rational choice theory) would not regard the gap as being an indelible slur on human rationality: as noted above, no one seriously holds the position that everybody always thinks logically. That would be to regard human thought as infallible, and cast us as the demon/god. Theorists who argue for a rationality with occasional blips are called Panglossians by Stanovich, after Voltaire's character Dr Pangloss, who liked to declare that, in this best of all possible worlds, all is for the best. Panglossians thus regard humans as essentially rational, save for the odd slip.

Performance errors – slips – are, by definition, random, unsystematic. This kind of error is not the same thing as bias; a bias is a systematic deviation from the norm. Two empirical predictions follow from the performance error hypothesis. The first is that there should not be any *patterns* of error at the task level either within or between tasks (errors, by their nature, will be scattered randomly) and nor should errors correlate with each other (again because they are random). The second prediction is that there should be no systematic relation between errors and persons. Of course, there will be individual differences, as people will differ in their liability to slip, but this will not be related to problem types, again because error is random.

The second possible explanation for the gap is *cognitive limitations*. We have already addressed this matter above, in looking at bounded rationality. Ascriptions of rationality should take into account what the mind is capable of, not hold humans to unattainable standards. Normative theories should only be considered *prescriptive* of what people ought to do when cognitive capacity is acknowledged. Aside from this general point, there is also the fact that people differ in their cognitive capacities: they produce different scores on tests of ability such as IQ tests, or in their measured working memory capacity (working memory being the 'workspace' that you have available to use for active thinking at any one time). It follows from this proposal that there should be a correlation between task performance and cognitive ability.

Thirdly, there is the possibility of *applying the wrong norm*: judging people's performance against the wrong standard. We have seen examples of this kind of explanation in previous chapters here: for instance, in explaining the conjunction fallacy as people's justified application of the logic of conversation to a probabilistic task (see Chapter 1), or in Oaksford and Chater's recasting of the Wason selection task in terms of belief revision rather than logical inference (see Chapter 6).

Fourthly, and relatedly, there is the idea that people in experiments may be using an *alternative problem construal*, justified or not, and responding rationally to that. This is a problem when designing research: you have to make sure that the problem you set your participants is the same from their point of view as it is from yours. Alternative problem construal is different from applying the wrong norm, in that with the latter both participant and experimenter interpret the task in the same way, but the experimenter judges performance against the wrong standard. Of course, alternative construal substitutes one possible rational ascription for another, because some task construals are clearly more rational than others. We can assess this kind of rationality from the perspectives of both researcher and participant. In the first case, we appear to depend on the consensus of experts. However, as Stanovich points out, experts do not always arrive at a consensus, and in any case the consensus is subject to historical and cultural variation (cf. Elqayam, 2010). Thus rational task construal from the researcher's standpoint is not an objective matter.

Participants' task construal is addressed by Stanovich using the dual process theory (see Chapters 6 and 9). To recap briefly, this proposes that we have two general kinds of thinking systems (or two minds, in the view of Evans, 2003, 2009, 2010): intuitive (Type 1) and analytical (Type 2). People differ in the degree to which they use one or the other, both as a trait of personality (Epstein, Pacini, Denes-Raj & Heier, 1996) and in response to the demands of a given task. This turns out to be a crucial step in Stanovich's argument, as we shall see shortly.

Let us look at the patterns of individual differences reported in the research of Stanovich and West. This will have to be a rather compressed summary, as the research is so extensive; there is more detail in Chapter 6. The first finding to report is one that disposes of the performance error hypothesis: in two studies, Stanovich and West found that there were significant correlations between

Scholastic Aptitude Test (SAT) scores and performance on a range of thinking and reasoning problems, including such old favourites as syllogisms, the selection task and tests of probability judgment. Stanovich and West (2000) call this 'positive manifold' among these different tasks. There would be no such positive manifold if the gap between normative prescription and observed performance were down to random error; when events are random, there is, by definition, no systematic pattern to be detected.

Secondly, it is easy to forget, when reading about all the evidence for error and bias in human thinking, that even in the case of problems such as the selection task, which most people get (logically) wrong, there are always some people who get them right. Stanovich and West discovered that these tend to be the people highest in general intelligence; this was indexed by their SAT scores, as the work was done in the USA where these are readily available. Although this link is hardly surprising, we have to ask why it is there: what is it that clever people are doing that enables them to score more highly than the less cognitively endowed on thinking problems? Stanovich invokes what he calls the understanding/acceptance assumption: that if you grasp a normative principle, you are likely to go along with it. This idea had been introduced much earlier, by Slovic and Tversky (1974). Rational task construal may have something to do with the observed performance difference: high-ability people are more likely to see the Wason selection task as a logical problem rather than as one of belief revision, for instance.

Which only raises yet another question: why do these people do this? This is where the dual process theory comes in, and once again we can use research on the selection task to explain what is going on. In Chapter 3 the research on the original form of the task was reviewed: this was the version in which people have to reason about the truth or falsity of a conditional statement, which is usually about neutral contents such as letter–number combinations. It is known as the indicative task. In Chapter 4 there was detailed discussion of a later adaptation of the task: the deontic form. Here, people are given meaningful conditional rules about permissions or obligations, and their task is to detect possible transgressions.

Only a minority produce answers that follow logical norms with the indicative task, but the situation flips with the deontic task: most people choose normatively. Stanovich and West (2000; see also Stanovich, 1999) report that performance is associated with intelligence in the case of the indicative task, but not with the deontic task. They argue that this is because of the actions of Type 1 and Type 2 thinking. If you look back at Chapter 6, you will find a dual process account of the selection task and an account of Stanovich's interpretation of it. He proposes that we have a *fundamental computational bias*: to compute the context of a problem and be guided by the beliefs that it evokes in us. Thus, we will immediately gravitate to the surface features of the indicative selection task: the meaning of *If*, and the p and q items mentioned in the sentence. That is Type 1 working, and it will lead you to the classical selection task error: failing to select the *not-q* card. To get to the logical solution, you need to do more than that, and think about the hidden items and their implications. That is a Type 2 activity, and it seems that only high-ability people are able to *override* Type 1 in this way and deploy their Type 2 processes.

The deontic task, on the other hand, is different. Here, Type 1 and Type 2 thinking both cue the same response. Using Type 2 will therefore produce no performance advantage. Cognitive ability differences thus seem to reside in the ability to recognise the need for, and to use, Type 2. When the two systems point to different solutions, the task will correlate with ability; when they point in the same direction, it will not.

Dysrationalia

The previous discussion shows that not all cognitive task performance is associated with intelligence. Stanovich (2009b; Stanovich et al., 2010) gives numerous other examples. A factor that is common to some of them gives a clue as to what determines whether or not there is an association with intelligence: it is whether an experiment is conducted in between-subjects or within-subjects (repeated measures) form. These terms will be familiar to you if you have had courses in research design. Just in case you need a reminder: a between-subjects experiment is where different factors are tested on different people; within-subjects experiments involve testing the same people under different conditions. Sometimes, it appears that intelligence only predicts performance in within-subjects experiments.

An example is the framing effect, which we met in Chapter 8. You will recall that this is the effect of description on decision: values tend to change depending on how they are portrayed – for example, as gains or losses. Falling for the framing effect is only influenced by intelligence with within-subject designs. Stanovich explains this by appealing to the override construct. The within-subject setup contains cues, in the shape of the differences in the tasks' features, that prompt you to get past immediate appearances and do some deeper thinking, whereas in the between-subject format it may never occur to you that description is an issue at all, because you only see the problem described in one way.

In Chapter 6 we saw that in Stanovich's version of dual process theory great importance is attached to the ability to override the Type 1 elements of a thinking problem. Indeed, it led to a distinction that goes beyond dual processes, introducing a Type 3 system, the reflective mind, in addition to the algorithmic mind, which is assigned to Type 2. Figure 6.8 in Chapter 6 shows this architecture. The algorithmic mind is the aspect that is indexed to intelligence. The reflective mind, on the other hand, is indexed to personality variables known as *dispositions*. One thinking disposition is a propensity or inclination to engage the algorithmic mind. Issues of rationality only arise at the level of the reflective mind.

A particular example of such a disposition is *need for cognition*, identified by Cacioppo and Petty (1982; Cacioppo, Petty, Feinstein & Jarvis, 1996), who also developed a test for it that has become widely used. Another term for it is cognitive motivation. It refers to your tendency to ask questions, seek information or reflect on problems. Stanovich reports that this disposition, and others such as conscientiousness and curiosity, are related to intelligence only weakly, if at all.

What this distinction opens up is the possibility of a sharp dissociation between intelligence and rationality, and Stanovich has pursued this idea with great vigour recently (see especially Stanovich, 2009b). The result is the construct of *dysrationalia*: thinking that is less rational than might be expected, given the person's level of intelligence. It is a play on the word *dyslexia*: reading ability that is below par for the person concerned. To see how it is possible to predict, on the basis of the Stanovich theory, that clever people might sometimes do stupid things, let us trace the various routes to irrationality that the theory signposts for us.

First, we need to note the broad circumstances under which irrationality might emerge. These will be when the Type 1 (intuitive) response is not the right one, where the 'right' one is the one that best furthers our goals, as would be confirmed by serious Type 2 thinking. Where the task environment promotes the use of the Type 1 response, and where that leads to the most favourable outcome, then rationality will be most likely to be seen, and most people will display it: we have seen examples of this in the shape of the deontic selection task (see above) and in the kinds of situations described by Gigerenzer's team (see above, and Chapter 9).

Sometimes, indeed often, however, we need to go beyond our immediate Type 1 impressions if we are to think properly about a problem, and not just in laboratory settings. We need to get beyond the jazzy advert, the person's appearance or the political spin, otherwise we might find ourselves in situations we would prefer to avoid. We need firstly to have some skilled cognition available: for instance, the ability to judge probability accurately. Stanovich calls this expertise *mindware*, by analogy with a computer's software. If you lack the requisite bit of mindware, you will not be equipped to escape the Type 1 intuitive, heuristic response. Probability judgment is a prime example of this: there is a saying that a gambler in Roman times, armed with the modern probability calculus, could have won all of Gaul. In Chapter 1 we saw that probability theory is quite a recent cultural development; it was simply not available as mindware earlier. Similarly, in Chapter 8 there was the example of insurance, where you can be gulled into paying a higher premium just by the mention of specific risks – if you lack a bit of mindware that tells you about subadditivity.

Thus, the first route to irrationality is a mindware gap. But this is not the only one. To show you the others, here are two problems adapted from versions that appear in Stanovich (2009b). Call the first one the Patti problem:

> George is looking at Patti but Patti is looking at Eric.
>
> George is married but Eric is not.
>
> Is a married person looking at an unmarried person?
>
> Yes
>
> No
>
> Can't tell.

The second one is the Batty problem:

> A bat and a ball cost $1.10 in total. The bat costs $1 more than the ball. How much is the ball?

We pause while you have a go at these.

Now for the answers. Stanovich reports that around 80% of people given the Patti problem get it wrong: they say *can't tell*, when the answer is actually *yes*. If you are among the majority, you will be wondering how it can possibly be yes. Here is a hint: think back to the THOG problem, in Chapter 3, to which Patti bears some resemblance. Solving THOG required you to consider the range of possible disjunctive (either–or) alternatives, and that is what you have to do with Patti too. There are two alternatives: she is either married or unmarried. If she is married, then the answer is yes, because she (married) is looking at Eric (unmarried); if she is unmarried, then it's also yes, as George (married) is looking at her.

It is quite likely that you got the Batty problem wrong too. The immediate Type 1 response is to say that the ball costs $0.10; this value just pops out at you, through simple subtraction, or possibly just matching. But that cannot be right, because then the bat would cost $1.10, and the total would be $1.20. The answer must be $0.05. Then the bat costs $1.05, and the total is $1.10, as specified.

The Batty problem shows us the second route to the erroneous Type 1 heuristic response: many people fail to detect the need to override it in the first place, because the answer supplied by Type 1 seems so clear. The Patti problem may also do this, but it seems more likely to awaken the need for override. However, doing so only presents the solver with another problem, because you need to be able to manage what Stanovich calls *sustained decoupling*: you need to park the heuristic response while you work through the alternative scenarios that the problem presents. That is, you need to engage in some systematic hypothetical thinking (see Chapter 7). You did not have a mindware gap when contemplating Patti: you know what a disjunctive is, and (I hope) found the explanation of the problem quite straightforward. It was the need to get past the 'obvious' answer and then the mental work required to do so that caused you pain. The need to achieve sustained decoupling is the third path to irrationality. It is hard to do, and if you lack the capacity for it you will fall back into the arms of Type 1 responding.

That is all very well for toy problems, you might object, but is there any evidence for this kind of paradoxical clever/stupid irrationality in the real world? There is. Stanovich (2009b) presents us with a litany of such cases, from high-IQ conspiracy theorists and Ponzi scheme victims to US presidents. He makes the point that no IQ test measures the kinds of abilities you need if you are to be able to think rationally, the kinds of abilities we have reviewed in this book. That is because IQ is Type 2: the algorithmic mind. Rationality depends on Type 3 thinking, the reflective mind. Being intelligent is not the same as being *smart*.

Delusional thinking: extreme irrationality

Right at the start of our examination of rationality, it was mentioned that people can be committed for medical treatment on the grounds of irrationality. Indeed, sometimes a person's beliefs or inferences can be so out of tune with what seems justified that they can be judged to have something wrong with them. They seem to be *deluded*.

Delusions commonly take the form of tenaciously held bizarre beliefs that are immune to contrary evidence. Although this sounds clear enough, the two key terms, *bizarre* and *evidence*, only open up further questions. What is called bizarre is clearly a subjective matter, and is subject to change. The idea that humans descended from apes was greeted as a bizarre belief 150 years ago, but it is now widely (though not universally) accepted, so that it is bizarre now to believe otherwise. If you (an adult) really believe that the goodies that come your way at Christmas arrive through the good offices of a jolly red-clad man via your chimney, then you are deluded; a little child who believes in Santa Claus is not. And that tells us something about the nature of evidence: we do not have to gather it ourselves every time. Much of what we believe, we believe because others tell us about it and we have no reason to disbelieve them (Nickerson, 2008). A bizarre belief is one that is out of line with this consensus.

Lisa Bortolotti (2009) provides an extensive review of the construct of delusion from both philosophical and psychological perspectives, if you want to go further into these matters. She gives examples of common delusions. Perhaps the best known is the persecutory delusion: the belief that someone is out to get you. People who have this kind of paranoid delusion tend to exhibit an extreme form of confirmation bias (see Chapter 7): taking notice of evidence only if it supports their belief, or interpreting data so that they are seen as confirming. In the clinically deluded, this extends to *creating* 'evidence' (e.g. in seeing coded messages in TV programmes, car registration numbers or in ordinary things people say).

You may also have heard of a similar type, erotomania: the belief that someone you don't know, such as a celebrity, is in love with you. Cases of this appear in the media from time to time. Again, the sufferer will see signs of this 'love' everywhere, and will deny contrary evidence: one of the signal properties of delusions is their incorrigibility. Delusions can even be combined, as when a person with erotomania suspects family members of plotting to keep them apart from the object of their desire. People with delusions can have their everyday lives turned upside down: quitting their jobs or moving house in order to escape persecutors or to be closer to their fantasy lover, for instance. It is when delusional beliefs interfere with a person's functioning that they are regarded as clinically deluded.

This last point has an important implication: not all delusional beliefs are as destructive as this. A delusional belief does not even have to be false. As the old saying goes, just because you're paranoid, it doesn't mean they are *not* out to get you (Nirvana, 1991, used a similar line in one of their songs). And there are lots of people who believe, without good cause, that someone is in love with them; we might describe them as arrogant or just mistaken, rather than deluded. According to the continuity model of psychosis (see Claridge, 1988, 1997; van Os, Hansen, Bijl & Ravelli, 2000; van Os, Linscott, Myin-Germeys, Delespaul & Krabbendam, 2009), the kinds of thinking that characterise clinical conditions such as schizophrenia and paranoia can be found at less extreme levels in the general population. Thus we might expect to find sub-clinical delusional thinking quite widely. The kinds of thinking disorders that resemble schizophrenia but do not reach clinical levels of seriousness come under the heading of *schizoptypy*, and this includes delusions.

Delusional thinking and reasoning have been studied together for about 20 years. This research has not been extensive, and awaits a truly integrative review and theory, but there is an emerging pattern to the findings that certainly adds to our understanding of the relation between rationality and personality, which is where its interest to cognitive psychology lies: we want to know about the cognitive processes that are associated with delusional thinking.

Researchers have converged on an important bias that characterises delusional thinking: the *jump to conclusions* (JTC) bias. This is a familiar everyday phrase: if you jump to a conclusion, you make an inferential leap on the basis of too little evidence. JTC is therefore a data-gathering bias. The best known early study of this bias was reported by Huq, Garety and Hemsley (1988). They used an existing probability judgment task, where people are given two jars of coloured beads in different proportions: 85 black, 15 white; or 85 white, 15 black. Beads are drawn by the experimenter, and participants have to judge which jar they were being drawn from. The participants with delusions (they were clinical schizophrenia patients) required significantly fewer beads – often only one or two – before making up their minds which jar was their source than did healthy control participants.

This finding has been replicated a number of times (see Garety & Freeman, 1999), and the beads task has been seen as the most reliable measure of the JTC bias (Fine, Gardner, Craigie & Gold, 2007). Dudley, John, Young and Over (1997) found that it is a true *data-gathering* bias: when all the information was presented to participants, deluded and non-deluded people's performance did not differ; it was only when they had to decide for themselves how much information to use that the bias emerged. Dudley and Over (2003) review JTC research and link it to the constructs of dual rationality (see above). It is not necessarily the case that people with delusions have a reasoning deficit, that is, they may not have a reduced rationality$_2$. However, they may have different goals and may fail to attain these goals, as when they try to persuade someone that they are being followed, or become so obsessive that their ordinary lives are interfered with. In that way, they would to some degree be irrational$_1$.

There are two questions about this research that we need to pick up on, in the light of the themes of this section. The first is whether we will see the same kind of biased thinking in people who are not diagnosed as clinically deluded, and the second is that the beads task is rather artificial: will we see anything similar to JTC when we use more realistic reasoning problems?

Fortunately, there are measures available to enable schizotypy to be assessed in the general population. Examples are the Oxford–Liverpool Inventory of Feelings and Experiences (O–LIFE: Mason, Claridge & Jackson, 1995) and the Peters et al. Delusions Inventory (PDI: Peters, Day & Garety, 1996). Using the PDI and a task in which a coin had to be tossed a number of times to test whether it was biased to heads or tails, Linney, Peters and Ayton (1998) found the JTC bias in high-scoring but non-clinical people. They thought that this might indicate that people high in delusional ideation would be less sensitive to the importance of sample size when making this kind of judgment.

In extending this research beyond beads and coins, Sellen, Oaksford and Gray (2005) tested people on causal conditional reasoning using realistic statements (see Chapter 4, where this form of reasoning is reviewed). Using the O–LIFE, they found that high scorers tended to consider fewer possible counter-examples when reasoning about cause–effect relationships: they sampled less evidence. Niall Galbraith and his colleagues (Galbraith, Manktelow & Morris, 2010) used the 'explorer' task invented by Nisbett, Krantz, Jepson and Kunda (1983), described in

Chapter 7. This was where people imagined arriving on a remote island and encountering different-sized samples of rocks, birds and tribespeople. Nisbett et al. found that people take into account the variability of the class when generalising from samples: they will happily generalise about rocks from just one sample, but they will be less confident generalising about the physique of a whole community upon encountering just one fat man. Galbraith et al. found that high PDI scorers were more confident in generalising from small samples with highly variable properties such as body size and aggression than were people low in delusional ideation, confirming the proposal of Linney et al. Thus one process underlying the JTC bias might be that people fail to see the need for larger samples, and so make inferences from smaller numbers. Since such inferences will be inherently less reliable than those from larger numbers, this increases the probability of forming a bizarre belief.

This is not the only possible route to delusional beliefs. In a major review of cognition in mental illness, Johnson-Laird, Mancini and Gangemi (2006) dismiss entirely the idea that faulty reasoning may cause psychological illness. They do not, however, include delusional thinking in their review, focussing instead on those disorders, such as obsessive–compulsive disorder (OCD), phobias and depression, that can be seen as arising from emotions. Their theory proposes hyper-emotional responses that are appropriate in kind to the situation but inappropriate in their intensity. Thus an excessive disgust response to dirt might lead to OCD with regard to, say, hand-washing. Is there any evidence for the role of feelings in delusional thinking?

Some authors have proposed just that. For instance, delusion-prone individuals have an exaggerated focus on the self, particularly threats to the self (Blackwood, Bentall, Fytche, Simmons, Murray & Howard, 2004; Dudley & Over, 2003). Galbraith, Manktelow and Morris (2008) confirmed that this self-referent bias affected how people judged arguments: they rated objections to arguments that referred to themselves as stronger than other kinds of arguments. Two studies using the beads task have also addressed feelings in relation to the JTC bias in delusion-prone (non-clinical) people. McKay, Langdon and Coltheart (2006) found that high PDI scorers showed the JTC bias, and that there was also a relation with need for closure: the desire to have a definite answer. However, scores on JTC and need for closure did not correlate, which undermines the idea that one causes the other. White and Mansell (2009) tested for another factor: perceived rushing. Again using the PDI, they found that greater JTC bias resulted when people felt they were being rushed into a judgment. So perhaps a feeling of needing to rush produces both heightened need for closure and the JTC bias, but does so independently.

We saw in Chapter 9 how important feelings are in making decisions, and this section has shown that the relation between rationality and personality is also to do with the kinds of emotion we experience when confronting problems, and vice versa: the kind of emotion we experience is partly a matter of the kind of person we are. In extreme cases, our thinking can become utterly disconnected from the real world owing to these factors. Even when not at this end of the spectrum, it is clear that different people treat information, and make inferences, differently. Although we now know quite a bit about factors such as the JTC bias, there is clearly a lot left still to be done. In the next section, we encounter another equally important area of research where the same can be said.

Thinking, reasoning and culture

The kind of person you are is not a mere accident. In previous chapters, we have seen that it partly has to do with your biological heritage: the sections on evolutionary theorising in Chapters 4, 6 and 9 concern this heritage, and Steven Pinker in a series of books has explored this evolutionary inheritance across many areas of psychology (e.g. Pinker, 1997, 2002). It is also to do with where you come from, the culture in which you were raised. As with delusional thinking, researchers on thinking and reasoning have turned their attention to this factor increasingly in the last two decades, which means that while some striking findings have emerged there is plenty more still to be found out.

Actually, 'returned to this factor' might be a better way of putting it, since psychologists have been interested in the thinking processes of people from different parts of the world for over a century. As Michael Cole (1977) remarks, much of the earlier work seemed to concern itself with apparent deficiencies in thinking among uneducated tribal people compared to that observed in educated people from industrialised societies. Cole and his colleague Sylvia Scribner (Cole & Scribner, 1974; Scribner, 1977); conducted a series of studies among the Vai and Kpelle peoples of the West African state of Liberia, one outcome of which was a serious questioning of the methods used to assess thinking in these contexts. Psychologists use experiments, of course, which means that they have to be very careful that their methods are appropriate to the people participating and to the thinking under investigation. Cole, even back in the 1970s, had serious misgivings about this. As he recalls his own initiation into field research in Africa, he carried with him 'an invisible cargo of assumptions about human nature' (Cole, 1977, p. 468). He goes on to report how much of this cargo had to be jettisoned in the light of his encounter with real thinking in its real context when he tried to assess it using his Western psychologist's tools.

An example of this kind of problem can be seen in some of Scribner's research. She tested syllogistic and conditional reasoning (see Chapters 2 and 3) among what she calls traditional people in Liberia. In Table 10.2 you can see a snippet of an exchange between an experimenter, E, and a participant, P, a Kpelle farmer. As Scribner points out, the farmer appears to get the problem wrong, by rejecting the modus ponens inference, which is almost universally made in standard reasoning experiments conducted in the West.

However, Scribner does not jump to the conclusion that this demonstrates that these people are unable to think logically. She draws our attention to the protocol that follows E's request to go on with the reason, and distils this passage into a more familiar (to us) syllogistic form (Scribner, 1977, pp. 487–488):

Sumo's drinking gives people a hard time
Saki's drinking does not give people a hard time
People do not get vexed when they are not given a hard time
The Town Chief is a person (implicit premise)

Therefore, the Town Chief is not vexed at Saki

Table 10.2 A Kpelle farmer's response to a conditional reasoning problem

E: If Sumo or Saki drinks palm wine, then the Town Chief gets vexed. Sumo is not drinking palm wine. Saki is drinking palm wine. Is the Town Chief vexed?
P: People do not get vexed with two persons.
E: (Repeats the problem)
P: The Town Chief was not vexed on that day.
E: The Town Chief was not vexed? What is the reason?
P: The reason is that he doesn't love Sumo.
E: He doesn't love Sumo? Go on with the reason.
P: The reason is that Sumo's drinking is a hard time [sic]. That is why when he drinks palm wine, the Town Chief gets vexed. But sometimes when Saki drinks palm juice he will not give a hard time to people. He goes to lie down to sleep. At that rate people do not get vexed with him. But people who drink and go about fighting – the Town Chief cannot love them in town.

Note: E, Experimenter; P, Participant
Source: Based on Scribner (1977)

This, Scribner notes, is an elegant piece of logical reasoning (one of many she recorded), albeit not from the exact materials presented by the experimenter. This is a continuing theme of Cole's and Scribner's work, and of the work of other researchers, such as that of the pioneering Russian psychologist A.R. Luria, reported in the 1970s (see Luria, 1971, 1977) but conducted in the 1930s, in Uzbekistan. Of course, educated Western participants are not immune from the effects of knowledge on their reasoning – we call it belief bias or facilitation, depending on the direction of the effect (see above, and especially Chapters 4 and 6). But there is something extra going on here. Non-educated 'traditional people' seem not to be prepared to detach problems from their context and reason abstractly to the same extent that educated Western people are. This turns out also to be the central observation of the modern phase of research into culture and thinking, although in this case we are dealing with people just as educated as the standard Western participant. Time, then, to look at this research.

Western and Eastern thinking

The study of the relation between culture and thinking is potentially vast in scope, so our review here will be quite tightly constrained to the themes of this book. We shall not, therefore, be much concerned with attitudes, beliefs, customs and so on. Besides which, the claim that people from different cultures might have different beliefs is hardly the stuff of front-page news. What is interesting, though, is the claim that different cultures might produce different thinking *processes*. We have just seen early evidence for this, in the Kpelle people's greater propensity to import everyday experience into their thinking about problems with supposedly fictitious content. Since the 1990s, evidence has been accumulating that something similar might be characteristic of Eastern as well as African thought, and that it might not be a matter of lack of education but indicative of a deeper *cultural* influence on how people think.

Much of this work has been conducted by Richard Nisbett and his associates, and a summary of the first decade of it is given by Nisbett (2003), in a book written for the non-specialist. Nisbett enlarges on the cargo of assumptions that had troubled Cole a generation earlier. These assumptions can be grouped under a general heading: *universality*. Despite the work of people such as Luria, and Cole and Scribner, Nisbett admits that most psychologists at the turn of the 21st century held that everyone everywhere has the same basic cognitive processes, and that these processes operate in the same way irrespective of what they are operating on (Nisbett & Norenzayan, 2002). He looks back to the title of his brilliant early book, *Human Inference* (Nisbett & Ross, 1980): not Western human, but all human, he and Ross assumed at the time. Atran and Medin (2008), in a major review of the ways in which different peoples think about the natural world (see Chapter 7 for examples of this work), put it even more strongly: '[Western] cognitive psychology does not search for universality, but rather assumes it' (p. 5).

However, in his own work Nisbett found that learning and training could change the ways in which (Western) people think (see Nisbett, 1992): we are perfectly capable of acquiring new mindware, in Stanovich's terms. That being so, it should not be hard to detect different ways of thinking in people who have lifetime – and ancestral – histories of thinking in different ways about different things. What follows is a summary of the main findings of the research programme that developed from these insights. We shall then go on to their wider implications.

Perhaps the most often quoted finding reported in Nisbett (2003) is not a study of thinking as such, but a study of perception. It is worth including here because it vividly illustrates the issues. Masuda and Nisbett (2001) gave university students pictures of aquariums. After viewing these scenes, they were simply asked to describe them. Some of the participants were from Kyoto, Japan and some were from Michigan, USA. The scenes were all similar, in that they showed one focal fish – bigger, faster moving, more brightly coloured – and various other fish, animals and background features. Both sets of participants referred to the boss fish about as often, but the Americans tended to do so earlier than did the Japanese, who often opened with a statement about the background. The Japanese made 60–70% more references to the background, and twice as many references to the relations between objects, than the Americans did.

Thus the Eastern participants seemed to be much more sensitive to context; as Nisbett (2003) puts it, they seem to view the world through a wide-angle lens, compared to the apparent tunnel vision of Westerners. This was more than a purely perceptual difference: it affected people's memory too. The participants were shown objects that had appeared in the original scenes along with new objects, with the 'old' objects presented sometimes against their original background and sometimes against a different one. Their task was one of recognition memory: had they seen the object before? The context manipulation only affected the Japanese: they found the objects harder to recognise when they were in a new context. The Americans were unaffected.

Does Westerners' greater preparedness to abstract an object from its context affect reasoning and thinking as well as perception and memory? There is a lot of evidence that it does. Here are some examples from the kinds of thinking that have featured in previous chapters here.

An obvious place to start is with *belief bias*, mentioned earlier in this chapter and in greater detail in Chapter 6. Norenzayan, Smith, Kim and Nisbett (2002, Expt. 4) gave Korean and European-American students syllogistic problems similar to the ones used by Evans et al. (1983) in their classic investigation (see Chapter 6). The believability of the conclusions was pre-tested in the two populations, so that valid and invalid arguments with believable and unbelievable conclusions could be constructed. Because of Westerners' greater propensity to set aside problem content, it was predicted that belief bias would be stronger in the Koreans; the instructions stressed the need to determine whether the conclusion followed logically from the premises. And stronger it was, although we have to be a little cautious about this because the interaction of belief bias with culture only happened on valid arguments. This is strange, as in previous experiments with Western-only participants the effect is usually much stronger with invalid arguments. Norenzayan et al. explain this difference by pointing to their finding that the believable conclusions were significantly less believable for the Koreans than they were for the Americans, leaving less room for the bias to emerge when the arguments were also invalid.

Another experiment reported in the Norenzayan et al. paper led to the same kind of result. In this case, they looked at the sorts of *category-based arguments* that were reviewed in detail in Chapter 7. This kind of thinking involves judgments of argument strength when there is a premise and a conclusion such as:

> Birds have ulnar arteries
> ―――――――――――――――――
> Eagles have ulnar arteries

Sloman (1998) had found that there was a difference between judgments about arguments like this, compared to arguments like the following:

> Birds have ulnar arteries
> ―――――――――――――――――
> Penguins have ulnar arteries

This is a typicality effect: eagles are more typical birds than penguins are. Sloman found that the effect disappeared when the implicit premise, that eagles/penguins are birds, was made explicit: then, people judged all such arguments as perfectly strong, which logically they are. Norenzayan and colleagues predicted that this logical step would be more available to Western participants than to Easterners, so that the typicality effect would be stronger among their Korean participants than their Americans. Once again, they found exactly that.

Probability judgment has also been found to be influenced by culture. One of the clearest cases of this influence is with a phenomenon called *hindsight bias*. This also goes under the name of the knew-it-all-along effect: whenever you hear someone say, after the fact, that that was predictable (even though they didn't predict it), you can suspect the presence of this bias. It was identified by Fischhoff (1975; see also Hawkins & Hastie, 1990), who gave people accounts of events from history and asked them to assign a probability to an outcome. They did this under two conditions: either without knowing the outcome, or knowing the outcome but being asked to think back and assess the probability they would have given had they not known it. Significantly higher probabilities were estimated in the outcome condition. Choi and Nisbett (2000) predicted that Easterners would be more prone to the bias than Westerners would, for reasons that will now be familiar: Easterners pay more attention to the context – outcome knowledge, in this case – and will be less likely to produce an explicit causal model (see Chapter 4) that would bring the outcome's non-occurrence more into focus. Their prediction was confirmed: hindsight bias was indeed stronger in Korean than in American participants.

The roots of cultural influence

The above results, just a fraction of the number that you can find in this literature, raise a further question: if Eastern and Western people come to different conclusions and judgments in these situations, why do they? Nisbett and colleagues (2003; Nisbett & Norenzayan, 2002; Nisbett, Peng, Choi & Norenzayan, 2001) locate the source firmly in what they call *systems of thought*. These systems they term *holistic*, characteristic of Eastern thought, and *analytic*, characteristic of Western thought. 'Holistic' is derived from a Greek word denoting whole or entire, so holistic thinkers are those who attend to and think about the whole field, not just the object. You can see how this fits the results that have just been reviewed.

Nisbett and colleagues review in great detail various aspects of thought and research on them to back up their contention that Eastern and Western thought diverges according to these two thought systems. Rather than add to the list of empirical findings at this point (I shall leave you to go into the literature if you want to find out more about these), let us focus on the heart of the matter as Nisbett and colleagues describe it: Eastern and Western ways of reasoning.

We can use the two cultures' approach to *contradiction* to provide this focus. Contradiction is an inherent property of logic as it is understood in the Western tradition. You will recall from Chapters 2 and 3 that logic is two-valued: a proposition can be either true or false, with nothing in between (the law of excluded middle). Something is either p or *not-p*. It is this property that enables true deduction, as we saw in those early chapters: soundly constructed arguments, such as quantified or conditional syllogisms, produce conclusions that can be drawn with certainty. You will also be aware, however, that cracks have appeared in this façade lately, with the appearance of the 'new paradigm' approach to the psychology of reasoning, which has at its heart the recognition that in the real world very few propositions can be held with the degree of certainty necessary for logic and deduction (see Chapter 6). The question naturally arises: how is contradiction dealt with in Eastern thought?

This question was addressed in a series of experiments reported by Peng and Nisbett (1999). We first have to ask what we would predict about Eastern approaches to contradiction. What do Easterners do when having to decide whether something is p or *not-p*, when there is apparent support for both? For instance, suppose there is an argument for keeping long-term prisoners locked up because they are the ones who have committed the gravest crimes, versus an argument for their early release on the grounds that older prisoners are less likely to reoffend.

As Peng and Nisbett point out, there are four possible responses to apparent contradictions such as this. You can deny that there is a contradiction, discount both arguments, decide in favour of one proposition and against the other, or accept the contradiction and see the merits in both arguments. Westerners are inclined to take the third course: they will look to find reasons to believe one or the other. They like to see a winner. Easterners are more likely to favour the fourth strategy: they seek to navigate between the two poles of the argument and find a compromise solution. For Easterners, the middle is not excluded.

The reason for the Eastern acceptance of contradiction and compromise seems to lie in a different tradition of argument. Easterners favour *dialectical* thinking. Dialectical thinking is the kind of thought that embraces contradiction, not so much as a problem to be overcome but as a means to further understanding. As just mentioned, this tends to take the form of an attempt to find the truth in both sides. Peng and Nisbett point to three principles of dialectical thinking as it is found in the East:

- *The principle of change*. Reality is in a state of constant flux, and so the concepts that reflect it must also be fluid. Apparent stability is a signal of likely change.
- *The principle of holism*. This was mentioned above. Nothing exists in isolation; every thing is connected to other things. It makes no more sense to consider a thing by itself than it does to study a melody by analysing each individual note.
- *The principle of contradiction*. Because of the interconnectedness of things, and the ever-changing world, paradoxes and contradictions constantly arise. Opposites are only apparent, and are best seen as complements. There is no light without dark, or good without bad.

Preferences for dialectical as opposed to logical (excluded middle) resolution of contradiction among Eastern (in this case, Chinese) participants were found on a variety of argument forms by Peng and Nisbett. Westerners (Americans) were more likely to prefer two-valued logical solutions. The prison arguments above were used in one of their studies, along with other scientific arguments, and they also considered both more formal and more informal arguments. The Eastern preference for dialectical solutions was apparent throughout.

These findings, yet again, lead to further questions. In this case, what is it about Eastern and Western cultures that leads to these seemingly profound differences in ways of thinking? Nisbett and his colleagues trace the ancestry of this division back over the millennia, to ancient Greek and Chinese philosophical traditions. The ancient Greeks are credited with emphasising the idea of personal agency and selfhood, which led to the tradition of debate. Indeed, as we saw in Chapter 2, the original laws of logic, handed down to us in the form of the syllogism, were reputed to have been developed by Aristotle as an objective means, rather than relying on mere opinion, to decide when someone was talking rubbish. Debate and confrontation are discouraged in the Chinese tradition. The Greeks can be credited with the idea of science, as conventionally practised: categorising objects, isolating variables, creating causal models and lawful explanations. The

Chinese did not develop an idea of 'nature' as distinct from humanity, and so could not develop natural science.

Chinese thought, on the other hand, places great emphasis on harmony and interrelationships. This extends not just to the kind of holism described above, but also to the relation between individual and community. An early study illustrating this aspect of Eastern thought was reported by Cousins (1989). He asked Japanese and American people basic 'who am I?' questions. Americans tended to answer this question by referring to personality traits (friendly, serious) or activities (camping, musical tastes), whereas the Japanese would more often refer to themselves in relation to others: I am serious *at work*, for instance. Markus and Kitayama (1991) similarly found that twice as many Japanese as American self-descriptions contained references to other people (e.g. I play music versus I play music with my friends).

This difference has been summed up in general social terms: societies of European origin are said to be *individualistic* while East Asian societies are said to be *collectivistic* (Hofstede, 1980; Triandis, 1989, 1995). Indeed, individualism–collectivism has emerged as a quantifiable personality dimension, and there are psychometric scales you can use to measure it. These are reviewed by Brewer and Chen (2007), who point out that there is a wide range of ways in which the dimension is represented and elaborated in these scales (see also Oyserman, Coon & Kemmelmeier, 2002). They are particularly bothered by loose definitions of what constitutes the collective in collectivism, and urge us to distinguish between interpersonal relationships and social groups when relating these concepts to cognition. As Oyserman et al. (2002) note, it is not mere awareness of group membership that marks out Eastern collectivism, but attention to group *harmony*.

A study by Knight and Nisbett (2007) confirms the need to be careful when generalising about culture. They studied different groups in one country, Italy. Northern Italians were found to be more analytic thinkers than were southern Italians, who were more holistic. This seemed to go with a cultural difference: the authors found that northern Italian culture emphasised more independence (individualism) whereas southern Italian culture emphasised more interdependence (collectivism). Furthermore, there was a similar difference in the South (but not in the North) between social classes, where working class participants were more holistic in their thinking than were middle class participants.

As we have seen, in this area one question often leads to another. There is evidence that there are differences between societies in terms of their propensity for holistic or analytic thinking, and that this can be linked to systems of thought (dialectical or logical) that can in turn be linked to social structures (collectivist or individualist). Given that there are these latter differences, where do they come from? Why are some cultures individualistic and some collectivistic?

Several authors, notably Nisbett and colleagues and, earlier, Triandis, have used an ecological argument in explaining the ultimate origins of the different systems of thought (see also Diamond, 1997). What this means is that the environment in which people live, and the ways in which people work in order to survive and prosper, condition the ways in which their systems of thought develop. If we go back to the Greek/Chinese dichotomy promoted by these authors, we can see how this ecological argument works. As Nisbett (2003) points out, China even today is a relatively uniform society: some 95% of its population come from one ethnic group, the Han. In pre-industrial times China was an agrarian society, with rice as a staple food, then as now. Agriculture, in particular rice farming with its need for massive irrigation systems, depends on a high degree of cooperation between people and communities. This requires harmonious relationships and facilitates central control, something also favoured by ethnic uniformity.

Greece, on the other hand, is and was a mountainous country, with little by way of fertile arable land. Its people lived by herding and hunting, and became prosperous by trading and, in former times, piracy. Its geographical location, at a confluence of trade routes in the Mediterranean, was a factor in this. These activities are much less conducive to cooperation and harmony than are those of the Chinese. Triandis also points to cultural complexity and affluence as drivers of individualism, both factors that would have been prevalent in Greece through its trading activities; Greece even 3000 years ago would have been a multicultural society. Knight and Nisbett's work on northern and southern Italy is consistent with this claim: the North is more prosperous, and more individualistic, than the South, and in the South, middle class people were more individualistic than the working class. The more complex a society you live in, the more in-groups you can be a member of and the less allegiance you need feel to any of them. You are just you.

Culture and thought and the dual process theory

You might be wondering, in view of the discussion earlier in this chapter and in earlier chapters, whether the systems of thought talked about by the cultural psychologists have anything to do with the systems of thought talked about by dual process theorists such as Evans, Sloman and Stanovich. Are holistic and analytic thought the same thing as heuristic – analytic, System 1–System 2 or implicit–explicit thought? A number of authors have addressed this question. It is not just important theoretically: if we were just to assume that they were the same thing, some uncomfortable conclusions might follow. Can it really be true that high-order, abstract reasoning is conducted mainly by Westerners, while Asians and Africans are trapped in a lower-order context-bound form of thought? The contemporary and historical evidence of cultural richness, technological prowess and economic clout in the East is against the very idea. We have a paradox on our hands.

This question has recently been addressed by Hiroshi Yama and his colleagues (Yama, Nishioka, Horishita, Kawasaki & Taniguchi, 2007) and by one of Nisbett's associates, Ara Norenzayan (Buchtel & Norenzayan, 2009). Both sets of authors acknowledge that there are similarities between the dual systems in the two areas, but go on to make important distinctions and elaborations.

Buchtel and Norenzayan argue that the relation between the two dualities counts as support for dual process theory. What the cultural researchers have uncovered, they say, is not different abilities that are differently available in the East and the West, but different habits of thought. They direct our attention to the list of contrasts that authors commonly provide in distinguishing dual thinking processes, a summary of which you can see in Table 6.2, Chapter 6. Evans (2008) grouped these into clusters, and Buchtel and Norenzayan argue that the holistic–analytic dimension overlaps with the System1–System 2 dimension in some of these clusters but not, crucially, in others.

The main area of overlap is with the contextual–abstract contrast: as we have seen, Westerners are more prepared to decontextualise than Easterners are. However, the automatic–controlled contrast does not overlap with the holistic–analytic contrast at all. In the West, the use of analytic thinking and overriding System 1 does indeed seem to be a trainable skill, and the more we do it the better we become. Buchtel and Norenzayan argue that this is also true of holistic thinking in the East: it can also be practised and perfected, just the same. Take the case of person perception. Western people have been found to commit the *fundamental attribution error*: when explaining someone else's actions we tend to appeal to their dispositions (personal traits), whereas when explaining our own we appeal to the situation we found ourselves in (Ross, 1977). Easterners are less prone to this bias (Choi, Nisbett & Norenzayan, 1999). However, in both cultural groups, people have an automatic dispositional bias that they have to override in order to take situational factors into account (Miyamoto & Kitayama, 2002); it is just that Easterners find this easier, as they have had more practice at monitoring contextual variables. Holism is also an acquired skill.

Yama and colleagues look more closely at the processes involved in holistic and analytic thinking. They focus on another of the contrasts in Table 6.2: the evolutionary one. Adopting the terms of Stanovich, they propose that there are gene-installed goals of thinking and also meme-acquired goals (a meme is a piece of knowledge that reproduces itself and spreads through the culture, by analogy with genes that replicate and spread through plant and animal populations through breeding). The gene-installed goals are universal across cultures, whereas the meme-acquired goals vary with culture. System 1 (or TASS, again to use Stanovich's terms; see above and Chapter 6) will contain both sets of processes. Since minds, cultures and environments interact, there will be selection pressures favouring particular thought systems that stem from both biology and culture (see also Norenzayan & Heine, 2005, on the interplay between evolution and culture in determining what psychological capacities are universal across the human species). You can see how this scheme fits the ecological explanations outlined above. In further research, Yama applied this theory to hindsight bias and argued that Westerners are less prone to the bias than Easterners because they have learned, through cultural experience, a rule to suppress the bias (Yama, Manktelow, Mercier, van der Henst, Do, Kawasaki & Adachi, 2010).

Thus holistic and analytic thinking systems are not low- and high-level abilities that are assigned to people by accident of origin: they are strategies, styles or, in Yama's terms, adaptations. One final point should convince you of this. What is the most abstract, analytic reasoning puzzle there is, one that has become a meme in itself and spread around the world? Sudoku. Where was it invented? Japan. As Johnson-Laird (2006; Lee, Goodwin & Johnson-Laird, 2008) notes, this fact gives the lie to any lingering notion that abstract analytic thought might be the sole province of Western thinkers.

There is a nice quotation from the American poet Mark van Doren that opens the paper by Norenzayan and Heine (2005, p. 763) reviewing the evidence for cognitive universals:

There are two statements about human beings that are true: that all human beings are alike, and that all are different. On these two facts is all human wisdom founded.

That is not a bad motto to carry around as you contemplate the unending mysteries of human thought and reason, not just in their cultural context but in all the aspects reviewed in this book. I hope you have enjoyed the ride.

Summary

1   Rationality has to be bounded if the construct is to have any explanatory validity. Complete normative rationality, as assumed by rational choice theory, is impossible.
2   Bounded rationality theories make use of the idea of satisficing: searching for an optimal rather than a maximal solution.
3   Dual rationality theory distinguishes between rationality of purpose (rationality$_1$), which is concerned with the achievement of goals, and rationality of process (rationality$_2$), which is thinking in line with a normative theory such as logic.
4   Dilemmas pose a problem for this scheme, because when goals conflict there can be no prescription for rationality$_1$.
5   Stanovich and West have shown that there are strong influences of individual differences on reasoning and thinking. These can consist of differences in intellectual ability or in thinking dispositions. This distinction explains the phenomenon of dysrationalia: intelligent people doing apparently stupid things.
6   Delusional thinking is an extreme case of irrationality. People with bizarre beliefs have been found to have particular biases in their thinking, such as the jump-to-conclusions bias and a self-reference bias.
7   A major influence on the way a person thinks is the culture they grow up in. There is a split between Eastern and Western thought, traceable to philosophical systems and ecology. The dual process theory has been linked to the effects of culture, to argue that these thought systems are adaptations or strategies rather than abilities.

Notes

5 Explaining reasoning: the classic approaches

1   See www.tcd.ie/Psychology/Ruth_Byrne/mental_models

7 Hypothetical thinking: induction and testing

1   Phagocytes is a term from cell biology.
2   'Seiche' is a real word, used by geographers to refer to brief movements in otherwise standing water.
3   You can find out more about John Snow from: www.ph.ucla.edu/ epi/snow.html
4   See the 'Recent research on Faraday' section of Tweney's website: http://personal.bgsu.edu/~tweney/

8 Decision making: preference and prospects

1   The $ sign in this chapter does not refer to any particular currency, but merely indicates 'units of money'.
2   Another way is to start from $4000 and work out what you stand to gain or lose relative to this figure if you gamble; see later for more on this.
3   The 50/50 element is crucial: in the usual four-choice situation there is only a .25 probability of guessing right, which shifts the expected value in favour of quitting.
4   Allais died while this book was being written, in October 2010, aged 99.
5   More information is available at: Darwin-online.org

10 Thinking, reasoning and you

1   Apologies if you are not. You can use this thought experiment with anything that a person with a reasonable level of school education could be expected to know.
2   This saying comes from the 18th century English poet William Cowper.

References

Ackerman, J.M., Nucera, C.C. & Bargh, J.A. (2010). Incidental haptic sensations influence social judgments and decisions. *Science, 328,* 1712–1715.

Adams, M.J. (1984). Aristotle's logic. In G.H. Bower (ed.), *The psychology of learning and motivation, Vol. 18.* New York: Academic Press.

Adler, J.E. & Rips, L.J. (eds.) (2008). *Reasoning: Studies of human inference and its foundations.* Cambridge: Cambridge University Press.

Ahn, W.-K. & Bailenson, J. (1996). Causal attribution as a search for underlying mechanisms: An explanation of the conjunction fallacy and the discounting principle. *Cognitive Psychology, 31,* 82–123.

Ahn, W.-K. & Graham, L.M. (1999). The impact of necessity and sufficiency in the Wason four-card selection task. *Psychological Science, 10,* 237–242.

Ahn, W.-K. & Kalish, C.W. (2000). The role of covariation vs. mechanism information in causal attribution. In R. Wilson & F. Keil (eds.), *Cognition and explanation.* Cambridge, MA: MIT Press.

Ahn, W.-K., Kalish, C.W., Medin, D.L. & Gelman, S.A. (1995). The role of covariation versus mechanism information in causal attribution. *Cognition, 54,* 299–352.

Ali, M. (1977). Probability and utility estimates for racetrack bettors. *Journal of Political Economy, 85,* 803–815.

Allais, M. (1953). Le comportement de l'homme rationnel devant le risque: Critique des postulates et axioms de l'école américaine (Rational human behaviour under risk: Critique of the postulates and axioms of the American school). *Econometrica, 21,* 503–546.

Alter, A.L. & Oppenheimer, D.M. (2006). From a fixation on sports to an exploration of mechanism: The past, present, and future of hot hand research. *Thinking & Reasoning, 12,* 431–444.

Anderson, J.R. (1990). *The adaptive character of thought.* Hillsdale, NJ: Lawrence Erlbaum Associates.

Anderson, J.R. (1991). Is human cognition adaptive? *Behavioral and Brain Sciences, 14,* 471–485.

Anderson, J.R. & Sheu, C.-F. (1995). Causal inferences as perceptual judgments. *Memory and Cognition, 23*, 510–524.

Ariely, D. (2008). *Predictably irrational: The hidden forces that shape our decisions*. New York: HarperCollins.

Arkes, H.R. (1996). The psychology of waste. *Journal of Behavioural Decision Making, 9*, 213–224.

Arkes, H.R. & Ayton, P. (1999). The sunk cost and Concorde effects: Are humans less rational than lower animals? *Psychological Bulletin, 125*, 591–600.

Arkes, H.R. & Blumer, C. (1985). The psychology of sunk cost. *Organizational Behavior and Human Decision Processes, 35*, 124–140.

Atran, S. & Medin, D.L. (2008). *The native mind and the construction of nature*. Cambridge, MA: MIT Press.

Ayton, P., Pott, A. & Elwakiri, N. (2007). Affective forecasting: Why can't people predict their emotions? *Thinking & Reasoning, 13*, 62–80.

Bailenson, J.N., Shum, M.S., Atran, S., Medin, D.L. & Coley, J.D. (2002). A bird's eye view: Biological categorization and reasoning within and across cultures. *Cognition, 84*, 1–53.

Ball, L.J., Lucas, E.J., Miles, J.N.V. & Gale, A.G. (2003). Inspection times and the selection task: What do eye-movements reveal about relevance effects? *Quarterly Journal of Experimental Psychology, 56A*, 1053–1077.

Ball, L.J., Phillips, P., Wade, C.N. & Quayle, J.D. (2006). Effects of belief and logic in syllogistic reasoning; Eye-movement evidence for selective processing models. *Experimental Psychology, 53*, 77–86.

Barbey, A.K. & Sloman, S.A. (2007). Base-rate respect: From ecological rationality to dual processes. *Behavioral and Brain sciences, 30*, 241–297.

Bargh, J.A. & Chartrand, T.L. (1999). The unbearable automaticity of being. *American Psychologist, 54*, 462–479.

Baron, J. (1985). *Rationality and intelligence*. Cambridge: Cambridge University Press.

Baron, J. (1994). Nonconsequentialist decisions. *Behavioral and Brain Sciences, 17*, 1–42.

Baron, J. (2008). *Thinking and deciding, 4th edition*. Cambridge: Cambridge University Press.

Baron, J. & Ritov, I. (1994). Reference points and omission bias. *Organizational Behavior and Human Decision Processes, 59*, 475–478.

Barrouillet, P. & Gauffroy, C. (2010). Dual processes in the development and understanding of conditionals. In K.I. Manktelow, D.E. Over & S. Elqayam (eds.), *The science of reason: Essays in honour of Jonathan StB.T. Evans*. Hove: Psychology Press.

Barrouillet, P., Gauffroy, C. & Lecas, J.-F. (2008). Mental models and the suppositional account of conditionals. *Psychological Review, 115*, 760–772.

Barrouillet, P., Grosset, N. & Lecas, J.-F. (2000). Conditional reasoning by mental models: Chronometric and developmental evidence. *Cognition, 75*, 237–266.

Bayes, T. & Price, R. (1970). An essay towards solving a problem in the doctrine of chances. In. E.S. Pearson & M.G. Kendall (eds.), *Studies in the history of statistics and probability*. London: Griffin. (Original work published 1763)

Bechara, A. (2011). Human emotions in decision making: Are they useful or disruptive? In O. Vartanian & D.R. Mandel (eds.), *Neuroscience of decision making*. Hove: Psychology Press.

Bechara, A., Damasio, A.R., Damasio, H. & Anderson, S.W. (1994). Insensitivity to future consequences following damage to human prefrontal cortex. *Cognition, 50*, 7–12.

Begg, I. & Denny, J.P. (1969). Empirical reconciliation of atmosphere and conversion interpretations of syllogistic reasoning errors. *Journal of Experimental Psychology, 81*, 351–354.

Bell, D.E. (1982). Regret in decision making under uncertainty. *Operations Research, 30*, 961–981.

Binmore, K. (2007). *Game theory: A very short introduction*. Oxford: Oxford University Press.

Birnbaum, M.H. & Chavez, A. (1997). Tests of theories of decision making: Violations of branch independence and distribution independence. *Organizational Behavior and Human Decision Processes*, *71*, 161–194.

Blackwood, N.J., Bentall, R.P., Fytche, D.H., Simmons, A., Murray, R.M. & Howard, R.J. (2004). Persecutory delusions and the determination of self-relevance: An fMRI investigation. *Psychological Medicine*, *34*, 591–596.

Blastland, M. & Dilnot, A. (2007). *The tiger that isn't: Seeing through a world of numbers*. London: Profile Books.

Bond, M. (2009). Risk school. *Nature*, *461*, 1189–1192.

Boninger, D.S, Gleicher, F. & Strathman, A. (1994). Counterfactual thinking: From what might have been to what may be. *Journal of Personality and Social Psychology*, *67*, 297–307.

Bonnefon, J.-F. & Hilton, D.J. (2005). Putting *Ifs* to work: Goal-based relevance in conditional directives. *Journal of Experimental Psychology: General*, *134*, 388–405.

Bortolotti, L. (2009). Delusion. *Stanford encyclopedia of philosophy* Retrieved March 2011, from http://plato.stanford.edu/entries/delusion/

Braine, M.D.S. (1990). The 'natural logic' approach to reasoning. In W.F. Overton (ed.), *Reasoning, necessity, and logic: Developmental perspectives*. Hillsdale, NJ: Lawrence Erlbaum Associates.

Braine, M.D.S. & O'Brien, D.P. (1991). A theory of If: A lexical entry, reasoning program, and pragmatic principles. *Psychological Review*, *98*, 182–203.

Braine, M.D.S. & O'Brien, D.P. (eds.) (1998). *Mental logic*. Mahwah, NJ: Lawrence Erlbaum Associates.

Braine, M.D.S., O'Brien, D.P., Noveck, I.A., Samuels, M.C., Lea, B.L., Fisch, S.M. & Yang, Y. (1995). Predicting intermediate and multiple conclusions in propositional inference problems: Further evidence for a mental logic. *Journal of Experimental Psychology: General*, *124*, 263–292.

Braine, M.D.S., Reiser, B.J. & Rumain, B. (1984). Some empirical justification for a theory of mental propositional logic. In G. Bower (ed.), *The psychology of learning and motivation: Advances in research and theory, Vol. 18*. New York: Academic Press.

Brandstätter, E., Gigerenzer, G. & Hertwig, R. (2006). The priority heuristic: Making choices without trade-offs. *Psychological Review*, *113*, 409–432.

Breiman, L., Friedman, J.H., Ohlson, R.A. & Stone, C.J. (1993). *Classification and regression trees*. New York: Chapman & Hall.

Brewer, M.B. & Chen, Y.-R. (2007). Where (who) are the collectives in collectivism? Toward conceptual clarification of individualism and collectivism. *Psychological Review*, *114*, 133–151.

Brickman, P., Coates, D. & Janoff-Bulman, R. (1978). Lottery winners and accident victims: Is happiness relative? *Journal of Personality and Social Psychology*, *36*, 917–927.

Brockner, J. & Rubin, J.Z. (1985). *Entrapment in escalating conflicts*. New York: Springer.

Bröder, A. & Schiffer, S. (2003). Take the best versus simultaneous feature matching: Probabilistic inferences from memory and effects of representation format. *Journal of Experimental Psychology: General*, *132*, 277–293.

Brown, W.M. & Moore, C. (2000). Is prospective altruist-detection an evolved solution to the adaptive problem of subtle cheating in cooperative ventures? Supportive evidence using the Wason selection task. *Evolution and Human Behavior*, *21*, 25–37.

Bruner, J.S., Goodnow, J.J. & Austin, G.A. (1956). *A study of thinking*. New York: John Wiley & Sons.

Bucciarelli, M. & Johnson-Laird, P.N. (1999). Strategies in syllogistic reasoning. *Cognitive Science*, *23*, 247–303.

Buchtel, E.E. & Norenzayan, A. (2009). Thinking across cultures: Implications for dual processes. In J.StB.T. Evans & K. Frankish (eds.), *In two minds: Dual processes and beyond*. Oxford: Oxford University Press.

Buehler, R., Griffin, D. & Ross, M. (1994). Exploring the 'planning fallacy': Why people underestimate their task completion times. *Journal of Personality and Social Psychology*, *67*, 366–381.

Buehler, R., Griffin, D. & Ross, M. (2002). Inside the planning fallacy: The causes and consequences of optimistic time prediction. In T. Gilovich, D. Griffin & D. Kahneman (eds.), *Heuristics and biases: The psychology of intuitive judgment*. Cambridge: Cambridge University Press.

Buehner, M.J. & Cheng, P.W. (2005). Causal learning. In K.J. Holyoak & R.G. Morrison (eds.), *The Cambridge handbook of thinking and reasoning*. Cambridge: Cambridge University Press.

Byrne, R.M.J. (2005). *The rational imagination*. Cambridge, MA: MIT Press.

Byrne, R.M.J. (2007). Précis of *The rational imagination*. *Behavioral and Brain Sciences*, *30*, 439–477.

Byrne, R.M.J. & McEleney, A. (2000). Counterfactual thinking about actions and failures to act. *Journal of Experimental Psychology: Learning, Memory, and Cognition*, *26*, 1318–1331.

Byrne, R.M.J. & Tasso, A. (1999). Deductive reasoning with factual, possible and counterfactual conditionals. *Memory and Cognition*, *27*, 724–740.

Cacioppo, J.T. & Petty, R.E. (1982). The need for cognition. *Journal of Personality and Social Psychology*, *42*, 116–131.

Cacioppo, J.T., Petty, R.E., Feinstein, J. & Jarvis, W. (1996). Dispositional differences in cognitive motivation: The life and times of individuals varying in need for cognition. *Psychological Bulletin*, *119*, 197–253.

Camerer, C.F. (1997). Progress in behavioural game theory. *Journal of Economic Perspectives*, *11*, 167–188.

Camerer, C.F. (2003). *Behavioral game theory: Experiments in strategic interaction*. Princeton, NJ: Princeton University Press.

Canessa, N., Gorini, A., Cappa, S.F., Piattelli-Palmarini, M., Danna, M., Fazio, F. & Perani, D. (2005). The effect of social content on deductive reasoning: An fMRI study. *Human Brain Mapping*, *26*, 30–43.

Carey, S. (1985). *Conceptual change in childhood*. Cambridge, MA: MIT Press.

Carlson, W.B. & Gorman, M.E. (1990). Understanding invention as a cognitive process: The case of Thomas Edison and early motion pictures. *Social Studies of Science*, *20*, 387–430.

Chapman, L.J. & Chapman, J.P. (1959). Atmosphere effect re-examined. *Journal of Experimental Psychology*, *58*, 220–226.

Chase, W.G. & Simon, H.A. (1973). Perception in chess. *Cognitive Psychology*, *4*, 55–81.

Chater, N. & Oaksford, M.R. (1996). Deontic reasoning, modules and innateness: A second look. *Mind and Language*, *11*, 191–202.

Chater, N. & Oaksford, M.R. (1999). The probability heuristics model of syllogistic reasoning. *Cognitive Psychology*, *38*, 191–258.

Chater, N. & Oaksford, M.R. (eds.) (2008). *The probabilistic mind: Prospects for a Bayesian cognitive science*. Oxford: Oxford University Press.

Chater, N., Oaksford, M., Nakisa, M. & Redington, M. (2003). Fast, frugal and rational: How rational norms explain behavior. *Organizational Behavior and Human Decision Processes*, *90*, 63–86.

Chen, M. & Bargh, J.A. (1999). Consequences of automatic evaluation: Immediate behavioral predispositions to approach or avoid the stimulus. *Personality and Social Psychology Bulletin*, *25*, 215–224.

Cheng, P.W. (1997). From covariation to causation: A causal power theory. *Psychological Review*, *104*, 367–405.

Cheng, P.W. & Holyoak, K.J. (1985). Pragmatic reasoning schemas. *Cognitive Psychology*, *17*, 391–416.

Cheng, P.W. & Holyoak, K.J. (1989). On the natural selection of reasoning theories. *Cognition*, *33*, 285–313.

Cheng, P.W., Holyoak, K.J., Nisbett, R.E. & Oliver, L.M. (1986). Pragmatic versus syntactic approaches to training deductive reasoning. *Cognitive Psychology*, *18*, 293–328.

Cheng, P.W. & Novick, L.R. (1990). A probabilistic contrast model of causal induction. *Journal of Personality and Social Psychology*, *58*, 545–567.

Cheng, P.W. & Novick, L.R. (1991). Causes versus enabling conditions. *Cognition*, *40*, 83–120.

Cheng, P.W. & Novick, L.R. (1992). Covariation in natural causal induction. *Psychological Review*, *99*, 365–382.

Cheng, P.W. & Novick, L.R. (2005). Constraints and nonconstraints in causal learning: A reply to White (2005) and to Luhmann and Ahn (2005). *Psychological Review*, *112*, 694–709.

Choi, I. & Nisbett, R.E. (2000). Cultural psychology of surprise: Holistic theories and recognition of contradiction. *Journal of Personality and Social Psychology*, *79*, 890–905.

Choi, I., Nisbett, R.E. & Norenzayan, A. (1999). Causal attribution across cultures: Variation and universality. *Psychological Bulletin*, *125*, 47–63.

Christensen-Szalanski, J. & Beach, L. (1982). Experience and the base-rate fallacy. *Organizational Behavior and Human Performance*, *29*, 270–278.

Claridge, G.S. (1988). Schizotypy and schizophreia. In P. Bebbington & P. McGuffin (eds.), *Schizophrenia: The major issues*. Oxford: Heinemann Professional.

Claridge, G.S. (1997). *Schizotypy: Implications for illness and health*. Oxford: Oxford University Press.

Cohen, L.J. (1981). Can human irrationality be experimentally demonstrated? *Behavioral and Brain Sciences*, *4*, 317–370 (including commentaries).

Cole, M. (1997). An ethnographic study of cognition. In P.N. Johnson-Laird & P.C. Wason (eds.), *Thinking: Readings in cognitive science*. Cambridge: Cambridge University Press.

Cole, M. & Scribner, S. (1974). *Culture and thought: A psychological introduction*. New York: Wiley.

Colman, A.M. (1995). *Game theory and its applications*. Oxford: Butterworth-Heinemann.

Colman, A.M. (2003). Cooperation, psychological game theory, and limitations of rationality in social interaction. *Behavioral and Brain Sciences*, *26*, 139–198 (including commentaries).

Copeland, D.E. (2006). Theories of categorical reasoning and extended syllogisms. *Thinking & Reasoning*, *12*, 379–412.

Cosmides, L. (1989). The logic of social exchange: Has natural selection shaped how humans reason? Studies with the Wason selection task. *Cognition,31*, 187–316.

Cosmides, L. & Tooby, J. (1989). Evolutionary psychology and the generation of culture. Part II. Case study: A computational theory of social exchange. *Ethology and Sociobiology*, *10*, 51–97.

Cosmides, L. & Tooby, J. (1992). Cognitive adaptations for social exchange. In J.H. Barkow, L. Cosmides & J. Tooby (eds.), *The adapted mind*. Oxford: Oxford University Press.

Cosmides, L. & Tooby, J. (1996). Are humans good intuitive statisticians after all? Rethinking some conclusions from the literature on judgment under uncertainty. *Cognition*, *58*, 1–73.

Cousins, S.D. (1989). Culture and self-perception in Japan and the United States. *Journal of Personality and Social Psychology*, *56*, 124–131.

Cummins, D.D. (1995). Naïve theories and causal deduction. *Memory and Cognition*, *23*, 646–658.

Cummins, D.D. (1996a). Evidence for the innateness of deontic reasoning. *Mind and Language*, *11*, 160–190.

Cummins, D.D. (1996b). Dominance hierarchies and the evolution of human reasoning. *Minds and Machines, 6,* 463–480.

Cummins, D.D. (1996c). Evidence of deontic reasoning in 3- and 4-year-old children. *Memory and Cognition, 24,* 823–829.

Cummins, D.D., Lubart, T., Alksnis, O. & Rist, R. (1991). Conditional reasoning and causation. *Memory and Cognition, 19,* 274–282.

Czerlinski, J., Gigerenzer, G. & Goldstein, D.G. (1999). Betting on one good reason: The take the best heuristic. In G. Gigerenzer, P.M. Todd & the ABC Research Group (eds.), *Simple heuristics that make us smart.* Oxford: Oxford University Press.

Damasio, A.R. (1994). *Descartes' error: Emotion, reason and the human brain.* London: Vintage.

Dawes, R.M. (1988). *Rational choice in an uncertain world.* New York: Harcourt Brace Jovanovich.

Dawes, R.M. (2001). *Everyday irrationality: How pseudo-scientists, lunatics, and the rest of us systematically fail to think rationally.* Oxford: Westview Press.

Dawkins, R. & Carlisle, T.R. (1976). Parental investment, mate desertion and a fallacy. *Nature, 262,* 131–133.

De Neys, W. & Goel, V. (2011). Heuristics and biases in the brain: Dual neural pathways for decision making. In O. Vartanian & D.R. Mandel (eds.), *Neuroscience of decision making.* Hove: Psychology Press.

Diamond, J. (1997). *Guns, germs, and steel: The fates of human societies.* New York: Norton.

Dickstein, L. (1978). The effect of figure on syllogistic reasoning. *Memory and cognition, 6,* 76–83.

Dittmar, H. (2001). Impulse buying in ordinary and 'compulsive' consumers. In E.K. Weber, J. Baron & G. Loomes (eds.), *Conflict and tradeoffs in decision making.* Cambridge: Cambridge University Press.

Doherty, M.E., Mynatt, C.R., Tweney, R.D. & Schiavo, M.D. (1979). Pseudodiagnosticity. *Acta Psychologica, 43,* 111–121.

Dominowski, R. (1995) Content effects in Wason's selection task. In J.StB.T. Evans & S.E. Newstead (eds.), *Perspectives on thinking and reasoning: Essays in honour of Peter Wason.* Hove: Lawrence Erlbaum Associates.

Dudley, R.E.J., John, C.H., Young, A. & Over, D.E. (1997). Normal and abnormal reasoning in people with delusions. *British Journal of Clinical Psychology, 36,* 243–258.

Dudley, R.E.J. & Over, D.E. (2003). People with delusions jump to conclusions: A theoretical account of research findings on the reasoning of people with delusions. *Clinical Psychology and Psychotherapy, 10,* 263–274.

Dunbar, K. (1995). How scientists really reason: Scientific reasoning in real-world laboratories. In R.J. Sternberg & J. Davidson (eds.), *Mechanisms of insight.* Cambridge, MA: MIT Press.

Dunbar, K. (2001). The analogical paradox: Why analogy is so easy in naturalistic settings, yet so difficult in the psychology laboratory. In D. Gentner, K.J. Holyoak & B. Kokinov (eds.), *Analogy: Perspectives from cognitive science.* Cambridge, MA: MIT Press.

Dunbar, K. & Fugelsang, J. (2005). Scientific thinking and reasoning. In K.J. Holyoak and R.G. Morrison (eds.), *The Cambridge handbook of thinking and reasoning.* Cambridge: Cambridge University Press.

Eddy, D.M. (1982). Probabilistic reasoning in clinical medicine: Problems and opportunities. In D. Kahneman, P. Slovic & A. Tversky (eds.), *Judgment under uncertainty: Heuristics and biases.* Cambridge: Cambridge University Press.

Elqayam, S. (2010). Grounded rationality: A relativist framework for normative rationality. In K.I. Manktelow, D.E. Over & S. Elqayam (eds.), *The science of reason: Essays in honour of Jonathan StB.T. Evans.* Hove: Psychology Press.

Epstein, S., Lipson, A., Holstein, C. & Huh, E. (1992). Irrational reactions to negative outcomes: Evidence for two conceptual systems. *Journal of Personality and Social Psychology, 62,* 328–339.

Epstein, S., Pacini, R., Denes-Raj, V. & Heier, H. (1996). Individual differences in intuitive-experiential and analytic-rational thinking styles. *Journal of Personality and Social Psychology, 71*, 390–405.

Evans, J.StB.T. (1972). Interpretation and matching bias in a reasoning task. *Quarterly Journal of Experimental Psychology, 24*, 193–199.

Evans, J.StB.T. (1984). Heuristic and analytic processes in reasoning. *British Journal of Psychology, 75*, 451–468.

Evans, J.StB.T. (1989). *Bias in human reasoning: Causes and consequences*. Hove: Lawrence Erlbaum Associates.

Evans, J.StB.T. (1993). Bias and rationality. In K.I. Manktelow & D.E. Over (eds.), *Rationality: Psychological and philosophical perspectives*. London: Routledge.

Evans, J.StB.T. (1996). Deciding before you think: Relevance and reasoning in the selection task. *British Journal of Psychology, 87*, 223–240.

Evans, J.StB.T. (1998). Matching bias in conditional reasoning: Do we understand it after 25 years? *Thinking & Reasoning, 4*, 45–82.

Evans, J.StB.T. (2002). Logic and human reasoning: An assessment of the deduction paradigm. *Psychological Bulletin, 128*, 978–996.

Evans, J.StB.T. (2003). In two minds: Dual process accounts of reasoning. *Trends in Cognitive Sciences, 7*, 454–459.

Evans, J.StB.T. (2004). History of the dual process theory of reasoning. In K.I. Manktelow & M.C. Chung (eds.), *Psychology of reasoning: Theoretical and historical perspectives*. Hove: Psychology Press.

Evans, J.StB.T. (2006). The heuristic-analytic theory of reasoning: Extension and evaluation. *Psychonomic Bulletin and Review, 13*, 378–395.

Evans, J.StB.T. (2007a). *Hypothetical thinking: Dual processes in reasoning and judgment*. Hove: Psychology Press.

Evans, J.StB.T. (2007b). On the resolution of conflict in dual-process theories of reasoning. *Thinking & Reasoning, 13*, 321–329.

Evans, J.StB.T. (2008). Dual-process accounts of reasoning, judgment, and social cognition. *Annual Review of Psychology, 59*, 255–278.

Evans, J.StB.T. (2009). How many dual process theories do we need? One, two, or many? In J.StB.T. Evans & K. Frankish (eds.), *In two minds: Dual processes and beyond*. Oxford: Oxford University Press.

Evans, J.StB.T. (2010). *Thinking twice: Two minds in one brain*. Oxford: Oxford University Press.

Evans, J.StB.T., Barston, J.L. & Pollard, P. (1983). On the conflict between logic and belief in syllogistic reasoning. *Memory and Cognition, 11*, 295–306.

Evans, J.StB.T., Clibbens, J. & Rood, B. (1996). Bias in conditional inference: Implications for mental models and mental logic. *Quarterly Journal of Experimental Psychology, 48A*, 392–409.

Evans, J.StB.T. & Frankish, K. (2009). The duality of mind: An historical perspective. In J.StB.T. Evans & K. Frankish (eds.), *In two minds: Dual processes and beyond*. Oxford: Oxford University Press.

Evans, J.StB.T., Handley, S.J. & Harper, C. (2001). Necessity, possibility and belief: A study of syllogistic reasoning. *Quarterly Journal of Experimental Psychology, 54A*, 935–958.

Evans, J.StB.T., Handley, S.J. & Over, D.E. (2003a). Conditionals and conditional probability. *Journal of Experimental Psychology: Learning, Memory, and Cognition, 29*, 321–335.

Evans, J.StB.T., Handley, S.J., Perham, N., Over, D.E. & Thompson, V.A. (2000). Frequency versus probability formats in statistical word problems. *Cognition, 77*, 197–213.

Evans, J.StB.T. & Lynch, J.S. (1973). Matching bias in the selection task. *British Journal of Psychology, 64*, 391–397.

Evans, J.StB.T., Newstead, S.E. & Byrne, R.M.J. (1993a). *Human reasoning*. Hove: Lawrence Erlbaum Associates.

Evans, J.StB.T. & Over, D.E. (1996). *Rationality and reasoning*. Hove: Psychology Press.

Evans, J.StB.T. & Over, D.E. (2004). *If*. Oxford: Oxford University Press.

Evans, J.StB.T., Over, D.E. & Handley, S.J. (2003b). A theory of hypothetical thinking. In D. Hardman & L. Macchi (eds.), *Thinking: Psychological perspectives on reasoning, judgment and decision making*. Chichester: John Wiley & Sons.

Evans, J.StB.T., Over, D.E. & Handley, S.J. (2005). Suppositions, extensionality, and conditionals: A critique of the mental model theory of Johnson-Laird and Byrne (2002). *Psychological Review, 112*, 1040–1052.

Evans, J.StB.T., Over, D.E. & Manktelow, K.I. (1993b). Reasoning, decision making, and rationality. *Cognition, 49*, 165–187. Reprinted in Adler & Rips (2008).

Evans, J.StB.T. & Wason, P.C. (1976). Rationalisation in a reasoning task. *British Journal of Psychology, 63*, 205–212.

Fairley, N., Manktelow, K. & Over, D. (1999). Necessity, sufficiency, and perspective effects in causal conditional reasoning. *Quarterly Journal of Experimental Psychology, 52A*, 771–790.

Farris, H. & Revlin, R. (1989). The discovery process: A counterfactual study. *Social Studies of Science, 19*, 497–513.

Feeney, A. (2007). Individual differences, dual processes, and induction. In A. Feeney & E. Heit (eds.), *Inductive reasoning: Experimental, developmental and computational approaches*. Cambridge: Cambridge University Press.

Feeney, A., Coley, J.D. & Crisp, A. (2010). The relevance framework for category-based induction; Evidence from garden-path arguments. *Journal of Experimental Psychology: Learning, Memory, and Cognition, 36*, 906–919.

Feeney, A., Evans, J.StB.T. & Venn, S. (2008). Rarity, pseudodiagnosticity and Bayesian reasoning. *Thinking & Reasoning, 14*, 209–230.

Feeney, A. & Heit, E. (eds.) (2007). *Inductive reasoning: Experimental, developmental and computational approaches*. Cambridge: Cambridge University Press.

Fiddick, L. (2003). Is there a faculty of deontic reasoning? A critical re-evaluation of abstract deontic versions of the Wason selection task. In D.E. Over (ed.), *Evolution and the psychology of thinking: The debate*. Hove: Psychology Press.

Fiddick, L. (2004). Domains of deontic reasoning: Resolving the discrepancy between the cognitive and moral reasoning literatures. *Quarterly Journal of Experimental Psychology, 57A*, 447–474.

Fiddick, L., Cosmides, L. & Tooby, J. (2000). No interpretation without representation: The role of domain-specific representations and inferences in the Wason selection task. *Cognition, 77*, 1–79.

Fiedler, K. (1988). The dependence of the conjunction fallacy on subtle linguistic factors. *Psychological Research, 50*, 123–129.

Fiedler, K. (2000). Beware of samples! A cognitive-ecological sampling approach to judgment biases. *Psychological Review, 107*, 659–676.

Fillenbaum, S. (1974). OR: Some uses. *Journal of Experimental Psychology, 103*, 913–921.

Fine, C., Gardner, M., Craigie, J. & Gold, I. (2007). Hopping, skipping, or jumping to conclusions? Clarifying the role of the JTC bias in delusions. *Cognitive Neuropsychiatry, 12*, 46–77.

Fischhoff, B. (1975). Hindsight ≠ foresight: The effect of outcome knowledge on judgment under uncertainty. *Journal of Experimental Psychology: Human Perception and Performance, 1*, 288–299.

Fisk, J.E. (2004). Conjunction fallacy. In R.F. Pohl (ed.), *Cognitive illusions: A handbook of fallacies and biases in thinking, judgment, and memory*. Hove: Psychology Press.

Ford, M. (1994). Two modes of representation and problem solution in syllogistic reasoning. *Cognition, 54*, 1–71.

Fox, C.R. & Tversky, A. (1998). A belief-based account of decision under uncertainty. *Management Science, 44*, 879–895.

Frankish, K. & Evans, J.StB.T. (2009). The duality of mind: An historical perspective. In J.StB.T. Evans & K. Frankish (eds.), *In two minds: Dual processes and beyond*. Oxford: Oxford University Press.

Fugelsang, J.A., Stein, C.B., Green, A.B. & Dunbar, K. (2004). Theory and data interactions of the scientific mind: Evidence from the molecular and the cognitive laboratory. *Canadian Journal of Experimental Psychology, 58*, 86–95.

Fugelsang, J.A. & Thompson, V.A. (2003). A dual-process of belief and evidence interactions in causal reasoning. *Memory and Cognition, 31*, 800–815.

Fugelsang, J.A., Thompson, V.A. & Dunbar, K.N. (2006). Examining the representation of causal knowledge. *Thinking & Reasoning, 12*, 1–30.

Gächter, S. (2004). Behavioral game theory. In D.J. Koehler and N. Harvey (eds.), *Blackwell handbook of judgment and decision making*. Oxford: Blackwell.

Galbraith, N., Manktelow, K. & Morris, N. (2008). Subclinical delusional ideation and a self-reference bias in everyday reasoning. *British Journal of Psychology, 99*, 29–44.

Galbraith, N.D., Manktelow, K.I. & Morris, N.G. (2010). Subclinical delusional ideation and appreciation of sample size and heterogeneity in statistical judgment. *British Journal of Psychology, 101*, 621–635.

Gale, M. & Ball, L.J. (2006). Dual-goal facilitation in Wason's 2–4–6 task: What mediates successful rule discovery? *Quarterly Journal of Experimental Psychology, 59*, 873–885.

Gale, M. & Ball, L.J. (2009). Exploring the determinants of dual goal facilitation in a rule discovery task. *Thinking & Reasoning, 15*, 294–315.

Garety, P.A. & Freeman, D (1999). Cognitive approaches to delusions: A critical review of theories and evidence. *British Journal of Clinical Psychology, 38*, 113–54.

Gavanagh, H. (1990). Human error in the air. *New Scientist*, 17 November, issue no. 1743, 23–24.

Geis, M.C. & Zwicky, A.M. (1971). On invited inferences. *Linguistic Inquiry, 2*, 561–566.

Gigerenzer, G. (1993). The bounded rationality of probabilistic mental models. In K.I. Manktelow & D.E. Over (eds.), *Rationality: Psychological and philosophical perspectives*. London: Routledge.

Gigerenzer, G. (1996). On narrow norms and vague heuristics: A reply to Kahneman and Tversky (1996). *Psychological Review*, 103, 592–596.

Gigerenzer, G. (2002). *Reckoning with risk*. London: Penguin. Published in the USA as *Calculated risks*. New York: Simon & Schuster.

Gigerenzer, G. (2004a). Fast and frugal heuristics: The tools of bounded rationality. In D.J. Koehler and N. Harvey (eds.), *Blackwell handbook of judgment and decision making*. Oxford: Blackwell. Reprinted in Gigerenzer (2008).

Gigerenzer, G. (2004b). Striking a blow for sanity in theories of rationality. In M. Augier & J,G. Marsh (eds.), *Models of man: Essays in memory of Herbert A Simon*. Cambridge, MA: MIT Press. Reprinted in Gigerenzer (2008).

Gigerenzer, G. (2006). Bounded and rational. In R.J. Stainton (ed.), *Contemporary debates in cognitive science*. Oxford: Blackwell. Reprinted in Gigerenzer (2008).

Gigerenzer, G. (2007). *Gut feelings*. London: Penguin.

Gigerenzer, G. (2008). *Rationality for mortals: How people cope with uncertainty*. Oxford: Oxford University Press.

Gigerenzer, G., Czerlinski, J. & Martignon, L. (2002). How good are fast and frugal heuristics? In T. Gilovich, D. Griffin & D. Kahneman (eds.), *Heuristics and biases: The psychology of intuitive judgment*. Cambridge: Cambridge University Press.

Gigerenzer, G. & Goldstein, D.G. (1996). Reasoning the fast and frugal way: Models of bounded rationality. *Psychological Review, 103*, 650–669.

Gigerenzer, G., Hertwig, R., van den Broek, E., Fasolo, B. & Katsikopoulos, K.V. (2005). 'A 30 per cent chance of rain tomorrow': How does the public understand probabilistic weather forecasts? *Risk Analysis, 25*, 623–629. Reprinted in Gigerenzer (2008).

Gigerenzer, G. & Hoffrage, U. (1995). How to improve Bayesian reasoning without instruction: Frequency formats. *Psychological Review, 102*, 684–704.

Gigerenzer, G. & Hoffrage, U. (2007). The role of representation in Bayesian reasoning: Correcting common misconceptions. *Behavioral and Brain Sciences, 30*, 264–267.

Gigerenzer, G., Hoffrage, U. & Ebert, A. (1998). AIDS counseling with low-risk clients. *AIDS Care, 10*, 197–211.

Gigerenzer, G., Hoffrage, U. & Kleinbölting (1991). Probabilistic mental models: A Brunswikian theory of confidence. *Psychological Review, 98*, 506–528.

Gigerenzer, G. & Hug, K. (1992). Domain-specific reasoning: Social contracts, cheating and perspective change. *Cognition, 43*, 127–171.

Gigerenzer, G. & Regier, T. (1996). How do we tell an association from a rule? Comment on Sloman (1996). *Psychological Bulletin, 119*, 23–26.

Gigerenzer, G. & Selten, R. (eds.) (2001). *Bounded rationality: The adaptive toolbox.* Cambridge, MA: MIT Press.

Gigerenzer, G, Swijtink, Z., Porter, T., Daston, L., Beatty, J & Krüger, L. (1989). *The empire of chance: How probability changed science and everyday life.* Cambridge: Cambridge University Press.

Gigerenzer, G. & Todd, P.M. (1999a). *Simple heuristics that make us smart.* Oxford: Oxford University Press.

Gigerenzer, G., & Todd, P.M. (1999b). Fast and frugal heuristics: The adaptive toolbox. In G. Gigerenzer & P.M Todd (eds.), *Simple heuristics that make us smart.* Oxford: Oxford University Press.

Gilbert, D.T. (2006). *Stumbling on happiness.* London: Harper Press.

Gillies, D. (2000). *Philosophical theories of probability.* London: Routledge.

Gilovich, T.D. Griffin, D. & Kahneman, D. (eds.) (2002). *Heuristics and biases: The psychology of intuitive judgment.* Cambridge: Cambridge University Press.

Gilovich, T., Vallone, R. & Tversky, A. (1985). The hot hand in basketball: On the misperception of random sequences. *Cognitive Psychology, 17*, 295–314. Reprinted in Gilovich et al. (2002).

Girotto, V., Blaye, A. & Farioli, F. (1989). A reason to reason: Pragmatic bases of children's search for counterexamples. *European Journal of Cognitive Psychology, 9*, 227–231.

Girotto, V. & Gonzalez, M. (2001) Solving probabilistic and statistical problems: A matter of information structure and question form. *Cognition, 78*, 247–276.

Girotto, V. & Johnson-Laird, P.N. (2004). The probability of conditionals. *Psychologia, 47*, 207–225.

Girotto, V. & Legrenzi, P. (1989). Mental representation and hypothetico-deductive reasoning: The case of the THOG problem. *Psychological Research, 51*, 129–135.

Girotto, V. & Legrenzi, P. (1993). Naming the parents of THOG: Mental representation and reasoning. *Quarterly Journal of Experimental Psychology, 46A*, 701–713.

Girotto, V., Legrenzi, P. & Rizzo, A. (1991). Event controllability in counterfactual thinking. *Acta Psychologica, 78*, 111–133.

Gladwell, M. (2005). *Blink: The power of thinking without thinking.* London: Penguin.

Goel, V. (2005). Cognitive neuroscience of deductive reasoning. In K.J. Holyoak & R.G. Morrison (eds.), *The Cambridge handbook of thinking and reasoning.* Cambridge: Cambridge University Press.

Goel, V. (2008). Anatomy of deductive reasoning. *Trends in Cognitive Sciences, 11*, 435–440.

Goel, V., Buchel, C., Frith, C. & Dolan, R.J. (2000). Dissociation of mechanisms underlying syllogistic reasoning. *Neuroimage, 12*, 504–514.

Goel, V. & Dolan, R.J. (2003). Explaining modulation of reasoning by belief. *Cognition, 87*, B11–B22.

Goel, V., Gold, B., Kapur, S. & Houle, S. (1997). The seats of reason? An imaging study of inductive and deductive reasoning. *NeuroReport, 8*, 1305–1310.

Goldstein, D.G. & Gigerenzer, G. (1999). The recognition heuristic: How ignorance makes us smart. In G. Gigerenzer & P.A. Todd (eds.), *Simple heuristics that make us smart*. Oxford: Oxford University Press.

Goldstein, D.G. & Gigerenzer, G. (2002). Models of ecological rationality: The recognition heuristic. *Psychological Review, 109*, 75–90.

Goldvarg, Y. & Johnson-Laird, P.N. (2001). Naïve causality: A mental model theory of causal meaning and reasoning. *Cognitive Science, 25*, 565–610.

Goodwin, R.Q. & Wason, P.C. (1972). Degrees of insight. *British Journal of Psychology, 63*, 205–212.

Gopnik, A. (1998). Explanation as orgasm. *Minds and Machines, 8*, 101–118.

Gopnik, A. (2000). Explanation as orgasm and the drive for causal understanding: The evolution, function and phenomenology of the theory-formation system. In F. Keil & R. Wilson (eds.), *Cognition and explanation*. Cambridge, MA: MIT Press.

Gorman, M.E. (1992). *Simulating science: Heuristics, mental models, and technoscientific thinking*. Bloomington, IN: Indiana University Press.

Gorman, M.E. (1995). Confirmation, disconfirmation, and invention: The case of Alexander Graham Bell and the telephone. *Thinking & Reasoning, 1*, 31–53.

Green, L.A. & Mehr, D.R. (1997). What alters physicians' decisions to admit to the coronary care unit? *Journal of Family Practice, 45*, 219–226.

Grice, H.P. (1975). Logic and conversation. In P. Cole & J.L. Morgan (eds.), *Studies in syntax. Vol. 3: Speech acts*. New York: Academic Press.

Griffin, D. & Brenner, L. (2004). Perspectives on probability judgment calibration. In D.J. Koehler and N. Harvey (eds.), *Blackwell handbook of judgment and decision making*. Oxford: Blackwell.

Griffin, D. & Buehler, R. (1999). Frequency, probability, and prediction: Easy solutions to cognitive illusions? *Cognitive Psychology, 38*, 48–78.

Griffin, D. & Tversky (1992). The weighing of evidence and the determinants of confidence. *Cognitive Psychology, 24*, 411–435.

Griggs, R.A. (1995). The effects of rule clarification, decision justification, and selection instruction on Wason's selection task. In J.StB.T. Evans & S.E. Newstead (eds.), *Perspectives on thinking and reasoning: Essays in honour of Peter Wason*. Hove: Lawrence Erlbaum Associates.

Griggs, R.A. & Cox, J.R. (1982). The elusive thematic-materials effect in Wason's selection task. *British Journal of Psychology, 73*, 407–420.

Griggs, R.A., Platt, R.D., Newstead, S.E. & Jackson, S.L. (1998). Attentional factors in a deductive reasoning task. *Thinking & Reasoning, 4*, 1–14.

Hammerton, M. (1973). A case of radical probability estimation. *Journal of Experimental Psychology, 101*, 252–254.

Handley, S.J., Evans, J.StB.T. & Thompson, V.A. (2006). The negated conditional: A litmus test for the suppositional conditional? *Journal of Experimental Psychology: Learning, Memory, and Cognition, 32*, 559–569.

Hardin, G. (1968). The tragedy of the commons. *Science, 162*, 1243–1248.

Hardin, G. (1978). Political requirements for preserving our common heritage. In H.P. Bokaw (ed.), *Wildlife and America*. Washington, DC: Council on Environmental Quality.

Hardman, D.K. (2009). *Judgment and decision making*. Oxford: Blackwell.

Harman, G. (1995). Rationality. In E.E. Smith & D.N. Osherson (eds.), *Thinking: Invitation to cognitive science*. Cambridge, MA: MIT Press.

Harman, G. (1999). *Reasoning, meaning and mind*. Oxford: Clarendon Press.

Harris, P. & Nuñez, M. (1996). Understanding of permission rules by preschool children. *Child Development, 67*, 1572–1591.

Hassin, R., Uleman, J. & Bargh, J. (eds.) (2005). *The new unconscious*. Oxford: Oxford University Press.

Hawkins, S.A. & Hastie, R. (1990). Hindsight: Biased judgments of past events after the outcomes are known. *Psychological Bulletin, 107*, 311–327.

Heider, F. (1958). *The psychology of interpersonal relations.* New York: John Wiley & Sons.

Heit, E. (1998). A Bayesian analysis of some forms of inductive reasoning. In M.R. Oaksford & N. Chater (eds.), *Rational models of cognition.* Oxford: Oxford University Press.

Heit, E. (2000). Properties of inductive reasoning. *Psychonomic Bulletin and Review, 7*, 569–572. Reprinted in Adler & Rips (2008).

Heit, E. & Rubinstein, J. (1994). Similarity and property effects in inductive reasoning. *Journal of Experimental Psychology: Learning, Memory, and Cognition, 20*, 411–422.

Hertwig, R. & Chase, V.M. (1998). Many reasons or just one: How response mode affects reasoning in the conjunction problem. *Thinking & Reasoning, 4*, 319–352.

Hertwig, R. & Gigerenzer, G. (1999). The 'conjunction fallacy' revisited: How intelligent inferences look like reasoning errors. *Journal of Behavioral Decision Making, 12*, 275–305.

Hilton, D.J., McClure, J.L. & Slugoski, B.R. (2005). The course of events. In D.R. Mandel, D.J. Hilton & P. Catellani (eds.), *The psychology of counterfactual thinking.* London: Routledge.

Hilton, D.J. & Slugoski, B.R. (1986). Knowledge-based causal attribution: The abnormal-conditions-focus model. *Psychological Review, 93*, 75–88.

Hiraishi, K. & Hasegawa, T. (2001). Sharing-rule and detection of free-riders in cooperative groups: Evolutionarily important deontic reasoning in the Wason selection task. *Thinking & Reasoning, 7*, 255–294.

Hoch, S.J. & Loewenstein, G.F. (1991). Time-inconsistent preferences and consumer self-control. *Journal of Consumer Research, 17*, 1–16.

Hoffrage, U., Gigerenzer, G., Krauss, S. & Martignon, L. (2002). Representation facilitates reasoning: What natural frequencies are and what they are not. *Cognition, 84*, 343–352.

Hofstede, G. (1980). *Culture's consequences.* Beverly Hills, CA: Sage.

Hogarth, R.M (2008). On the learning of intuition. In H. Plessner, C. Betsch & T. Betsch (eds.), *Intuition in judgment and decision making.* London: Lawrence Erlbaum Associates.

Holland, J.H., Holyoak, K.J., Nisbett, R.E. & Thagard, P.A. (1986). *Induction.* Cambridge, MA: MIT Press.

Hsee, C.K. (1998). Less is better: When low-value options are valued more highly than high-value options. *Journal of Behavioral Decision Making, 11*, 107–121.

Hsee, C.K. (2000). Attribute evaluability: Its implications for joint–separate evaluation reversals and beyond. In D. Kahneman & A. Tversky (eds.), *Choices, values, and frames.* Cambridge: Cambridge University Press.

Hsee, C.K. & Hastie, R. (2006). Decision and experience: Why don't we choose what makes us happy? *Trends in Cognitive Sciences, 10*, 31–37.

Hsee, C.K., Loewenstein, G.F., Blount, S. & Bazerman, M.H. (1999). Preference reversals between joint and separate evaluations of options: A review and theoretical analysis. *Psychological Bulletin, 125*, 576–590. Reprinted in Lichtenstein & Slovic (2006).

Hume, D. (1978). *A treatise of human nature.* Oxford: Oxford University Press. (Original work published 1739)

Huq, S.F., Garety, P.A. & Hemsley, D.R. (1988). Probabilistic judgments in deluded and non-deluded subjects. *Quarterly Journal of Experimental Psychology, 40A*, 801–812.

Inhelder, B. & Piaget, J. (1958). *The growth of logical thinking.* New York: Basic Books.

Iyengar, S.S. (2010). *The art of choosing.* London: Little, Brown.

Iyengar, S.S. & Lepper, M.R. (2000). When choice is demotivating: Can one desire too much of a good thing? *Journal of Personality and Social Psychology, 79*, 995–1006. Reprinted in Lichtenstein & Slovic (2006).

Jackson, S.L. & Griggs, R.A. (1990). The elusive pragmatic reasoning schemas effect. *Quarterly Journal of Experimental Psychology, 42A*, 353–374.

James, O. (2007). *Affluenza*. London: Vermilion.

Johnson, E.J., Hershey, J., Meszaros, J. & Kunreuther, H. (1993). Framing, probability distortions, and insurance decisions. *Journal of Risk and Uncertainty, 7*, 35–51. Reprinted in Kahneman & Tversky (2000).

Johnson-Laird, P.N. (1983). *Mental models*. Cambridge: Cambridge University Press.

Johnson-Laird, P.N. (1994). A model theory of induction. *International Studies in the Philosophy of Science, 8*, 5–29.

Johnson-Laird, P.N. (2004). The history of mental models. In K.I. Manktelow & M.C. Chung (eds.), *Psychology of reasoning: Theoretical and historical perspectives*. Hove: Psychology Press.

Johnson-Laird, P.N. (2005). Mental models and thought. In K.J. Holyoak and R.G. Morrison (eds.), *The Cambridge handbook of thinking and reasoning*. Cambridge: Cambridge University Press.

Johnson-Laird, P.N. (2006). *How we reason*. Oxford: Oxford University Press.

Johnson-Laird, P.N. (2008). Mental models and deductive reasoning. In J.E. Adler and L.J. Rips (eds.), *Reasoning: Studies of human inference and its foundations*. Cambridge: Cambridge University Press.

Johnson-Laird, P.N. (2010). The truth about conditionals. In K.I. Manktelow, D.E. Over & S. Elqayam (eds.), *The science of reason: Essays in honour of Jonathan StB.T. Evans*. Hove: Psychology Press.

Johnson-Laird, P.N. & Bara, B. (1984). Syllogistic inference. *Cognition, 16*, 1–61.

Johnson-Laird, P.N. & Byrne, R.M.J. (1991). *Deduction*. Hove: Psychology Press.

Johnson-Laird, P.N. & Byrne, R.M.J. (2002). Conditionals: A theory of meaning, pragmatics, and inference. *Psychological Review, 109*, 646–678.

Johnson-Laird, P.N., Byrne, R.M.J. & Schaeken, W. (1992). Propositional reasoning by model. *Psychological Review, 99*, 418–439.

Johnson-Laird, P.N., Legrenzi, P., Girotto, V., Legrenzi, M.S. & Caverni, J.P. (1999). Naïve probability: A mental model theory of extensional reasoning. *Psychological Review, 106*, 62–88

Johnson-Laird, P.N., Legrenzi, P. & Legrenzi, M.S. (1972). Reasoning and a sense of reality. *British Journal of Psychology, 63*, 395–400.

Johnson-Laird, P.N., Mancini, F. & Gangemi, A. (2006). A hyper-emotion theory of psychological illnesses. *Psychological Review, 113*, 822–841.

Johnson-Laird, P.N. & Steedman, M.J. (1978). The psychology of syllogisms. *Cognitive Psychology, 10*, 64–99.

Johnson-Laird, P.N. & Tagart, J. (1969). How implication is understood. *American Journal of Psychology, 82*, 367–373.

Johnson-Laird, P.N. & Wason, P.C. (1970). A theoretical analysis of insight into a reasoning task. *Cognitive Psychology, 1*, 134–148.

Kahneman, D. (1993). New challenges to the rationality assumption. *Journal of Institutional and Theoretical Economics, 150*, 18–36. Reprinted in Kahneman & Tversky (2002).

Kahneman, D. (2000a). Experienced utility and objective happiness: A moment-based approach. In D. Kahneman & A. Tversky (eds.), *Choices, values, and frames*. Cambridge: Cambridge University Press.

Kahneman, D. (2000b). Evaluation by moments: Past and future. In D.Kahneman & A. Tversky (eds.), *Choices, values, and frames*. Cambridge: Cambridge University Press.

Kahneman, D. (2002). *Maps of bounded rationality: A perspective on intuitive judgment and choice*. Nobel Prize lecture. Stockholm: Nobel Foundation.

Kahneman, D. (2003a). Maps of bounded rationality: Psychology for behavioural economics. *American Economic Review*, December, 1449–1475.

Kahneman, D. (2003b). A perspective on judgment and choice: Mapping bounded rationality. *American Psychologist, 58*, 697–720

Kahneman, D. & Frederick, S. (2002). Representativeness revisited: Attribute substitution in intuitive judgment. In T.D. Gilovich, D. Griffin & D. Kahneman (eds.), *Heuristics and biases: The psychology of intuitive judgment*. Cambridge: Cambridge University Press.

Kahneman, D., Fredrickson, B.L., Schreiber, C.A. & Redelmeier, D.A. (1993). When more pain is preferred to less: Adding a better end. *Psychological Science, 4*, 401–405.

Kahneman, D. & Klein, G. (2009). Conditions for intuitive expertise: A failure to disagree. *American Psychologist, 64*, 515–526.

Kahneman, D., Knetsch, J.L. & Thaler, R. (1990). Experimental tests of the endowment effect and the Coase theorem. *Journal of Political Economy, 98*, 1325–1348.

Kahneman, D., Knetsch, J.L. & Thaler, R. (1991). Anomalies: The endowment effect, loss aversion, and status quo bias. *Journal of Economic Perspectives, 5*, 193–206.

Kahneman, D., Slovic, P. & Tversky, A. (eds.) (1982). *Judgment under uncertainty: Heuristics and biases*. Cambridge: Cambridge University Press.

Kahneman, D. & Tversky, A. (1972). Subjective probability: A judgment of representative-ness. *Cognitive Psychology, 3*, 430–454. Reprinted in Kahneman, Slovic & Tversky (1982).

Kahneman, D. & Tversky, A. (1973). On the psychology of prediction. *Psychological Review, 80*, 237–251. Reprinted in Kahneman, Slovic & Tversky (1982).

Kahneman, D. & Tversky, A. (1979a). Intuitive prediction: Biases and corrective procedures. *TIMS, Studies in Management Science, 12*, 313–327.

Kahnemann, D. & Tversky, A. (1979b). Prospect theory: An analysis of decision under risk. *Econometrica, 47*, 263–291. Reprinted in Kahneman & Tversky (2000).

Kahneman, D. & Tversky, A. (1982a). The simulation heuristic. In D. Kahneman, P. Slovic & A. Tversky (eds.), Subjective probability: a judgment or representativeness. Cambridge: Cambridge University Press.

Kahneman, D. & Tversky, A. (1982b). Variants of uncertainty. In D. Kahneman, P. Slovic & A. Tversky (eds.), *Judgment under uncertainty: Heuristics and biases*. Cambridge: Cambridge University Press.

Kahneman, D. & Tversky, A. (1982c). Intuitive prediction: Biases and corrective procedures. In D. Kahneman, P. Slovic & A. Tversky (eds.), *Judgment under uncertainty: Heuristics and biases*. Cambridge: Cambridge University Press.

Kahneman, D. & Tversky, A. (1996). On the reality of cognitive illusions. *Psychological Review, 103*, 582–591.

Kahneman, D. & Tversky, A. (eds.) (2000). *Choices, values, and frames*. Cambridge: Cambridge University Press.

Kahneman, D. & Varey, C.A. (1990). Propensities and counterfactuals: The loser that almost won. *Journal of Personality and Social Psychology, 59*, 1101–1110.

Kareev, Y., Halberstadt, N. & Shafir, D. (1993). Improving performance and increasing the use of non-positive testing in a rule discovery task. *Quarterly Journal of Experimental Psychology, 39A*, 29–41.

Katz, J., Redelmeier, D.A. & Kahneman, D. (1997) Memories of painful medical procedures. Paper presented at the American Pain Society 15th Annual Scientific Meeting.

Keeney, R.L. (1992). *Value-focused thinking: A path to creative decision making*. Cambridge, MA: Harvard University Press.

Keeney, R.L. & Raiffa, H. (1976). *Decisions with multiple objectives*. New York: John Wiley & Sons.

Kelley, H.H. (1973). The processes of causal attribution. *American Psychologist, 28*, 107–128.

Kemp, C. & Tenenbaum, J.B. (2003). Theory-based induction. *Proceedings of 25th annual conference of the Cognitive Science Society*. Mahwah, NJ: Lawrence Erlbaum Associates.

Kilpatrick, S.G., Manktelow, K.I. and Over, D.E. (2007). Power of source as a factor in deontic inference. *Thinking & Reasoning, 13*, 295–317.

Kirby, K.N. (1994). Probabilities and utilities of fictional outcomes in Wason's four-card selec-tion task. *Cognition, 51*, 1–28.

Klauer, K.C., Musch, J. & Naumer, B. (2000). On belief bias in syllogistic reasoning. *Psychological Review, 107*, 852–884.

Klauer, K.C., Stahl, C. & Erdfelder, E. (2007). The abstract selection task: New data and an almost comprehensive model. *Journal of Experimental Psychology: Learning, Memory, and Cognition, 33*, 680–703.

Klayman, J. (1995). Varieties of confirmation bias. *The psychology of learning and motivation, Vol. 32*. New York: Academic Press.

Klayman, J. & Ha, Y.W. (1987). Confirmation, disconfirmation, and information in hypothesis testing. *Psychological Review, 94*, 211–228.

Klayman, J. & Ha, Y.W. (1989). Hypothesis testing in rule discovery: Strategy, structure, and content. *Journal of Experimental Psychology: Learning, Memory, and Cognition, 15*, 596–604.

Klein, G. (1998). *Sources of power: How people make decisions.* Cambridge, MA: MIT Press.

Klein, G. (2009). *Streetlights and shadows: Searching for the keys to adaptive decision making.* Cambridge, MA: MIT Press.

Klein, G., Orasanu, J., Calderwood, R. & Zsambok, C.E. (1993). *Decision making in action: Models and methods.* Norwood, NJ: Ablex.

Kleiter, G.D. (1994). Natural sampling: Rationality without base rates. In G.H. Fischer & D. Laming (eds.), *Contributions to mathematical psychology, psychometrics, and methodology.* New York: Springer.

Knetsch, J.L. (1989). The endowment effect and evidence of nonreversible indifference curves. *American Economic Review, 79*, 1277–1284.

Knight, N. & Nisbett, R.E. (2007). Culture, class and cognition: Evidence from Italy. *Journal of Cognition and Culture, 7*, 283–291.

Koehler, J.J. (1996). The base rate fallacy reconsidered: Descriptive, normative, and methodological challenges. *Behavioral and Brain Sciences, 19*, 1–53.

Koenig, C.S. & Griggs, R.A. (2004). Facilitation and analogical transfer in the THOG task. *Thinking & Reasoning, 10*, 355–370.

Koenig, C.S. & Griggs, R.A. (2010). Facilitation and analogical transfer on a hypothetico-deductive reasoning task. In K.I. Manktelow, D.E. Over & S. Elqayam (eds.), *The science of reason: Essays in honour of Jonathan StB.T. Evans.* Hove: Psychology Press.

Kruglanski, A.W. & Gigerenzer, G. (2011). Intuitive and deliberate judgments are based on common principles. *Psychological Review, 118*, 97–109.

Lagnado, D. & Sloman, S.A. (2004). The advantage of timely intervention. *Journal of Experimental Psychology: Learning, Memory, and Cognition, 30*, 856–876.

Lea, R.B., O'Brien, D.P., Noveck, I.A., Fisch, S.M. & Braine, M.D.S. (1990). Predicting propositional logic inferences in text comprehension. *Journal of Memory and Language, 29*, 361–387.

Lee, N.Y.L., Goodwin, G.P. & Johnson-Laird, P.N. (2008). The psychological puzzle of Sudoku. *Thinking & Reasoning, 14*, 342–364.

Lichtenstein, S., & Fischhoff, B. (1977). Do those who know more also know more about how much they know? *Organizational Behavior and Human Decision Processes, 20*, 159–183.

Lichtenstein, S., Fischhoff, B. & Phillips, B. (1982). Calibration of probabilities: The state of the art to 1980. In D. Kahneman, P. Slovic & A. Tversky (eds.), *Judgment under uncertainty: Heuristics and biases.* Cambridge: Cambridge University Press.

Lichtenstein, S. & Slovic, P. (1971). Reversal of preference between bids and choices in gambling decisions. *Journal of Experimental Psychology, 89*, 46–55. Reprinted in Lichtenstein & Slovic (2006).

Lichtenstein, S. & Slovic, P. (eds.) (2006). *The construction of preference.* Cambridge: Cambridge University Press.

Lichtenstein, S., Slovic, P., Fischhoff, B., Layman, M. & Combs, B. (1978). Judged frequency of lethal events. *Journal of Experimental Psychology: Human Learning and Memory, 4*, 551–578.

Lindsey, S., Hertwig, R. & Gigerenzer, G. (2003). Communicating statistical DNA evidence. *Jurimetrics: The Journal of Law, Science and Technology, 43*, 147–163.

Linney, Y.M., Peters, E.R. & Ayton, P. (1998). Reasoning biases in delusion-prone individuals. *British Journal of Clinical Psychology, 37*, 285–307.

Lober, K. & Shanks, D.R. (2000). Is causal induction based on causal power? Critique of Cheng (1997). *Psychological Review, 107*, 195–212.

Loomes, G. & Sugden, R. (1982). Regret theory: An alternative theory of rational choice under uncertainty. *Economic Journal, 92*, 805–824.

Lopes, L.L. (1996). When time is of the essence: Averaging, aspiration and the short run. *Organizational Behavior and Human Decision Processes, 65*, 179–189.

Lopez, A., Atran, S., Coley, J.D., Medin, D.L. & Smith, E.E. (1997). The tree of life: Universal and cultural features of folkbiological taxonomies and inductions. *Cognitive Psychology, 32*, 251–295.

Lowenthal, D. (1993). Preference reversals in candidate evaluation. Unpublished study cited by Hsee (2000).

Lucas, E.J. & Ball, L.J. (2005). Think-aloud protocols and the selection task: Evidence for relevance effects and rationalisation processes. *Thinking & Reasoning, 11*, 35–66.

Luhmann, C.C. & Ahn, W.-K. (2005). The meaning and computation of causal power: Comment on Cheng (1997) and Novick & Cheng (2004). *Psychological Review, 112*, 685–683.

Luhmann, C.C. & Ahn, W.-K. (2007). BUCKLE: A model of unobserved causal learning. *Psychological Review, 112*, 657–677.

Luria, A.R. (1971). Towards the problem of the historical nature of psychological processes. *International Journal of Psychology, 6*, 259–272.

Luria, A.R. (1977). *The social history of cognition*. Cambridge, MA: Harvard University Press.

Mackie, J.L. (1974). *The cement of the universe*. Oxford: Oxford University Press.

Mandel, D.R. (2003). Judgment dissociation theory: An analysis of differences in causal, counterfactual, and covariational reasoning. *Journal of Experimental Psychology: General, 132*, 419–434.

Mandel, D.R. (2005). Counterfactual and causal explanation: From early theoretical views to new frontiers. In D.R. Mandel, D.J. Hilton & P. Catellani (eds.), *The psychology of counterfactual thinking*. London: Routledge.

Mandel, D.R. & Lehman, D.R. (1996). Counterfactual thinking and ascription of cause and preventability. *Journal of Personality and Social Psychology, 71*, 450–463.

Manktelow, K.I. (2004). Reasoning and rationality: The pure and the practical. In K.I. Manktelow & M.C. Chung (eds.), *Psychology of reasoning: Theoretical and historical perspectives*. Hove: Psychology Press.

Manktelow, K.I. & Evans, J.StB.T. (1979). Facilitation of reasoning by realism: Effect or non-effect? *British Journal of Psychology, 70*, 477–488.

Manktelow, K.I. & Fairley, N. (2000) Superordinate principles in reasoning with causal and deontic conditionals. *Thinking & Reasoning, 1*, 41–66.

Manktelow, K.I. & Over, D.E. (1990). Deontic thought and the selection task. In K. Gilhooly, M. Keane, R. Logie & G. Erdos (eds.), *Lines of thought: Reflections on the psychology of thinking, Vol. 1*. Chichester: John Wiley & Sons.

Manktelow, K.I. & Over, D.E. (1991). Social roles and utilities in reasoning with deontic conditionals. *Cognition, 39*, 85–105.

Manktelow, K.I. & Over, D.E. (1995) Deontic reasoning. In S.E. Newstead & J.St.B.T. Evans (eds.), *Perspectives on thinking and reasoning: Essays in honour of Peter Wason*. Hove: Lawrence Erlbaum Associates.

Manktelow, K.I., Over, D.E. & Elqayam, S. (2010a). Paradigms shift: Jonathan Evans and the psychology of reasoning. In K.I. Manktelow, D.E. Over & S. Elqayam (eds.), *The science of reason: Essays in honour of J.StB.T. Evans*. Hove: Psychology Press.

Manktelow, K.I., Over, D.E. & Elqayam, S. (2010b). *The science of reason: Essays in honour of J.StB.T. Evans*. Hove: Psychology Press.

Manktelow, K.I., Sutherland, E.J. & Over, D.E. (1995). Probabilistic factors in deontic reasoning. *Thinking & Reasoning, 1*, 201–220.

Markus, H. & Kitayama, S. (1991). Culture and the self: Implications for cognition, emotion, and motivation. *Psychological Review, 98*, 224–253.

Mason, O., Claridge, G.S. & Jackson, M. (1995). New scales for the assessment of schizotypy. *Personality and Individual Differences, 18*, 7–13.

Masuda, T. & Nisbett, R.E. (2001). Attending holistically vs. analytically: Comparing the context sensitivity of Japanese and Americans. *Journal of Personality and Social Psychology, 81*, 922–934.

McKay, R., Langdon, R. & Coltheart, M. (2006). Need for closure, jumping to conclusions, and decisiveness in delusion-prone individuals. *Journal of Nervous and Mental Disease, 194*, 422–426.

McKenzie, C.R.M., Ferreira, V.S., Mikkelson, L.A., McDermott, K.J. & Skrable, R.P. (2001). Do conditional hypotheses target rare events? *Organizational Behavior and Human Decision Processes, 85*, 291–301.

Medin, D.L., Coley, J.D., Storms, G. & Hayes, B.K. (2003). A relevance theory of induction. *Psychonomic Bulletin and Review, 10*, 517–532.

Medvec, V.H, Madley, S.F. & Gilovich, T. (1995). When less is more: Counterfactual thinking and satisfaction among Olympic medallists. *Journal of Personality and Social Psychology, 69*, 6–3–610. Reprinted in T. Gilovich, D. Griffin & D. Kahneman (eds.) (2002), *Heuristics and biases: The psychology of intuitive judgment*. Cambridge: Cambridge University Press.

Meehl, P.E. & Rosen, A. (1955). Antecedent probability and the efficiency of psychometric signs, patterns, or cutting scores. *Psychological Bulletin, 52*, 194–216.

Mellers, B.A. (2000). Choice and the relative pleasure of consequences. *Psychological Bulletin, 126*, 910–924.

Michotte, A. (1963). *The perception of causality*. New York: Harper.

Mill, J.S. (1973). A system of logic ratiocinative and inductive. In J.M. Robson (ed.), *The collected works of John Stuart Mill*. Toronto: University of Toronto Press. (Original work published 1843)

Miyamoto, Y. & Kitayama, S. (2002). Cultural variation in correspondence bias: The critical role of attitude diagnosticity of socially constrained behavior. *Journal of Personality and Social Psychology, 83*, 1239–1248.

Moreno-Rios, S., Garcia-Madruga, J.A. & Byrne, R.M.J. (2004). The effects of linguistic mood on if: Semifactual and counterfactual conditionals. Unpublished paper cited in Byrne (2005).

Morley, N.J., Evans, J.StB.T. & Handley, S.J. (2004). Belief bias and figural bias in syllogistic reasoning. *Quarterly Journal of Experimental Psychology, 57A*, 666–692.

Murphy, A.H., Lichtenstein, S., Fischhoff, B. & Winkler, R.L. (1980). Misinterpretations of precipitation probability forecasts. *Bulletin of the American Meteorological Society, 61*, 695–701.

Myers, D.G. (2002). *Intuition: Its powers and perils*. New Haven, CT: Yale University Press.

Mynatt, C.R., Doherty, M.E. & Dragan, W. (1993). Information relevance, working memory, and the consideration of alternatives. *Quarterly Journal of Experimental Psychology, 46A*, 759–778.

Newell, B.R. & Shanks, D.R. (2003). Take the best or look at the rest? Factors influencing 'one-reason' decision making. *Journal of Experimental Psychology: Learning, Memory, and Cognition, 29*, 53–65.

Newstead, S.E. (1995). Gricean implicatures and syllogistic reasoning. *Journal of Memory and Language, 34*, 644–664.

Newstead, S.E., Legrenzi, P. & Girotto, V. (1995). The THOG problem and its implications for human reasoning. In J.StB.T. Evans & S.E. Newstead (eds.), *Perspectives on thinking and reasoning: Essays in honour of Peter Wason*. Hove: Lawrence Erlbaum Associates.

Nickerson, R.S. (2008). *Aspects of rationality: Reflections on what it means to be rational and whether we are*. Hove: Psychology Press.

Nirvana (1991). Territorial pissings. *Nevermind*. Seattle, WA: Sub Pop/MCA.

Nisbett, R.E. (ed.) (1992). *Rules for reasoning*. Hillsdale, NJ: Lawrence Erlbaum Associates.

Nisbett, R.E. (2003). *The geography of thought*. London: Nicholas Brealey.

Nisbett, R.E., Krantz, D.H., Jepson, D. & Kunda, Z. (1983). The use of statistical heuristics in everyday inductive reasoning. *Psychological Review*, *90*, 339–363.

Nisbett, R.E. & Norenzayan, A. (2002). Culture and cognition. In D.L. Medin (ed.), *Stevens' handbook of experimental psychology, 3rd edition*. New York: John Wiley & Sons.

Nisbett, R.E., Peng, K., Choi, I. & Norenzayan, A. (2001). Culture and systems of thought: Holistic versus analytic cognition. *Psychological Review*, *108*, 291–310.

Nisbett, R.E. & Ross, L. (1980). *Human inference: Strategies and shortcomings of social judgment*. Englewood Cliffs, NJ: Prentice Hall.

Nisbett, R.E. & Wilson, T.D. (1977). Telling more than we can know: Verbal reports on mental processes. *Psychological Review*, *84*, 231–259.

Nobles, R. & Schiff, D. (2005). Misleading statistics within criminal trials: The Sally Clark case. *Significance*, March, 17–19.

Norenzayan, A. & Heine, S.J. (2005). Psychological universals: What are they, and how can we know? *Psychological Bulletin*, *131*, 763–784.

Norenzayan, A., Smith, E.E., Kim, B. & Nisbett, R.E. (2002). Cultural preferences for formal versus intuitive reasoning. *Cognitive Science*, *26*, 653–684.

Norman, D.A. & Shallice, T. (1986). Attention to action: Willed and automatic control of behavior. In R. Davidson, R. Schwartz & D. Shapiro (eds.), *Consciousness and self-regulation: Advances in research and theory*. New York: Plenum Press.

Noveck, I.A., Chierchia, G., Chevaux, F., Guelminger, R. & Sylvestre, E. (2002). Linguistic-pragmatic factors in interpreting disjunctions. *Thinking & Reasoning*, *8*, 297–326.

Noveck, I.A. & O'Brien, D.P. (1996). To what extent do pragmatic reasoning schemas affect performance on Wason's selection task? *Quarterly Journal of Experimental Psychology*, *49A*, 463–489.

Novick, L.R. & Cheng, P.W. (2004). Assessing interactive causal inference. *Psychological Review*, *111*, 455–485.

Oaksford, M.R. & Chater, N. (1993). Reasoning theories and bounded rationality. In K.I. Manktelow & D.E. Over (eds.), *Rationality*. London: Routledge.

Oaksford, M.R. & Chater, N. (1994a). A rational analysis of the selection task as optimal data selection. *Psychological Review*, *101*, 608–631.

Oaksford, M.R. & Chater, N. (1994b). Another look at eliminative and enumerative behaviour in a conceptual task. *European Journal of Cognitive Psychology*, *6*, 149–169.

Oaksford, M.R. & Chater, N. (1995a). Information gain explains relevance which explains the selection task. *Cognition*, *57*, 97–108.

Oaksford, M.R. & Chater, N. (1995b). Theories of reasoning and the computational explanation of everyday inference. *Thinking & Reasoning*, *1*, 121–152.

Oaksford, M.R. & Chater, N. (eds.) (1998). *Rational models of cognition*. Oxford: Oxford University Press.

Oaksford, M.R. & Chater, N. (2003). Optimal data selection: Revision, review and re-evaluation. *Psychonomic Bulletin and Review*, *10*, 289–318.

Oaksford, M.R. & Chater, N. (2007). *Bayesian rationality*. Oxford: Oxford University Press.

Oaksford, M.R. & Chater, N. (2009). Précis of *Bayesian Rationality*. *Behavioral and Brain Sciences*, *32*, 69–120.

Oaksford, M., Chater, N., Grainger, B. & Larkin, J. (1997). Optimal data selection in the reduced array selection task (RAST). *Journal of Experimental Psychology: Learning, Memory, and Cognition*, *23*, 441–458.

Oaksford, M., Chater, N. & Larkin, J. (2000). Probabilities and polarity biases in conditional inference. *Journal of Experimental Psychology: Learning, Memory, and Cognition*, *26*, 883–889.

Oaksford, M.R. & Moussakowski, M. (2004). Negations and natural sampling in data selection: Ecological versus heuristic explanations of matching bias. *Memory and Cognition*, *32*, 570–581.

Oaksford, M.R. & Stenning, K. (1992). Reasoning with conditionals containing negated constituents. *Journal of Experimental Psychology: Learning, Memory, and Cognition*, *18*, 835–854.

Oberauer, K., Geiger, S.M., Fischer, K. & Weidenfeld, A. (2007). Two meanings of 'if'? Individual differences in the interpretation of conditionals. *Quarterly Journal of Experimental Psychology*, *60*, 790–819.

Oberauer, K. & Oaksford, M. (2008) What must a psychological theory of reasoning explain? Comment on Barrouillet, Gauffroy, and Lecas (2008). *Psychological Review*, *115*, 773–778.

Oberauer, K., Weidenfeld, A & Hörnig, R. (2004). Logical reasoning and probabilities: A comprehensive test of Oaksford and Chater (2001). *Psychonomic Bulletin and Review*, *11*, 521–527.

Oberauer, K. & Wilhelm, O. (2003). The meaning(s) of conditionals: Conditional probabilities, mental models, and personal utilities. *Journal of Experimental Psychology: Learning, Memory, and Cognition*, *29*, 680–693.

Oberauer, K., Wilhelm, O. & Dias, R.R. (1999). Bayesian rationality for the Wason selection task? A test of optimal data selection theory. *Thinking & Reasoning*, *5*, 115–144.

O'Brien, D.P. (1993). Mental logic and irrationality: We can put a man on the moon, so why can't we solve those logical reasoning problems? In K.I. Manktelow and D.E. Over (eds.), *Rationality: Psychological and philosophical perspectives*. London: Routledge.

O'Brien, D.P. (1995). Finding logic in human reasoning requires looking in the right places. In J.StB.T. Evans & S.E. Newstead (eds.), *Perspectives on thinking and reasoning: Essays in honour of Peter Wason*. Hove: Lawrence Erlbaum Associates.

O'Brien, D.P., Noveck, I.A., Davidson, G.M., Fisch, S.M., Lea, R.H. & Freitag, J. (1990). Sources of difficulty in deductive reasoning. *Quarterly Journal of Experimental Psychology*, *42A*, 329–352.

Oda, R., Hiraishi, K. & Matsumoto-Oda, A. (2006). Does an altruist-detection cognitive mechanism function independently of a cheater-detection cognitive mechanism? Studies using Wason selection tasks. *Evolution and Human Behavior*, *27*, 366–380.

Offer, A. (2006). *The challenge of affluence*. Oxford: Oxford University Press.

Oppenheimer, D.M. (2003). Not so fast! (and not so frugal!): Rethinking the recognition heuristic. *Cognition*, *90*, B1–B9.

Osherson, D.N., Perani, D., Cappa, S., Schnur, T., Grassi, F. & Fazio, F. (1998). Distinct brain loci in deductive versus probabilistic reasoning. *Neuropsychologia*, *36*, 369–376. Reprinted in Adler & Rips (2008).

Osherson, D.N., Smith, E.E., Wilkie, O., Lopez, A. & Shafir, E.B. (1990). Category-based induction. *Psychological Review*, *97*, 185–200. Reprinted in Adler & Rips (2008).

Ostrom, E. (1990). *Governing the commons*. Cambridge: Cambridge University Press.

Over, D.E. (ed.) (2003). *Evolution and the psychology of thinking: The debate*. Hove: Psychology Press.

Over, D.E. (2009). New paradigm psychology of reasoning. *Thinking & Reasoning*, *15*, 431–438

Over, D.E. & Green, D.W. (2001). Contingency, causation and adaptive inference. *Psychological Review*, *108*, 682–684.

Over, D.E., Hadjichristidis, C., Evans, J.StB.T., Handley, S.J. & Sloman, S.A. (2007). The probability of causal conditionals. *Cognitive Psychology*, *54*, 62–97.

REFERENCES

Over, D.E. & Manktelow, K.I. (1993). Rationality, utility and deontic reasoning. In K.I. Manktelow & D.E. Over (eds.), *Rationality: Psychological and philosophical perspectives*. London: Routledge.

Oyserman, D., Coon, H.M. & Kemmelmeier, M. (2002). Rethinking individualism and collectivism: Evaluation of theoretical assumptions and meta-analyses. *Psychological Bulletin, 128*, 3–72.

Paris, S.G. (1973). Comprehension of language connectives and propositional logical relationships. *Journal of Experimental Child Psychology, 16*, 278–291.

Pearl, J. (2000). *Causality: Models, reasoning and inference.* Cambridge: Cambridge University Press.

Peng, K. & Nisbett, R.E. (1999). Culture, dialectics, and reasoning about contradiction. *American Psychologist, 54*, 741–754.

Perham, N. & Oaksford, M. (2005). Deontic reasoning with emotional content: Evolutionary psychology or decision theory? *Cognitive Science, 29*, 681–718.

Peters, E.R., Day, S. & Garety, P.A. (1996). The Peters et al. Delusions Inventory (PDI): New norms for the 21-item version. *Schizophrenia Research, 18*, 118.

Piaget, J. (1972). Intellectual evolution from adolescence to adulthood. *Human Development, 15*, 1–12.

Pinker, S. (1994). *The language instinct.* London: Penguin.

Pinker, S. (1997). *How the mind works.* London: Allen Lane.

Pinker, S. (2002). *The blank slate: The modern denial of human nature.* London: Allen Lane

Platt, J. (1973). Social traps. *American Psychologist, 28*, 641–651.

Plessner, H., Betsch, C. & Betsch, T. (eds.) (2008). *Intuition in judgment and decision making.* Hove: Lawrence Erlbaum Associates.

Poletiek, F.H. (1996). Paradoxes of falsification. *Quarterly Journal of Experimental Psychology, 49A*, 447–462.

Poletiek, F.H. (2001). *Hypothesis-testing behaviour.* Hove: Psychology Press.

Politzer, G. (1986). Laws of language use and formal logic. *Journal of Psycholinguistic Research, 15*, 47–92.

Politzer, G. (2001). Premise interpretation in conditional reasoning. In D. Hardman & L. Macchi (eds.), *Thinking: Psychological perspectives on reasoning, judgment and decision making.* Chichester: John Wiley & Sons.

Politzer, G. (2004). Some precursors of current theories of syllogistic reasoning. In K.I. Manktelow & M.C. Chung (eds.), *Psychology of reasoning: Theoretical and historical perspectives.* Hove: Psychology Press.

Politzer, G. and Bourmaud, G. (2002). Deductive reasoning from uncertain conditionals. *British Journal of Psychology, 93*, 345–381.

Politzer, G. & Nguyen-Xuan, A. (1992). Reasoning about conditional promises and warnings: Darwinian algorithms, mental models, relevance judgments or pragmatic schemas? *Quarterly Journal of Experimental Psychology, 46A*, 401–412.

Politzer, G. & Noveck, I.A. (1991). Are conjunction rule violations the result of conversational rule violations? *Journal of Psycholinguistic Research, 20*, 83–103.

Pollard, P. & Evans, J.StB.T. (1983). The role of 'representativeness' in statistical inference: A critical appraisal. In J.StB.T. Evans (ed.), *Thinking and reasoning: Psychological approaches.* London: Routledge.

Popper, K. (1959a). The propensity interpretation of probability. *British Journal for the Philosophy of Science, 10*, 25–42.

Popper, K. (1959b). *The logic of scientific discovery, 3rd edition.* London: Hutchinson.

Purves, D., Brannon, E.M., Cabeza, R., Huettel, S.A., LaBar, K.S., Platt, M.L. & Woldorff, M.G. (2008). *Principles of cognitive neuroscience.* Sunderland, MA: Sinauer.

Quiggin, J. (1982). A theory of anticipated utility. *Journal of Economic Behavior and Organization, 3*, 323–343.

Read, D. (2007). Experienced utility: Utility theory from Jeremy Bentham to Daniel Kahneman. *Thinking & Reasoning, 13*, 45–61.

Redelmeier, D. & Kahneman, D. (1996). Patients' memories of painful medical treatment: Real-time and retrospective evaluations of two minimally invasive procedures. *Pain*, *116*, 3–8.

Reed, L. (1989). Strawman. *New York*. New York: Sire Records.

Rehder, B. (2006). When similarity and causality compete in category-based property induction. *Memory and Cognition*, *34*, 3–16.

Rehder, B. (2007). Property generalization as causal reasoning. In A. Feeney & E. Heit (eds.), *Inductive reasoning: Experimental, developmental and computational approaches*. Cambridge: Cambridge University Press.

Revlis, R. (1975). Syllogistic reasoning: Logical decisions from a complex data base. In R.J. Falmagne (ed.), *Reasoning: Representation and process*. New York: John Wiley & Sons.

Rips, L.J. (1975). Inductive judgments about natural categories. *Journal of Verbal Learning and Verbal Behavior*, *14*, 665–681.

Rips, L.J. (1994). *The psychology of proof*. Cambridge, MA: MIT Press.

Rips, L.J. (2001). Two kinds of reasoning. *Psychological Science*, *12*, 129–134.

Rips, L.J. (2008). Causal thinking. In J.E. Adler and L.J. Rips (eds.), *Reasoning: Studies of human inference and its foundations*. Cambridge: Cambridge University Press.

Rips, L.J. & Marcus, S.L. (1977). Suppositions and the analysis of conditional sentences. In P.A. Carpenter & M.A. Just (eds.), *Cognitive processes in comprehension*. Hillsdale, NJ: Lawrence Erlbaum Associates.

Ritov, I. & Baron, J. (1990). Reluctance to vaccinate: Omission bias and ambiguity. *Journal of Behavioural Decision Making*, *3*, 263–277.

Ritov, I. & Baron, J. (1999). Protected values and omission bias. *Organizational Behavior and Human Decision Processes*, *64*, 119–127.

Roberge, J.J. (1976a). Reasoning with exclusive disjunction arguments. *Quarterly Journal of Experimental Psychology*, *28*, 417–427.

Roberge, J.J. (1976b). Effects of negation of adults' disjunctive reasoning abilities. *Journal of General Psychology*, *94*, 23–28.

Roberge, J.J. (1978). Linguistic and psychometric factors in propositional reasoning. *Quarterly Journal of Experimental Psychology*, *30*, 705–716.

Roberts, M.J. (1998). Inspection times and the selection task: Are they relevant? *Quarterly Journal of Experimental Psychology*, *51A*, 781–810.

Roberts, M.J. (2005). Expanding the universe of categorical syllogisms: A challenge for reasoning researchers. *Behavior Research Methods*, *37*, 560–580.

Roberts, M.J., Newstead, S.E. & Griggs, R.S. (2001). Quantifier interpretation and syllogistic reasoning. *Thinking & Reasoning*, *7*, 173–204.

Roberts, M.J. & Sykes, E.D.A. (2005). Categorical reasoning from multiple premises. *Quarterly Journal of Experimental Psychology*, *58A*, 333–376.

Rosch, E. (1973). On the internal structure of perceptual and semantic categories. In T.E. Moore (ed.), *Cognitive development and the acquisition of language*. New York: Academic Press.

Rosch, E. (1978). Principles of categorization. In E. Rosch & B. Lloyd (eds.), *Cognition and categorization*. Hillsdale, NJ: Lawrence Erlbaum Associates.

Ross, L. (1977). The intuitive psychologist and his shortcomings. In L. Berkowitz (ed.), *Advances in experimental social psychology, Vol. 10*. New York: Academic Press.

Ross, M. & Sicoly, F. (1979). Egocentric biases in availability and attribution. *Journal of Personality and Social Psychology*, *37*, 322–336.

Rottenstreich, Y. & Tversky, A. (1997). Unpacking, repacking and anchoring: Advances in support theory. *Psychological Review*, *104*, 406–415. Reprinted in Gilovich et al. (2002).

Sanjana, N.E. & Tenenbaum, J.B. (2003). Bayesian models of inductive generalization. In S. Becker, S. Thrun & K. Obermayer (eds.), *Advances in neural processing systems 15*. Cambridge, MA: MIT Press.

Savage, L.J. (1954). *The foundations of statistics*. New York: John Wiley & Sons.

Schroyens, W. & Schaeken, W. (2003). A critique of Oaksford, Chater and Larkin's (2000) conditional probability model of conditional reasoning. *Journal of Experimental Psychology: Learning, Memory, and Cognition, 29,* 140–149.

Schroyens, W., Schaeken, W. & d'Ydewalle, G. (2001). The processing of negations in conditional reasoning: A meta-analytic case study in mental logic and/or mental model theory. *Thinking & Reasoning, 7,* 121–172.

Scribner, S. (1977). Modes of thinking and ways of speaking: Culture and logic reconsidered. In P.N. Johnson-Laird & P.C. Wason (eds.), *Thinking: Readings in cognitive science.* Cambridge: Cambridge University Press.

Schwartz, B. (2004). *The paradox of choice.* New York: Ecco.

Sedlmeier, P., Hertwig, R. & Gigerenzer, G. (1998). Are judgments of the positional frequency of letters systematically biased due to availability? *Journal of Experimental Psychology: Learning, Memory, and Cognition, 24,* 745–770.

Sellen, J.S., Oaksford, M. & Gray, N.S. (2005). Schizotypy and conditional reasoning. *Schizophrenia Bulletin, 31,* 105–116.

Shafir, E.B. (1993). Choosing versus rejecting: Why some options are both better and worse than others. *Memory and Cognition, 21,* 546–556.

Shafir, E.B. & Tversky, A. (1992). Thinking through uncertainty: Nonconsequential reasoning and choice. *Cognitive Psychology, 24,* 449–474.

Shanks, D.R. & Dickinson, A. (1987). Associative accounts of causality judgment. In G.H. Bower (ed.), *The psychology of learning and motivation, Vol. 21.* San Diego, CA: Academic Press.

Shiffrin, R.M. & Schneider, W. (1977). Controlled and automatic human information processing: 2. Perceptual learning, automatic attending, and a general theory. *Psychological Review, 84,* 127–190.

Simon, H.A. (1957). *Models of man: Social and rational,* New York: John Wiley & Sons.

Simon, H.A. (1978). Rationality as a process and product of thought. *American Economic Review, 68,* 1–16.

Simon, H.A. (1983). *Reason in human affairs,* Stanford, CA: Stanford University Press.

Sloman, S.A. (1993). Feature-based induction. *Cognitive Psychology, 25,* 231–280.

Sloman, S.A. (1994). When explanations compete: The role of explanatory coherence in judgments of likelihood. *Cognition, 52,* 1–21. Reprinted in Adler & Rips (2008).

Sloman, S.A. (1996). The empirical case for two systems of reasoning. *Psychological Bulletin, 119,* 3–22. Reprinted in Gilovich et al. (2002).

Sloman, S.A. (1998). Categorical inference is not a tree: The myth of inheritance hierarchies. *Cognitive Psychology, 35,* 1–33.

Sloman, S.A. (2005). *Causal models.* Oxford: Oxford University Press.

Sloman, S.A. (2007). Taxonomizing induction. In A. Feeney & E. Heit (eds.), *Inductive reasoning: Experimental, developmental and computational approaches.* Cambridge: Cambridge University Press.

Sloman, S.A. & Lagnado, D. (2005a). Do we 'do'? *Cognitive Science, 29,* 5–39.

Sloman, S.A. & Lagnado, D.A. (2005b). The problem of induction. In K.J. Holyoak and R.G. Morrison (eds.), *The Cambridge handbook of thinking and reasoning.* Cambridge: Cambridge University Press.

Sloman, S.A. & Over, D.E. (2003). Probability judgment from the inside and out. In D.E. Over (ed.), *Evolution and the psychology of thinking: The debate.* Hove: Psychology Press.

Sloman, S.A., Over, D.E. & Slovak, L. (2003). Frequency illusions and other fallacies. *Organizational Behavior and Human Decision Processes, 91,* 296–306.

Slovic, P. (1995). The construction of preference. *American Psychologist, 50,* 364–371. Reprinted in Kahneman & Tversky (2002).

Slovic, P., Finucane, M., Peters, E. & MacGregor, D.G. (2002). The affect heuristic. In T.D. Gilovich, D. Griffin & D. Kahneman (eds.), *Heuristics and biases: The psychology of intuitive judgment.* Cambridge: Cambridge University Press. Reprinted in Lichtenstein & Slovic (2006).

Slovic, P. & Tversky A. (1974). Who accepts Savage's axiom? *Behavioral Science, 19*, 368–373.

Smyth, M.M. & Clark, S.E. (1986). My half-sister is a THOG: Strategic processes in a reasoning task. *British Journal of Psychology, 77*, 275–287.

Spellman, B.A. (1997). Crediting causality. *Journal of Experimental Psychology: General, 126*, 323–348.

Spellman, B.A. & Kincannon, A. (2001). The relation between counterfactual ('but for') and causal reasoning: Experimental findings and implications for jurors' decisions. *Law and Contemporary Problems, 64*, 241–264.

Sperber, D., Cara, F. & Girotto, V. (1995). Relevance theory explains the selection task. *Cognition, 57*, 31–95.

Sperber, D. & Girotto, V. (2002). Use or misuse of the selection task? Rejoinder to Fiddick, Cosmides, and Tooby. *Cognition, 85*, 277–290.

Sperber, D. & Wilson, D. (1995). *Relevance: Communication and cognition, 2nd edition.* Oxford: Blackwell.

Stahl, C., Klauer, K.C. & Erdfelder, E. (2008). Matching bias in the selection task is not eliminated by explicit negations. *Thinking & Reasoning, 14*, 281–303.

Stanovich, K.E. (1999). *Who is rational? Studies of individual differences in reasoning.* Mahwah, NJ: Lawrence Erlbaum Associates.

Stanovich, K.E. (2004). *The robot's rebellion: Finding meaning in the age of Darwin.* Chicago: Chicago University Press.

Stanovich, K.E. (2009a). Distinguishing the reflective, algorithmic, and autonomous minds: Is it time for a tri-process theory? In J.StB.T. Evans and K. Frankish (eds.), *In two minds: Dual processes and beyond.* Oxford: Oxford University Press.

Stanovich, K.E. (2009b). *What intelligence tests miss: The psychology of rational thought.* New Haven: Yale University Press.

Stanovich, K.E. & West, R.F. (2000). Individual differences in reasoning: Implications for the rationality debate? *Behavioral and Brain Sciences, 23*, 645–726.

Stanovich, K.E., West, R.F. & Toplak, M.E. (2010). Individual differences as essential components of heuristics and biases research. In K.I. Manktelow, D.E. Over & S. Elqayam (eds.), *The science of reason: Essays in honour of Jonathan StB.T. Evans.* Hove: Psychology Press.

Staw, B.M. & Ross, J. (1989). Understanding behavior in escalating situations. *Science, 246*, 216–220.

Stein, E. (1996). *Without good reason: The rationality debate in philosophy and cognitive science.* Oxford: Clarendon Press.

Stenning, K. (2002). *Seeing reason.* Oxford: Oxford University Press.

Stenning, K. & van Lambalgen, M. (2004a). The natural history of hypotheses about the selection task. In K.I. Manktelow & M.C. Chung (eds.), *Psychology of reasoning: Theoretical and historical perspectives.* Hove: Psychology Press.

Stenning, K. & van Lambalgen, M. (2004b). A little logic goes a long way: Basing experiment on semantic theory in the cognitive science of conditional reasoning. *Cognitive Science, 28*, 481–529.

Stenning, K. & van Lambalgen, M. (2008a). *Human reasoning and cognitive science.* Cambridge, MA: MIT Press.

Stenning, K. & van Lambalgen, M. (2008b). Interpretation, representation, and deductive reasoning. In J.E. Adler & L.J. Rips (eds.), *Reasoning: Studies of human inference and its foundations.* Cambridge: Cambridge University Press.

Stewart, N., Chater, N. & Brown, G.D.A (2006). Decision by sampling. *Cognitive Psychology, 53*, 1–26.

Stewart, N. & Simpson, K. (2008). A decision-by-sampling account of decision under risk. In N. Chater & M.R. Oaksford (eds.) (2008), *The probabilistic mind: Prospects for a Bayesian cognitive science.* Oxford: Oxford University Press.

Sutherland, S. (1992). *Irrationality: The enemy within.* Harmondsworth: Penguin.

Tavris, C. & Aronson, E. (2008). *Mistakes were made (but not by me)*. London: Pinter & Martin.

Teigen, K.H., Kanten, A.B. & Terum, J.A. (2011). *Thinking & Reasoning, 17*, 1–29.

Tenenbaum, J.B., Kemp, C. & Shafto, P. (2007). Theory-based models of inductive reasoning. In A. Feeney & E. Heit (eds.), *Inductive reasoning: Experimental, developmental and computational approaches*. Cambridge: Cambridge University Press.

Tetlock, P.E. & Mellers, B.A. (2002). The great rationality debate. *Psychological Science, 13*, 94–99.

Thagard, P.A. (2007). Abductive inference: from philosophical analysis to neural mechanisms. In A. Feeney & E. Heit (eds.), *Inductive reasoning: Experimental, developmental and computational approaches*. Cambridge: Cambridge University Press.

Thagard, P.A. & Nisbett, R.E. (1982). Variability and confirmation. *Philosophical Studies, 42*, 379–394.

Thaler, R. (1980). Toward a positive theory of consumer choice. *Journal of Economic Behavior and Organization, 1*, 39–60.

Thaler, R. (1999). Mental accounting matters. *Journal of Behavioural Decision Making, 12*, 183–206.

Thaler, R.H. & Shefrin, H.M. (1981). An economic theory of self-control. *Journal of Political Economy, 89*, 392–406.

Thatcher, M. & Manktelow, K. (2007). The cost of individualism. *Counselling Psychology Review, 22*, 31–42.

The Doors (1967). People are strange. *Strange days*. New York: Elektra Records.

Thompson, V.A. (1994). Interpretational factors in conditional reasoning. *Memory and Cognition, 22*, 742–758.

Thompson, V.A. (1995). Conditional reasoning: The necessary and sufficient conditions. *Canadian Journal of Experimental Psychology, 49*, 1–58.

Thompson, V.A. (2000). The task-specific nature of domain-general reasoning. *Cognition, 76*, 209–268.

Thompson, V.A. (2009). Dual-process theories: A metacognitive perspective. In J.StB.T. Evans & K. Frankish (eds.), *In two minds: Dual processes and beyond*. Oxford: Oxford University Press.

Thompson, V.A. & Byrne, R.M.J. (2002). Reasoning about things that didn't happen. *Journal of Experimental Psychology: Learning, Memory, and Cognition, 28*, 1154–1170.

Todd, P.M. & Gigerenzer, G. (2000). Précis of *Simple heuristics that make us smart*. *Behavioral and Brain Sciences, 23*, 727–780.

Triandis, H.C. (1989). The self and behavior in differing cultural contexts. *Psychological Review, 96*, 506–520.

Triandis, H.C. (1995). *Individualism and collectivism*. Boulder, CO: Westview Press.

Tsuji, T. & Watanabe, S. (2009). Neural correlates of dual-task effect on belief-bias syllogistic reasoning: A near-infrared spectroscopy study. *Brain Research, 1287*, 118–125.

Tsuji, T. & Watanabe, S. (2010). Neural correlates of belief-bias reasoning under time pressure: A near-infrared spectroscopy study. *Neuroimage, 50*, 1320–1326.

Tversky, A. (1969). Intransitivity of preferences. *Psychological Review, 76*, 31–48.

Tversky, A. (1972). Elimination by aspects: A theory of choice. *Psychological Review, 79*, 281–299.

Tversky, A. & Kahneman, D. (1973). Availability: A heuristic for judging frequency and probability. *Cognitive Psychology, 4*, 207–232.

Tversky, A. & Kahneman, D. (1981). The framing of decisions and the psychology of choice. *Science, 211*, 453–458.

Tversky, A. & Kahneman, D. (1982a). Evidential impact of base rates. In D. Kahneman, P. Slovic & A. Tversky (eds.), *Judgment under uncertainty: Heuristics and biases*. Cambridge: Cambridge University Press.

Tversky, A. & Kahneman, D. (1982b). Judgments of and by representativeness. In D. Kahneman, P. Slovic & A. Tversky (eds.), *Judgment under uncertainty: Heuristics and biases*. Cambridge: Cambridge University Press.

Tversky, A. & Kahneman, D. (1983). Extensional versus intuitive reasoning: The conjunction fallacy in probability judgment. *Psychological Review, 90*, 293–315.

Tversky, A. & Kahneman, D. (1992). Advances in prospect theory: Cumulative representations of risk and uncertainty. *Journal of Risk and Uncertainty, 5*, 297–323. Reprinted in Kahneman & Tversky (2000).

Tversky, A. & Koehler, D.J. (1994). Support theory: A nonextensional representation of probability. *Psychological Review, 101*, 547–567. Reprinted in Gilovich et al. (2002).

Tversky, A., Sattath, S. & Slovic, P. (1988). Contingent weighting in judgment and choice. *Psychological Review, 95*, 371–384. Reprinted in Lichtenstein & Slovic (2006).

Tversky, A. & Shafir, E.B. (1992). The disjunction effect in choice under uncertainty. *Psychological Science, 3*, 305–309.

Tversky, A. & Simonson, I. (1993). Context-dependent preferences. *Management Science, 39*, 177–185. Reprinted in Kahneman & Tversky (2000).

Tversky, A., Slovic, P. & Kahneman, D. (1990). The causes of preference reversal. *American Economic Review, 80*, 204–217. Reprinted in Lichtenstein & Slovic (2006).

Tweney, R.D. (1985). Faraday's discovery of induction: A cognitive approach. In D. Gooding & F.A.J.L. James (eds.), *Faraday rediscovered: Essays on the life and work of Michael Faraday, 1791–1867*. London: MacMillan.

Tweney, R.D., Doherty, M.E. & Kleiter, G.D. (2010). The pseudodiagnosticity trap: Should participants consider alternative hypotheses? *Thinking & Reasoning, 16*, 332–345.

Tweney, R.D., Doherty, M.E. & Mynatt, C.R. (1981). *On scientific thinking*. New York: Columbia University Press.

Tweney, R.D., Doherty, M.E., Worner, W.J., Pliske, D.B., Mynatt, C.R., Gross, K.A. & Arkkelin, D.L. (1980). Strategies of rule discovery in an inference task. *Quarterly Journal of Experimental Psychology, 32*, 109–123.

Vallée-Tourangeau, F., Austin, N.G. & Rankin, S. (1995). Inducing a rule in Wason's 2–4–6 task: A test of the information-quantity and goal-complementarity hypotheses. *Quarterly Journal of Experimental Psychology, 48A*, 895–914.

Vallée-Tourangeau, F. & Krüsi Penney, A. (2005). The impact of external representation in a rule discovery task. *European Journal of Cognitive Psychology, 17*, 820–834.

Vallée-Tourangeau, F. & Payton, T. (2008). Graphical representation fosters discovery in the 2–4–6 task. *Quarterly Journal of Experimental Psychology, 61*, 625–640.

Van Os, J., Hansen, M., Bijl, R.V. & Ravelli, A. (2000). Strauss (1969) revisited: A psychosis continuum in the general population? *Schizophrenia Research, 45*, 11–20.

Van Os, J., Linscott, R.J., Myin-Germeys, I, Delespaul, P. & Krabbendam, L. (2009). A systematic review and meta-analysis of the psychosis continuum: Evidence for a psychosis proneness–persistence–impairment model. *Psychological Medicine, 27*, 455–465.

Vartanian, O. & Mandel, D.R. (eds.) (2011). *Neuroscience of decision making*. Hove: Psychology Press.

Villejoubert, G. & Mandel, D.R. (2002). The inverse fallacy: An account of deviations form Bayes's theorem and the additivity principle. *Memory and Cognition, 30*, 171–178.

Von Mises, R. (1950). *Probability, statistics and truth*. London: Allen & Unwin.

Von Neumann, J. & Morgenstern, O. (1944). *Theory of games and economic behavior*. Princeton, NJ: Princeton University Press.

Wason, P.C. (1960). On the failure to eliminate hypotheses in a conceptual task. *Quarterly Journal of Experimental Psychology, 12*, 129–140

Wason, P.C. (1966). Reasoning. In B.M. Foss (ed.), *New horizons in psychology 1*. Harmondsworth: Pelican.

Wason, P.C. (1968a). Reasoning about a rule. *Quarterly Journal of Experimental Psychology*, *20*, 273–281.

Wason, P.C. (1968b). On the failure to eliminate hypotheses: Second look. In P.C. Wason & P.N. Johnson-Laird (eds.), *Thinking and reasoning*. Harmondsworth: Penguin.

Wason, P.C. (1969a). Structural simplicity and psychological complexity: Some thoughts on a novel problem. *Bulletin of the British Psychological Society*, *22*, 281–284.

Wason, P.C. (1969b). Regression in reasoning? *British Journal of Psychology*, *60*, 471–480.

Wason, P.C. (1977). Self-contradictions. In P.N. Johnson-Laird & P.C. Wason (eds.), *Thinking: Readings in cognitive science*. Cambridge: Cambridge University Press.

Wason, P.C. & Brooks, P.J. (1979). THOG: The anatomy of a problem. *Psychological Research*, *41*, 79–90.

Wason, P.C & Evans, J.StB.T. (1975). Dual processes in reasoning? *Cognition*, *3*, 141–154.

Wason, P.C. & Green, D.W. (1984). Reasoning and mental representation. *Quarterly Journal of Experimental Psychology*, *36A*, 597–610.

Wason, P.C. & Johnson-Laird, P.N. (1972). *Psychology of reasoning: Structure and content*. London: Batsford.

Wason, P.C. & Shapiro, D.A. (1971). Natural and contrived experience in a reasoning problem. *Quarterly Journal of Experimental Psychology*, *23*, 63–71.

Wasserman, E.A., Dorner, W.W. & Kao, S.-F. (1990). Contributions of specific cell information to judgments of interevent contingency. *Journal of Experimental Psychology: Learning, Memory, and Cognition*, *16*, 509–521.

Wasserman, E.A., Elek, S.M. Chatlosh, D.L. & Baker, A.G. (1993). Rating causal relations: Role of probability in judgments of response-outcome contingency. *Journal of Experimental Psychology: Learning, Memory, and Cognition*, *19*, 174–188.

Weidenfeld, A., Oberauer, K. & Hörnig, R. (2005). Causal and noncausal conditionals: An integrated model of interpretation and reasoning. *Quarterly Journal of Experimental Psychology*, *58A*, 1479–1513.

Wetherick, N.E. (1962). Eliminative and enumerative behaviour in a conceptual task. *Quarterly Journal of Experimental Psychology*, *14*, 246–249.

Wetherick, N.E. & Gilhooly, K.J. (1990). Syllogistic reasoning: Effects of premise order. In K. Gilhooly, M. Keane, R. Logie & G. Erdos (eds.), *Lines of thinking: Reflections on the psychology of thought, Vol. 1*. Chichester: John Wiley & Sons.

Wharton, C.M., Cheng, P.W. & Wickens, T.D. (1993). Hypothesis-testing strategies: Why two rules are better than one. *Quarterly Journal of Experimental Psychology*, *46A*, 750–758.

White, L.O. & Mansell, W. (2009). Failing to ponder? Delusion-prone individuals rush to conclusions. *Clinical Psychology and Psychotherapy*, *16*, 111–124.

White, P.A. (1989). A theory of causal processing. *British Journal of Psychology*, *80*, 431–454.

White, P.A. (1995). *The understanding of causation and the production of action: From infancy to adulthood*. Hove: Lawrence Erlbaum Associates.

White, P.A. (2005). The power PC theory and causal powers: Comment on Cheng (1997) and Novick & Cheng (2004). *Psychological Review*, *112*, 675–684.

Wilkins, M.C. (1928). The effect of changed material on ability to do formal syllogistic reasoning. *Archives of Psychology*, *102*.

Woodworth, R.S. & Sells, S.B. (1935). An atmosphere effect in syllogistic reasoning. *Journal of Experimental Psychology*, *18*, 451–460.

World Health Organization (2009). What are the health risks associated with mobile phones and their base stations? Retrieved October 2010, from www.who.int/features/qa/30/en/

Wu, G., Zhang, J. & Gonzalez, R. (2004). Decision under risk. In D.J. Koehler & N. Harvey (eds.), *Blackwell handbook of judgment and decision making*. Oxford: Blackwell.

Yama, H. (2001). Matching versus optimal data selection in the Wason selection task. *Thinking & Reasoning*, *7*, 295–311.

Yama, H., Manktelow, K.I., Mercier, H., van der Henst, J.-P., Do, K.-S., Kawasaki, Y. & Adachi, K. (2010). Across-cultural study of hindsight bias and conditional probabilistic reasoning. *Thinking & Reasoning, 16*, 346–371.

Yama, H., Nishioka, M., Horishita, T., Kawasaki, Y. & Taniguchi, J. (2007). A dual process model for cultural differences in thought. *Mind & Society, 6*, 143–172.

Zajonc, R.B. (1980). Feeling and thinking: Preferences need no inferences. *American Psychologist, 35*, 151–175.

Zeelenberg, M., van der Bos, K., van Dijk, E. & Pieters, R. (2002). The inaction effect in the psychology of regret. *Journal of Personality and Social Psychology, 82*, 314–327.

Author index

Subject index